The
Flint River

A RECREATIONAL GUIDEBOOK TO THE FLINT RIVER AND ENVIRONS

The Flint River

A RECREATIONAL GUIDEBOOK TO THE FLINT RIVER AND ENVIRONS

Fred Brown and Sherri M. L. Smith

Preface by
Jimmy Carter

Illustrations by
Roel Wielinga

Book and cover design by Dori Nicholson

*Funding provided by Dougherty and Lee Counties, Georgia,
in cooperation with the Georgia Department of Community Affairs
and the Georgia Power Company*

PUBLISHING
Atlanta

Grateful acknowledgment is made to the following for permission to reprint previously published material:
Florida Classics Library: Excerpts from *The Other Florida* by Gloria Jahoda. Copyright © 1967 by Gloria Jahoda. Garden Club of Georgia: Excerpts from *Indian Heritage of Georgia* by Marion R. Hemperley. Copyright © 1994 by Garden Club of Georgia. Historic Chattahoochee Commission: Excerpts from *Perilous Journeys: A History of Steamboating on the Chattahoochee, Apalachicola and Flint Rivers, 1828–1928* by Edward A. Mueller. Copyright © 1990 by Historic Chattahoochee Commission. Excerpts from *This So Remote Frontier: The Chattahoochee Country of Alabama and Georgia* by Mark Fretwell. Copyright © 1990 by Historic Chattahoochee Commission. Excerpts from *The Old Beloved Path–Daily Life Among the Indians of the Chattahoochee River Valley* by William W. Winn. Copyright © 1992 by The Chattahoochee Historic Commission and The Columbus Museum. Maston O'Neal: Excerpts from *Prologue* by Maston O'Neal. Copyright © 1985 by Maston O'Neal. Menasha Ridge Press: Excerpt from *A Paddler's Guide to Southern Georgia* by Bob Sehlinger and Don Otey. Copyright © 1980 by Menasha Ridge Press. Penguin Books: Excerpts from *Travels* by William Bartram. Copyright © 1988 by Penguin Books. Pineapple Press, Inc.: Excerpt from *The Young Naturalist's Guide to Florida* by Peggy Sias Lantz and Wendy A. Hale. Copyright © 1994 by Peggy Sias Lantz and Wendy A. Hale. Robert A. Jordan: Excerpt from *There Was a Land, A History of Talbot County* by Judge Robert A. Jordan. Copyright © 1971 by Robert A. Jordan. The Institute of Community and Area Development, The Roosevelt Warm Springs Institute for Rehabilitation: Excerpts from *The Squire of Warm Springs* by Theo Lippman, Jr. The University of Alabama Press: Excerpts from *Fair to Middlin,' The Antebellum Cotton Trade of the Apalachicola / Chattahoochee River Valley* by Lynn Willoughby. Copyright © 1993 by the University of Alabama Press. Excerpts from *Flowing Through Time, A History of the Lower Chattahoochee River* by Lynn Willoughby. Copyright © 1999 by The University of Alabama Press. The University of Georgia Press: Excerpts from *A History of Georgia* edited by Kenneth Coleman. Copyright © 1991 by The University of Georgia Press. Excerpts from *Knights of Spain, Warriors of the Sun* by Charles Hudson. Copyright © 1997 by Charles Hudson. Excerpts from *Georgia Rivers* edited by George Hatcher. Copyright © 1962 by Atlanta Newspapers, Inc. Excerpts from *The Atlas of Georgia* by Thomas W. Hodler and Howard A. Schretter. Copyright © 1986 by The Institute of Community and Area Development, The University of Georgia. Westville Historic Handicrafts, Inc.: Excerpt from *The Magic of Westville* text by William W. Winn. Copyright © 1999 Westville Historic Handicrafts, Inc. W. H. Wolfe Associates: Excerpts from *Decatur County, Georgia, Past and Present* by the Decatur County Historical Society. Excerpts from *Cornerstone of Georgia, Seminole County 1920–1991* by Seminole County Historical Society.

ISBN 1-58072-003-X

Printed in Canada

First edition, first printing.

CI Publishing, 52 Walton Street, Suite 211, Atlanta, Georgia 30303
www.cipublishing.com

Contents

Dedication

We may have been able to do this book without them,
But it would have been a lot less informed
And a whole lot less fun.

This book is dedicated to
Tom and Barbara Morgan,
Who know and love
The Flint River,
Particularly, the sections in
Meriwether, Pike, Talbot and Upson Counties

Acknowledgments

PAT SAMFORD, the former editor of *Guide to Georgia*, came up with the idea for a Flint River guidebook. She had read *The Riverkeeper's Guide to the Chattahoochee* that Sherri Smith and I had written in 1996 and thought that a similar book should be done about the Flint River, a waterway she had known as a child growing up in Albany, Georgia. She took the idea to Lieutenant Governor Mark Taylor, himself a native of Albany. The Lieutenant Governor immediately saw that a Flint River guidebook had the potential to identify and stimulate nature-based and cultural tourism in the Flint River Corridor and, thereby, serve as an economic stimulus for the region, particularly in the southwestern portion of the state through which the Flint River flows. He brought State Senator George Hooks into the discussion. Senator Hooks, a native of Americus in Sumter County, also in the Flint watershed, and the chairman of the Georgia senate's finance committee, helped us coordinate the book project through Dougherty and Lee Counties in cooperation with the Georgia Department of Community Affairs. Georgia Power Company added its support to the underwriting of the book.

This is the third book I have written or edited that has been all, or partially, funded by the Georgia Power Company. The first was the 1990 publication of *The Georgia Conservancy's Guide to the North Georgia Mountains* that I edited with Nell Jones and which contained an introduction by President Jimmy Carter. That book went through three editions in its original form, then was acquired by Longstreet Press and served as the prototype for Longstreet's successful Highroads guidebook series.

The second project was *The Riverkeeper's Guide to the Chattahoochee*, published in 1996 in cooperation with the Upper Chattahoochee Riverkeeper. The Atlanta Press Club gave that book their Authors of the Year award—a recognition that Sherri and I readily acknowledged to be for the subject and timeliness of the book rather than its literary merits.

If books like the mountain guide and the Chattahoochee guide and now this Flint River guide are to be of genuine value to the regions about which they are written and to the readers who read them, they must be thoroughly researched *in the field*—a process that is tremendously time consuming. After all, the potential for finding and packaging good information, not widely known or distributed, is what makes guidebooks worth doing in the first place. The dollar and logistical commitments required to thoroughly develop this information is more than most publishers want to invest. Also, books like this involve the (costly) talents of many people: contributing researchers and writers, photographers, illustrators, designers, copy editors, proofreaders and printers. Books like this are, in a word, expensive. The financial commitment required to produce them is more than most publishers can justify, given the projected financial return on investment.

It is only as a result of the participation of companies such as Georgia Power, and, in the case of this Flint River guide, Lieutenant Governor Mark Taylor, Senator George Hooks, the Georgia Department of Community Affairs and Dougherty and Lee Counties, that books like this are possible.

Funding a book is a good starting point, but it is only a starting point. Producing it takes the help, support and cooperation of many individuals who bring a wide range of talents and expertise to the table.

Morgan Murphy, recently retired chairman of Regions Bank of South Georgia and currently a consultant and chairman of the Southwest Georgia Water Resource Task Force; Dr. Liz Blood, associate scientist at the Joseph Jones Ecological Center; Paul DeLoach, manager of community affairs for Miller Brewing Company in Albany; and Kay Reid, editor of the *Albany Herald*, were early supporters of this book project. They provided a solid foundation of advice and contacts that we built on throughout the research and writing period.

Paul DeLoach is also a nationally recognized cave diver, who has explored the Floridan aquifer caves beneath the Flint River. His knowledge of the Flint, particularly between Albany and Bainbridge, is expert and he was always glad to share it with us, often on river trips in his boat.

John Sperry, retired city engineer for the City of Albany, also traveled the river with us and shared his expert knowledge about the Flint. Richard Huggins of Huggins Outboard in Albany provided an 18-foot Alumacraft jon boat with a 65-hp Mercury jet engine for our research.

Richard Crowdis, county administrator of Dougherty County, and Randall Dowling, county administrator of Lee County, efficiently processed correspondence and paperwork involving the book's funding that allowed it to proceed through the county and state government systems efficiently.

Bob Callaway, Laura Jones, Glenn Dowling, Sid Linton, Mildred Slayton, Gigi Leverett and Carmen Alexander in Lieutenant Governor Mark Taylor's office provided political advice, logistical support and, periodically, motivating suggestions that kept research and production reasonably on schedule.

Bill Archer, Georgia Power Company's executive vice president of external affairs, and Ben Harris, vice president of the land department, have been consistent supporters of CI Publishing projects involving Georgia's rivers and mountains. Both are inspiring examples of senior corporate executives who love the outdoors and are working in practical ways to balance economic development with the preservation of natural resources.

A key group of individuals in the Flint-Chattahoochee Watershed helped us "see" the "Land Between the Rivers" and understand the potential for the development of nature-based and cultural tourism in the region. That group included: James Lee Adams, Becky Basset, Joe and Beverley Burke, Peter Bowden, Jennifer Elliott, Claude Fullerton, Tommy Gregors, Tina Hardin, Joy Jinks, Karen Kimbell, Caroln Maschke, Mack Moye, Joe Nichols, Pattie Pennington, Brenda Price, Kip Purvis, India Taylor, Michael Taylor, Lindsay Thomas, Linton Thompson, Charles Tyson and Billy Winn.

A long list of individuals provided interviews, photographs and other types of information about the river. These included M. T. Allen and staff at Peachtree City Library, Maxwell Duke, William Godfrey, Richard Green, W. C. Rip Holman, Jr., Charles Irwin, Ben Kirkland, Joseph Kitchens, Jim McDaniel, Dr. Bruce O'Connor, Keith O"Mary, Frank Schnell, Claude Terry, Matt Thomas, Billy Townsend, Reece Turrentine and Jack Wingate. A special thanks to Faye Perdue at the Carter Center for coordinating the logistics that resulted in President Carter writing a preface for this book.

Finally, thanks to the hard core editorial production team that contributed writing, photographs, design, illustrations and printing expertise, the sine qua non of a project like this. These included: writers Eric Smith, Hal Jacobs, Liz Stubbs and Edie Cohen; illustrator Roel Wielinga; designer Dori Nicholson; proofreader Kim Blass; and printers Dave Avesian and Andy Laflamme.

Foreword: Discovering the Flint River

By Fred Brown

IN THE 1970S AND 80S, I edited and published a monthly recreational guidebook to Georgia and the surrounding states. Over the past 25 years, I have written extensively about nature-based and cultural tourism in Georgia and the South. In addition to that, I have edited the guidebook writing of others; and because of my interest in the subject and the region, I have read much that is written by experts more knowledgeable than I. During those years, most of my attention was focused on the southern coast, the southern mountains and Atlanta—regions of the South that are the best known and which are considered to have the most potential for the kind of go-see-and-do experiences that have been my main interest. Until fairly recently, I am ashamed to say, I knew very little about the part of Georgia, Alabama and Florida defined by the Flint, Chattahoochee and Apalachicola Watershed.

Fortunately for me, about four years ago I had the opportunity, along with my co-author Sherri Smith, to research and write a guidebook about the Chattahoochee River from its headwaters in North Georgia to where it becomes the Apalachicola River at the Georgia and Florida border and continues for another 106 miles to the Gulf of Mexico.

It was an eye-opening experience. During the time that Sherri and I worked on *The Riverkeeper's Guide to the Chattahoochee*, I learned that the entire Chattahoochee (and Apalachicola) River Basin is a marvelous recreational resource, filled with nature-based and cultural tourism opportunities.

The two years that Sherri and I have spent researching and writing this Flint River guidebook not only confirm what I had come to understand about the Chattahoochee-Apalachicola Watershed but enlarge it and add what is, for me, a new and paradigm-shifting dimension.

Of all the rivers I know in Georgia—including the Chattahoochee—the Flint is, to me, the most scenically beautiful, the most diverse, the most user friendly. In terms of simply physically enjoying a river, the Flint provides opportunities that no other river in my experience does. From canoeing *upstream* between Flat Shoals and the Sea, to *walking* the river through the Fall Line that separates the Georgia Piedmont from the Coastal Plain to swimming in the 68-degree springs that flow into the Flint from the Floridan aquifer, I have never felt *connected* to a river to the degree that I have felt a part of the Flint. The experience of putting our boat in Lake Seminole at Lunker Lodge below Bainbridge and locking through at the Jim Woodruff Dam to explore the Apalachicola River or cruising 106 miles to Apalachicola Bay lingers in my memory. It is like suddenly discovering that Georgia has two seacoasts instead of one.

But as satisfying as those Flint River experiences have been, what was even more gratifying was discovering that the Flint matches up with the Chattahoochee and Apalachicola, like three pieces of a puzzle, to form one of the most interesting recreational regions in Georgia. And one that is virtually undiscovered. Knowing the Flint, Chattahoochee and Apalachicola Rivers is like knowing three sisters from the same family. Each has a different look and a distinct personality but all three share a common natural and cultural history.

As a result of our combined experience on the Flint and Chattahoochee Rivers, the introduction to this book is not just about the Flint River but about how the Flint, Chattahoochee and

Apalachicola Watershed tell one story. And what a fascinating story it is: Native Americans, explorers, pioneers and settlers, three presidents, riverboating, early industry, agriculture. The region's history was determined more by the watershed than by the state boundaries.

In addition, along with six chapters on the Flint River, we have included two additional chapters: one on "The Land Between the Rivers," a region defined by Pine Mountain on the north, the Flint River on the east, the Chattahoochee River on the west and Lake Seminole on the south; and another chapter on the Apalachicola River.

We hope you will read and use this book to explore the Flint River—a rare natural treasure of Georgia. At the same time, we hope you will see and explore the Flint as part of the Flint-Chattahoochee-Apalachicola Watershed, one of the great undiscovered recreational areas of the South.

Preface: Preserving A Georgia Treasure

By Jimmy Carter

A S A BOY GROWING UP IN ARCHERY, I worked fields that drained into Choctahatchee (or as we called it, Chock-li-hatchet) Creek. Choctahatchee Creek joins Kinchafoonee Creek, which merges with Muckalee Creek and flows into the Flint River just above Albany. The Choctahatchee was where I fished. It was where I learned about the out-of-doors, where I learned to explore and where I learned how not to get lost. It's where my playmates and I, and occasionally my father, had many hours and days together. We had an immersion in the natural world that has marked my whole existence. The Choctahatchee drainage is really the origin of my life. I still feel more at home and more in a natural element and closer to God when I'm out in the woods by myself, or just with Rosalynn, than at any other time.

During those childhood years on the Choctahatchee, I developed an appreciation for the protection of at least part of the world the way God made it. It affected my life when, as a state senator, I had to deal with natural resources. It was a part of my attitude when I became governor. I was one of the founders of the Georgia Conservancy; I advocated the protection of the Chattahoochee River, particularly in the Atlanta area, and, as governor, I created the Georgia Heritage Trust, which had a budget of $11 million the first year.

While I was governor, I had two major altercations involving the environment and natural resources. One was the designation of wetlands to be drained. This was a standard program that had never been challenged before I went into office. There were 535 projects for draining wetlands in the process of being approved when I took office as governor. During the four years I was in office, none of those projects was approved.

The other altercation concerned the Flint River.

There was a period of time during the economic evolution of our state's and our nation's history, when it was inevitable that many of our dams would be built and naturally free-flowing streams would be obstructed. The primary reason for these dams was power production, and in some areas, flood control. Later, to some degree, recreation became a justification.

At that time there was a system in Washington that aligned U. S. congressmen and the U. S. Corps of Engineers in a process that led inexorably to the construction of more and more dams. It worked for all congressmen but particularly for southern congressmen, most of whom were democrats and almost none of whom were challenged once they became an incumbent. One of a congressman's highest goals in life was to have built in his district a notable dam at federal government expense that would create a lake that could be named for him. There was a standard procedure. The process began when a newly elected legislator went in as a junior member of congress. He would put his name on the list to get a dam built in his district. That dam might be at the bottom of 500 dams to be constructed in America. But as the congressman got re-elected time after time, eventually his particular project would move up to the top of the list.

As a result of this system, the Corps of Engineers, part of the United States Army, was subverted in its basic integrity. The motivation for the Corps was not to make an objective analysis of costs of a project versus its benefits, but to make sure that it pleased the members of Congress by guaranteeing that the computed benefits of each dam was always far in excess of the costs. At least on paper. The Corps of Engineers abandoned its basic integrity, uniformly over the whole country, in order to justify those projects; to please the congressmen who supervised the operations of the Corps and who also appropriated funds for its operation; and to justify its own existence. So there were hundreds and hundreds of dams being built around the country over a 10-year period. Almost all of them were unnecessary, yet, at the same time, they were quite attractive to the local communities involved as presented in the economic benefits analysis prepared by the Corps.

The Flint River dam at Sprewell Bluff fell into this Washington pork barrel pattern. In the case of the Flint, the major factor considered by the Corps in assessing the value of the proposed dam at Sprewell Bluff was recreation potential. The Flint is the longest-remaining free-flowing major river in Georgia. It is free flowing until it gets down to Lake Blackshear in Crisp County some 200 miles from its headwaters. Congressman Jack Flint, a good man so far as I know, wanted to dam up the Flint River near Thomaston, which was in his district.

When I became governor, I became aware of this. As an environmentalist, I was interested in the identification and preservation of natural areas. I was becoming more and more involved with people who enjoyed the streams and the out-of-doors in its natural state. I became an avid canoeist. I learned how to kayak. I learned how to roll a kayak in the Georgia State University swimming pool. I began to go down the Chattooga River, which was the setting for the movie *Deliverance*.

At the time, the Flint River was basically ignored. But when the idea of the dam came along, I was urged by a few outdoorsmen, fishermen and environmentalists to take a critical look at the project to see if it was justified. I personally canoed down the river twice. I went fishing on the river for shoal bass, a species indigenous to the Flint. I began to see what would change about the upper Flint if the dam at Sprewell Bluff was built.

I started a commitment—which was quite time-consuming but not unpleasant—of meeting with groups who were interested in the Flint River. I met with 50 different groups in the governor's office. I met with concrete manufacturers and salesmen. I met with people who anticipated building a big recreation center in the neighborhood of Griffin and Thomaston. I met with chamber of commerce people who pointed out that during the dam construction period, which might last two or three years, there were going to be as many as 200 jobs created. These were people I had worked with in the past. I understood their point of view. I had been a businessman in a rural community myself.

On the other side there were environmental groups and sportsmen groups who raised contrasting issues. It used to be that canoeists and fishermen, who wanted to wade down a river to catch some fish with a fly rod, were a small group and quite often not vocal. Those times have changed, and I think they have changed for the better.

Jack Flint was furious that any investigation or question was raised. But I was impervious to that displeasure.

My next step was to ascertain the accuracy of the facts and figures of the Corps of Engineers, which I didn't have any reason to doubt. I considered the Corps an element of the military. I presumed that the officers of the Corps of Engineers were telling me the truth. But, as I investigated their figures, I found that sometimes—if there was a question about economic benefits of the Sprewell Bluff project—they would triple the alleged benefits with no substantiating data to back up the change. They kept emphasizing the need for another broadwater lake in the vicinity, despite the fact that within 50 miles of the Sprewell Bluff site there were already a half dozen or more lakes. None of those lakes had realized the Corps of Engineers projections' for economic benefits of tourism or for surface use. If anybody wanted to go back and look at the Corps of Engineers' analysis of benefits that would accrue in tourism, they would find that those benefits are just a complete passel of lies and exaggerations to justify a project the Corps wanted to construct and that a member of congress wanted to have constructed. It would give the Corps work to do and justify its existence, and they thought nobody would question it.

The Corps brought up flood control. They said that the dam would prevent flooding in the lower reaches of the Flint River. This proved to be totally unfounded. The only way you can control flooding with a dam of this kind, I learned at the time, is to reduce the water level in the lake by 10 feet in anticipation of heavy rain so that when the rains fall, instead of running downstream, the rain would fill up the lake. Well, you can't anticipate that. By the Corps' own estimates, Sprewell Bluff dam would have had little effect in flood control below Lakes Blackshear and Chehaw. For instance, had the project been built prior to the 1925 Albany flood, damages of $2,000,000 would have been reduced by only $35,700. (A similar marginal difference in flood impact would have been the case in the 1994 flood.) In Bainbridge, a 10-year flood interval would have been increased to 12 years with river depth being lowered from 33.5 feet to 32.5 feet.

I finally decided to call a press conference on October 1, 1974, and announce that my final judgement was that this dam should be vetoed. There was a furor raised—primarily by the chambers of commerce and the folks dedicated to Congressman Flint.

When I became President of the United States, the Sprewell Bluff dam event was a very important memory for me, an experience that was instructive. I began to look on all the Corps of Engineers projects in the other 49 states that were moving inexorably toward final approval and that were not being questioned. I began to question those dams. As President, I had the prerogative to veto them, and I began to do that. I wasn't a dictator, and I have to admit that some of the ill-advised projects were approved. But, overwhelmingly, they were disapproved. It created one of the most difficult confrontations between me and members of Congress of anything I did while I was in office. I was also instrumental in helping get the law changed so that for a project, such as the one the Corps proposed at Sprewell Bluff, local people would have to put up 25 percent of the money; before, it was 100 percent Washington financing.

So, it's likely that my experience at Sprewell Bluff has basically changed the U.S. national attitude toward dams and their ill-advised nature in many cases. Nowadays, the big altercation is how many of these enormous dams should be removed. The Corps of Engineers is now devoting part of its time to analyzing how it can take some of these dams out. Not only have many dams served their original purposes, but they are now becoming filled with sediment. Instead of the water being 90 feet deep at the dam, it is now only 20 feet deep; in 50 more years it's going to be two feet deep.

Sometimes Rosalynn and I stop in Thomaston on our way from Atlanta to Plains. I have had many people come up to me and confess that they cursed me profoundly when I vetoed the dam. But now they are thankful for my having done it. They are glad that the river was saved. I think it has been worth all the confrontations and the debates and sometimes disharmonies that have resulted from what is still an ongoing process in America of preserving things instead of trying to modify them in an unnecessary fashion.

Those people have—we all have—a precious possession along that river. It is not adequately used now. But anyone who wants to experience the way Georgia was when God made it or the way it was when it was first settled by white people can go to the upper parts of the Flint River and see how beautiful it is. It is breathtaking in its beauty. And the wildlife that exists in that river corridor: otter, fox, muskrat, beaver, bobcat....You cannot describe it. It is a treasure. A treasure that is appreciated by an increasing number of people as the generations pass. Lakes and dams are everywhere. But to experience something that is undisturbed and has its natural beauty? You hope and pray that it will be there a thousand years in the future, still just as beautiful and undisturbed.

Introduction:
A Recreational Guidebook to the Flint River and Environs

By Sherri M. L. Smith

AMERICA

From the Flint River to the Chattahoochee River is a land that is tightly intertwined with the history of Georgia and America. Within this region sprang events with national scope. What was occurring in America was reflected in what was happening in the region, and events that occurred in the region greatly effected the policies of an emerging nation.

Some of the first European explorers to come to America made their way up the Flint River and found a society of people who had been inhabiting this land for thousands of years—cutting paths through the forests, canoeing the waters and planting the fields. George Washington sent Benjamin Hawkins to serve as Indian Agent when the clash of these two cultures seemed imminent, but Hawkins could not ward off the inevitable. This part of the country was necessary to the manifest destiny of Thomas Jefferson, and was the proving ground for the fierce nationalism of Andrew Jackson.

The stories here are woven into an intricate tapestry: a story of the American frontier and a general, Jackson, who brutally and methodically moved a nation out so that another nation might survive. A story of the antebellum South where cotton was king. Here was one of the largest slaveholding regions of the country, and the beginnings of the Civil Rights Movement. A story of rivers, and of water power and of mills and industry. And here is the story of three Presidents—Jackson, Franklin D. Roosevelt and Jimmy Carter. As president Jackson would deliver the final blow to Southeast Indians with his Indian Removal Act, which appropriated funds for negotiating treaties and relocating Indians to the West—thus securing Georgia lands for white settlement. Witnessing the struggle of this area during the 1920s and '30s, Roosevelt was inspired to formulate his New Deal policies that brought the country out of its greatest depression. Carter, who grew up loving this land, was enlightened enough to see the harm in harnessing the wild river that ran through it.

THE NATIVE AMERICANS

Prehistoric Indians

It is estimated that at the time of first European contact, more than 90 million people inhabited North and South America. Anthro-

---

De Soto's First Crossing of the Flint

In 1540, explorer Hernandez de Soto and his band of 700—including priests, carpenters, musicians, sword cutlers, Cuban Indian slaves, horses, dogs and pigs—left La Florida and entered the land that is now Georgia, looking for cities of gold.

"…on March 5, passing near present-day Cairo and Camilla, Georgia, the vanguard arrived at a large river in the vicinity of present-day Newton. The remainder of the army caught up with the vanguard on March 6 or 7, after a march of four or five days.

"The Spaniards found themselves standing on the bank of the Flint River, deep and swift, and so wide—about 250 feet—that Cristobal Mosquera, the best stone-thrower among them, could not throw a stone to the opposite bank. They cut down some trees, sawed them into planks, and built a piragua, which was a simple, flat-bottomed boat, usually long and narrow in shape, used to transport people and goods, mainly on rivers and lakes. They at first attempted to pull the boat back and forth across the river using their slave chains, the segments of which they connected together with iron S-hooks. But the current of the river was so strong that twice it broke the chain. Finally, they twisted several ropes together, forming them into two hawsers. They fastened one hawser to the bow and the other to the stern of the boat, and in this way they pulled the boat back and forth across the river, ferrying the men and supplies across. They got the horses across by tying ropes around their necks and pulling to assist them while they swam. Had they not been anxious about obtaining food, De Soto and his men could have traveled due north up the eastern side of the Flint River, thereby avoiding this river crossing."

Knights of Spain, Warriors of the Sun by Charles Hudson

pologists have grouped these Native American societies, or American Indians as they are known, into several culture areas. The Indian societies occupying land from the Atlantic coast west to central Texas were dubbed the Southeastern culture and included the Cherokee, Choctaw, Chickasaw, Seminole and Creek people—the Creeks being the Indians who lived in the valleys and river bottoms of the Flint and Chattahoochee Rivers.

The Creeks, like all other Native Americans, appear to have descended from Asian peoples who migrated across the Bering Strait, a 50-mile long land bridge between Asia and Alaska, created during the Ice Age about 30,000 to 50,000 years ago. Those who made the crossing were not explorers or settlers or adventurers. They were simply hungry men and women following the game on which their livelihood depended. Over the centuries, their descendants spread out over the two continents, from Alaska to the tip of South America, from the Arctic Circle to the subtropics. People had to learn to live in frozen tundra, in forests, on grassy plains and in arid deserts, in high mountains and in deep canyons, along rugged coastlines and lakeshores and in fertile river valleys.

Some of them ended up in the fertile valleys of the Flint and Chattahoochee Rivers about 10,000 years ago. Known as the Paleo Indians, they were nomadic hunters of large mammals who roamed the region looking for food in a time when ice still covered much of the earth. Their daily routine centered around hunting. They traveled in small bands, or families, searching for the large animals of their day —mastodon, the giant bison, the mammoth. These animals provided them with meat and fat for food, skins for clothing and bones for tools. The Indians stayed in one place for only a few days, eating the animals and plants in the area and moving on. They built shelters only if they found enough food in an area to last a few weeks or months.

By the Archaic Period, from 8000 B.C. to 1000 B.C., the ice had retreated, the climate had gradually warmed and the large animals roaming the region had disappeared. White-tailed deer, boars, black bear and many small animals, which can still be found today, appeared. These Indians were hunters and gatherers who utilized the new foods as well as shellfish and seasonal plants. Rivers and their rich food sources became available. Nut-bearing trees, extending from the Fall Line to the upper Coastal Plain, were probably of great importance to these people, providing them with needed protein and fatty acids. The large stands of hickory and oak trees growing in the region were probably as important in bringing these Indians into the area as the large amounts of game.

The first steps to farming were taken when hunters began to understand more and more about the plants and animals they used for food. They possibly noticed that a plant would grow where seeds had fallen on the ground, or learned how to raise animals by taking care of young animals whose mothers they had killed. In the region, it is

Standing Boy Flint Industry

Archaic Indians, who inhabited the Flint and Chattahoochee River Valley between 8000 and 1000 B.C., created something of a tool manufacturing industry at Standing Boy Creek, using stone quarried from the Flint River.

"We know Archaic man was in the [Chattahoochee-Flint] Valley because there is clear evidence of his occupation in the area just north of present-day Columbus where Lake Oliver is now located. There in 1959, on a sandy knoll on the north bank of Standing Boy Creek in an area now covered by the waters of the lake, archaeologists found numerous ancient artifacts flaked from a light-colored, heavily weathered flint. Among these were endscrapers, unifacial and bifacial knives, and small, triangular, beveled and notched knives, originally thought to be projectile points, called spinner points by collectors. The flaking done to create the tools is of such a nature as to suggest a highly specialized approach, one reason archaeologists believe the site was the location of what is now called the Standing Boy Flint Industry. Experts date the site back to at least 7500 to 6500 B.C., and point out that similar tool assemblages have been found further down the Chattahoochee in Houston County, Alabama, at the Stanfield-Worley shelter cave in northwest Alabama, to the east near Macon, Georgia, and at various other sites in the Southeast.

"The Standing Boy site appears to have been the location of a tool industry, involving quartz as well as flint, for many hundreds of years, and may, in fact, have its roots in the preceding Paleo Period. Interestingly, much of the flint used as the Standing Boy site came from the Flint River. Apparently it was acquired in a crudely flaked form and then was finished locally."

The Old Beloved Path by William W. Winn

known that during the Woodland Period, 1000 B.C. to A.D. 900, people planted sunflower, marsh elder and goosefeet—plants considered weeds today. Eventually, squash and gourds and later corn and beans were cultivated. The Indians also learned to make pottery, which was a monumental step, as it was used to cook and store food and transport water. People began to live in villages at least part of the year. After thousands of years as hunters, these Woodland people no longer had to roam to obtain food. Farmers settled in one area for several years at a time and built villages near their cropland, living there as long as the crops grew well and the firewood lasted. Once the land became unproductive, the Indians moved to a new area.

During the Mississippian Period, A.D. 900 to European contact in the mid-1500s, the Indians built large villages, usually on rivers or streams, using the rich bottomlands for farming and the rivers and streams for transportation. Village areas surrounded huge, flat-topped temple mounds where social and religious ceremonies took place. The Mississippian Indians still hunted and gathered, but this culture discovered that the bottomland soils produced better crops and the periodic flooding that occurred restored the nutrients in the soil. They cultivated seed plants, pumpkins, beans and squash, probably tobacco and especially corn. So important was the staple corn that the Mississippians gave it religious significance, connecting it to the king-gods, who led them. The great mounds they built, full of burial plots and artifacts, still stand, some protected as public property. There are two big Mississippian sites just south of the Fall Line. Rood Creek Indian Mounds (see page 205) on the Chattahoochee in Stewart County was one of the largest in prehistoric Georgia. At its peak, the population of Rood's Landing was an estimated 3,500 people. Another important mound site is the Kolomoki Mounds State Historic Site near Blakely (see page 201).

The decade that followed their contact with Europeans brought cultural devastation to the native people of the Southeast. The earliest known meeting between Southeastern Indians and Europeans occurred in 1513 when a Spaniard named Juan Ponce de Leon landed with his ship on the coast of Florida. Other Europeans followed. Hernando de Soto and his band of Spanish explorers first stepped foot into the Flint River Valley in 1540. These explorers were surprised to find an established culture of people. But with these explorers came measles, tuberculosis, typhus, smallpox and other old world diseases, far worse than anything that could have been inflicted upon the Indians with mere weapons or military force. Despite the tragic consequences of disease, the survivors persevered and so began a 300-year-era of Indian, black and white interactions in the region.

The Greatest Naturalists

From 1000 B.C. to A.D. 700, Woodland Indians swam and fished the rivers and streams, waded the swamps and searched for nuts and berries in the vast forests of the Flint and Chattahoochee River Valley.

"In the daily struggle for survival, and in the simple fact of existence, the Woodland Indians became the greatest naturalists the Valley has ever known. They made use of almost everything and wasted nothing. There was scarcely an animal or a plant in the Valley that was not utilized by the Woodland people. Animals not only provided food, but their skins, bones and sinews were used to fashion useful articles, including clothing, bow strings, drills, hoes, tool handles, needles and the like. Fish provided flesh for food. Their teeth, scales, and bones were made into arrowheads, cutting and puncturing tools, and articles of adornment. Wild plants which we consider to be weeds were a vital source of food, medicine, and raw material for domestic use and manufacture. Never before or since have the people of the Valley known so much about their surroundings—or turned them to such useful purpose—as during the Woodland Period."

The Old Beloved Path by William W. Winn

The Creeks

The Creek people are believed to be the Southeastern descendants of the Moundbuilders of the Mississippian Period. These indigenous people of composite origin spoke a family of related languages referred to as Muskogean. They called themselves the Muskogee Nation—Muskogees or Muscogulges. (The word Muskogee, or Muscogee, signifies land that is wet or prone to flooding; "ulge" designates a nation or people.) But English-speaking white men called them Creeks because they lived and roamed the many rivers, streams and swamps that ran through their territory—a territory that extended from the Atlantic to the Tombigbee River, through parts of Georgia, Florida, Alabama and Mississippi.

By the 18th century the Creeks were the dominant tribe in a confederacy with a membership of about 30,000. The confederacy occupied most of what are now the states of Georgia and Alabama. After the Cherokee, the Creeks were the most powerful grouping of Native Americans south of New York.

The Creek Nation included approximately 60 towns and was divided into two geopolitical divisions, which the Europeans called the Upper and Lower Towns. Forty Upper Towns lay along the Tallapoosa-Coosa-Alabama River System and 20 Lower Towns were scattered on the Ocmulgee, Flint and Chattahoochee Rivers of Georgia. This division predated trading relations between the Creeks and the British Colonies, but originated with the relative position of the two main trading paths that linked the Creeks with South Carolina: the Upper Creek Trading Path and the Lower Creek Trading Path. These two divisions differed not only geographically, but politically. They respected their kinship with each other but held separate councils, claimed separate territories and very often pursued different foreign policy—a difference that would ultimately affect their survival. Besides that, Creeks also divided their towns into two types—red, or war towns, and white, or peace towns.

The Creek town, or tulwa, was the center of political, social and economic life. Each town contained a public square, which was its governmental and ceremonial center, and 25 to 100 log houses. Creek temples were impressive dome-shaped structures made of thatch. The town was governed by a mico, or town king, who was so associated with his town that his given name was forsaken and he became known as Coweta Mico or Cussita Mico. The Creek were an agricultural tribe: Creek women cultivated corn, squash, beans and other crops. The men hunted and fished.

Long before the Europeans disrupted Native American life, trade took place among the different tribes. Well-traveled trading paths linked villages. Furs, flint, copper, silver, clay pipes, salt, conch shells, feathers—all were common goods for trade. But once the first Carolina traders entered the Indian town of Coweta in 1685, carrying glass beads, bells and brightly colored cloth, as well as steel knives and

William Bartram and the Flint

While collecting plants in the Southeast for an English patron, naturalist William Bartram wrote and illustrated a diary of Indian life that captured the imagination of Europe, inspiring the poetry of Wordsworth and the politics of Voltaire. Bartram reached the Flint River near the present-day GA 127 on July 5, 1775, and then moved on several miles to camp for the night on a creek, a tributary of the Flint.

"The adjacent low grounds and Cane swamp afforded excellent food and range for our horses, who, by this time, through fatigue of constant travelling, heat of the climate and season, were tired and dispirited, we came to camp sooner than usual and started later next day, that they might have time to rest and recruit themselves. The territory lying upon this creek and the space between it and the river, present every appearance of a delightful and fruitful region in some future day, it being a rich soil and exceedingly well situated for every branch of agriculture and grazing, diversified with hills and dales, savannas and vast Cane meadows, and watered by innumerable rivulets and brooks, all contiguous to the Flint river: an arm of the great Chata Uche or Apalachucla offers an uninterrupted navigation to the bay of Mexico and Atlantic ocean, and thence to the West India Islands and over the whole world."

Travels by William Bartram

muskets, the focus changed. The Creeks soon established strong trading links with Charles Town [Charleston] in the Colony of Carolina: Indian deerskins and other produce for flintlock muskets, metal tools and European textiles. This trade was certainly a lucrative proposition for the Carolina colony as hides and furs from the interior Indian tribes became its major export.

After the American Revolution (1775–1783), the Creeks, who had supported the British, were faced with land-hungry American settlers eager to push into Creek territory and an American government somewhat intent on manifest destiny. In 1796, President George Washington appointed Colonel Benjamin Hawkins as Indian Agent on the Flint River. Hawkins's philosophy to integrate the Indians into the white culture by teaching them the skills of modern farming and industry was noble but difficult to implement. Some Creeks, mostly in the Lower Towns, realized the advantages of cooperating with the Americans, but other, younger Creeks, mostly living in the Upper Towns, rejected contact with whites and the consequent abandonment of their own Indian culture.

All Creeks resented the relentless encroachment on their land. Encouraged by the Spanish in Florida and the British in Canada, who promised to provide arms and supplies, many Creeks prepared for war against the United States, which was now building roads from Georgia into the Alabama settlements. Tecumseh, a Shawnee Indian chieftain from the northern tribes, conceived a plan to organize all tribes from the Great Lakes to the Gulf of Mexico and force out the white man. In 1811, he visited the Creeks, including Red Eagle, leader of the militant Red Sticks (named as such because they painted their war sticks a bright red) to recruit warriors and gain support for his campaign. As Tecumseh stirred their fears and hatreds, the Creek Nation became more and more divided and the threat of Civil War loomed between the Upper and Lower tribes.

Desultory raids on white settlements along the American border by the Upper tribes widened the split within the Creek Nation. Finally, on August 30, 1813, Red Eagle and 1,000 Creek followers of Tecumseh descended upon Fort Mims, a white stronghold located about 40 miles from Mobile, butchering about 500 men, women and children.

So began the Creek War of 1813–1814. In the long history of Indians in North America, the Creek War was the turning point in their ultimate destruction. The irreversible step toward obliterating tribes as sovereign entities within the United States now commenced. The Creek Nation would be irreparably shattered. All other tribes would soon experience the same melancholy fate.

Hawkins and Tecumseh

In 1811, the great Shawnee chief Tecumseh traveled to the Creek Council to urge them to join other tribes in rising up against the whites. Indian Agent Benjamin Hawkins also attended, hoping to keep peace.

"The day after the conference convened, Tecumseh with twenty-four of his warriors, hideously covered with black paint marched dramatically into the Square. Tenseness and an air of impending violence hung over the town.

"Hawkins, with calmness waited for Tecumseh to address the Council. Each morning a Shawnee warrior would announce that his chief would speak at noon and each noon the speech was put off until the following day. Tecumseh chose to bide his time. He knew the agent's influence was a power to reckon with, that his hopes of arousing the Indians would be obstructed as long as this man remained among them. He waited.

"Finally, after almost a week, Hawkins, disheartened, decided that the council could have no important outcome. He warned the Creeks in his speech, against taking unfriendly actions toward the United States, and departed for his home on the Flint.

"It was an error in judgement, based perhaps on his belief that the Creeks would remain firm in their loyalty to him and to the nation he represented. But as soon as the agent set out from Tuckabatchee the Shawnee chief with eloquence and impressive mysticism loosed his terrible hatred of the whites. His words and gestures flicked life fire over the disgruntled Creeks. He won them completely. With shouts, brandishing their weapons, they roared frenzied approval of war to the death against the land stealing Americans."

This So Remote Frontier by Mark E. Fretwell

GEORGIA

Great Britain's 13th colony became one of the first 13 states after the Revolution, and for several decades was part of America's vast Indian territory and frontier. As Georgia's boundaries were pushed further and further west with the Indian land cessions and removal from their land, the Georgia frontier quickly became settled with people moving from Virginia, the Carolinas and the Georgia coast looking for fertile farm lands. Three Indian land cessions, created by three different treaties, opened up land for white settlement in the Flint and Chattahoochee River Valley: the 1814 Treaty of Fort Jackson ceded land for the 1820 Land Lottery; the 1821 Treaty of Indian Springs ceded land for the 1821 Land Lottery; and the 1825 Treaty of Indian Springs ceded land for the 1827 Land Lottery. The only state in the country to use a lottery to distribute public domain, Georgia rushed in settlers in order to push out Indians and secure the land. The lottery was a logical system that gave every qualified Georgian equal chance to obtain new land, with surveyors marking off a rectangular plot before actual distribution. Between 1820 and the beginning of the Civil War in 1861, numerous counties were carved out of the "Land Between the Rivers." After the war, counties continued to be created until the last new county in Georgia, Peach County, was formed in 1924.

TRANSPORTATION

Indian Trails

When De Soto came to explore the interior of America, there was a already a vast network of trails. Indian trails sprawled across the region just as they did throughout America. Some trails connected vast stretches of country, just as interstates do today. Other trails went to the nearest village or cut through the woods to the best river crossing. Many of these trails, especially the ones that went to the shallow fords across rivers and streams, were first trod by the mastodon and other prehistoric animals on their relentless search for water and food. The paths which connected longer distances were part of a great trading system where many items were traded from one area to another.

Paths began to evolve into roads as more Europeans and later Americans entered the Indian Territory. By nature, the paths were narrow, allowing only single-file traveling by the Indians or traders; but as time progressed, and permanent white settlers began crossing the Indian lands in wagons carrying their goods, trails had to be widened. Trees had to be cut and stumps removed. It was a laborious process. Sometimes a road would diverge from the original path for some reason, but for the most part, the newer, wider roads followed the existing footpaths.

The Land Lottery

All land within the Flint River Valley and the Land Between the Rivers was distributed by land lotteries. People who secured land through the lottery system could either cultivate it themselves or sell it. Many families today still hold title to land that their ancestors secured through the lottery.

"The new land-granting system enacted in 1803 provided for the complete surveying of land in any Indian cession and laying it out in lots of 202 1/2 or 490 acres, depending upon its value. The land was then distributed by a lottery in which all citizens were eligible to participate. Every free white male citizen of the United States who was a Georgia resident for the past twelve months was allowed one chance in the lottery, as was every family of orphans under twenty-one years of age. Every man with a wife and minor child and every widow with minor children secured two chances. The land given in the lottery was free except for fees of $4.00 per hundred acres....

"As new lands were granted and settled, the legislature usually provided commissioners to lay out county seats, reserve land for public buildings, sell town lots, and create a county academy with the money derived from lot sales. This system secured better-planned towns and cities and established important public services at once; delayed services would have prevailed if town planning had been left to the settlers. Georgia probably received less than ten cents an acre for land distributed under the lottery system, compared with the minimum price of $1.25 an acre received by the federal government for its public lands."

A History of Georgia by Kenneth Coleman

Generally, Georgia's main Indian trails ran from east to west with a few connecting to other areas north and south. Today's Augusta was the main east-west gateway into Georgia with many major trails branching out across the state from there because it was a good place to cross the Savannah River. From Augusta the path led to the coastal town of Charles Town (Charleston, South Carolina), a major colonial trading port.

Probably the best-known and most-heavily traveled Indian trail in Georgia was the Lower Creek Trading Path. From the trading center of Augusta, it ran westward across the state, following the geographical Fall Line, which millions of years ago was the seacoast. The Fall Line, which cuts directly through the Flint and Chattahoochee River Valleys, crosses every major river at its lowest good crossing point. The route was formed thousands of years ago by herds of large animals migrating across the region and crossing the rivers at the shallows. It was only natural that the Indians following those animals would use the same crossing points. The trading path crossed the Flint River where Col. Hawkins would establish his Creek Indian Agency around 1800 and continued westward to Columbus and then onward into Alabama.

With the Louisiana Purchase in 1803, President Thomas Jefferson recognized the importance of the most-direct route possible between Washington and New Orleans. In 1805 Congress passed an act to establish a post road from "Washington City by Athens, Georgia, to New Orleans," Later that year, as part of the Treaty of Washington with the Creek Indian Nation, the Federal government secured the right of way for a wagon road through the Creek Territory, which would closely follow the route of the Lower Creek Trading Path:

"that the government of the United States shall forever hereafter have a right to a horse path, through the Creek country, from the Ocmulgee to Mobile, in such direction as shall, by the President of the United States, be considered most convenient, and to clear out the same, and lay logs over the creeks; and the citizens of said State shall at all times have a right to pass peaceably on said path, under such regulations and restrictions as the government of the United States shall from time to time direct; and the Creek chiefs will have boats kept at the several rivers for the conveyance of men and horses, and the houses of entertainment established at suitable places on said path for the accommodation of travelers; and the respective ferriages and prices of entertainment for men and horses shall be regulated by the present agent, Col. Hawkins, or by his successor in office, or as usual among white people."

As much as anything, this agreement, signed by such Creek leaders as William McIntosh, ultimately led to the downfall of the Creek Nation.

By 1809, faced with the threat of war with Britain, the U.S. government determined that the Old Horse Path, as the wagon road had

The Creeks and the Federal Road

What began as a wagon road through Indian Territory, known as the Old Horse Path, soon became a military road, marking the beginning of the end for the Creek Indians in the Flint and Chattahoochee River Valley.

"The 1805 treaty, with its provision for a federal road to be built through the lands of the Upper Creeks, caused an uproar among the towns of the Coosa and Tallapossa Rivers. The westernmost Creeks did not want to invite more whites to tramp over their lands, cutting down their trees, killing their animals, and coming into contact with their headstrong youth who might too easily resort to violence. The older townsmen understood that any violence that erupted along the road could be used to extort a further land cession. Because of their opposition, the completion of the road was delayed until 1811.

"What alarmed the conservative group of Creeks most about the federal road was that whites were not just passing through Creek lands. Though it was illegal, whites began to settle in Alabama south of most of the Upper Creek settlements. The sight of scores of wagons daily spewing dust into the Chattahoochee Valley convinced many that the white man's frontier was not isolated only to the east of the Creek Nation. It was beginning to surround them. But instead of blaming the whites, resentment focused more on the assimilated Indians and mestizos."

Flowing through Time, A History of the Lower Chattahoochee River by Lynn Willoughby

become known, would have to be upgraded to a military road for the purpose of moving supply wagons, cannons and men on horse and foot. Over the protests of the Indians, the U.S. military began widening the Old Horse Path for that purpose. Completed in 1812, the Federal Road, as it was now called, was built in anticipation of conflict with the British, but sparked the Creek War of 1813–14.

The Upper Creek Trading Path, or Oakfuskee Trail as it was more commonly called, was one of the oldest, longest and most important trails, economically speaking, in Georgia. It paralleled the path of the Lower Creek Trading Path, connecting with it at both its eastern and western terminus, but diverged in between to the north where it connected many of the Upper Creek Indian villages. The path crossed the Flint at Flat Shoals and the Chattahoochee just below the mouth of Wehadke Creek. In time, the Oakfuskee Trail became a pioneer's trace and some segments of it eventually grew into noted stagecoach roads, but it never gained the significance of its lower counterpart.

Numerous paths in the Flint and Chattahoochee River Valleys diverged from the main trails, sometimes looping back and sometimes going off into a new direction. A number of old paths were known as Barnard's Trails, named because they ran to or past the residence of Timothy Barnard, a Creek Indian of mixed ancestry who lived on the Flint River at today's Montezuma. He was, for a number of years, assistant to Creek Indian Agent Benjamin Hawkins. McIntosh Road was a road built by Indian Chief William McIntosh to connect his plantations across Georgia and Alabama. From his plantation at Indian Springs, the road ran northwestward near today's Griffin, Brooks and Peachtree City, across Whitewater and Line Creeks onward to his home, the McIntosh Reserve, near today's Newnan. Herod's Trail was one of a large network of old Indian paths that intersected at Leesburg and then eventually went through the old community of Herod and on into Fort Gaines, when it was a Creek Indian War fort that protected Georgia's western frontier.

Not to be confused with the Federal Road was the Federal Trail, which ran southward from today's Albany on the east side and parallel to the Flint River. United States troops used the path during the Creek War of 1813–14. Although there was little fighting in Georgia during that war, troops moved up and down the road between Fort Early and other military stations. Later, in 1816, Fort Scott was constructed and Gen. Andrew Jackson moved his troops from Fort Scott down the trail into Florida to fight the Seminoles in 1818. Another Indian path that paralleled the Federal Trail on the opposite or west side of the Flint was also used by Jackson during the Seminole War and became known as Jackson's Trail.

Ferries

Trails that led to the Flint always found their way to the shallowest point possible in order for travelers to ford the river. Initially, travelers

The Ferryman

Underwood's Ferry was just one name given to the ferry that crossed the Flint just west of Marshallville— the last ferry to operate in the state of Georgia.

"Lester Cromer took over the job of running Underwood's Ferry early in 1961 when his brother became seriously ill; his brother had operated the ferry for seven years. 'I don't know how old this ferry is,' said Mr. Cromer, 'but it's old. Lots of people cross this ferry just to see how it rides.' The ferry is guided by two large cables attached to trees on each side of the river. When the ferry's car motor is started, the cables turn around a drum—and the ferry moves to the opposite bank. A crossing takes only a minute and 10 seconds.

"'Saturday and Sunday are the busiest days,' Mr. Cromer says. 'Some Sundays I go back and forth all day. I'm on call seven days a week, 24 hours a day. I live in that house where I can see the cars come from both directions; if a driver wants to cross at night, he just blows his horn and I get up and go take him across.

"'Once a car almost rolled off because the driver forgot to put on his brakes. He had gotten out, but his wife was still in the car when it started rolling. I caught hold of the car and yelled—and the man jumped in and yanked on his brakes just in time.'"

"The Flint" by Katherine Barnwell from *Georgia Rivers* edited by George Hatcher

crossed by walking or riding horses over the rocky shoals. The first ferries built were usually just logs tied together to form a raft-like vehicle that was often pulled by horses. Later most ferries were large wooden barges operated by a system of cables and pulleys and powered mainly by the river's current, with additional encouragement from a long wooden pole in the hands of a muscular ferryman. Horses were sometimes used.

How many ferries crossed the Flint is hard to determine, but there were plenty. In Macon County alone there were at least four ferries, at one time or another, crossing the Flint. The real heyday of ferries was in the 19th century, although some continued to operate well into the 20th century. In 1920, the Georgia Highway Department took over the state road system and the ferries on those roads were purchased from private individuals who had been operating them. Toll charges were abolished at state-owned ferries. One by one though, bridges replaced the ferries.

The last ferry crossing in Georgia was on the Flint near Marshall-ville. At first, a wooden barge was used at the ferry, which was known over the years by various names, including the Miona Ferry, the Marshallville Ferry, Underwood's Ferry and the Flint River Ferry. Later the craft in use was a 55-foot metal barge with a plank floor, powered by a six-cylinder 1954 Chevrolet engine rigged up to cables. The crossing was safe, smooth and only took a couple of minutes. Unless the river was extremely high or there were problems with snags and floating logs, 24-hour service was available until 1988 when the ferry discontinued service.

Steamboats

Transportation improvements throughout Georgia were almost always aimed at aiding agriculture. By 1820 steam navigation on Georgia's rivers was just beginning. The first steamboat to travel the Apalachicola-Flint-Chattahoochee River System appeared in 1828. Steamboats regularly traveled the Chattahoochee as far as Columbus, the head of navigation on that river, and served more than a 100-mile stretch of the lower Flint. By 1860 more than 26 steamboat landings dotted the Flint between its junction with the Chattahoochee and Bainbridge—all loaded with cotton waiting for a trip down the river to the port of Apalachicola and northern markets. Navigation above Bainbridge was more difficult, but smaller boats and barges traveled the water from Bainbridge to Albany. In fact, Nelson Tift founded Albany as a purely financial venture to ship cotton to market on the Flint. Steamboats continued to thrive in the 1850s despite the competition of railroads, and remained in operation until about 1928.

Railroads

The area's future, as well as that of the rest of the state's, lay not with steamboats but with railroads. Georgians throughout the Land

The River Was the Highway

By 1832, Apalachicola had become the third-largest port city on the Gulf and the third-largest cotton port in the United States.

"The pulse of this community was quieted or quickened according to the state of its major artery, the river. The waterway originated at two Georgia streams, the Chattahoochee and the Flint Rivers, which flowed from north Georgia in a southwesterly direction roughly paralleling each other through southwest Georgia until they converged at the Florida and Alabama boundaries. From this point of their confluence to where the waters reached the Gulf of Mexico, the river was known as the Apalachicola. In Florida a smaller stream known as the Chipola originated west of the larger course near the Alabama line and paralleled the Apalachicola for about fifty miles before the two united and wound their way to the Gulf.

"The river was the highway that linked the port with the rich cotton fields of Georgia and Alabama and, beyond them, the industrial and commercial city of Columbus, Georgia. Until the railroads came in from east and west to break up this unit in the 1850s, residents throughout the valley seemed to face inward toward the river that would take the cotton to market or mill. It was not a perfect transportation network. In the dry summer months the streams dwindled to a thread, carrying less than two feet of water in many places. Every summer commerce halted until the river again resumed its usable state."

Fair to Middlin'–The Antebellum Cotton Trade of the Apalachicola/Chattahoochee River Valley by Lynn Willoughby

Between the Rivers were eager to lay the twin ribbons of iron that would bind together the state and the markets for their agricultural products. Like the steamboats preceding them, railroads primarily linked established commercial areas. In 1857, the first train of cars over the Georgia and Florida Railroad arrived at Albany and the Upson County Railroad – built, financed and operated by Upson County citizens – was completed. By the end of the Civil War, much of the rail lines in Southwest Georgia were twisted into Sherman's bow ties, like most of the track in Georgia. But the railroads bounced back as large amounts of money for repairs came from northern businesses and banks desiring to get the South's industry and railroads back on its feet. Manchester and Americus were two of the many towns that grew up along a repaired and extended rail system.

PRESIDENTS

Andrew Jackson

As the Creek warriors descended upon Fort Mims, little did they know that this would be the death knell of the entire Creek Confederacy, for it set U.S. General Andrew Jackson on his course to enlarge the territory of his newly found nation while annihilating that of the Creek Indians.

Jackson was a child of the American Revolution. Born in 1767, he was a veteran of the war and the victim of intense personal suffering by the time he reached the age of 15. He grew up with a loathing of the British, a determination that America would prosper, a hatred of the Spanish and a paternalistic attitude towards the Indians.

With the massacre at Fort Mims, Jackson recognized that his long-awaited opportunity for military glory had arrived. With 2,500 volunteers and militia authorized by Governor William Blount of Tennessee, Jackson set out from Nashville, one of four armies that would enter the Creek Nation. The strategy was to kill the Red Sticks, burn their villages and destroy their crops. As they marched south, the army would build forts about one day's march apart in order to divide the Creek Nation.

Although plagued by desertions, lack of food and supplies and demands from Governor Blount to abandon the expedition, Jackson drove forward. By the close of 1813, he had battled twice with the Creeks. On March 27, 1814, on the Tallapoosa, where the winding river sweeps in a great loop at Horseshoe Bend, he struck them with fury. By Jackson's side were Indian fighter Davy Crockett and a young officer named Sam Houston. When the battle ended, U.S. troops had slain more than 700 warriors, breaking the spirit of Creek resistance. Creek prophets had said they could never be driven from the ground at Horseshoe Bend. But most of the defenders were dead and the homeplace lay in ruins.

After Horseshoe Bend, the Creek War was all but over.

Although the Federal government sent army general Thomas

Flint

Prehistoric Indians learned that they could take a piece of the dark-colored rock with the waxy luster that they found in a stream bed, chip it and fashion it into weapons and tools with sharp edges.

The rock was flint, a form of silica—the same material which makes up sand. And the Indians used it to make spears, knives and arrowheads. Most flint is found in the form of fine-grained, dark-gray lumps mixed with chalk and limestone. Pure flint is so hard and even-grained that it chips in smooth curved flakes. Later people learned that flint gave a spark when it was struck against some hard metal, and they began using it to start fires. The pioneers fired their flintlock rifles by striking flint against iron. Today, flint is principally used as an ingredient of fine pottery.

Pinckney and Indian Agent Benjamin Hawkins to arrange a peace treaty with the Creeks, Jackson dictated the terms at the negotiations. From them, he demanded the equivalent of all expenses incurred by the United States in prosecuting the war. By Jackson's calculation this came to 23 million acres of land—more than half of the old Creek domain, and roughly three-fifths of the present state of Alabama and one-fifth of Georgia.

By this treaty, the entire Creek Nation, even the Indians who had fought on Jackson's side, had to pay the enormous indemnity. All were required to remove themselves from their land and become wards of the Federal government. The treaty removed the threat of attack from the borders of Tennessee and Georgia and confined the Creeks to a manageable area where they could be watched and guarded and where they were separated geographically from the evil influence of the Spanish in Florida and Indians who had fled.

At Jackson's urging, the boundaries were drawn and the land sold to settlers as quickly as possible—a measure that would ensure the security of the frontier.

Horseshoe Bend was not the end of Jackson's conflict with the Indians, for now he would go after the Seminoles. But the Creek War and the Treaty of Fort Jackson set up a pattern of land seizure and removal that ensured the ultimate destruction of not only the Creek Nation, but of all Indians throughout the South and Southwest. And the man responsible was Andrew Jackson.

Franklin D. Roosevelt

A little more than 100 years after Andrew Jackson stepped foot in Georgia, Franklin D. Roosevelt did as well. A wealthy aristocrat and nationally known Democratic political leader at the time, he was looking for a way to fight the polio that was crippling his body. He sought relief at the warm springs in Meriwether County. Between therapeutic sessions in the warm springs pool, Roosevelt would fish the waters of the Flint River, drive the countryside between Manchester, Greenville and Gay, visit the Cove for bootlegged whiskey and fiddle playing and spend hours on Dowdell's Knob just thinking as he looked out over the great river valley below him. He would see an impoverished land where people lived as sharecroppers on unmechanized farms, where planting, harvesting and maintenance were done with the aid of mules and black field hands, who worked for a dollar and a half a day. The roads were unpaved, there was no electricity, radio reception was poor and staticky, electricity was available on a very erratic basis and most farms had no electrical appliances.

Those years were years when the entire country would be plunged into the greatest depression it had ever known and then into the greatest world war ever known. During those years, Roosevelt bought farmland and woodland in Harris and Meriwether Counties expressly

Roosevelt's Moonshine

It's known that President Franklin D. Roosevelt liked to serve liquor at the Little White House and it's believed he got much of his moonshine in "The Cove" on the Flint River.

"Moonshine was illegal even after Repeal. It was unaged corn whisky made in hidden spots along the Flint River. One such still was forever after referred to as 'Roosevelt's still,' because, according to legend at least, he occasionally drove there with a Secret Service agent to chat and pick up the supplies for a party. This criminal behavior, if it did indeed occur, was not routine procedure for stocking the liquor cabinet at the Little White House. More often, the illicit corn was brought over by a friend like Henry Toombs, who preferred it to commercial liquor, as did many Georgians. This traffic was also criminal, technically, but the county sheriff was not feared, since he was an occasional supplier to the President, himself. Or so the historians believe."

The Squire of Warm Springs by Theo Lippman, Jr.

to demonstrate to other farmers that a farm could be profitable—that they could grow something other than cotton. Roosevelt experimented with cattle and goat raising, timbering, peach and apple orchards, various vegetables and grapes. During those years, Roosevelt would serve an unprecedented three terms as president of the United States and many of the New Deal policies that he would formulate to lead the country out of the Depression and financial ruin would stem from what he saw and learned from the rural people that touched his life in Warm Springs.

Jimmy Carter

In 1924, the same year that Franklin D. Roosevelt first visited Warm Springs, Jimmy Carter was born in Plains, Georgia. Carter grew up during the Great Depression on his family's 360-acre farm just west of Plains. Carter's family turned to some of the very practices that President Roosevelt was espousing concerning farming. They shifted away from the growing of cotton, and turned to peanuts, cattle and sheep, geese, wheat, oats, rye and some sugar cane. Life was hard on the unmechanized farm. As a boy, Carter and his family plowed, cultivated and harvested the fields with only the help of mules. FDR's Rural Electrification Administration brought electricity to the area and the Carter farm in 1938, when Carter was 14.

Carter learned an appreciation for protecting the world that had been given to him. He said the stewardship of nature—of preserving the quality of the land, the beauty of the woodland and the abundance of wildlife—was immediately and dramatically tied in with his belief in God. As governor of Georgia he demonstrated those beliefs when he vetoed the building of a dam at Sprewell Bluff on the Flint River. As president, he continued to fight the unnecessary building of dams on rivers across the United States.

TOWNS

Settlements sprang up as the first traders began to enter the Indian Territory between the Flint and Chattahoochee Rivers. Most grew up along the banks of the river where river crossings were easier, or at an intersection where major Indian paths converged.

With the land cessions and subsequent removal of the Creeks, settlers rushed in, many times establishing a white settlement around what had been a frontier fort or on or near the location of what was once an Indian town. No matter what the culture or purpose, people tend to look for the same traits in settling a village or town: land near water; land on high ground for protection; land with good fertile soil for growing crops. The Indian town of Chehaw became Albany. Pucknawhitla became Burgess Town, which became Fort Hughes, which became Bainbridge. Chemocheechobee became Fort Gaines the fort, which later became Fort Gaines the town.

Land Distribution in Georgia

Georgia initially used the "headright" system to distribute land to settlers, but later, turned to the land lottery—becoming the only state to employ the lottery system in distributing land.

"Georgia employed a unique system of land distribution that used two distinct methods, separately as well as simultaneously. Variations of the old English system of land selection and tenure were used from 1733 until 1909. Known as the 'headright' system, that method allowed a certain number of acres on the 'right of a person's head' and used a random metes and bounds type of survey (where boundary lines to a parcel of land are precisely drawn) prior to the granting of the land.

"Though the headright method was being used in the state's settled areas, in 1805, Georgia's newer section was distributed by six different lotteries. The lottery method used a rectangular survey before actual distribution. The land lottery was a logical system that gave every qualified Georgian equal chance to obtain new land. Only Georgia distributed the public domain by lottery.

"All Georgia surveys and grants were issued in the 44 original counties. Generally, headright lands were east of the Oconee River, and the lottery method distributed the remaining area of the state."

The Atlas of Georgia by Thomas W. Hodler and Howard A. Schretter

But white settlers were more industrial minded than the Creeks. Towns grew up around the gristmills that were built on rocky streams. Towns grew up around river landings where area farmers brought their cotton for shipment to Apalachicola. Towns grew up wherever the tracks of a railroad terminated.

AGRICULTURE

When de Soto arrived in what would become Georgia, he did not find the nomadic savages he perhaps expected, but rather villages of Indians who had been farming the rich bottomland of the river valley, cultivating corn, squash, beans and other crops. In many cases, villages had already relocated several times because years of planting crops around the village had eroded and depleted the soil of nutrients.

But the destiny of much of the Flint and Chattahoochee River Valley was bound in cotton. King Cotton. In fact, cotton was one of the first crops specified to be grown in the Georgia colony when James Oglethorpe and the colonists first arrived at Yamacraw Bluff in 1733. And cotton was the reason planters and farmers flocked to the Flint River Valley as soon as the Indian threat lessened. Cotton had sorely depleted the soils in the eastern part of the state and beyond in the Carolinas. The Flint River Valley was land that had never been touched by cotton. At first, cotton, which was labor intensive, was only profitable for the very large planters who owned hundreds of slaves supplying the labor needed to plant, pick and hand remove the seeds from the short staple fiber. But after Eli Whitney's invention of the cotton gin in 1893, the economics changed. The gin cleaned cotton as fast as 50 persons. Cotton became profitable to produce on small farms, using only family labor, as well as large slaveholding plantations. Both types of farmers grabbed up the Land Between the Rivers, and by 1860 Georgia was the world's largest producer of cotton, with much of that production coming from the Flint River Valley.

But the Civil War did much to change the agricultural economy of the region. Plantations were divided into tenant farms. Farmers were growing corn, tobacco and peanuts, but cotton still ruled. Farmers ignored agrarian leaders across the South who warned of cotton's effect on the soil and of the farmer's dependency on cash crops.

By the 1920s, severe erosion, soil depletion, the boll weevil menace and the Depression wrecked havoc on the state's agriculture. Between 1920 and 1925, 3.5 million acres of cotton land were abandoned throughout Georgia and the number of farms fell from 310,132 to 249,095. It would take new ways of farming, new farm programs resulting from President Franklin D. Roosevelt's New Deal Programs and a world war to turn the agricultural economy around in this region, as well as in the rest of the South. The rule of cotton in Georgia would be over. Peanuts, peaches and soybeans would become

Coweta County

The eastern half of Coweta County —from the west bank of Line Creek to the ridge that separates the Chattahoochee and the Flint River Basins—lies within the Flint River Watershed.

"Coweta County was created in 1826. Georgia's 67th county bears the name of the Coweta Indians, a Creek tribe headed by William McIntosh, Jr., the half-Scott, half Creek who relinquished lands to the Federal government in the 1825 Treaty of Indian Springs. The county has seven municipalities. Newnan, the largest of these municipalities and the county seat, was named for General Daniel Newnan who fought in the Indian Wars, the War of 1812, and later served in the Georgia General Assembly. The county's other incorporated municipalities are Grantville, Haralson, Moreland, Senoia, Sharpsburg and Turin."

From *Georgia County Snapshots*, Georgia Department of Community Affairs

For tourism information for towns in Coweta County, see Resources page 300.

some of the crops that would replace King Cotton in the Land Between the Rivers.

By the time Plains peanut farmer Jimmy Carter was elected President of the United States in 1976, peanuts and soybeans—combined with traditional row crops, such as corn, cotton, wheat and vegetables—were important crops grown in Southwest Georgia. Dairying as well as cattle, hogs and pigs also became important to the area's agricultural economy.

INDUSTRY

All along the Flint River and its tributaries settlers to the area built gristmills, the first real industries of the area. Until the early 20th century, most mills used water from nearby streams to power gears and machinery. The hilly Piedmont or the Fall Line section of the river, where the water rushes over rock outcroppings and shoals, were ideal locations for mills.

Today, many times only place names, such as Lee's Mill, Terrell Mill and Mundy's Mill in Clayton County, remain. In some places, such as Flat Shoals, ruins can be spotted. At a few sites, a structure may still stand, such as Starr's Mill in Fayette County. At one time all of these mills were important community centers. Farmers traveled for miles to the nearest mill to grind grain, saw timber, hull rice or gin cotton. They fished the pond, swapped news and stories or picked up some supplies as they waited their turn to grind their corn. Many times a town grew up around the mill itself.

With cotton such an all-important crop in the area, it was only natural that textile mills would spring up where there was water power and logical to bring cotton mills to the cotton fields. A number of settlers came to Upson County from northern states for the express purpose of establishing textile mills. The first cotton mill in Upson County, Franklin Factory, was built on Tobler Creek in 1833. A total of four textile mills, all water-powered, were built before the Civil War, making Upson the center of the textile industry in Middle Georgia.

The textile mills in Thomaston, as well as the mills in Columbus on the Chattahoochee, were extremely important to the Confederacy during the Civil War, making such items as gray uniform tweed, osnaburg cloth, cotton duck for tents and cotton jeans. One of the goals of the Union Army as it swept through Georgia in the waning days of the Civil War was to destroy as many mill sites as possible. On April 16, 1865, in one of the last major land battles of the war, 13,000 Federal cavalry troops invaded Columbus from Alabama and burned all of the war-related mills, warehouses and foundries. They then moved across the land between the two rivers—burning plantations and destroying railroads—to the Flint, crossed it via the old Double Bridges and completely destroyed all four textile plants and several gristmills in Upson County.

Spalding County

The western half of Spalding County, including Griffin, its county seat, lies within the Flint River Watershed.

"Spalding County was formed in 1851 from parts of Fayette, Henry and Pike counties. The 96th county created in the state was named after Thomas Spalding, the first Georgian known to have successfully harvested cotton and sugar cane. There are three municipalities in the county: Sunny Side, Orchard Hill and Griffin, the county seat. Griffin was named for General L. Griffin, the first president of the Monroe Railroad. This railroad later became the Central of Georgia."

From *Georgia County Snapshots*, Georgia Department of Community Affairs

For tourism information for towns in Spalding County, see Resources page 300.

The textile industry, however, was one of the few industries in the South to rebound quickly after the war. New mills were built in both Columbus and Thomaston. As the technology of mill building changed—turbines connected to electrical generators, instead of paddle wheels connected to mechanical gears—the mills no longer had to be close to the rivers to receive their energy supply.

THE FLINT RIVER

More than 300 years ago a Creek Indian village existed near what is now Albany. It was called Thronateeska. The word in the Creek language means "flint picking up place" and, over time, the name came to be applied to the river that ran by the village.

The Flint River flows southerly across Georgia in a wide eastward arc from its headwaters at the southeastern edge of Atlanta for 350 miles to its junction with the Chattahoochee River at Lake Seminole.

It is part of the Apalachicola-Flint-Chattahoochee River System, which drains a total area of 19,600 square miles into the Gulf of Mexico. Eight thousand seven hundred and seventy square miles lie along the Chattahoochee River arm and 8,460 square miles lie along the Flint River arm. The remaining 2,370 square miles of the watershed lies along the Apalachicola River below the confluence of the Chattahoochee and Flint.

A major continental divide between the Flint and the Ocmulgee River to its east separates the Gulf of Mexico and the Atlantic Ocean drainage.

The upper reaches of the Flint flow through a plateau characterized by rolling red hills known as the Piedmont. At the Fall Line, the river drops about 400 feet over a distance of 50 miles. The Yellow Jacket Shoals area, between GA 36 and Po Biddy Road Bridge, has slopes of 50 feet per mile. The lower Flint flows through the soft, sandy sediments and limestone that make up the Coastal Plain.

For more than 200 miles, the Flint is a wild and free-flowing river. It is one of only 40 U.S. rivers with 125 miles or more of unimpeded flow. The Crisp County power dam on Lake Blackshear, approximately 220 miles from the headwaters, is the first dam on the Flint and one of only three dams on the river—the others being the Georgia Power Dam at Lake Chehaw and the Jim Woodruff Dam at Lake Seminole.

This river, its watershed, its physical alliance with the Chattahoochee and Apalachicola Rivers and its history—all combine to tell a fascinating story with universal themes—a story of people, of Georgia and of America.

Throughout this book run the threads of all these stories.

Thronateeska

"While 'Thronateeska' is almost universally recognized and used by Southwest Georgians as a poetic or Indian name for the Flint River, I do not believe it ever appeared on an early map of historical significance. A friendly challenge is offered to any professional historian who can show one.

"The reader must remember two important things in this connection. The Indian, except the Cherokee of more modern times, had no written language. So, when the white man heard him pronounce something, the individual white man wrote it as he thought it sounded from the lips of that particular Indian. This accounts for many different ways the same Indian word is spelled.

"Frank S. Jones, author of the History of Decatur County *once wrote to Henry T. McIntosh, editor and columnist of the* Albany Herald *that Benjamin Hawkins, U.S. Agent for Indian Affairs, in one of his writings (found in the University of Georgia Library) states that the Indian name for the Flint was Lonatiskahatchee and that the word Lonato meant Flint.'*

"The de Soto Expedition Commission of the Smithsonian Institution uses the word Capachequi in every reference to the river in the same location of the Flint. In Arrondo's Spanish Title to Georgia *by Herbert E. Bolton, there is a map showing the Flint River as the Rio Pedernales. Phillipeaux's map of the English Colonies as late as 1781, but drawn for French use, calls the Flint River 'Riviere au Callaux.' In London, however as long ago as 1719 in Herman Moll's* Atlas, *the word Flint is used for the river. William Bartram in his widely known and respected 'Travels' says he crossed the Flint River back in 1776.*

"The use of the name 'Thronateeska' seems to have started in the early 19th century after the Indians were gone."

Prologue by Maston O'Neal

Section 1

The Headwaters to Line Creek

We meet Rio. He takes us to the headwaters of the Flint River near Atlanta's Hartsfield International Airport. We visit Newman Wetlands Center in Clayton County and see how Mother Nature uses natural wetlands to help clean up rivers.

From the Headwaters to Line Creek, use the Guidebook Section beginning on page 40 to explore: William H. Reynolds Memorial Nature Preserve, the Newman Wetlands Center and its Wetlands Trail, the rocky shoals of Line Creek Nature Area and Starr's Mill.

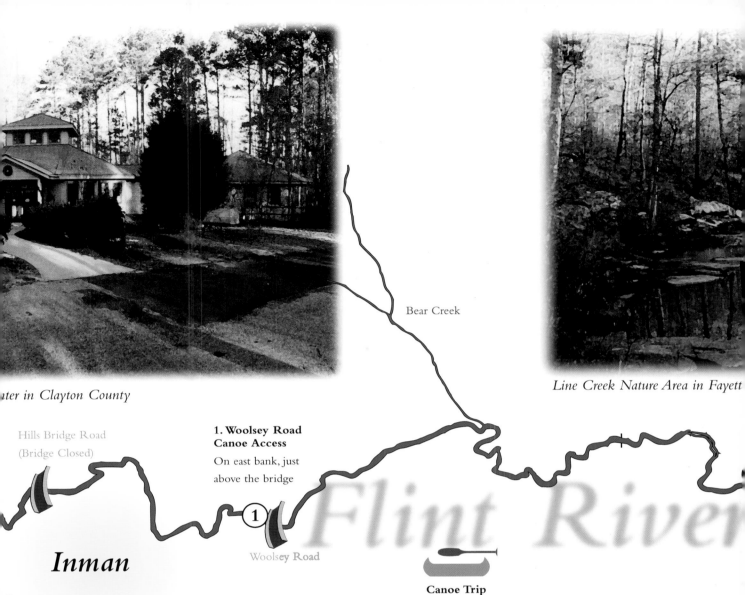

Bear Creek

ater in Clayton County

Line Creek Nature Area in Fayett

1. Woolsey Road Canoe Access

On east bank, just above the bridge

Hills Bridge Road (Bridge Closed)

Inman

Inman
About 1 mile west of the river via Hills Bridge Road

Woolsey Road

Woolsey

Woolsey
About 1 mile west of the river via Woolsey Road

Canoe Trip

Below the Woolsey Road Bridge, the Flint becomes canoeable. Up until this point, deadfalls, which are largely the result of beavers, restrict paddling.

Heading downstream from the Woolsey Road Bridge, Class I riffles and small ledges combine with deadfalls to keep the paddler awake. The stream continuously winds and is well insulated in a canopy of willow, ash, birch and silver maple. One-half mile below the GA 92 Bridge is a dam that must be portaged. Beyond the GA 16 Bridge west of Griffin, deadfalls completely block the stream in several places and also must be portaged. Not until the Flint passes beneath the GA 362 Bridge east of Alvaton does the channel become generally clear of obstructions.

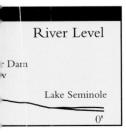

River Level

Dam

Lake Seminole

0'

Hills Bridge Road
River miles above mouth: 322.3
Counties: Fayette and Clayton

Woolsey Road
River miles above mouth: 319.4
Counties: Fayette and Clayton

The Flint River first sees the light of day at the mouth of a concrete culvert on the south side of Virginia Avenue in Hapeville, just north of Hartsfield Atlanta International Airport. From this inauspicious beginning, its first few miles are inauspicious, too. Captured again by culverts, it flows under the airport runways. It flows through a half dozen industrial parks on the south side of Hartsfield and under Riverdale Road, a typical American suburban highway lined with strip malls, car washes and fast food restaurants.

But soon, thanks to tributaries, beaver dams and wetlands, the Flint River begins to look like a river. By the time it reaches the GA 362 Bridge between Meriwether and Pike Counties, 53.7 miles from its source, it has transformed itself by its own regenerative powers into a diverse and endlessly fascinating river with steep quartzite shoals, trackless swamps, sandy beaches and blue springs flowing out of limestone caverns. The Nature Conservancy and others have recog-

Reynolds Nature Preserve

1. William H. Reynolds Nature Preserve
Hardwood forests, streams, wetlands and five spring-fed ponds make up this 146-acre nature preserve on Jester's Creek.

Beaver

Beaver Dam

Riverdale

Riverdale
City Hall is about 1.5 miles west of the river via Riverdale Road.

GA 85	**Upper Riverdale Road**	**Valley Hill Road**	**GA 138**
River miles above mouth: 343.5	*River miles above mouth: 341.2*	*River miles above mouth: 339.8*	*River miles abo*
County: Clayton	*County: Clayton*	*County: Clayton*	*County: Clayto*

Sherri Smith at the headwaters

Atlanta

Atlanta

The headwaters of the Flint are just
south of the Atlanta city limits.

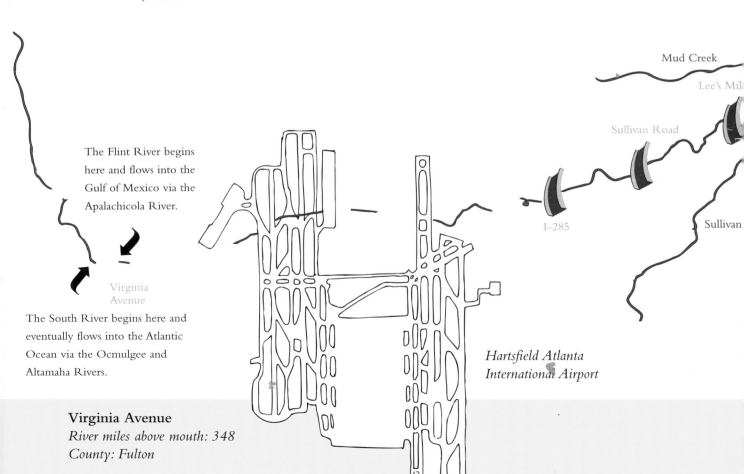

The Flint River begins
here and flows into the
Gulf of Mexico via the
Apalachicola River.

Virginia
Avenue

The South River begins here and
eventually flows into the Atlantic
Ocean via the Ocmulgee and
Altamaha Rivers.

Mud Creek

Lee's Mil

Sullivan Road

I-285

Sullivan

Hartsfield Atlanta
International Airport

Virginia Avenue
River miles above mouth: 348
County: Fulton

Griffin

Griffin

About 9 miles east of the river via GA 16

County

2. GA 92 Canoe Access

On east bank, just above the bridge

GA 92

2 **3**

3. New Salem Road Canoe Access

On east bank, about 0.25 mile below
the GA 92 Bridge

Wildcat Creek

4. McIntosh Road Canoe Access

On east bank, just above the bridge

McIntosh Road

rton Creek

4

GA 16

5

Brooks

5. GA 16 Canoe Access

On west bank, just above
the bridge

Brooks

About 2 miles west of the river via Vaughn Road

GA 92	McIntosh Road	GA 16
River miles above mouth: 313.2	*River miles above mouth: 308.3*	*River miles above mouth: 304.4*
Counties: Fayette and Spalding	*Counties: Fayette and Spalding*	*County: Spalding*

nized the region where the Flint and Chattahoochee Rivers meet to form the Apalachicola as one of the most uniquely bio-diverse regions in the entire United States.

The case can be made that the Flint flows from the most densely urban area of the South—what is more dense and urban than the busiest airport in the world?—to some of its wildest and most pristine.

This fold-out map and the seven others that follow at intervals through the book follow the Flint on its transforming journey.

The river flows north to south. The foldout maps "flow" west to east, or horizontally, across the page. Locator maps on each page show the north-to-south orientation and the change in elevation and provide a "You Are There" position on the river.

River miles related to specific bridges found on state highway maps are shown along the bottom of each page.

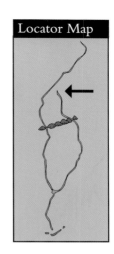

Locator Map

Jonesboro

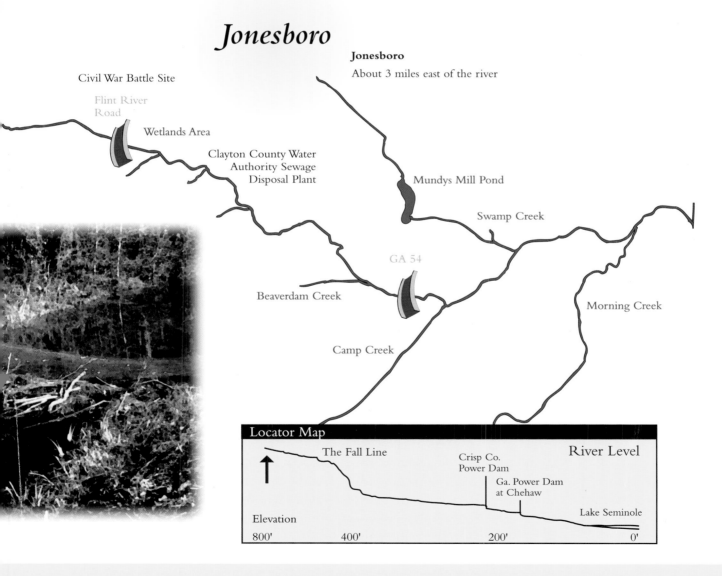

Civil War Battle Site

Flint River Road

Wetlands Area

Clayton County Water Authority Sewage Disposal Plant

Jonesboro
About 3 miles east of the river

Mundys Mill Pond

Swamp Creek

GA 54

Beaverdam Creek

Morning Creek

Camp Creek

Locator Map

The Fall Line

Crisp Co. Power Dam

River Level

Ga. Power Dam at Chehaw

Lake Seminole

Elevation

800'   400'   200'   0'

GA 54
River miles above mouth: 333.7
Counties: Fayette and Clayton

mouth: 338.1

See the Guidebook sections for additional information and directions to locations listed on this page.

Tara Country

Margaret Mitchell's Fitzgerald grandparents' farm, the original inspiration for Tara in *Gone With the Wind*, was located on this part of the river.

Shoal Creek

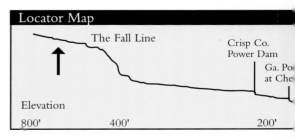

Melvin L. Newman Wetlands C

Hurricane Creek

Site of Civil War skirmish

North Bridge Road

McDonough Road

Murphy Creek

Gay Creek

Fayetteville

Fayetteville

About 4 miles west of the river via GA 54

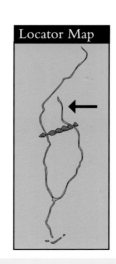

Locator Map

Locator Map

The Fall Line

Crisp Co.
Power Dam

Ga. Po
at Che

Elevation

800'   400'   200'

McDonough Road
River miles above mouth: 330.6
Counties: Fayette and Clayton

North Bridge Road
River miles above mouth: 325.7
Counties: Fayette and Clayton

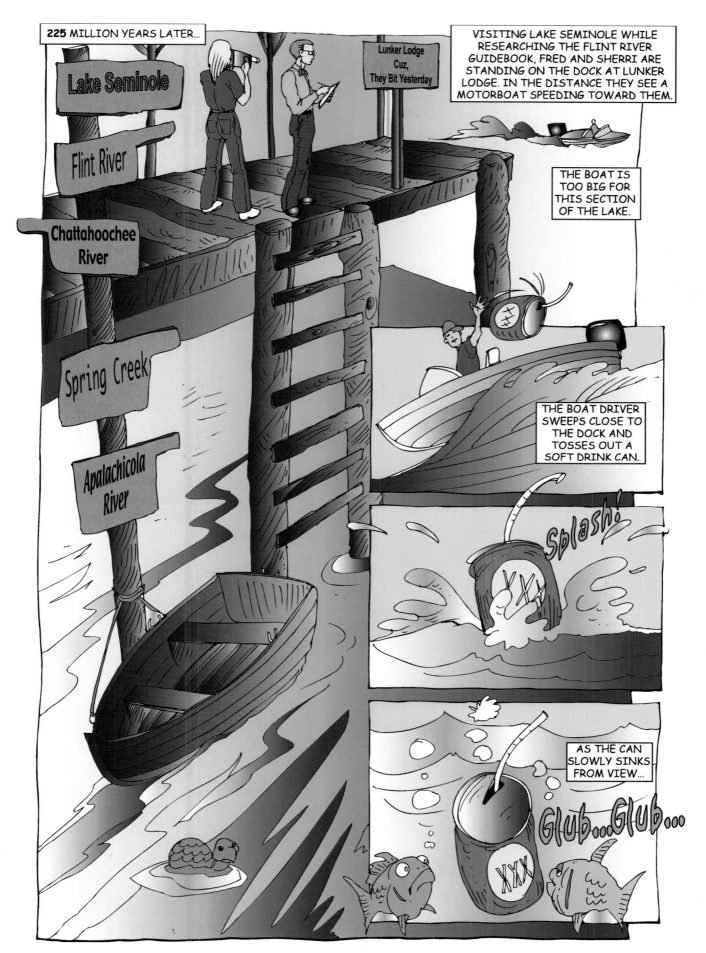

35

225 MILLION YEARS LATER...
Lake Seminole
Flint River
Chattahoochee River
Spring Creek
Apalachicola River
Lunker Lodge Cuz, They Bit Yesterday
VISITING LAKE SEMINOLE WHILE RESEARCHING THE FLINT RIVER GUIDEBOOK, FRED AND SHERRI ARE STANDING ON THE DOCK AT LUNKER LODGE. IN THE DISTANCE THEY SEE A MOTORBOAT SPEEDING TOWARD THEM.
THE BOAT IS TOO BIG FOR THIS SECTION OF THE LAKE.
THE BOAT DRIVER SWEEPS CLOSE TO THE DOCK AND TOSSES OUT A SOFT DRINK CAN.
Splash!
AS THE CAN SLOWLY SINKS FROM VIEW...
Glub...Glub...

BUT SOON **MOTHER NATURE** BEGINS TO WORK HER MAGIC.

THESE BEAVER DAMS HELP CLEAN THE WATER.

THESE WETLANDS PURIFY THE RIVER, TOO.

NEWMAN WETLANDS CENTER IN CLAYTON COUNTY IS A GOOD PLACE TO SEE HOW MOTHER NATURE'S WETLANDS CLEAN UP THE MESS THAT HUMANS MAKE.

CLICK

WETLANDS NOT ONLY BENEFIT THE RIVER, THEY PROVIDE HOMES AND FOOD FOR MANY ANIMALS. IT'S THE ONLY HOME MOST OF THEM HAVE.

Section 1

Headwaters to Line Creek

NATURE-BASED EDUCATIONAL CENTERS

William H. Reynolds Memorial Nature Preserve

On a typical summer's day, dozens of turtles swim and sun on logs on Azalea Pond, bluebirds and woodpeckers fly overhead, deer drink from numerous streams and squirrels scamper from tree to tree along Hickory Stump Trail at Reynolds Nature Preserve. Hardwood forests, streams, wetlands and five spring-fed ponds make up this 146-acre nature preserve that sits next to Jester's Creek, a tributary of the Flint.

The property, which was once the homestead of a prominent Clayton County public official, William Reynolds, is now a plant and wildlife sanctuary with four miles of wide, pine bark-covered hiking trails, a butterfly and hummingbird garden and an interpretive trail where Georgia native plants grow. The Reynolds's home, an 1867 farmhouse (which is private and not open to the public) and barn still stand on the grounds. You can walk through a Heritage Garden behind the barn where peppermint, yarrow, chives, tomatoes and coneflowers, as well as other vegetables and herbs typically grown during the late 1800s, are grown today. At the end of the garden stands one of Clayton County's oldest trees, a White Oak believed to be more than 300 years old.

Building bluebird and bat houses, making grapevine wreaths and vine baskets, walking for fun and fitness, composting and soil management and backyard vegetable gardening are just a few of the varied year-round classes that the preserve's Interpretive Center offers. Scout Merit Badge courses, guided hikes and summer nature camps are also available. The preserve also sponsors two annual events, the Yule Log Celebration in December and the Earthday Celebration in April.

Reynolds Preserve publishes a quarterly newsletter, *The Legacy*, which features news about the preserve and its events and programs, as well as informative articles on wildlife and plants. *The Legacy* is distributed to members and is available to visitors.

Facilities: *Interpretive Center, 4 miles of hiking trails laid out in 0.5, 1.0 and 1.5 mile loops, the wheelchair accessible Georgia Native Plants Trail, picnic areas and restrooms.* **Days/Hours**: *Preserve trails and grounds — open daily, 8:30 a.m. until dusk. Interpretive Center — Monday through Friday, 8:30 a.m. to 5:30 p.m.* **Directions**: *Clayton County. From Atlanta, take I-75 south to Exit (233), GA 54. Turn left on GA 54 and go to the 4th*

The Piedmont

The Piedmont is the hilly, upland region of the eastern United States between the Atlantic Coastal Plain and the Appalachians and stretching from southeast New York to central Alabama. In Georgia, the Piedmont cuts a swath through the upper half of the state. It is usually further defined as the Upper Piedmont, which is the more mountainous, and the Lower Piedmont, where the Fall Line runs.

The familiar red clay soil characterizes the Piedmont throughout Georgia. In general, deciduous hardwoods are the predominant vegetative growth. Writings of naturalist William Bartram and early settlers indicate that during the late 1700s in the eastern Piedmont (as far west as the Ogeechee River), there were numerous fields, second-growth forests and occasional stands of pines attributable to Indian agriculture and to Indian use of fire. Later, heavy settlement and farming throughout the Georgia Piedmont resulted in loss of much of its topsoil as well as serious gully erosion. Outside of its urban centers, as you drive across the Piedmont today, you'll see many old fields grown up or planted with loblolly pine and second-growth deciduous hardwood and hardwood-pine forests.

Rivers cut through the Piedmont's hard rock in narrow, well-defined channels. In *The Natural Environments of Georgia*, Dr. Charles H. Wharton attributes three general appearances to Piedmont rivers: "shoales, sometimes with whitewater and falls; gently meandering slower runs and strongly meandering slow water." Flood plains here are usually one half mile or less wide.

The Flint River has its headwaters in the Piedmont. It and the Chattahoochee are the only South Georgia Coastal Plain rivers draining into the Gulf to originate from this hilly area.

traffic light, which is Reynolds Road. Turn left on Reynolds Road. The preserve entrance is 1 mile on the left. **More Information**: *William H. Reynolds Memorial Nature Preserve, 5665 Reynolds Road, Morrow, GA 30260. 770/603-4188; fax: 770/603-4190.*

Melvin L. Newman Wetlands Center

What is your watershed address? That is a major question at the Newman Wetlands Center in Clayton County. Here you can learn about the characteristics, wildlife and plants in a wetland and how to preserve these environments. The Wetland Center does not share the Flint River Watershed address—it sits just 2 miles east of US 19/41 on a ridge that divides the Flint from the Ocmulgee Watershed. Yet wetlands are common to *all* watersheds, and this is an excellent facility for both children and adults to visit to learn of their importance.

In the central exhibit area, you can watch a video on wetlands and see displays on the water cycle, watersheds, wetland wildlife, wildflowers, common wetland plants, wetland soils and wading birds. You can test your wetland I.Q., learn how wetlands purify and filter water and how they provide a place to raise the young of migratory birds and other wildlife. You can also wander the wetlands trail, where more than 130 bird species have been identified and beaver, river otter, fox, raccoon, muskrat, deer, wild turkey, opossum, mink and many species of reptiles, insects and amphibians live.

Staff members give guided tours of the wetlands to groups of 10 or more, as well as to school groups. All groups should call in advance for reservations. During the summer months, the staff offers weekday guided walks for visitors without reservations, summer birdwatching walks, various programs and field trips and a Wetlands and Watershed Festival in June. The Atlanta Audubon Society holds Sunday morning bird walks here during the spring and fall migrations.

Opened in 1995, the center is owned and operated by the Clayton County Water Authority. The center is named for Melvin L. Newman, a past general manager of the Authority and a nationally recognized expert in innovative water and wastewater technology.

Facilities: *4,888 square-foot building complex with central exhibit and learning lab area, 50-seat auditorium, offices and conference facility; nature trail with boardwalk (see page 43) and picnic area. The entire facility, including the trail, is handicap accessible.* **Admission**: *No general admission but group programs require fees.* **Days/Hours**: *Wetlands Center – open March through October, Monday through Saturday, 8:30 a.m. to 5 p.m.; November through February, Monday through Friday, 8:30 a.m. to 5 p.m. Trail – open daily, 8:30 a.m. to 5 p.m.; June through August, 8:30 a.m. to 7 p.m.* **Directions**: *Clayton County. From Jonesboro, take US 19/41 south about 5 miles to McDonough Road. Turn left and go to Freeman Road. Follow Freeman Road about 1 mile. The Wetlands Center is on the left.* **More Information**: *Newman Wetlands Center, 2755 Freeman Road, Hampton, GA 30228. 770/603-5606; fax, 770/603-5602. Website: www.ccwa1.com*

River Otter

One of the few carnivorous aquatic animals in Georgia is the river otter. Fish, crayfish, frogs, turtles and birds fill an otter's diet. Its long, slender body, powerful tail and webbed feet allow for quick and graceful swimming. In clear water, it uses its excellent swimming ability to capture fish by sight, while in murky water it relies on its whiskers to "feel" its prey. During a dive, the river otter's small ears and nose pad close tight and its pulse slows to a tenth of its normal rate to conserve oxygen.

They are active mostly at dawn and dusk, spending large amounts of time playing—wrestling, sliding on snow, ice and mud and the repeated capture and release of live prey. King James I of England kept a pack of tame otters to catch fish for his table and even appointed a "Keeper of the King's Otters" to tend them. A thick undercoat and coarse outer coat make otters nearly impervious to cold. Having no blubber, the thick fur keeps them warm and dry—making the otter's pelt very popular with trappers.

Otters require a large amount of space to live. They often occupy 50 or more miles of stream per year, relocating from one area to another. Their home range depends on a number of variables, including age, gender and food supply. Most of the year, they utilize the abandoned dens of beavers and other animals rather than digging their own. The presence of beavers in an area is important to otters, not just because of their dens, but because the ponds created by beavers make an ideal habitat. You can see otters, as well as beavers, in their habitat at the Newman Wetlands Center.

HISTORIC SITES

Starr's Mill

At one time numerous gristmills for grinding grain operated along the Flint River and its tributaries above the Fall Line (see "How Rivers Work" on page 282). These were some of the region's earliest industry. Starr's Mill, located on Whitewater Creek in Fayette County, is one of the few gristmills that remain standing in the area.

In all, 16 property owners and three mills have been part of the Starr's Mill history. Hananiah Gillcoat, the property's second owner, constructed the first mill sometime between 1822 and 1827, just after the region was opened to settlement in 1821. Records indicate that the second millhouse to stand on the site burned to the ground around 1900, supposedly by arson. In 1907 the property's 13th owner, William T. Glower, built the present wooden millhouse, on the same foundation, and the concrete dam.

Over the years, the mill, as well as the community that grew up around it, became known as Starr's Mill, after 10th owner Hilliard M. Starr, who acquired the property in 1866. An 1870 census lists H. M. Starr Mill as having a maximum capacity of 100 bushels per day, $5,000 capital, two water wheels and 30 horsepower.

A cotton gin that served the community once stood at the opposite end of the dam. It was capable of ginning one bale of cotton per hour. Gates on each end of the dam opened and closed to regulate the necessary flow of water needed to drive the gin's machinery, as well as the mill. The gin operated until the mid-1940s and was blown down by a wind storm in 1955. In 1959 Starr's Mill ceased production and the remains of the old cotton gin were torn down.

Like other mill ponds, the mill pond at Starr's Mill was the center of community activities. Fishing, swimming, camping and family reunions took place around the pond. The April 15, 1904, *Fayetteville News* reported that Col. A. O. Blalock caught the biggest fish of the season, a 17 pound carp, at Starr's pond, "a fine pull as the water was ten feet deep where he caught it."

In 1991, Fayette County purchased the mill for use as a water system reservoir. You aren't allowed to swim there anymore, but on a June day, fishermen trying their hand can still be seen fishing among the lily-padded tail waters of the Starr's Mill dam.

Facilities: Picnic tables and lights. **Days/Hours**: *Open daily, 6:30 a.m. to 6:00 p.m. and 6:30 a.m. to 8:30 p.m. DST.* **Directions**: *Fayette County. From Fayetteville, take GA 85 south about 9 miles. You will see the red painted wood mill on the right. Turn right onto Waterfall Way, a gravel road right before GA 85's intersection with GA 74.* **More Information**: *Fayette County Water System, 245 McDonough Road., Fayetteville, GA 30214. 770/461-1146.*

Fayette County Gristmills

Mills, much like ferries, usually took on the name of their owner. Through the years, one mill could change hands—and names—many times.

Lee's Mill on Whitewater Creek was built in the 1840s but got its commonly known name from Jim Lee, who bought it in 1915. It was run by an overshot waterwheel that generated 20 horsepower, and, according to the 1870 census, the mill could grind 100 bushels of corn and wheat a day. By 1915, the mill also had machinery for shelling corn, sawing logs, planing lumber and making shingles. Lee's Mill burned to the ground in 1957.

William Bennett built Bennett's Mill on Whitewater Creek in 1837. The mill, which was run by one 48-horsepower waterwheel, is now a restaurant called The Olde Mill Steakhouse.

Wynn's Mill was established along Line Creek on the Fayette and Coweta County line and operated until sometime in the 1940s. Powered by two waterwheels that generated 20 horsepower, it could grind 100 bushels of wheat and corn a day.

Leach's Mill, built in the 1850s by Edward William Leach, was a corn mill powered by the waters of Flat Creek in a location that is now part of Peachtree City's Flat Creek Golf Course. In 1870 it could produce 40 bushels of corn mill a day. The mill was also commonly called Tinsley Mill, after its last owner, and burned down in 1989.

North's Mill, which ground corn and wheat, was located on the Flint River at North Bridge (see page 46). Owners Edward and Saphronia North also had a sawmill there and a large plantation that grew cotton, sugarcane, sorghum, corn and wheat.

Banks Mill, a corn and wheat mill owned by Warren Lockett Banks, was also located on the Flint River near North Bridge during the early 1900s.

HIKES AND WALKS

The Wetlands Trail

Anyone who wants to learn more about wetland environments and how to preserve them should spend an hour walking the Wetlands Trail at Newman Wetlands Center. The trail is well interpreted with signage, and the Wetlands Center has two trail guides—one specifically for children and another on wetland plants—that are filled with good information about what you will find along the trail.

Distance: This is a 0.5 mile long, easy-to-walk trail over crushed stone and boardwalks that are handicap accessible. Benches, covered areas and water fountains are found frequently along the trail.

Trailhead Location: Melvin L. Newman Wetlands Center (see page 41). The well-marked entrance to the trail is just off the parking area and to the left of the exhibit center.

Features: Until the 1930s this area was farmed extensively in cotton, and there are remnants of plowing terraces and second-growth forest as the trail winds down to the wetlands.

The wetlands are only about a foot deep, but Pate's Creek, which flows through the area, is 12 to 13 feet deep. Dam and sluice gates control the water level. You are likely to spot otters, turtles, large fish and maybe wood ducks and kingfishers along the creek. Much of the water is covered with a layer of tiny green plants, known as duckweed (see sidebar on this page).

Along the path are dogwood, red mulberry, sweetgum, tulip poplar, chestnut oak and umbrella magnolia. You'll see several types of ferns, including maidenhair and Christmas fern on Beech Hill, and sensitive fern throughout. Hammock Overlook is a transitional area between the mixed hardwood upland forest and the lowland wet region.

Look for the gray bat roosting box and woodpecker and wood duck nest boxes, as well as the beaver lodge. More than 130 species of birds have been identified in the wetlands, including different types of herons, osprey, mallard, wild turkey and hawks.

Line Creek Nature Area

Whether you decide to hike or wade the Line Creek shoals, this is a good place to see large rock shoals and outcroppings, as well as trees and vegetation unique to the Georgia Piedmont. Owned and maintained by a non-profit organization called the Southern Conservation Trust, the nature area takes in about 70 acres of land along Line Creek, a tributary of the Flint River, as it flows through Peachtree City.

Distance: Ridge Trail is an 0.8-mile loop that mostly follows a ridge along Line Creek's east bank. Creek Trail is an easy to medium walk that follows the creek bed a distance of 1.2 miles one way.

Trailhead Location: Line Creek Nature Area in Peachtree City. A sign to the right as you enter the nature area parking lot marks the

Duckweed

The floating green plant often confused for pond scum is thought to be one of the most promising environmental technologies of the future, doubling as both wastewater treatment and a high protein food source for animals. Duckweed is the layer of green you often see on still or slow-moving freshwater bodies and is very apparent on the water at the Newman Wetlands Center. It is actually a network of extremely tiny plants made of a small floating disc of photosynthetic tissue. It is the smallest of flowering plants, but the flowers are very difficult to see.

Duckweed grows best in water with high levels of nitrogen and phosphate. Wetland biologists use the plant as a cheap and efficient way to help filter nitrates from water, removing excess nutrients that cause algae and other problems. Preventing the growth of algae is beneficial, since an overgrowth of algae will eventually die and decay, reducing the oxygen content in the water to harmful levels for fish. As it has no anchoring root system, duckweed can be easily skimmed off the surface or eaten by fish, making it an economical feed source for fish farming.

Most importantly, scientists are beginning to use duckweed as a new form of wastewater treatment. Combined with conventional methods, wastewater lagoons covered with duckweed effectively purify and concentrate nutrients. The duckweed then becomes a source of more protein per square meter than soybeans. It grows rapidly, doubling its size in a few days. Easily harvested, the duckweed can be used to feed fish, poultry, cattle and even humans, making it extremely useful to developing countries.

entrance to the trail. Trail maps are located in a marked box and signs point the way to the Ridge Trail and the Creek Trail.

Features: For the most part, large rock shoals and outcroppings stretch the entire width and length of this part of Line Creek. The Creek Trail is a rocky walk and at many points you can easily step out onto the shoals. The ruins of an old bridge used by both Yankee and Confederate troops to cross Line Creek can be spotted on the east bank of the creek near the beginning of the Creek Trail. From the Ridge Trail, there are good views of Line Creek, especially in the winter when the trees are bare.

A stocked fishing pond, gazebo and picnic area are located at the beginning of the trails. The nature area is well-marked around the pond area but the trails are not.

Directions: *Fayette County. From the intersection of GA 74 and GA 54 in Peachtree City, take GA 54 west about 0.25 mile. Sign for the Line Creek Nature Area is on the left just before the Days Inn motel. Turn left into the Days Inn parking lot and take an immediate left onto the gravel drive between the two brick entrance markers for the nature area. Follow the gravel drive to the parking lot area.*

BRIDGES

Virginia Avenue Bridge

This bridge, located on the north side of the Hartsfield Atlanta International Airport could be considered the first bridge over the Flint River. The headwaters of the Flint, covered by thousands of yards of concrete, see the light of day for the first time as they pour from the culverts under Virginia Avenue. After this initial entry into the sunlight, the Flint runs through a series of concrete draining ditches and underground culverts as it makes its way across the airport runways—26R, 26L, 27R—emerging from another culvert near runway 27L, then southward to the I-285 Bridge. **Location**: *In Fulton County where Virginia Avenue crosses the Flint just to the east of the Delta Airline Headquarters.*

I-285 Bridge

There is no way to ever catch a glimpse of the Flint as you travel around I-285, Atlanta's perimeter highway, but the river is fighting to make its way out from under the concrete. **Location**: *In Clayton County where I-285 crosses the Flint River.*

Terrell Mill Road Bridge Ruins

Now in ruins, this bridge once crossed the Flint near the site of the old Terrell Mill. This is one of the first locations from which you can see the Flint actually looking like a stream. An interesting place, it is difficult to get to. Kudzu grows waist-high along the path to the bridge and wisteria, columbine vine and wild blackberries grow

Beaver

A beaver's ability to change the landscape is second only to a human's. Known as the "Engineer" of the animal kingdom, beavers dam streams, raising the water level to surround their lodge with a protective moat to create the deep water needed for winter food storage. Native Americans called beavers the "sacred center" of the land because they create such rich habitats for other animals. Since beavers prefer to dam streams in shallow valleys, much of the flooded area becomes wetlands. Amazingly, these wetlands have a biodiversity that can rival tropical rain forests (see "How Rivers Work" on page 290). Almost half of endangered and threatened species in North America rely upon wetlands for survival. Beavers create and maintain these wetlands, which can sponge up floodwaters, prevent erosion, raise the water table and act as the "earth's kidneys" to purify water.

They also contributed more to the early development of the United States and Canada than any other animal. A beaver's coat consists of a fine, dense underfur covered by an outer coat of coarse hair. The search for this thick, glossy fur motivated much of the early 19th-century explorations of western North America when beaver pelts were a standard currency.

Among the largest rodents in North America, beavers eat only plants. Soft bark is their primary food source; a special flap of skin behind the front teeth allows the beaver to gnaw the bark underwater without getting a mouthful of wood chips or water. Their front incisors never stop growing because they are continually worn down with use. Beavers are hard at work all along the upper Flint River as well as at the Newman Wetlands Center (see page 41).

profusely around the ruins. Cherokee rose, the state flower of Georgia, can also be found blooming all along the path in summer. **Location**: *In Clayton County where Terrell Mill Road once crossed the Flint River near Forest Park.*

Sullivan Road Bridge

Built in 1984, this is the first bridge over the Flint headwaters that is fairly accessible and from which you can see the river—surrounded by mimosa and kudzu in all its urban setting glory. **Location**: *In northwest Clayton County where Sullivan Road crosses the Flint River about 1 mile south of I-285.*

Lee's Mill Road Bridge

This highly industrialized area was once an area of mills. Built in 1989, Lee's Mill Road Bridge crosses the river near the site of the old Lee's Mill. **Location**: *In northwest Clayton County where Lee's Mill Road crosses the Flint.*

Atlanta South Parkway Bridge

Built in 1991, this bridge, surrounded by mimosa trees, is in the Atlanta South Business Park. This nicely landscaped area is a fairly safe and quiet place to look at the river, especially on a weekend when there is less traffic. The river is narrow here, running over and around large, flat rocks. At times it looks and sounds like a mountain stream. **Location**: *In Clayton County where Atlanta South Parkway crosses the Flint just past the entrance to the Atlanta South Business Park.*

GA 85 Bridge

Sullivan Creek merges with the Flint here as the river passes under this 1974 bridge in a very high-volume traffic area. Now officially a part of urban sprawl, the Flint runs parallel with GA 85, passing between the towns of Lake City, Morrow, Riverdale and Jonesboro. **Location**: *In northwest Clayton County where GA 85 crosses the Flint.*

Upper Riverdale Road Bridge

The river begins to widen as it passes under this bridge. A plaque on the bridge reads: "In Memory of W. C. "Bill" Benefield (March 15, 1885–October 23, 1977). He planted seeds of trust, faith and friendship that build bridges of love, respect and goodwill. Board of Commissioners: Charley Griswell, Chairman; Loren B. Cheaves, Vice chairman; Annie Ruth Ford; Raymond Johnson; Ernest Wright." **Location**: *In Clayton County where Upper Riverdale Road crosses the Flint just east of Clayton General Hospital in the town of Riverdale.*

Valley Hill Road Bridge

The river is wider and less rocky as it passes under this bridge and

Fayette County

Created in 1821, Fayette County was one of the first counties formed after the 1821 Treaty of Indian Springs, which ceded Creek Indian land between the Ocmulgee and Flint Rivers to Georgia. The boundary in the upper portion of this cession was actually Line Creek, rather than the Flint, and Fayette County's western border was set at Line Creek (named such because it was the boundary line between white settlement and the Indians). This land then became part of the 1821 Land Lottery.

"Fayette County was formed in 1821 from parts of the Creek Indian Territory. Georgia's 49th county and its county seat, Fayetteville, were named for the Marquis de LaFayette, one of General George Washington's commanders in the Revolutionary War. The Fayette County Courthouse in Fayetteville was built in 1825, making it the oldest courthouse in the state...."

From *Georgia County Snapshots*, Georgia Department of Community Affairs

For tourism information for towns in Fayette County, see Resources page 300.

there is even access to the river from a fishing trail along the west bank. **Location**: *In Clayton County where Valley Hill Road crosses the Flint in Riverdale.*

GA 138 Bridge

The floodplain around this bridge is flat and wider and has been cleared. **Location**: *In Clayton County where GA 138 crosses the Flint River near Jonesboro.*

Flint River Road Bridge

From this bridge, built in 1987, look north and you will see pilings from another bridge that once stood here. On August 31, 1864, a Southern brigade created a diversion here when they charged Union cavalry, barricaded on the east side of the river with four artillery pieces, then drove the Federals across the Flint. A state historical marker about the battle is located on the corner of Flint River Road and Roberts Road, just east of the river. A deeply rutted dirt road on the southwest bank leads to a grassy area where fishermen can park and access the river. A grassy area on the east side of the river is wetlands that are managed by the Clayton County Water Authority. **Location**: *In Clayton County where Flint River Road crosses the Flint River Road near Jonesboro.*

GA 54 Bridge

Built in 1999, these double bridges cross the river and floodplain near the old Mundy's Mill area. **Location**: *On Fayette and Clayton County line where GA 54 crosses the Flint River.*

McDonough Road Bridge

This bridge, built in 1956, is in the heart of Tara Country. Margaret Mitchell's grandparents owned a plantation along the Flint just north of here. Their real-life homestead, called Rural Home, was the inspiration for the fictional Tara in her novel, Gone With the Wind. The History of Fayette County relates that a brief skirmish was fought here when a group of Rebel pickets attempted to burn a covered bridge over the Flint River to prevent Yankees from crossing during the Civil War. Pilings from an earlier bridge can be seen downstream and there are fishing trails on both banks. **Location**: *On Fayette and Clayton County line where McDonough Road crosses the Flint between Fayetteville and Lovejoy.*

North Bridge Road Bridge

There has been a bridge at this site ever since the area was first settled. First, the Glass family and then the North family owned a large plantation here and built and maintained a bridge. According to *The History of Fayette County*, a skirmish took place between Union

Gone With the Wind

After being told by the Tarleton twins that Ashley Wilkes was to marry his cousin Melanie Hamilton, Scarlett O'Hara stood on the road to Tara awaiting her father, Gerald O'Hara's, return from Twelve Oaks, the plantation across the Flint River where Ashley lived.

"Her eyes followed the winding road, blood-red now after the morning rain. In her thought she traced its course as it ran down the hill to the sluggish Flint River, through the tangled swampy bottoms and up the next hill to Twelve Oaks where Ashley lived. That was all the road meant now—a road to Ashley and the beautiful white-columned house that crowned the hill like a Greek temple."

The Flint is only a 20-foot wide, winding stream between Fayette and Clayton Counties, but this portion of it has played an integral part in literary history. Here, is where it flows along the western edge of Tara, the fictional home of Scarlett O'Hara—and perhaps the most famous home in all of American literature.

In reality, these Flint River bottomlands were part of a 2,527-acre cotton plantation owned by author Margaret Mitchell's Irish great-grandfather, Philip Fitzgerald. Margaret roamed the land as a child, and when she sat down to write *Gone With the Wind*, the Flint and her grandfather's plantation, named Rural Home, evolved into Tara.

and Confederate cavalry along this road during the Atlanta Campaign of the Civil War. **Location**: *On Fayette and Clayton County line where North Bridge Road crosses the Flint between Fayetteville and Lovejoy.*

Hills Bridge Road Bridge

This bridge in Inman has been impassable for many years but is still a good place to see the river. **Location**: *On Fayette and Clayton County line where Hills Bridge Road crosses the Flint in Inman.*

Woolsey Road Bridge

This bridge is the first good place to put a canoe into the Flint. **Location**: *On Fayette and Clayton County line where Woolsey Road crosses the Flint on the east side of Woolsey.*

GA 92 Bridge

Location: *On Fayette and Spalding County line where GA 92 crosses the Flint River between Fayetteville and Griffin.*

McIntosh Road Bridge

This bridge is surrounded by the rolling countryside of south Fayette County just east of the little town of Brooks. **Location**: *On Fayette and Spalding County line where McIntosh Road crosses the Flint 2 miles east of Brooks.*

GA 16 Bridge

Built in 1960, this bridge provides access to the river from a fishing trail on the southwest side. **Location**: *In Spalding County where GA 16, also known as Newnan Road, crosses the Flint between the communities of Digbey and Zetella.*

Line Creek Road Bridge

If you look upstream, you will see the pilings from another bridge that once stood here. You might even catch a glimpse of a beaver or two building a dam. There is access to the Flint from fishing trails on the west side of the river. **Location**: *In southwest corner of Spalding County where Line Creek Road crosses the Flint near Blanton's Mill.*

Hollonville Road Bridge

Line Creek empties into the Flint about one mile below this bridge which was built in 1966. **Location**: *On Pike and Spalding County line where Hollonville Road crosses the river near Hollonville.*

Clayton County and Jonesboro

Created in 1858 from parts of Fayette and Henry Counties, Clayton County was named for Judge Augustin Smith Clayton, a Superior Court judge and a U.S. representative. Jonesboro, the county seat, was chartered in 1859; but its history goes back to 1823 when it was first settled and called Leaksville. When the Central Railroad line reached the town, its name was changed to Jonesboro in honor of Captain Samuel Jones, one of the line's surveying engineers.

By 1860 Jonesboro was a prosperous community surrounded by farms and plantations. Countless bales of cotton stood near the depot, awaiting shipment to Atlanta and other points.

During the Civil War, the railroad became the focus of Union troops during the final days of the Atlanta Campaign in 1864. Running right down the middle of Main Street, it was the main supply line to Confederate troops, defending Atlanta against General William Sherman's Army. Unable to gain Atlanta by siege from the north, Sherman sent his troops around the city to the south to destroy the railroad line from Jonesboro. Federal troops crossed the Flint River into Jonesboro in a front formation that was six miles long. Massively outnumbered, the Confederates managed to hold the railroad lines free until the evacuation of the doomed Confederate Army was complete. Local legend says that trains ran all night on August 31, right down the middle of Jonesboro, while soldiers from both sides—witnessing the defeat of a great army—looked the other way.

Many of the old downtown brick exteriors still stand, surviving Sherman's torch as their interiors burned. For information on a driving tour of historic Jonesboro and Clayton County, see Resources page 300.

Section 2

Line Creek to Potato Creek

RIO CONVINCES US that he is… well… different. We follow him to Flat Shoals, where an Indian trading path once crossed the Flint. We find out that two U.S. Presidents were influenced by tributaries of the Flint and that they, in turn, had a tremendous impact on the region through which the FLint River flows.

Between Line Creek and Potato Creek, use the Guidebook Section beginning on page 60 to explore: The Sea, Flat Shoals, Dripping Rocks, The Cove, Tally Gap, Sprewell Bluff State Park, Yellow Jacket Shoals, Big Red Oak Creek Covered Bridge, the Old South Farm Museum, Joe Kurz Wildlife Management Area, Big Lazer Creek Wildlife Management Area, Camp Thunder, Goat Mountain and the Flint River Outdoor Center.

MERIWETHER COUNTY

PIKE COUNTY

THE OAKFUSKEE INDIAN TRAIL, OR WHAT WAS CALLED THE UPPER CREEK TRADING PATH, CROSSED THE FLINT HERE.

STONE TOOLS, ARROWHEADS AND POTTERY FOUND ON THE BANKS TELL A STORY OF EARLY INHABITANTS OF THIS REGION DATING BACK TO STONE AGE PEOPLE.

FLAT SHOALS

SETTLERS CHOSE ROCKY SHOALS LIKE THESE ON RIVERS AND CREEKS AS SITES TO BUILD THEIR GRISTMILLS.

IN SOME PLACES, LIKE POTATO CREEK AND TOBLER CREEK NEAR **THOMASTON**, THE GRISTMILLS GREW INTO SOME OF GEORGIA'S EARLIEST MANUFACTURING PLANTS.

WARM SPRINGS FLOWS INTO ROCKY FORD BRANCH, WHICH FLOWS INTO CANE CREEK, WHICH FLOWS INTO THE FLINT RIVER.

BECAUSE OF WARM SPRINGS, THIS REGION POWERFULLY INFLUENCED **FRANKLIN ROOSEVELT'S NEW DEAL**, DURING ONE OF THE MOST IMPORTANT PERIODS IN AMERICAN HISTORY.

1N 1924 ROOSEVELT CAME TO WARM SPRINGS IN HOPES OF FINDING A CURE FOR HIS POLIO.

HE BUILT A SIMPLE WHITE FRAME COTTAGE NEAR THE SPRINGS.

AFTER HE WAS ELECTED PRESIDENT IN 1932, IT WAS CALLED THE LITTLE WHITE HOUSE. HE VISITED HERE OFTEN DURING HIS PRESIDENCY.

ROOSEVELT DROVE AROUND THE PINE MOUNTAIN REGION IN HIS SPECIALLY EQUIPPED '32 FORD CONVERTIBLE. HE GOT TO KNOW FARMERS AND THEIR PROBLEMS.

HE MET LOCAL MERCHANTS IN TOWNS LIKE MANCHESTER, GREENVILLE AND WOODBURY.

HE LOVED TO EXPLORE THE COUNTRYSIDE. THE PEOPLE HE MET AND THE LANDSCAPE HE SAW HELPED FORM HIS NEW DEAL POLICIES.

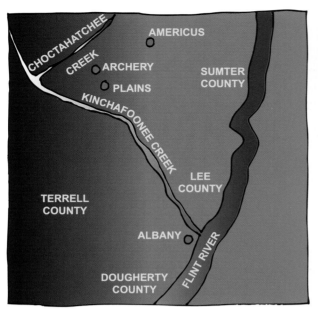

CHOCTAHATCHEE CREEK

AMERICUS

ARCHERY

PLAINS

SUMTER COUNTY

KINCHAFOONEE CREEK

LEE COUNTY

TERRELL COUNTY

ALBANY

FLINT RIVER

DOUGHERTY COUNTY

IN 1924, THE SAME YEAR THAT PRESIDENT-TO-BE FRANKLIN ROOSEVELT CAME TO WARM SPRINGS FOR THE FIRST TIME, **ANOTHER PRESIDENT-TO-BE** WAS BORN IN THE LITTLE TOWN OF PLAINS, GEORGIA.

HE GREW UP HUNTING AND FISHING ON **CHOCTAHATCHEE CREEK** IN THE FLINT RIVER WATERSHED.

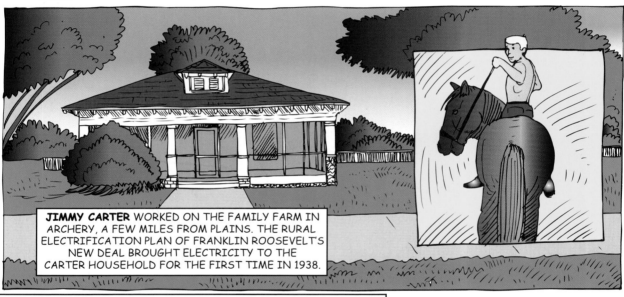

JIMMY CARTER WORKED ON THE FAMILY FARM IN ARCHERY, A FEW MILES FROM PLAINS. THE RURAL ELECTRIFICATION PLAN OF FRANKLIN ROOSEVELT'S NEW DEAL BROUGHT ELECTRICITY TO THE CARTER HOUSEHOLD FOR THE FIRST TIME IN 1938.

WHEN HE BECAME GOVERNOR OF GEORGIA IN 1970, THE U.S. ARMY CORPS OF ENGINEERS WANTED TO BUILD **A DAM ON THE FLINT RIVER AT SPREWELL BLUFF**. CARTER PERSONALLY CANOED AND FISHED THE FLINT TO SEE THE PROPOSED DAM SITE.

LET'S GO TO THE FLINT RIVER. **I WANT TO SEE THIS FOR MYSELF!**

GOVERNOR CARTER DISCOVERED THAT THE CORPS OF ENGINEERS OVERESTIMATED THE BENEFITS THAT WOULD RESULT FROM THE DAM AND **VETOED** THE SPREWELL BLUFF PROJECT

FOR WHAT RIO'S RIVER MARK MEANS, SEE PAGE 84.

A Canoe Trip Through Time

Editor's Note:

Here are three different stories about one section of the Flint River—the 25 miles between the GA 18 Bridge near Woodbury and the Po Biddy Road Bridge.

Two of the stories were written more than 25 years ago, and the third was written in 1996. But when I re-read them now, they are as fresh to me as a waterfall on Big Lazer Creek. Taken together, these stories tell a remarkable and very personal story of the Flint River from three different, but related, perspectives. They get to the heart of how and why people are drawn to rivers. They also tell an inspiring story of how citizen involvement combined with government leadership can protect river corridors and other features of our natural environment. FB

THE FLINT, NOW!

By Claude Terry

When Claude Terry wrote this story for Brown's Guide to Georgia *magazine in 1973, he was a professor of microbiology at Emory University. A scientist by training and an expert outdoorsman by nature, Claude was among a small number of pioneering Georgia environmentalists who helped Jimmy Carter and other state and federal government officials see and appreciate the Flint as well as other Georgia rivers. He was one of the original Friends of the River, the group that successfully lobbied for designation of a portion of the Chattahoochee River in Atlanta as a National Recreation Area. He founded and continues to operate Southeastern Expeditions, a rafting outfitter on the Chattooga River in northeast Georgia, and is president of CTA, an environmental consulting company.*

Take a river labeled "Georgia's Number One Scenic River" by the Natural Areas Council, add the spice of three controversial dams that will drown this river valley, cap that off with the fact that this stream offers the best whitewater canoeing in middle Georgia and you can only be talking about Georgia's unique Flint River. Fishermen float and hike the river, canoeists drift down the easy stretches or risk boat and limb in Yellow Jacket Shoals and hunters prowl the adjacent forests in large numbers to stalk the plentiful deer.

Near GA 18 the river meanders through some of the loveliest country in middle Georgia, with rolling hills and fat cattle grazing blue-green pastures. About three miles below GA 18 the country changes, Pine Mountain throws up a barricade to the river's passage, and resulting conflict between river and rock provides some of the most exciting scenic vistas along any Georgia river. The plants and animals of the mountains occur along this river valley, intermingled with coastal vegetation. As a result, you can see Spanish moss hanging over mountain laurel and rhododendron, a strange but beautiful combination. The river has walled off, or more properly, carved off a sweeping bend in the Pine Mountain escarpment, leaving a cove protected on three sides by mountains, and on the fourth by river. This river cove has provided isolation for plants, animals and people for thousands of years. Today it offers the best recreation potential in the middle of the state, if properly used.

Just above Sprewell Bluff, a large ridge on the southwest side of the river, the Flint offers a series of shoaly rapids, of no real consequence, but enough to pep up an otherwise placid run. (This is the site for the first and most controversial Flint River dam proposed by the Corps of Engineers.) A county park opposite Sprewell Bluff affords a take-out point for the upper trip, a place to enter the river for the lower stretch, or a picnicking and viewing point for the auto traveler. From Sprewell Bluff to GA 36 the river continues its good manners, with little gradient and no significant rapids.

Canoeist and rafters desiring an easy trip can get on the Flint at GA 18 and paddle down to Sprewell Bluff Park (14 miles) or on to GA 36 (21 miles). Those desiring more adventure should read on!

At GA 36 Bridge the river appears swift but smooth, a tempting place for an easy Sunday float. Don't you believe it! Around the first bend you begin to encounter a building series of rapids, climaxing in the twisting drop at the bottom of Yellow Jacket Shoals.

At high water (10 feet or greater on the GA 36 gauge) these rapids can build up some heavy water, with large waves, big holes and a better than even chance to swamp an open canoe. At about 10 to 11 feet the river can be run by decked boats and rafts manned by competent experienced paddlers.

At high levels, even these paddlers would probably be endangered. This spring [1973], I paddled the river at 11 feet and found the section from GA 18 to GA 36 okay for experienced open boaters, and the Yellow Jacket section okay for kayakers and rafters of moderate experience. However, we saw pieces of several flat-bottomed boats and canoes, and a local resident along the side informed me that 10 canoes and one life had been lost in the last couple of weeks on this stretch of river. To those of us with heavy water experience, the river would be class III at these high levels. However, to the area boaters who normally run flat rivers this tricky section could be hairy indeed! At lower water levels (about 8 feet) the river offers intricate maneuvering and long, steep drops down narrow chutes. Minimum levels have not been established since the gauge is new, but are probably about seven feet. Take-out for this run is at Po Biddy Road. The Yellow Jacket Shoals stretch with medium flow requires about three hours running time, a comfortable afternoon run.

I doubt if there is another river in the world where tupelo trees form part of the obstacles in a rapid, where Spanish moss drips onto mountain laurel, where water and rock have combined to give such a beautiful sweep to the traveler's vision.

To casually inundate such a treasure with the dam that the Corps of Engineers proposes would seem incomprehensible, particularly in a region where such mountain beauty is rare. Yet the proposal to build Sprewell Bluff Dam and a reregulating dam is still pushed by the Corps, some state officials, and various economic interests. But not by those whose land will be inundated. There is much local opposition by the young landowners who will be flooded out, and by sportsmen.

It now appears that the benefits in flood control and power production are negligible, and it is apparent that recreational benefits of a lake must be weighed against lost benefits of a unique river corridor. Lakes silt out in 50 to 200 years, leaving mud flats. Rivers just keep on "rollin' along" —at least until man in his infinite wisdom intervenes.

Georgians have a choice of a long narrow pool which will soon (is 100 years really very long?) be a mud flat or the infinite river. See the Flint River now, and let your children and grandchildren see it.

Canoe trip from GA 18 Bridge to Po Biddy Road Bridge
This section of river naturally divides itself into several different trips. From GA 18 to Sprewell Bluff (about 14 miles, six hours) is an easy trip with no significant rapids. From Sprewell Bluff to GA 36 (seven miles, three hours) is more of the same. From GA 36 to Po Biddy Bridge it's a different story. Just around the bend is Yellow Jacket Shoals. At 10 feet or more on the GA 36 gauge, these rapids can build up some heavy water with a better than even chance of swamping an open canoe. Boaters should check with the Flint River Outdoor Center (see page 81) at the GA 36 Bridge for information on water levels and shuttle service.

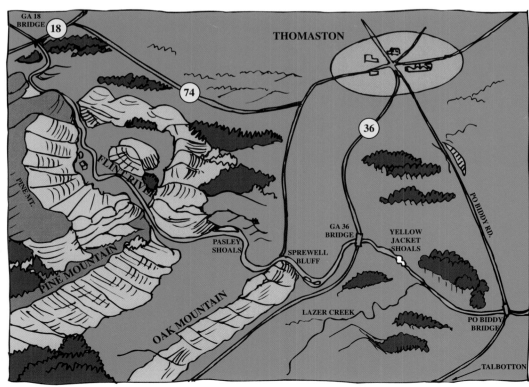

THE FIGHT TO SAVE THE FLINT

By Eugene H. Methvin

Eugene Methvin, a Georgia native, wrote this story for Readers Digest *in August, 1974. It picks up the story of the Flint where Claude Terry's canoe trip leaves off by describing the events surrounding Jimmy Carter's veto of the Sprewell Bluff dam in 1974. To get Carter's perspective on the events of those years, see his Preface on page 13.*

Throughout the spring and summer of 1972, Georgia's Gov. Jimmy Carter had been besieged with pleas to block a proposed federal dam and "save the Flint River." Finally, in August, the governor took an overnight canoe trip to see for himself the source of the uproar.

The Flint River rises in Atlanta. Leaving the city, it is a greasy, sticky industrial sludge. But after tumbling through the Piedmont Plateau for 30 miles, it becomes a healthy highland stream that cuts through four steep ridges, forming the beautiful Flint River gorges, before spilling out into the Coastal Plain. In this magnificent fall-line passage of singing waters and hardwood forest, teeming wildlife thrives. Fishermen flock to try the Flint River bass, a prized game fish that spawns nowhere else, while canoeists test themselves on swirling white-water rapids.

"If we are going to destroy all this natural beauty," Carter said to his fellow camper, Joe Tanner, commissioner of the state's Department of Natural Resources, "we better make sure that what we get in return is worth the price."

Back in the state capital, the two men began asking questions of federal planners—and soon found themselves grappling with gravely flawed government machinery for dealing with the twin crises of energy demands and environmental quality. The lessons they learned are vital to all Americans.

Carter and Tanner discovered that for nearly a decade no one had really questioned the dam project. As early as 1955, Rep. John J. Flynt, Jr., had introduced a proposal to plug the Flint gorges right at the mouth, near a place called Sprewell Bluff, flooding almost the entire valley. The Army Corps of Engineers backed Flynt's proposal with impressive statistics. For every dollar invested, the Corps claimed, the dam would return $1.60—in such benefits as hydroelectric power, lake recreation and downstream flood control—over a 100-year period.

Local economies were promised a boom, and the prospect of "free" federal dollars mobilized a formidable array of vested interests—land promoters, chambers of commerce and rural electric cooperatives. Congress authorized the project in 1963, and in ensuing years routinely voted 7 million of a total cost estimated at over $200 million. Construction was to begin in June 1974.

Carter's easiest course was to "go along." But he had begun to sense growing opposition, both in Congress and in the electorate, to the old manner of viewing natural resources through a pork barrel. In 1969, Congress had passed the National Environmental Policy Act (NEPA) which among other things ordered federal agencies to publish "impact statements" on every major section, detailing possible adverse effects on the environment and presenting thorough studies of alternatives. In so doing, Congress launched the nation on a painful educational voyage into the true costs of the resource exploitation that increasingly degrades our environment and our everyday lives. Across America, conservationists marched into courtrooms, stopping dams and other projects until the bureaucrats complied with NEPA. Which is what began to happen in Georgia.

In 1970, the Georgia Natural Areas Council surveyed 53 rivers to see which merited preservation under the New National Scenic Rivers Act. The survey made Georgians realize that they had precious few free stretches of river left: in fact, the Flint was the last major river in the state whose fall line remained undammed. Formally assigning the Flint top priority, the Council submitted a report to Carter and urged him to suspend the project.

Almost simultaneously, archeology student and Flint River buff Ron Miles formed the Flint River Preservation Society. Armed with the scenic-rivers report, Miles' group mobilized the Georgia Conservancy, Audubon Society, League of Conservation Voters and others. As a result, Carter received 6,000 letters, and visits from more than 50 citizens' delegations. "And that," says the governor with a grin, "is enough to get any politician's attention."

Under federal law, the governor of any state is entitled to see all Corps of Engineers reports to

Congress on projects within his state. But when Carter sought data in support of the Flint River project, he encountered only obfuscation and delay. He found the Corps' NEPA-ordered impact statement "little more than promotional literature supporting dam construction." Threatened with court action, the Corps announced plans for a revised statement.

Awaiting the report, the governor directed Commissioner Tanner to assemble geologists, archeologists, hydrologists, historians and plant and wildlife experts for an independent analysis. University students and professors pitched in with their own studies. In Washington, Georgia Sen. Herman Talmadge (D. GA) through a supporter of the project, asked the General Accounting Office (GAO) for its opinion on the Corps proposal.

When he received all the reports, Carter got a profound shock. Despite the clear command of NEPA for a detailed presentation of alternatives, the Corps' new impact statement brushed aside other possibilities with a bare mention. Additionally, the reports from Tanner and the GAO made clear that the Corps had omitted colossal costs and had wildly inflated benefits in an effort to "sell" the dam. Examples:

The project's 211-foot dam would totally submerge the Flint valley for 28 of its most scenic miles. Yet the Corps measured the devastation of 24,500 acres of magnificent hardwood forest at a mere $248,000 annually, the net value of the raw timber produced. And it ignored an annual loss to the state of $12 million in jobs and other income.

The dam would bottle up a self-purifying river, possibly forcing upstream cities to spend additional millions removing nutrients from sewage-treatment effluents. Yet nowhere in the Corps' impact statement was the danger acknowledged.

The Corps claimed a $127,000 annual "wildlife" benefit—the income expected from reservoir fishing permits. Yet the project would destroy one of Georgia's finest wildlife habitats, threatening extinction of the river's bass, and devastating deer, wild turkey and osprey populations.

Fourteen Mercer University student volunteers conducted a massive study of usage on Georgia's recreational lakes to test a Corps estimate of nearly $4 million in annual recreation benefits from the

proposed reservoir. They found that the new lake would compete with nine other large water impoundments, all within 50 miles, all operating at far below capacity. (One such federally financed lake, just 26 miles from Sprewell Bluff, was already going bankrupt from underuse.) Moreover, the state's own 1972 survey showed "a gigantic present deficit" of stream recreational opportunities, which it predicted would double within a decade.

Once the facts were clear, Carter called for a Congressional probe of the Corps' cost/benefit hocus-pocus and urged Congress to revoke the project's appropriation. "The Corps grossly misrepresented both benefits and costs," he declared. "It did not look for least-cost solutions, just dam solutions."

Embarrassed Corps officials suspended construction. But at the request of Congressman Flynt, Corps headquarters in Washington drafted a resolution for introduction in the Georgia legislature disavowing Carter's stand and calling on the Corps and Congress to build the Flint dam anyway. Last February, the Georgia house passed the resolution, but to the shock of traditional pork-barrelers, it was beaten twice in the senate by narrow margins of two and six votes.

Still the Corps wasn't ready to give up. It sent to the White House additional data to persuade President Nixon to include the Flint dam in his crash program to make the nation self-sufficient in energy by 1980. Unhappily for the Corps, Governor Carter's Naval career in nuclear engineering and submarine power plants equipped him to suggest an energy alternative to the Flint dam.

From the Atomic Energy Commission, Carter learned that for less than one third the Flint Project's cost, Uncle Sam could buy nuclear generating capacity that would supply seven times as much electricity. (Obscured in the Corps' design data was the astonishing reality that the Flint's meager flow could turn generators only the equivalent of 42 days a year.) Thus, for $140 million less, taxpayers could have sevenfold the electricity—and save a unique wilderness resource in the bargain.

So the Flint—thanks to NEPA, a wide mobilization of concerned citizens, and a courageous and technically trained governor—was saved from the bulldozers.

We must realize that our swamps and forests, our rivers and mountains, perform vital life-support functions that have monetary values we are only beginning to learn to calculate. We can never create water-cleansing mechanisms like the Flint River. We can only save those we have.

A RIVER MAKES UP ITS MIND
by Reece Turrentine

This third story in the series describes one man's appreciation for what was saved on the Flint when Jimmy Carter vetoed the dam at Sprewell Bluff.

Over the years I have canoed southern rivers with many different companions and I have assigned stories to and edited copy from many writers who were writing about southern streams. In all that time, I have never known anyone who, deep down at their core, really loved rivers more than Reece Turrentine. If there ever was a person for whom the description, "He has river water flowing through his veins," applied, that person is Reece. Not only does he have the spirit, he can describe it. Reece relates his river experiences in a way that communicates to everyone, whether or not they have ever paddled a canoe. A Methodist minister by profession, now retired, Reece can hear more of God's voice in an eddy current than most of us can find in the Old Testament.

Summer before last, my wife and I spent a couple of weeks canoeing, hiking and fishing around Yellowstone National Park. In the evening we were delighted to get back to the quaint elegance of the old Yellowstone Inn on the lake. Each evening meal was accompanied by a live string quartet and by "Bullwinkle," a huge Bull Moose who made nightly rounds.

One evening we heard more commotion than usual. Into the dining room strolled former President and Mrs. Jimmy Carter and their entourage. They were ushered to the table next to ours. The temptation was too great. As he approached, I stood up and offered a "down-home" introduction.

"President Carter," I said, "I'm Reece Turrentine and this is my wife, Onie. We're both from Thomasville."

My reference elicited the familiar smile, and brought both Carters over to talk. "Why that's just down from Plains," Mr. Carter said. "What are you doing way out here?" We chatted as we walked to the window to see "Bullwinkle."

"President Carter, I said," I want to thank you for saving the Flint River years ago. I was canoeing editor for *Brown's Guide* for years, and everyone was afraid we were about to lose the Flint."

"Thank you," he replied graciously, "for those articles and for what y'all did to keep the environmental issues of our state before everybody." After a few more "folksy" comments we left them to their privacy.

Back in the early 1970s when he was governor, Carter took a trip down the Flint, saw the unusual environmental and scenic wonders of the area, and suppressed the proposed dam. We are indebted to him for that. There's really nothing like it in middle Georgia. Canoeists have a mountain whitewater river, fishermen can fly fish, hikers can climb mountains and explore rock outcroppings found only hundreds of miles to the north.

The Flint River has a rather meager beginning. It starts from drainage and feeder streams around Hartsfield Airport, College Park and Forest Park. Once it survives that, it seems to gather its senses and decides to become a river. The upper stretches aren't too much for canoeing; too many deadfalls and urban trash. As it moves through Fayette County into Pike County, it gets down to business. After the GA 18 Bridge, west of Thomaston, the river begins to open through some of middle Georgia's loveliest rolling hills and blue-green pastures. Then comes the shocker. A few miles below the GA 18 Bridge, you think your canoe suddenly has become some kind of magic carpet and transported you far north into the mountains.

What strange forces have created a river like this in middle Georgia? To answer that, you'd have to ask Pine Mountain, and the forces that created it. Geologists could explain it. But whatever it was, something shot a ridge of mountains southward sharply into middle Georgia. So much so that the trees, plants, rocks and water all think they are still up there. So you've got this strange mixture. Tupelos are part of the obstacles in the rapids. Along the banks Spanish moss drips over rhododendron and mountain laurel. It is here the Flint has a hard time deciding what it is and wants to be, but is a wonderland for hikers, fishermen, hunters, canoeists and all who love the outdoors.

Soon after Carter halted the dam project, another young man appeared on the scene to watch and protect the Flint. Jim McDaniel, who was born and reared near the river, and his wife, Margie, opened the Flint River Outpost at the GA 36 Bridge. Jim and I have canoed several rivers together through the years, strange places, like Potato Creek, and the remote section of the Ochlockonee River in Florida. But I hadn't seen the Flint since the flood of 1994. I wondered what damage had been done. I picked up the phone. "Hey Reece," came his familiar voice, although several years had passed. "Where do you want to go?" I kinda hated to tell him I just wanted to canoe down to his place on the Flint. He sounded like he was expecting some exotic locale with a strange name. But he loves the Flint more than any place on earth, so he was ready to set the date.

Sprewell Bluff's massive rock outcroppings looked the same. Thank God they hadn't been touched by a dam builder's drills and explosives. The water was high and swift, swollen by recent rains. I imagined Yellow Jacket Shoals downstream would be running close to a Class IV rapid at this height. But we weren't going that far. Thank goodness. I've fought that monster in past years, and will again in less water. In this current, it wouldn't take long to go the five miles to the outpost at the bridge.

As we launched our canoes into the swift waters, I thought I felt an old familiar pull in the paddle. But that's foolish. Water is water, and rivers are rivers. When I get on a river my sentiments and feelings stimulate my imagination.

I was paddling tandem with Jim so I could ask him questions about recent happenings on the river. Jim and I talked about groups we've taken on rivers in the past. Neither of us has had much formal training in canoeing. We've just paddled a lot of rivers. You learn strokes, even if you don't know all the textbook names for them.

As we approached Owens Island, Jim told me about the old Confederate bridge that crossed there and was burned during the Civil War. A stagecoach road crossed it on the Old Alabama Road.

"There's an old well up on the riverbank where the stagecoaches would stop." Jim said.

"Do you know where it is?" I asked.

"I used to," he replied.

"Let's go look," I said as I executed what textbooks would call an across the bow draw-stroke. Jim followed with a reverse stroke that headed us toward the bank.

Soon we were up on the bank, tromping through the woods looking for an old stagecoach roadbed and a rock-lined water well.

We parted and walked alone to search. It took a minute for it to soak in. In an instant we had stepped out of the river, and back hundreds of years, looking for remnants of stagecoaches and wells. We found them, as well as some strange rockpiles, which Jim identified as Indian graves, or possibly slave graves. Then we separated again to see what else we could find. It was as if a time machine had transported us to another world. Once again, I felt the old exhilaration, or maybe inspiration is a better term. Whatever, such feelings have swept over me many times.

Through the years I've paddled rivers, camped by them, bathed in them, watched their moods and listened to their murmurings. I've been caressed by them and bruised by them. I've climbed their banks and marveled at the delicate but sturdy plant growth that lies hidden everywhere. The plant life and the amazing array of animals that call to you from a distance—it all makes you feel the energy and harm-ony of it all. It makes me want to reach out and claim kinship with the wholeness. But I can't do that.

I can't ignore the fact that I'm an outsider. I'm more of an intruder than a kinsman. I'm of a species that seems bent on destroying places like this. But I still get the old feeling. I knew Jim felt it. I could see him through the trees in the distance, walking slowly, looking at the ground and up in the trees, as if in deep thought. He was thinking it, or praying it in his own way, what every outdoorsman has felt: "O God, let it stay like this forever." With people like President Carter being a river leader, and Jim McDaniel a river lover, maybe it will.

Section 2

Line Creek to Potato Creek

SIGNIFICANT NATURAL AREAS

The Sea

Many times extensive shoaling in a river will act as a dam, creating a backup that results in a natural lake. This is the effect that the huge, granite rocks, protruding from the water at Flat Shoals, have had on a portion of the Flint about one mile upstream, known as the Sea. Here, the Flint River widens to about twice its normal width and forms a nearly circular lake.

Ever since the first pioneering families settled Meriwether and Pike Counties in the mid-1820s, the Sea has been a traditional recreational area for locals. People who have enjoyed swimming and fishing in the Sea estimate it to be about 35 feet at its deepest point.

Vegetation around the Sea is thick and grows close to the river's edge. Limbs of red maple reach out over the water while sweetgum, pine, river birch, hickory and oak crowd the Sea's perimeter. Trees and shrubs native to the Coastal Plain mix with those of the Piedmont. The water tupelo, or tupelo gum, as well as the southern catalpa have adapted to this Piedmont area. Several tupelo gums, with their long, straight trunks and bell bottom-like bases, can be spotted on the right bank as you paddle upstream from Flat Shoals to the Sea. The short-trunked southern catalpas are easier to find. Their branches of heart-shaped leaves hang low along the river banks.

Since the Sea is surrounded by private property, the only way to view it is from the water. You can put in at the David Knott Bridge (see map page 67) and head upstream about one mile.

Flat Shoals

Rocks. Hugh, flat and angular, gray to light brown in color. They protrude from beneath the shallow water of the Flint, extending from bank to bank. This is Flat Shoals. A stretch of river that is about 200 feet wide with granite outcrops on each side. An area rich with diverse plant life. A place where Indians have crossed and a president has fished.

The Flat Shoals area begins at the David Knott Bridge (see page 83) on Flat Shoals Road, three miles east of Gay in Meriwether County, and extends downstream about one river mile. The area is made up of two distinct rock shoal areas separated by about two acres of water and bisected by several islands. The river through Flat Shoals is wider

Freshwater Mussels

Freshwater mussels spend their entire life partially or wholly buried in mud, sand or gravel in permanent bodies of water. The vast majority of species are found in streams, but a few are present in ponds or lakes. They live in a variety of habitats but are most abundant on shoals, where they live in gravel or a mixture of sand, mud and gravel. If you walk the Flat Shoals area in low water, you will find lots of mussels.

A protective shell, made up of two similar pieces called valves, covers the mussel's body—which consists of various organs, including the foot, gills, heart and stomach. The valves are joined at one point by a hinge and can be opened and closed somewhat like a powder compact.

Freshwater mussels continuously pump water through their bodies, filtering food from the water. The food consists of detritus, which is organic matter found on the stream or lake bottom, and plankton, composed of microscopic plants and animals suspended in the water. Mussels are an important food source for many animals, including muskrats, minks, otters, fishes and some birds.

Freshwater mussels are considered to be "environmental monitors" of rivers, streams, ponds and lakes. They indicate the water quality in terms of their numbers within their particular niche. Since freshwater mussels are towards the bottom of the food chain, chemical pollutants will be present within their tissue. According to a 1992 American Fisheries study, of the 297 native American freshwater mussels, many are considered "endangered, threatened or of special concern. Only 70 percent are listed as currently stable."

For more about mussels living in Georgia and the Flint River, see map page 237.

because the rock shoals tend to act as a dam. The river also drops throughout this section. Water cascades over ledges and rocks, pools in places several feet deep and swirls around large, dry outcrops.

To get a good view of Flat Shoals, stand on the David Knott Bridge and look downstream. By definition, a shoal is anyplace in a river, or the ocean for that matter, where the water is shallow and difficult to navigate by boat. Historically, shoals have been natural places to cross a river. The huge rocks at Flat Shoals are so near the surface of the water that you can walk from one side of the river to the other. Animals discovered this natural bridge millions of years ago, as did the Native Americans (see page 65).

Flat Shoals is abundant with plant life. Aralia, cassia, sumac, plum, smilax, climbing moonseed vine and climbing milkweed bloom profusely on the wooded island that bisects the shoals under the highway bridge where you stand.

Flat Shoals is particularly rich with endemic, or native, plants that grow on wet and on dry rock outcrops. Outcrops are defined as rocks that emerge from the earth. The "flat-rock" outcrops that flank both sides of the Flint at Flat Shoals are granite, a coarse-grained igneous rock composed mostly of two minerals, quartz and feldspar. Granite is the most common intrusive rock exposed at the earth's surface.

A trip down the river at Flat Shoals is a worthwhile lesson in the ecosystems of a rock outcrop. Most rock outcrops have shallow pits of varying depth where soil has formed. Some have more soils than others, so they support different degrees, or levels, of plant development—from simple algae that have no roots, to shrubs and small trees. You can see some form of this on almost any outcrop you inspect at Flat Shoals. The rock shoals are slippery with algae. Lichens, which are formed by algae growing inside fungus, grow on bare rock; green mosses on wet rock. Then there are various succulent annuals that adapt to extremes in moisture—dry in low water levels, submerged at other times. Brown and spongy, they adhere to rocks above and below the water. As the soil on the outcrop becomes deeper, perennials take root—clumps of spiderwort, arrowhead lilies, sedges and rushes. If the outcrop is large enough and the soil is deep enough, shrubs and small trees will dominate. At Flat Shoals, shrubs, such as black titi with its finger-like clusters of white flowers and button bush with its white, ball-like flower, can be spotted at the top of outcrops. Winged elm, slippery elm, water oak, water hickory and willow oak grow all along the edge of the river and in the islands.

Deer tracks and those of large birds can be spotted in wet areas of an outcrop. Turtles sun themselves on the rocks. Birds feed on duckweed, a tiny, green plant—the smallest known flowering plant (see sidebar on page 43)—that floats in still water areas around the rocks.

Anytime is a good time for exploring Flat Shoals, but the best time is during low water. You can put in a canoe or small boat at the David Knott Bridge (see map page 67) and pass under the bridge to access

Southern Catalpa

With its broad, heart-shaped leaves and short trunk, the Southern catalpa *(Catalpa bignonioides Walter)* tree can be easily spotted along streams and gullies throughout Georgia. You'll find this tree hanging low along the Flint River in the area above Flat Shoals known as "The Sea" (see opposite page).

Rarely 50 feet high, the southern catalpa's trunk is one to two feet in diameter, terminating in a broad head. The Georgia Forestry Commission describes the tree as having "4-to 12-inch long heart-shaped leaves" and a fruit that is "a slender, cylindrical pod, 10 to 12 inches long." The bark is "light brown, tinged with red and separating on the surface into large, thin, irregular scales."

Catalpa flowers are white, tinged and dotted with violet or purple. Known as Indian pods, the long, bean-like pods succeed the flowers, sometimes hanging on the limbs all winter.

Originally, the catalpa only grew in a few counties in the Coastal Plain of Southwest Georgia. Today, however, it can be found throughout the state because it has been planted as an ornamental tree and for the culture of catalpa worms, a large black caterpillar, which is highly prized as fishbait. The tree's pods attract the caterpillars, which can completely defoliate the tree by early summer. Remarkably, the tree, which grows quickly in moist soil, can regenerate a new set of leaves by mid-summer—which the worms might also eat completely—and still survive.

the shoals directly below, but be aware and respectful of the private property that lines both sides of the Flint River at Flat Shoals.

Directions: *From Concord, take GA 18 south 2 miles to Flat Shoals Road. Turn right and go 4 miles. Boat ramp and limited parking is on the right just before the David Knott Bridge.*

Dripping Rocks

Just east of Woodbury, the Flint River begins to wind its way through the Pine Mountain range, the last vestige of the Southern Appalachian Mountains. Past the sweeping arc called Horseshoe Bend. Past Elkins Creek to the left. Past Buzzard's Roost to the right to an area known as Dripping Rocks. Here, within the next mile, the river's elevation drops from about 647 to 637 feet, as the bluffs on both sides rise to more than 1,100 feet, the highest bluffs along the Flint.

Dripping Rocks is a good place to see the crystalline rock known as Hollis quartzite, which makes up Pine Mountain. Quartzite is a metamorphosed, quartz-rich sandstone. It is extremely hard and resistant to erosion. This particular quartzite is named Hollis because the principal quartzite of this terrain was first found in Hollis, Alabama, in 1915. For millions of years, the Flint River has flowed over this mountain peak, cutting into and gradually—very gradually—wearing away the quartzite rock to form the steep cliffs on both sides of the river, as well as the river shoals in between.

This same erosion process has left natural shelter-like rock formations in the bluffs on both sides of the river. Large enough to offer protection to four to five people, there is evidence that these were once occupied by Native Americans. Waterfalls (see "How Rivers Work page 272) have also formed in the bluffs where water flowed from hard to softer, more easily eroded rock. An example of this is Moss Falls, which can be found along the Dripping Rocks Trail.

Dripping Rocks has an unusually large concentration of native and rare plants, such as the white-flowered Alabama azalea and rhododendron, a shrubby evergreen (see sidebar page 77). The ravine between Moss Falls at Dripping Rocks and the Flint is a good place to see plants and animals common to both northern and southern environments living side by side. Titi, a Coastal Plain shrub, grows alongside mountain rhododendron. Chestnut oak, common to the mountains and upper Piedmont, grows with tupelo gum, usually found in Coastal Plain river swamps. Oak, pine, hickory, red maple, river birch, beech, poplar, sweet gum, myrtle, mountain laurel, water willow and river cane all grow abundantly. Coral snakes have been found in the sandy floodplain environment, as well as purple salamander, which is native to the mountains. Woodsia fern and spike moss cover Moss Falls where water drips down the rocky cliff; and wildflowers, such as trillium, bloodroot, wild geranium, wild indigo and brown eyed Susan, bloom along Dripping Rocks Road.

The best way to explore Dripping Rocks is to walk the trail (see

Mountain Laurel

Mountain laurel (*Kalmia latifolia* L.) is one of the most beautiful of native flowering shrubs and is often used as an ornamental in parks. With a range from Maine south to north Florida, west to Louisiana and north to Indiana, it grows in elevations up to 4,000 feet—higher in the southern Appalachians. It is usually found in the understory of mixed forests on upland mountain slopes and valleys and in shrub thickets, sometimes called "laurel slicks."

As a shrub, this evergreen plant stands five to 10 feet tall. As a tree, it reaches heights of 30 feet or more. Its glossy, dark green leaves are oblong and pointed at the ends. Blooming April to July, mountain laurel has pink or white flowers, which may have purple markings. The stamens of the flowers have a spring-like mechanism which spreads pollen when tripped by a bee. The leaves are poisonous to livestock, and honey from the flowers is believed to be poisonous as well.

Mountain laurel is one of those plants native to northern environments that can be seen growing in thickets around Moss Falls at Dripping Rock (see this page) and in other areas along the Flint River Corridor as well as the Apalachicola River Bluffs (see page 241) in southwest Georgia and northern Florida. For an illustration of mountain laurel, see page 191.

page 77) that follows the river. Dripping Rocks is part of the Gerald I. Lawhorn Canoe Base (see page 80), owned by the Flint River Council of the Boy Scouts of America, but the trail is open to hikers.

The Cove

To really understand the geological significance of the Cove, it is best to look at a topographical map. On a topo it's easy to see that Pine Mountain stretches from Lake Harding on the Chattahoochee River northeast to Barnesville. When it reaches the Flint River, the mountain forms a definite circle—a circle of hard, crystalline rock called Hollis quartzite, which the Flint River cuts through on its way south. This circular ridge encloses a basin that is known by locals as "The Cove."

Geologists who have studied the formation of the Cove believe that it was once a dome of rock. Over time the center of the dome eroded, leaving a fertile basin surrounded by the erosion-resistant quartzite that makes up most of Pine Mountain. The Flint River wore its pathway through the Cove, entering just below Elkins Creek and exiting a little below Pigeon Creek.

Ridges around the Cove range in elevation from about 1,000 to 1,250 feet. Here, ravine forests consist of beech, sourwood, sweet gum, chestnut oak, longleaf pine, American holly, tulip poplar, red maple and dogwood. River cane, dwarf rhododendron, maple-leafed viburnum, flame azalea and oak-leaf hydrangea are common shrubs.

Tally Gap

After leaving the Cove, the Flint River continues its trek downstream through the Pine Mountain range. It skirts around Singers Hill and Goat Mountain and then heads for Tally Gap. The river follows Tally Gap between Rockhouse Mountain and Spring Mountain, two of the highest peaks along the Flint.

This is an area of extremely steep bluffs and deep ravines. The ravines, slopes and bluffs here support a mixture of both mountain and Coastal Plain plant life. Large beech trees, hazelnuts, silverbells, oak-leaf hydrangea and black haw grow in Tally Gap's wooded bottomland, as well as a profusion of common azalea and Alabama azalea. Numerous ferns, partridge berry, weeping sedge and grass of parnassus—plants more typical of mountain environments—grow near a small stream and waterfall that empty into the river.

As at Dripping Rocks, erosion has carved large, cave-like shelters from rocks on Rockhouse Mountain. Some of these appear to have been inhabited by Indians at one time. One such rock shelter is in the high bluffs near the river.

The best way to see this area is to hike the old jeep road that follows the Flint for about one mile from the mouth of Pigeon Creek to Tally Gap. You can access the trail through the Pigeon Creek tract of the Sprewell Bluff Public Hunting Area (see page 79), where hiking is permitted except during hunting season.

Coral Snake

Tending to be secretive and nocturnal, the coral snake does not strike, but bites, injecting a lethal poison, which acts primarily on the nervous system, by a pair of short fangs fixed in the front of the snake's mouth. When threatened, a coral snake usually curls its tail into a tight spiral and holds it upright; this behavior is thought to attract predators to the tail instead of the more vulnerable head.

About 50 species of coral snake are known but the one that can be found in the Flint River Corridor is the *eastern* coral snake, or *harlequin*. It generally ranges from 20 to 40 inches in length and lives in the southeastern United States and in extreme northeastern Mexico. Its body is encircled by broad black and red bands separated by narrow yellow ones. The snake has a black snout. Just behind the snout is a wide yellow band followed by a black band. Some of these coral snakes are covered with black spots that hide much of the red color. Some nonpoisonous snakes look like coral snakes because they have similar coloring. But coral snakes have red and yellow bands next to each other. The harmless snakes have red and black bands together. For an illustration of a coral snake, see page 191.

Most coral snakes feed on lizards and other small snakes.

Sprewell Bluff

From Pasley Shoals to Owens Island winds a four-mile stretch of river called Sprewell Bluff. About 21 miles downstream from Flat Shoals, this is the southern end of the high ridge portion of the Piedmont. From here, the river will tumble through the Fall Line, headed for the flat, sandy Coastal Plain.

Made primarily of gneiss, schist and quartzite crystalline rock, the bluffs on the west bank range from 700 to 1,000 feet while the bluffs on the east, where Pine Woods Ridge extends northward, range from 550 to 900 feet. A series of shoals stretch across the river's width, with one particular set on the northern end of Sprewell Bluff State Park forming a natural dam.

Like much of this part of the Piedmont, Sprewell Bluff is a unique botanical area—a mixture of mountain and coastal plants and Piedmont and Coastal Plain animals are common. The higher elevations have typical high-ridge flora—chestnut, yellow chestnut and black jack, along with hickory, wild cherry, sourwood and winged elm with an understory of staghorn, smooth and shining sumac and a wide array of composites and legumes. The lower elevations, which run along the river bed, are dense with river birch (see sidebar this page), ash, willow oak, styrax, Georgia hackberry, silverbell, azalea, swamp dogwood, wild crabapple, buckeye, fringe tree and sugar maple. Thickets of blue-stem palmetto (see sidebar page 79) grow about as far north as they are able to survive. Lavender, phlox, violets and ginger grow in the spring, while summer flowers include showy baptisia, meadow beauties and wild indigo.

White-tailed deer, wild turkey, grey squirrel and raccoon roam the woods. It is a regular stop for migratory songbirds, such as hooded warbler, Arcadian flycatcher, summer tanager, eastern wood-pewee and red-eyed vireo.

One of the best things about Sprewell Bluff is that the state park makes it accessible to everyone. There are two areas worth exploring if you want to get a good panoramic view of the Sprewell Bluff area. One is from the overlook on Pine Wood Ridge, just before you arrive at the entrance to Sprewell Bluff State Park (see page 70). This 900-foot overlook faces northward toward Pasley Shoals offering one of the most-photographed views of the entire Flint River. The other location is in the park at the overlook near the trailhead. Here, the river makes its final arc around the high bluffs on the west bank as it heads toward Owens Island.

Yellow Jacket Shoals

Once the Flint River passes under Wynn's Bridge on GA 36 between Talbot and Upson Counties, it begins its rapid descent through the Fall Line, the boundary that marks the edge of the ocean that once covered parts of Georgia, Alabama, South Carolina and Mississippi about 50 million years ago. Above the Fall Line is the red

River Birch

River Birch *(Betula nigra L.)* is typically a flood plain species that grows along streams, rivers and wet bottomland and, occasionally, along moist roadsides. It is common throughout Georgia, but is most prevalent in the Piedmont and less common in the Coastal Plain. River birch grows thick along the banks of the Piedmont area of the Flint, especially at Dripping Rocks and Sprewell Bluff.

One of the most distinguishing features of a river birch is its bark, which the Georgia Forestry Commission describes as "reddish brown, peeling off in thin, curling, papery layers." Birch wood is "rather hard, close-grained, light, strong, light brown with pale sapwood." It is used for furniture, veneer and cabinets. The tree is also frequently used as a specimen tree in landscaping.

clay soil and hard rock of the Piedmont. Below the Fall Line is the flat, sandy Coastal Plain. Within two and a half miles of the bridge, the river drops about 70 feet. A one-mile stretch of that, known as Yellow Jacket Shoals, drops about 40 feet, creating one of the most picturesque and unique sections of the Flint.

Here, the flat granite shoals stretch completely across the river. In this area of hardwood slope, river swamp and rock outcrop, Spanish moss hangs from shagbark hickory on the moist slopes and overcup oak in swampy areas. Trees such as white oak, beech, basswood, water gum and birch predominate, with an understory of the shrub-like pawpaw, as well as such northerly plants as golden alexanders, ginger, twisted stalk goldenrod, bellworts, rue anemone, harebells and pale vetchling. Carolina lilies sprout from rock outcrops along with yellow star grass, pussytoes and mountain harebell. Red bud and wax myrtle grow on drier slopes. Century plant and Michaux's lily can be found on the dry, rocky south-and-west facing bluffs. Summer months are particularly beautiful, with rare and endangered plants, such as the spider lily (see map page 101) and blue flag, blooming on the small rock islands.

Since Yellow Jacket Shoals creates Class III and IV rapids, exploring this section of river by canoe is not an option unless you are an expert canoeist. But during times of low water, and particularly during drought years, if you are willing to drag your boat a good part of the way, a canoe trip down Yellow Jacket Shoals offers unique opportunities to see the formation of the shoals and the vegetation.

Should you decide to canoe Yellow Jacket Shoals, the best place to put-in is at the Flint River Outdoor Center. You can take out at Big Lazer Creek WMA, which is about a two and a half-mile trip, or at the boat ramp on Po Biddy Road, which makes for about a six-mile trip. For boat ramp locations, see map page 101.

HISTORIC SITES

Flat Shoals

This is an area rich with layers of history. The flat shoals across this wide stretch of river have made this a historical river crossing for hundreds of years. Here, the Upper Creek Trading Path, known as the Oakfuskee Trail, entered what is now Meriwether County on its way from the Savannah River at Augusta to Oakfuskee Town, a Creek settlement on the Tallapoosa River in Alabama. White traders began crossing here in the early 1700s; by the 1830s pioneers were calling it the "Old Plank Road." After the area was settled, the path and river crossing developed into a leading stagecoach road known as the Greenville Stage Road.

If you stand on the David Knott Bridge (see page 83) and look downstream, the abutments of the former wooden bridge, which had a metal span in the middle, still loom from the water directly in front

Pike County

The Flint River forms the western border of Pike County, with Line Creek flowing into the river in the county's northwest corner.

"Pike County was created from part of Monroe County in 1822. Georgia's 57th county and its county seat, Zebulon, were named for Zebulon Montgomery Pike. An expedition led by Pike in 1805 attempted (and failed) to trace the Mississippi River to its source. He discovered Pike's Peak on the same expedition. In addition to Zebulon, Pike County has four incorporated municipalities, none of which exceeded 500 in population in 1990. These are Concord, Meansville, Molena, and Williamson. Agriculture and forestry are still the main industries in Pike County, though the county is feeling the effects of Atlanta's growth. The county is one of Georgia's major peach producers. The Pike County Courthouse, built in 1895, is listed on the National Register of Historic Places. Pike County has been the site for the filming of several motion pictures, including 'Murder In Coweta County,' 'Cold Sassy Tree,' and 'Tank.'"

From *Georgia Snapshots*, Georgia Department of Community Affairs

For tourism information for towns in Pike County, see Resources page 300.

of you. The ruins of an old mill with granite stones, hewn square and stacked without mortar, are on the west bank. The community of Flat Shoals, which grew up just north of the road on the Meriwether County side of the river, consisted of a post office, general store, church, the Pierce Female College, a boarding house, several large homes and cultivated farm lands.

A little further downstream on the right bank of the river is a very large, flat outcrop. This was a favorite place for President Franklin D. Roosevelt to come and fish when he stayed at Warm Springs in the 1930s and '40s. In fact, you can see a picture of him sitting on that rock on map page 67.

Directions to Flat Shoals: *Meriwether County. In Gay, take GA 85 south to the traffic light in the middle of town. After the light, turn left onto Flat Shoals Road. Go 3 miles to the David Knott Bridge over the Flint River. You can park alongside of the road and walk to the bridge.* **Directions to "Noted Indian Trail" Historical Marker**: *Meriwether County. From Gay, take GA 85 south about 2 mile. The Historical Marker is on the left, just before Magnolia Road.*

Big Red Oak Creek Covered Bridge

For more than 150 years people have driven over this bridge spanning Big Red Oak Creek as they travel between the community of Imlac and Flat Shoals Road. Built in the 1840s, Big Red Oak Creek Bridge, or the Imlac Bridge as it is sometimes called, is the oldest covered bridge in the state of Georgia and the longest wooden bridge.

Horace King, freed slave and prominent bridge builder (see sidebar this page), constructed it using a popular covered bridge design known as Town Lattice. Patented in 1820 by Connecticut architect Ithiel Town, Town Lattice is a style of covered bridge known for its simplicity and strength and for being one of the first truly American designs. The trusses, or sides of the bridge, are heart of pine boards, slanted and crisscrossed within a frame of heavy, horizontal timbers to form a lattice. Each plank making up the lattice is twice pinned with foot-long treenails, a very dry, wooden peg used to join timbers.

About 2,500 treenails hold the trusses together on the Big Red Oak Creek Bridge. The bridge's massive sill timbers, sawed from heart pine, are 15 inches by 15 inches and stretch between stone piers. The State Department of Transportation, which maintains covered bridges in Georgia, measures the total span of the bridge at 253.5 feet, 115 feet of which are covered. There is a 250-foot timber-decked approach on one end. The unsupported span length of bridge is 115 feet. The bridge is 12 to 15 feet wide, meaning only one vehicle can pass at a time.

Big Red Oak Creek Bridge is also believed to be one of the state's sturdiest bridges, after surviving 1994 flood waters where the water level was so high that a canoeist paddled through the bridge. A sign

Horace King

Born a slave in 1807, Horace King, not only eventually won his freedom, but also wrote himself into history books, building more than 100 covered bridges in Georgia and surrounding states. Upon his death in 1888, his funeral procession made its way around what is now LaFayette Square in LaGrange, Georgia. Businesses closed, and people of all colors arrived to show their respect. His obituary noted that he had "risen to prominence by force of genius and power." His unmarked grave was discovered again in 1978 and, today, a large granite headstone reminds us of the great man who lay resting—"Horace King, Master Covered Bridge Builder."

Along with his owner John Godwin, Horace was instrumental in opening up west Georgia and the Flint and Chattahoochee River Valley region to development with the construction of covered bridges. It is said that Godwin once promised King his freedom if he could build a bridge in a given amount of time. King succeeded and Godwin kept his promise. After Godwin's death, King carried on the trade and eventually handed down the skills to his sons.

"Laborer and Legislator his life was an astonishing symbolic bridge—a bridge not only between states, but between men. Like one of his stately Town lattice bridges, Horace King's life soars above the murky waters of historical limitations, of human bondage and racial prejudice. He did not change the currents of social history, but he did transcend them and stands as a reminder of our common humanity, the potential of human spirit, the power of mutual respect."

A speech by Dr. William H. Green from *Covered Bridges of Georgia* by Thomas L. French, Jr. and Edward L. French

 (continued on page 69)

Dripping Rocks

3. Dripping Rocks Natural Area

The river cuts through crystalline rock known as Hollis quartzite that makes up Pine Mountain, creating cliffs that rise 400 feet or more above the river surface. Merging the climates of northern and southern environments, the cliffs and river banks provide an environment in which plants and animals of both the Piedmont and Coastal Plain find a home.

3. Dripping Rocks Trail

A well-marked trail follows the river for approximately 2 miles to a line of cliffs carved out of Pine Mountain by the flowing water.

4. G

This
in Pl
Goat
strea
Own
Outd

Long Branch

Goat Mountain

Matt Branch

Double Branch

Dripping Rocks ③

④

Wright Branch

Singers Hill

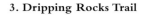

Pine Mountain

The Cove

Buck Creek

Buzzards Roost

Detail of topographical map showing the Cove

The Cove

A circle of hard crystalline rock about 3 miles in diameter that the river has cut through on its way south. Geologists believe the Cove was once a dome of rock. They say the center eroded over time, leaving a fertile basin surrounded by the hard Hollis quartzite.

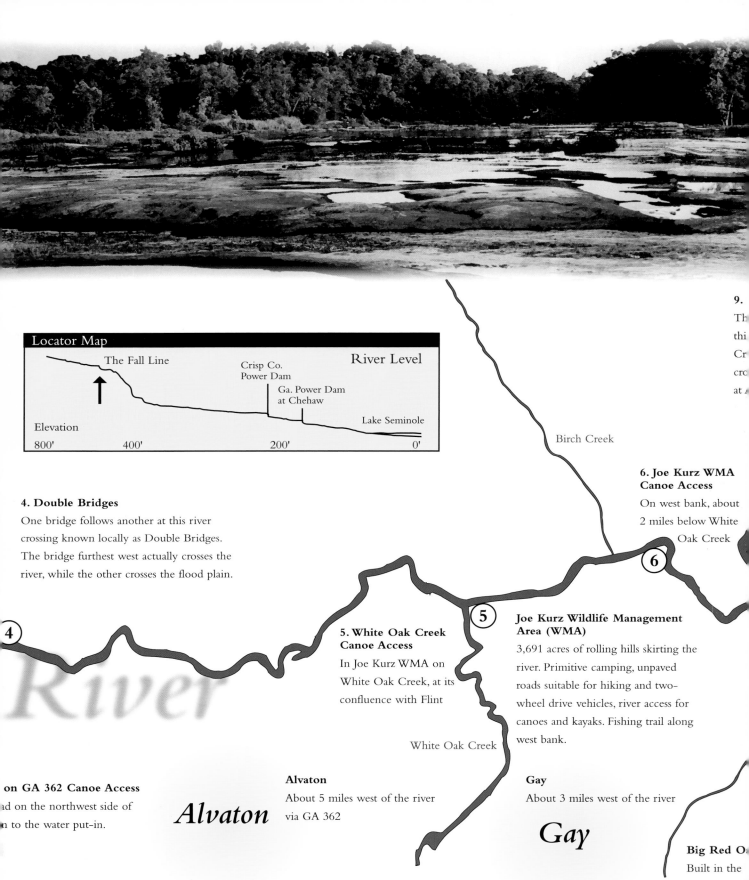

Locator Map

The Fall Line

Crisp Co.
Power Dam

Ga. Power Dam
at Chehaw

River Level

Lake Seminole

Elevation

800'   400'   200'   0'

9.

Th
thi
Cr
cro
at A

Birch Creek

**6. Joe Kurz WMA
Canoe Access**

On west bank, about
2 miles below White
Oak Creek

4. Double Bridges

One bridge follows another at this river
crossing known locally as Double Bridges.
The bridge furthest west actually crosses the
river, while the other crosses the flood plain.

**5. White Oak Creek
Canoe Access**

In Joe Kurz WMA on
White Oak Creek, at its
confluence with Flint

White Oak Creek

River

**Joe Kurz Wildlife Management
Area (WMA)**

3,691 acres of rolling hills skirting the
river. Primitive camping, unpaved
roads suitable for hiking and two-
wheel drive vehicles, river access for
canoes and kayaks. Fishing trail along
west bank.

on GA 362 Canoe Access
d on the northwest side of
 to the water put-in.

Alvaton

Alvaton

About 5 miles west of the river
via GA 362

Gay

About 3 miles west of the river

Gay

Big Red O

Built in the
builder Hora
bridge in Ge

above mouth: 295.3
eriwether and Pike

Concord

Concord
About 4 miles east of the river

Franklin D. Roosevelt at Flat Shoals

...at Shoals
...flat shoals across this wide stretch of river have made
...historical river crossing for hundreds of years. A
...k Indian trading route known as the Oakfuskee Trail
...ed the river here on its way from the Savannah River
...gusta to Oakfuskee Town, a Creek settlement on the
Tallapoosa River in
Alabama.

Big Branch

8. Flat Shoals Road Boat Ramp
A deeply rutted boat ramp for canoes
and small jon boats on east bank of river,
just above the David Knott Bridge

Still Branch

David Knott Bridge
on Flat Shoals Road

⑦   ⑧   ⑨

7. The Sea
Extensive shoaling downstream at Flat Shoals
acts as a natural dam for this area. Here, the
river widens to about twice its normal width
and forms a nearly
circular lake.

Canoe Trip
Use a lightweight canoe or sit-on-top to
explore the remarkable shoals and steep drop in the river, extending
from the David Knott Bridge to about a mile downstream. In low
water of summer and fall, this is mostly a river walk, but it's relatively
easy to return upstream (walking and towing your boat) to the put-in.
Note that there is another extensive set of shoals below the small
pond south of the shoals visible from the bridge. It is the second set
of shoals that backs up the water to form the pond.
In high water, this is a hazardous area.

Big Red Oak Creek

Canoe Trip
Paddle between
White Oak Creek
and Flat Shoals. In low
water of summer and
fall, put in at Flat
Shoals and paddle
upstream as far as
White Oak Creek then
return downstream to
the starting point.

...Creek Covered Bridge
...40s by master covered bridge
...King, this is the oldest covered
...gia and the longest wooden bridge.

Big Red Oak Creek Covered Bridge

Flat Shoals Road
River miles above mouth: 284.5
Counties: Meriwether and Pike

See the Guidebook sections for additional information and directions to locations listed on this page.

Sprewell Bluff, The Cove and Dripping Rocks

Molena

Molena

About 2 miles east of the river

Rock Ford Branch

Lawrence Lake

Red Oak Creek

Pappys Creek

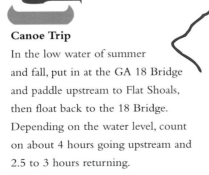

Canoe Trip

In the low water of summer and fall, put in at the GA 18 Bridge and paddle upstream to Flat Shoals, then float back to the 18 Bridge. Depending on the water level, count on about 4 hours going upstream and 2.5 to 3 hours returning.

Thomaston

About 3 miles east of

Thunder Scout Reservation

For the most part, Thunder Scout Reservation is reserved for Boy Scout troops. It is one of the largest Boy Scout camps in the United States, with hundreds of campers each summer from all over the country. But the camp welcomes all groups—Girl Scouts, youth and church groups, civic and corporate organizations—and individual mountain bicyclists and hikers are permitted to use the 8.5-mile loop trail.

Thunder Scout Reservation Biking Trail

An 8.5-mile biking trail winds thorough the 1,800 acre Thunder Scout Reservation. It follows the river for 1.8 miles before ascending approximately 1,100 feet up Dripping Rocks Mountain.

2. GA 18/74 Boat Ramp

This public boat ramp is the first concrete ramp on the river. It's only suitable for small boats that are light enough to be removed from a trailer by hand. On the west bank just below the bridge.

Elkins Creek

GA 18/74

1   2

1. GA 18/74 Bridge

If you stand on this 1990 bridge and look upriver, you can see the 1887 pilings from the Georgia Midland and Gulf Line that ran from Columbus to Atlanta and marked a period of prosperity for the nearby town of Woodbury.

Woodbury

Woodbury

About 3 miles west of the river via GA 18

Canoe Trip

GA 18 Bridge to Sprewell Bluff, the Flint River Outdoor Center at the GA 36 Bridge or Yellow Jacket Shoals. See page 54 for two narrative descriptions of this trip or contact the Flint River Outdoor Center, page 81 for information, maps, boat rental and shuttle.

GA 18/74

River miles above mouth: 278.0

Counties: Meriwether and Pike

Line Creek, Double Bridges and Flat Shoals

Flat Shoals

1. Line Creek Road Canoe Access

On west bank, just above the bridge

Starr's Mill

Starr's Mill on Whitewater Creek, which flows into Line Creek in Fayette County, is one of the few old time gristmills still standing in the area. Now owned by Fayette County as a water system reservoir, the picturesque red mill with its tin roof is a favorite location for area photographers and painters.

2. Hollonville Road Canoe Access

On east bank, just above the bridge

Hollonville Road

Line Creek

Flint

Starr's Mill

Line Creek Shoals

A good place to see large rock shoals and trees and vegetation characteristic of the Georgia Piedmont. The Line Creek Nature Area, owned by the Southern Conservation Trust, takes in about 70 acres of land along Line Creek in Peachtree City. The 0.8-mile Ridge Trail follows a ridge along the east bank of the creek. The Creek Trail is 1.2 miles one-way along the creek bed.

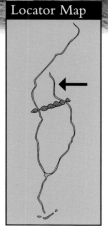

Locator Map

GA 362

3. Double Bridge

A rough, unpaved r
the bridge leads dov

Line Creek Road
River miles above mouth: 305.9
County: Spalding

Hollonville Road
River miles above mouth: 297.4
Counties: Pike and Spalding

GA 362
River miles
Counties: N

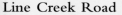

Sprewell Bluff Natural Area

Made primarily of gneiss, schist and quartzite crystalline rock, the bluffs on the west bank range from 700 to 1,000 feet while the bluffs to the east, where Pine Woods Ridge extends northward, range from 550 to 900 feet. A series of shoals stretch across the river's width with one particular set on the northern end of Sprewell Bluff State Park, forming a natural dam. Like much of this part of the Piedmont, Sprewell Bluff is a unique botanical area—a mixture of mountain and coastal plants. Both Piedmont and Coastal Plain animals are common.

Sprewell Bluff State Park Hiking Trail

A 1.5-mile hiking trail (one way) with good views of Sprewell Bluff. One of the most scenic natural areas along the river.

7 Islands

Table Rock

Dubignon Ferry Crossing

Owens Island

Rebel Chute

Pasley Shoals

Sprewell Bluff

Natural Dam

6

7

7. Sprewell Bluff State Park Boat Ramp

On the east bank, 3 miles below Pasley Shoals and 1 mile above Owens Island in Sprewell Bluff State Park

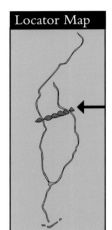

Locator Map

at Mountain Campground

rimitive camping area sits
sant Valley at the base of
Mountain on a little
called Long Branch.
d by the Flint River
or Center.

Tally Hole

5 Tally Gap

Hardy Branch

Rock House Mountain

6. Sprewell Bluff State Park

Boat ramp, pebble beach, picnic area with tables and grills, hiking trails, playground and restrooms with pit toilets. About 1,200 acres of the 1,372-acre park is devoted to a public hunting area.

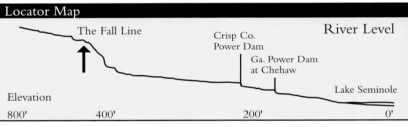

Locator Map

The Fall Line

Crisp Co. Power Dam

River Level

Ga. Power Dam at Chehaw

Lake Seminole

Elevation

800'   400'   200'   0'

Pigeon Creek

5. Tally Gap Natural Area

This is an area of extremely steep bluffs and ravines that support a mixture of both mountain and Coastal Plain plant life. The best way to see this area is to hike the old jeep road that follows the river for about 1 mile from the mouth of Pigeon Creek to Tally Gap.

Overlook near Sprewell Bluff

Manchester

About 6 miles west of the river

Manchester

(continued from page 66)

on the bridge indicates the high water mark.

Refurbished in 1999, the bridge, which is listed on the National Register of Historic Places, stands on Covered Bridge Road, a dirt road connecting Flat Shoals Road to GA 85 near the community of Imlac, north of Woodbury.

Directions: *Meriwether County. From Woodbury, take GA 85 north about 3 miles to the community of Imlac. Turn right onto Covered Bridge Road, a dirt road. Go about 1 mile to Big Red Oak Creek and the bridge. Parking is available alongside of the road.*

MUSEUMS

Old South Farm Museum and Agricultural Leaning Center

Sheep shearing. Chicken killing, Hog castration. The Old South Farm Museum is the real thing. "I'm just trying to preserve a little agricultural history," says owner and operator Paul Bulloch, and this hands-on museum does just that.

Farming and agriculture has played a major role in the lives of the people who settled the Flint River Valley; and the Old South Farm Museum is an incredible learning experience about living and earning a living on a farm in the early 1900s: thrashers, combines, tractors, wagons, silage cutters, corn binders, rows of plows, a cellar, a hitching post, sheep shears, a bone grinder for making bone meal, a cotton gin, ice boxes, old stoves, peanut pickers, peach packing shed, a German cabbage shredder for making sauerkraut, a clothes washer and hand ringer—more than 2,000 pieces of equipment from turn-of-the-century farms.

A retired County Extension Agent, Bulloch has been collecting farm equipment for years. He wants kids, particularly, to know what it was like to actually live on a farm. Says Bulloch, "In the early 1900s, more than 60 percent of Americans farmed, today only two percent do. Our kids don't know where their food comes from." So Bulloch and his wife Pam let school groups come in and gather eggs, milk cows, feed chickens, draw water from the well, grind wheat, shell corn, grind sugarcane, take a wagon ride and start up an old washing machine and ringer. The children get to see and do many of the things that they would have done had they grown up on a farm.

The museum and learning center caters mostly to student groups during the school year, but is open to all visitors. Two events a year draw people from all over the area: a Hog Killing on the first Saturday in February and Old South Farm Day on the third Saturday in June.

Days/Hours: *Open Monday through Saturday, 9 a.m. to 5 p. m. but it is best to call ahead if you are planning a trip.* **Fees**: *Adults, $3; Children, $1.* **Directions**: *Talbot County. From Talbotton, take GA 41 north about 8 miles to Woodland. About 0.5 mile past the GA 41 and GA 36 intersection, turn right onto Pleasant Valley Road. A red-and-white sign points the way. The museum is on the right about 150 feet from the highway.* **More**

Meriwether County

The Flint River enters Meriwether County at its northeast corner and continues flowing south, forming the county's eastern border.

"*Meriwether County was created in 1827, the 73rd county created. The county was named for General David Meriwether, a state militiaman often called on by the federal government to negotiate with the Indians. General Meriwether served in the Revolutionary War and was a state legislator and a member of congress. The county seat is Greenville, named for Revolutionary war hero General Nathaniel Greene. The largest municipality is Manchester, and others include Gay, Lone Oak, Luthersville, Warm Springs and Woodbury. Warm Springs—site of President Roosevelt's 'Little White House'—is in the county [see page 202].... The springs' waters stay naturally at 90 degrees, and were used by Indians as a healing spring and later as a spa for white settlers. More recently, Franklin D. Roosevelt, as well as other polio victims, have benefited from the therapeutic water. The Warm Springs Foundation opened its doors to people suffering from other types of crippling disease and conditions after the invention of the polio vaccination.*"

From *Georgia Snapshots*, Georgia Department of Community Affairs

For tourism information for towns in Meriwether County, see Resources page 300.

Information: Paul or Pam Bulloch, Old South Farm Museum and Agriculture Learning Center, Route 1, P.O. Box 191, Woodland, GA 31836. 706/674-2894.

PARKS

Sprewell Bluff State Park

It's June. Red, green and yellow canoes glide out into the Flint River. Swimmers climb on the protruding boulder-like river shoals and splash in the cool eddies. Fishermen quietly toss their line in search of the shoal bass that lurk under the rocky pools.

Scenes like this are taking place all along the river. But Sprewell Bluff State Park, 80 miles from the river's headwaters, is the first large area as you travel downstream that is designed for public river recreation, and it is the only state park on the Flint.

Opened in 1994, the state park sits on the east bank at one of the river's most beautiful natural areas—Sprewell Bluff (see page 64). Here, rocky shoals stretch the width of the river, and bluffs tower on both banks. Canoeists and kayakers paddling through this section can experience the fun of Class II rapids, but the shoals directly off the pebble beach in the park's day-use area are gentle enough for wading and tubing.

In the park, there are approximately three miles of hiking trails that follow the river's banks and climb into the bluffs; a large, grassy area for pitching horseshoes; and plenty of room to skip a rock across the water. In fact, a rock-skipping contest on Labor Day is a yearly park event. About 1,200 acres of the 1,372-acre park is devoted to a public hunting area (see page 79).

Facilities: Boat ramp (see map page 68), pebble beach, picnic area with tables and grills (no drinking water), hiking trails (see page 78), playground and restrooms with pit toilets. Kayaks and canoes can be rented at the Flint River Outdoor Center (see page 81). Primitive camping sites in the state park are closed, but camping is available at FDR State Park (see page 211) about 25 miles away. **Days/Hours***: Open daily, 7 a.m. until dark.* **Fees***: Parking, $2.* **Directions***: Upson County. From Thomaston, take GA 74 west 5.5 miles to Old Alabama Road. Turn left and go about 5 miles, following the signs into the park.* **More Information***: Sprewell Bluff State Park, 740 Sprewell Bluff Road., Thomaston, GA 30286. 706/646-6026. Georgia Department of Natural Resources, Georgia State Parks and Historic Sites, 205 Butler Street, Suite 1352 East, Atlanta, GA 30334. 404/656-3530. Website: www.gastateparks.org.*

WILDLIFE MANAGEMENT AREAS

Joe Kurz Wildlife Management Area

These 3,691 acres of rolling hills skirt the west bank of the Flint

A Record Shoal Bass

"The Flint is not noted for giving up big largemouth: 12- to 14-inch fish are the norm. In the case of the shoalies, 1- to 2-pound fish are considered good sized, but catches of 25 to 30 fish per day are possible.

"The river did, however, give up the state-record shoal bass on October 23, 1977, when David Hubbard of Williamson boated an 8-pound 3-ounce fish that was recognized as the world record for several years. Although that world standard was later bested, Hubbard continues to claim the state mark. He caught his fish a couple of miles downstream of the present site of Sprewell Bluff State Park. The shoal bass was 23 inches long and had a girth of 16.5 inches."

Bass Fishing in Georgia by Jimmy Jacobs

River in Meriwether County. Loblolly pines, oaks, hickory and sweetgum grow on the uplands of this former private hunting property; while water oak, overcup oak and red maple fill the bottomlands along White Oak Creek and the Flint River. This is a good area for hiking, bird watching (particularly along the sloughs and marshes), horseback riding and seasonal hunting. An unpaved road leads to the Flint where there is unofficial canoe and kayak access and a fishing trail along the river.

Managed by the Georgia Department of Natural Resources, the Joe Kurz WMA sponsors seasonal deer hunts (approximately 35-40 deer per square mile), as well as hunts for turkey, squirrel, rabbit, quail, dove and duck. For general WMA regulations, license requirements and hunting seasons, hunters should obtain a current copy of the "Georgia Hunting Seasons & Regulations" booklet, available at local outdoors stores and from the Georgia DNR. Hikers and birdwatchers should also check the booklet for the schedule of seasonal hunts. All visitors are encouraged to wear fluorescent orange during hunting season.

The Joe Kurz WMA Wetland Enhancement program is a cooperative wetland habitat project between the Department of Natural Resources Division and Ducks Unlimited.

Facilities: *Primitive camping area (see page 73); unpaved roads suitable for hiking (see page 76) and two-wheel drive vehicles; two unofficial river access points for canoes and kayaks (see map page 67).* **Days/Hours**: *Open daily, 24 hours. Roads in the WMA are open to foot traffic year-round. If a road is gated, it just means that vehicles are not allowed. All visitors should first go to the check-in station.* **Directions**: *Meriwether County. From the traffic light in Gay, turn right on Mt. Carmel Road and go 2.7 miles to check station.* **More Information**: *Georgia Department of Natural Resources, Wildlife Resources Division, 1014 Martin Luther King Jr. Boulevard, Fort Valley, GA 31030. 229/825-6354.*

Big Lazer Creek Wildlife Management Area

A fisherman wades in Big Lazer Creek, catching two decent-sized shoal bass within a few minutes. Another fishermen stands on the shoals casting his line. A family, loaded up with tubes, cooler, outdoor grill, beach towels and the family dog, head to the sandbar at the mouth of the creek. "We come every Sunday afternoon," says dad. "It's our family outing." Several father-son looking groups shoot pistols at the firing range. Boats back down the ramp at the public fishing lake, ready for a day on the lake. A wild turkey runs down the road just ahead (see sidebar this page).

Like other wildlife management areas, Big Lazer Creek WMA is designed for hunting and fishing, but nearly any other outdoor recreational activity can be enjoyed—hiking, picnicking, swimming, camping, canoeing, bird watching, biking, horseback riding. From mid-May to mid-August hunting is out of season, making it a perfect time for families to get out and enjoy the area. Rangers caution that

Wild Turkey

Perhaps while strolling through the woods you've heard the unmistakable guttural gobble of the wild turkey. Adult males use this deep, throaty sound as a mating call, attracting hens up to a mile away. Wild turkeys use a variety of clucks, yelps and putts to communicate. Just as a dog's bark can silence a flock's gobble, a loud noise during the early spring mating season can trigger the turkey's call.

Like many other species of plant and animal, the wild turkey was in abundance before the arrival of early settlers. At the height of colonization however, the population of the easily caught wild turkey was decimated. Loss of habitat through deforestation and the over-harvesting of these delicious birds were the biggest reasons for the dramatic reduction in wild turkey numbers. Today those numbers have been greatly improved and about 4 million of the birds exist in every state but Alaska. Numerous wild turkey roam the Flint River Valley and they are hunted in most wildlife management areas.

Wild turkeys consume a large variety of plant and animal matter. Poults, or baby turkeys, eat a tremendous amount of insects in order to get the protein necessary for rapid development, doubling their weight each week for the first four weeks. As the turkeys mature, plant matter becomes the primary source of food—making up about 90 percent of the turkey's diet. Chufa, tupelo, longleaf pine, clover and many other types of grasses, shrubs and trees make up the wild turkey's herbaceous diet. Occasionally, they'll also consume grasshoppers, small amphibians and reptiles for protein.

the deer hunting season in October and November is the only dangerous time for recreational activity at Big Lazer; during small game hunting seasons, recreationists are encouraged to wear fluorescent orange.

Big Lazer Creek WMA encompasses 5,864 acres of land between Big Lazer Creek, the Flint River and Po Biddy Road in Talbot County. Pine and hardwoods, such as maple, beech and oak, make up much of the forested terrain, which is generally hilly, and even steep in some places. Elevations peak at 500 to 600 feet with flatter bottomlands along the river and creeks. River Road, a main road through the WMA, winds around hills and along the Flint's bottomland before it reaches the point where the wide river cascades over Hightower Shoals near the mouth of Big Lazer Creek. Where the river and creek merge, a large sandbar is a staging area for swimmers and fishermen alike. From here you can wade in to catch the Flint River shoal bass, take out your canoe or kayak after running the series of Class III–IV shoals below the GA 36 Bridge or explore a pristine habitat that includes the shoal-spotted lily.

Operated by the Georgia Department of Natural Resources, the area maintains good populations of deer, turkey, gray squirrel and rabbit for the nearly 2,000 hunters who visit during a year. Woodcock, raccoon, opossum, fox and bobcat also make their home in this natural habitat. For general WMA regulations, license requirements and hunting seasons, hunters should obtain a current copy of the "Georgia Hunting Seasons & Regulations" booklet, available at local outdoors stores and from the Georgia DNR.

Most roads within the WMA are passable with two-wheel drive vehicles. A map available at the check station shows limited access roads that can be used as hiking trails. Hikers and birdwatchers should avoid off-road rambles while seasonal hunts are in progress.

Facilities: *Canoe access to Flint River (see map page 101); three primitive camping areas with no facilities; fishing lake (see page 75) with boat ramp, fishing pier, and restrooms; picnic area with tables and grills; hiking trail (see page 77) and eight-station shooting range for single projection ammunition.* **Days/Hours**: *Open daily, 24 hours. The lake is open from sunrise to sunset. All visitors must sign in at the check station.* **Directions**: *Talbot County. From Talbotton, take GA 80 east 4 miles to Po Biddy Road. Turn left and go 6.4 miles to Bunkham Road, the first dirt road on the left beyond Collinsworth Methodist Church. There is a sign for the WMA. Turn left and go 1.2 miles to the check station, a wooden building with a large front porch, on the left.* **More Information**: *Georgia Department of Natural Resources, Wildlife Resources Division, 1014 Martin Luther King Jr. Boulevard, Fort Valley, GA 31030. 229/825-6354.*

CAMPGROUNDS

Joe Kurz Campground

This primitive campground near the check station at Joe Kurz

Shoal Bass

"The shoal bass (also known as the Flint River smallmouth, or, in Florida, as the Chipola bass) is very much a creature of the river. Its natural range is in southeast Alabama, northwest Florida, and in Georgia. In the Peach State, the shoal bass is found in the drainage of the Chattahoochee and Flint Rivers, and it was transplanted into the Ocmulgee River in 1975. While it does show up in the headwaters of Lakes Seminole, Chehaw, and Blackshear, it rarely thrives in a lake environment. In fact, the range of shoal bass is quite small even in the rivers it inhabits. As their name implies, shoal bass are found almost exclusively in the moving waters of rapids, riffles, and shoals. These fish are rarely found in areas devoid of rocks. Although spotted bass often inhabit similar types of river areas as do shoal bass, where shoal bass are found, spots are absent, which indicates that the shoalies are the dominant fish."

Bass Fishing in Georgia by Jimmy Jacobs

WMA (see page 71) is only open during hunting season and fills quickly with campers.

Facilities: *Primitive camping area with no facilities.* **Days/Hours**: *Open daily, 24 hours during hunting season.* **Directions**: *Meriwether County. From the traffic light in Gay, turn right on Mt. Carmel Road and go 2.7 miles to check station.* **More Information**: *Georgia Department of Natural Resources, Wildlife Resources Division, 1014 Martin Luther King Jr. Boulevard, Fort Valley, GA 31030. 229/825-6354.*

Thunder Scout Reservation Campground

This area near the mouth of Elkins Creek and the Flint River has been a campsite for hundreds of years. Natural rock caves on Dripping Rocks sheltered prehistoric Indians. A Creek Indian village once stood near Thundering Springs, a natural spring at the eastern edge of the campground, giving rise to legends about the spring and the rumble it once made. The Confederate Army had a campground here during the Civil War. A hotel, known as the Thundering Springs Resort, housed visitors who came to enjoy the 76 degree waters of the warm springs.

But since 1938 it has been the Boy Scouts of America who have camped, fished, canoed and hiked in this scenic area. And in the early 1950s, the organization damned Thundering Springs to form Lake Ini-To, the centerpiece of the campground.

Currently, the Flint River Council, Boy Scouts of America, divides the 2,200-acre facility into two camps, operating with independent missions. Camp Thunder, the original camp, focuses on younger children and their development; the Gerald I. Lawhorn Canoe Base and Training Center (see page 80) educates organized groups on a range of "high adventure" activities that include canoeing, kayaking, hiking, biking, backpacking, climbing and rappelling.

For the most part, Thunder Scout Reservation is reserved for Boy Scout troops. It is one of the largest Boy Scout camps in the United States, with hundreds of campers each summer from all over the country. But the camp welcomes all groups—Girl Scouts, youth groups and church, civic and corporate organizations. Individual mountain bicyclists and hikers are permitted to use the 8.5-mile loop trail as well as the Dripping Rocks hiking trail.

Facilities: *Cabins, tent campsites and primitive campsites; bathhouses with flush toilets; pavilions with water and electricity and gas grills and burners; trading post; lake; hiking trail (see page 71); biking trail (see page 80); picnic area; activity fields.* **Days/Hours**: *Open daily, year-round. Office — Monday through Friday, 9 a.m. to 5 p.m.* **Fees**: *Call for organized group activity fees and information on pre-packaged programs.* **Directions**: *Upson County. From Woodbury, take GA 74 east about 6 miles. Turn south (right) at Thunder Scout Reservation sign. This is Thundering Springs Road. Go about 0.5 mile to Dripping Rocks Road and turn right. Follow road to Trading Post. Parking is available anywhere along the road near the Trading Post.*

Upson County

The Flint River flows into Upson County in its northwest corner and continues flowing south to form the county's western border.

"Upson County was created from parts of Pike and Crawford counties in 1824. Georgia's 59th county was named for Stephen Upson, a well-known lawyer and legislator of the time. In addition to Thomaston, the county seat, there is one other incorporated municipality, Yatesville. Thomaston was named for General Jett Thomas, the leader of the state militia in 1812 and the builder of the state capitol in Milledgeville."

From *Georgia Snapshots*, Georgia Department of Community Affairs

For tourism information for towns in Upson County, see Resources page 300.

More Information: *Thunder Scout Reservation, 1166 Dripping Rocks Road, Molena, GA 30258. 706/646-2255; fax, 706/646-2120. Website: www.thunderbsa.org. Gerald I. Lawhorn Canoe Base and Training Center, 706/647-6313. E-mail: canoe@thunderbsa.org.*

Goat Mountain Campground

Owned by the Flint River Outdoor Center, this is the halfway point and overnight spot for the two-day, 20-mile river trips that the Outdoor Center shuttles. This primitive camping area sits in Pleasant Valley at the base of Goat Mountain on a little stream called Long Branch. This area once had a reputation for making moonshine (see sidebar this page). A crystal, clear spring at the campsite was the water source for many a gallon of the unlawfully distilled whiskey made by locals.

Facilities: *Primitive camping site, picnic tables and outhouse. Spring provides drinking water. There is no parking for vehicles here. Vehicles must be left at the Flint River Outdoor Center (see page 81).* **Days/Hours**: *Open year-round. Call Flint River Outdoor Center for reservations.* **Fees**: *2 adults, $6; extra adults, $3 each; children, $1.50 each. Tent rentals available.* **Directions**: *Upson County. The campsite is located on the east side of the river at the mouth of Long Branch, approximately 10 miles below the GA 18 bridge.* **More Information**: *Flint River Outdoor Center, 4429 Woodland Road, Thomaston, GA 30286-3235. 706/647-2633.*

Flint River Outdoor Center Campground

Ninety miles from the Flint River's headwaters, this is the only full-service campground open to the public on the entire river until you reach Lake Blackshear, another 105 miles downstream. Bordering both sides of the river, campers enjoy the same relaxed setting and atmosphere typical of the Flint River Outdoor Center (see page 81).

Facilities: *25 RV and camper sites with full hookups, 18 tent campsites with water and electricity; picnic tables; grills; fire rings; restrooms; showers; drinking water; dump station and fish cleaning station; 27 acres of primitive camping on east bank of river across from Outdoor Center. Primitive camping at Goat Mountain Campground (see above).* **Days/Hours**: *Open daily, year-round. Call for reservations.* **Fees**: *RV, camper and tent campsites can be rented with or without various hookups. Call for current rates. Primitive camping – 2 adults, $6; extra adults, $3; children, $1.50 each. Tent rentals available.* **Directions**: *Upson County. From downtown Thomaston, take GA 36 west 8 miles. Cross the bridge and the Outdoor Center is on the left.* **More Information**: *Flint River Outdoor Center, 4429 Woodland Road, Thomaston, GA 30286-3235. 706/647-2633.*

Big Lazer Creek Campground

Three flat, grassy open areas designated for camping are located within the Big Lazer Creek Wildlife Management Area. This is

Moonshine

The mere utterance of the word brings to mind hushed tones and images of back-wood hoodlums determined to stay one step ahead of the law. Car chases and shoot-outs, whispers and distrust, makeshift stills and bootlegging. All were part of a time when alcohol was illegal—but drinking it was as popular as ever. It was said that President Franklin Roosevelt got his moonshine in the Cove when he came to the Little White House (see sidebar page 27). There were plenty of streams around the Flint River that were the source for moonshine stills—the remnants of which can still be found, if you know where to look.

Yet, moonshine, the illegally distilled 120 proof corn alcohol, was notorious long before Prohibition. Moonshine's popularity soared just after the Civil War. The Union had earlier imposed excise taxes on whiskey and tobacco in order to fund the Union Army, and kept them in place to help rebuild the nation afterwards. As taxes increased, so did the amount of moonshine.

The 1919 passing of the 18th Amendment and the subsequent Prohibition, changed the focus from taxation of liquor to eliminating it altogether. Prohibition also guaranteed the moonshiner's business. With legal alcohol out of the competition, the emphasis on production became quantity—quality of the liquor took a backseat. This was liquor that could "blind and paralyze."

The economic war subsided, and the moral war took hold. Moonshiners didn't care. The moonshine kept runnin.'

primitive camping only. Occupancy is first-come, first-serve and the areas fill quickly with hunters during hunting season.

Facilities: *Three primitive camping areas with no facilities. Restrooms are located near the Public Fishing Lake (see below) within the Big Lazer Creek Wildlife Management Area. For other facilities within the WMA see page 71.* **Days/Hours**: *Open daily, 24 hours. All campers must sign in at the check station.* **Directions**: *Talbot County. From Talbotton, take GA 80 east 4 miles to Po Biddy Road. Turn left and go 6.4 miles to Bunkham Road, the first dirt road on the left beyond Collinsworth Methodist Church. There is a sign for the WMA. Turn left and go 1.2 miles to the check station, a wooden building with a large front porch, on the left. Sign in here and pick up a map of the WMA with campgrounds indicated.* **More Information**: *Georgia Department of Natural Resources, Wildlife Resources Division, 1014 Martin Luther King Jr. Boulevard, Fort Valley, GA 31030. 229/825-6354.*

FISHING

Big Lazer Creek Public Fishing Area

Boats glide across the quiet water. Pole and lines are out. Large-mouth bass and channel catfish lurk among the tree stumps and brush piles of the lake. This is Big Lazer Lake—a 195-acre public fishing lake carved out of the Big Lazer Creek Wildlife Management Area (see page 71). Impounded by an earthen dam at Gum Creek, it is the focal point of the Big Lazer Creek Public Fishing Area.

Big Lazer is one of eight public fishing areas in the state. Public Fishing Areas (PFAs) are areas managed extensively for fishing by the Wildlife Resources Division of the Georgia Department of Natural Resources. Among other management activities, DNR rangers fertilize, lime and stock the lakes with largemouth bass, bream, bluegill, redear sunfish, channel catfish and crappie. The rangers sample fish populations and plant wildlife foods. These areas are designed for relaxed family recreation—fishing, picnicking, hiking, wildlife watching and camping (where designated). Regulations vary, but at Big Lazer Creek motorboats are restricted to idle speed; fishing is limited to pole and line with only two poles per person; legal limits on fish are posted; and swimming, alcoholic beverages and the use of personal watercraft, sailboats and sailboards are prohibited.

Anglers 16 years of age and older must possess a valid Wildlife Management Area license and a current fishing license to fish in a PFA. For more information, see special fishing regulations at the check station or pick up a copy of DNR's "Sport Fishing Regulations" from area fishing and hunting stores.

Facilities: *Concrete, two-lane boat ramp with wooden docks and tie downs; fishing pier with handicapped access; restrooms; and large, paved parking area. A picnic area with tables and grills is located near the dam. Primitive camping in designated areas of Wildlife Management Area (see page 75).* **Days/Hours**: *Open daily, sunrise to sunset. WMA – open daily, 24 hours.*

Shoal Bass Fishing

"*Most anglers who tackle the Flint's water prefer to float the stream in canoes or johnboats, stopping at the shallow rapids to get out and wade while fishing. The current-loving shoal bass are most at home in shoals like these. This type of angling is necessary anyway, since most of the shore is privately owned. The only truly riverine sections that are open to bank access are at Sprewell Bluff State Park on the east side of the river in Upson County and Big Lazer Creek Wildlife Management Area on the western shore in Talbot County. The Big Lazer site offers the best bank access to wadable shoals on the river.*"

Bass Fishing in Georgia by Jimmy Jacobs

All visitors must sign in at the check station. **Directions**: *Talbot County. From Talbotton, take GA 80 east 4 miles to Po Biddy Road. Turn left and go 6.4 miles to Bunkham Road, the first dirt road on the left beyond Collinsworth Methodist Church. There is a sign for the WMA. Turn left and go 1.2 miles to the check station, a wooden building with a large front porch, on the left. Sign in here and pick up a map of the WMA and the public fishing lake.* **More Information**: *Wildlife Resources Office in Manchester, 706/846-8448. Georgia Department of Natural Resources, Wildlife Resources Division, 1014 Martin Luther King Jr. Boulevard, Fort Valley, GA 31030. 229/825-6354.*

HIKES AND WALKS

Joe Kurz WMA Hiking Trails

Although not maintained for hiking, the trails within Joe Kurz Wildlife Management Area provide some enjoyable walking experiences and a look at some of the different habitats that can be found along the Flint River.

Distance: There are numerous miles of trails throughout the WMA as well as open pastures, fields and marshy areas.

Trailhead Location: Joe Kurz Wildlife Management Area (see page 71). From the check station head northeast on Mt. Carmel Road. After you cross White Oak Creek, there is a sign and parking area for the waterfowl management area, which is to the left.

Features: This particular trail leads to a pond and marsh that are in a waterfowl management area of the WMA. Beaver, otter, duck, woodcock and other wading birds are just some of the wildlife you will see here. January and February are usually good months to visit this area. There are numerous sloughs in this part of the floodplain that collect and hold rain water, as well as water from the periodic normal flooding of the river itself. This provides a good nesting habitat for waterfowl. Wear hip boots if you really want to get out and explore the marsh, as this area can be quite wet.

Across the road from the waterfowl area and along White Water Creek to its confluence with the Flint is a unique botanical area. A large number of hardwood trees grow along here, including basket oak, willow oak, southern red oak, water oak, sugar maple, red maple, pawpaw, sweet gum and river birch. There are also some very large overcup oak and water hickory. You'll see parsley, haw, wild crabapple, indigo bush, button bush, two species of high bush blueberries and deciduous holly in the understory. Look for atamasco lily, or Easter Lily, with its white, delicate flower tinged with pink blooming April through June, as well as colonies of wild indigo.

There are also numerous deer and turkey throughout Joe Kurz, so the chance is good for running into wildlife along the creek.

Flint River Fishing

"The Flint River is probably the most fabled stretch of flowing fishing water found in the Peach State. For years anglers have flocked to it for several reasons. First, this stream is the stronghold of the shoal bass. Although these fish are found in other rivers and creeks in Georgia, the fact that for many years they were called 'Flint River smallmouths' hints at their abundance in this stream. Second, the development that has gobbled up the shores of other rivers in the state has spared the Flint. Finally, on its northern half, this stream has numerous rocky shoals that are ideal for wading while fishing. While these assets have drawn anglers in great numbers, the fishing pressure on the Flint still never reaches heavy levels. Most angling on the Flint occurs in the spring and summer, but the water levels are equally good for fishing in the fall, and the fall flow tends to be clearer."

Bass Fishing in Georgia by Jimmy Jacobs

Dripping Rocks Trail

Walk along Dripping Rocks Trail in the winter when the trees are bare, and you can easily see what a river can do to a mountain. At one time, the Flint River flowed over the top of this mountain peak. But after millions of years, the river has eroded away the Hollis quartzite rock of Pine Mountain, leaving cliffs on both sides of the river that are 400 to 500 feet higher than the river.

Distance: This well-marked trail follows the river for approximately two miles. You can either double back or take one of the trails that leads away from the river and up onto the cliffs.

Trailhead Location: The Gerald I. Lawhorn Canoe Base (see page 80) at Thunder Scout Reservation (see page 73). The public is welcome to hike or bike the trails at Camp Thunder but rangers ask that you check in and out. A sign-up sheet is located at the Trading Post. As you come out of the Trading Post, the trailhead is on the right, through the canoe arch. Continue to the gated area that says private drive, no vehicles.

Features: The path follows the riverbed except for a short incline near the beginning of the hike, which takes you up to an overlook area. Here, it is an easy climb out to a ledge for a better view of the river. About a mile into the hike, the exposed quartzite walls become more prominent and there are wooden steps that lead up the cliff that is actually known as Dripping Rocks. The six-foot wide path varies from sandy to rocky to muddy, depending on where water comes off the rocks and runs across it. The Dripping Rocks natural area (see page 62) is believed to have the largest concentration of plant species found anywhere along the river. Moss Falls, a lush, moss-draped, 25-foot waterfall surrounded by thickets of rhododendron and mountain laurel, is located along a side trail that ascends Double Branch Creek. The remains of three moonshine stills along the creek attest to the area's infamous reputation in bygone days.

Big Lazer Creek Hiking Trail

This narrow path begins at the confluence of Big Lazer Creek with the Flint River and follows the winding path along the creek's west bank.

Distance: The trail follows the creek about 1 mile one way.

Trailhead Location: Big Lazer Creek Wildlife Management Area (see page 71). Once inside the WMA, stop at the check station, sign in and pick up a map of the area. Then continue to follow Bunkham Road (CR 9) about 2 miles, past the public fishing area and over the dam until you get to River Road. If the road sign is missing—which is sometimes the case—River Road can be identified by the two primitive camping areas which face each other at its intersection with Bunkham Road. Turn right, and follow River Road to the Flint, about another 2 miles. Here, the road will swing to the left and follow the river for about 1 mile until you reach a dead end and clearing

Rhododendron

Rhododendron is the name of a group of trees and shrubs that belong to the heath family. The name means *rose tree*. Rhododendrons are evergreen shrubs with leathery leaves and clusters of showy, bell-shaped flowers that arise from end buds formed the previous season. The thick, interlocking branches of rhododendrons can form thickets that are nearly impassable.

Rhododendrons grow mainly in more northern environments, including the North Georgia mountains, but several varieties can be seen in bluff areas of the Flint River Corridor, particularly at Dripping Rocks (see this page). Carolina Rhododendron (*Rhododendron minus* Michaux) is a three to eight feet high shrub with white to deep rose pink flowers, often spotted with olive green or orange (see illustration on page 191). It usually blooms April to July. It is also known as Piedmont and Small Rhododendron. Rosebay Rhododendron (*Rhododendron maximum* L.) is commonly five to 15 feet high. Its white to rose pink flowers, spotted with olive green to orange, bloom in June or July. Catawba Rhododendron (*Rhododendron catawbiense* Michaux), also called Purple Rhododendron and Mountain Rosebay, is usually four to 10 feet high. Its lilac purple to rose purple flowers are spotted with olive green and usually bloom from April to June.

that serves as a parking area. The trailhead is at the left of the parking area.

Features: The trail begins at the confluence of Big Lazer Creek and the Flint River. Near the beginning of the trail, look for a path that leads to the right. This will take you out to a sandbar at the confluence where you can get a good look at Hightower Shoals, one of the last sets of shoals on the Flint above the Fall Line. The rather-large island just downstream from the shoals is named Hickman Island. All along this trail are opportunities to get out on the shoals and play in the creek. Look for deer and raccoon tracks as well as mussel shells. This is a rocky area filled with fern and wildflowers, such as red trumpet honeysuckle, a vine which blooms profusely during summer. Maple, beech and hickory grow on the steep hillsides beside the trail.

Sprewell Bluff State Park Hiking Trail

No matter what time of year you choose to hike this trail, the views of Sprewell Bluff, one of the most scenic natural areas along the Flint River (see page 64), are the focus: fall's red, yellow and orange foliage; the barren winter slopes of Oak Mountain; springtime lavender, azalea and dogwood; the Flint's exposed shoals during summer's low-water periods.

Distance: The one and a half-mile hiking trail makes for a three-mile round-trip and is an easy hike except for a steep area near the overlook deck.

Trailhead Location: Sprewell Bluff State Park (see page 71). There are two different places to access the trail: a trailhead at the small parking lot off the entrance road and another near the restrooms in the day-use area. Trail maps are available at the bulletin board, located near the day use restrooms.

Features: The trail winds along the river through flat bottomlands, except for a small section along the bluffs near the main parking area. Near the trailheads, there is an overlook deck where you can see the river as it makes a wide, sweeping bend in front of the towering bluffs on the west. From there, follow the trail as it makes a steep descent to the riverbank. Notice the palmetto, a plant common to the Coastal Plain (see sidebar next page). This is about as far north as the plant can grow. The trail passes signs for three campsites, which are permanently closed. In several places, the trail was washed out during the 1994 flood and hasn't been repaired, so some detours along old four-wheel drive roads into the woods are necessary. All roads eventually lead back to the state park's main entrance road. Because the roads often fork at odd angles as they approach the river, using caution—and a compass—is advised, especially before dusk. The trail ends at "Natural Dam," a low, narrow shelf of rocks that crosses the river. Keep in mind that this is not a loop trail, so return by the same route.

Raccoon

From Big Lazer Creek to Lake Seminole to Apalachicola, you'll come across the paw prints of these masked-bandits, who are respected for their intelligence yet reviled for their peskiness. Their knack for finding food comes from their ability to solve problems and learn. Raccoons eat anything they can get their paws on, and human garbage is an easy feed; in the battle of wits, humans often lose. A raccoon learns much of what it knows from its mother, but is constantly learning and mastering new tricks throughout its life.

Raccoons can be found at night; turning over rocks and logs, watching for prey in shallow pools of water, foraging through garbage cans. Their preferred habitat is in the cavities of old trees, 10 to 60 feet up. Claw marks at the base of the tree and raccoon fur stuck to the bark is a sure sign a den is above. Piles of droppings at the base of the tree and paw prints, which look like small human hands, are other indications of nearby raccoons.

The raccoon's paws, or "hands," are extremely sensitive and nimble. Its agility allows a raccoon to reach into a pool of water, searching tiny cracks and crevices until it feels some movement. Then, with lightning reflexes, the raccoon lunges and snatches the creature from its hiding place. There is little evidence to support the stories of raccoons washing their food. They are known to douse some food items, but they'll eat their catch whether it's dirty or not.

HUNTING

Sprewell Bluff Public Hunting Area

The Flint River runs through the steep, wooded Piedmont terrain that makes up this nearly 3,000 acres of public hunting land managed by the Georgia Department of Natural Resources.

The main tract of land lies adjacent to Sprewell Bluff State Park on the east side of the river, where elevations range from 540 to 757 feet. Two other tracts lie across the river; the Pigeon Creek Tract extends along the west river bank from Singers Hill to Tally Gap, while the Nichols Tract fronts the Flint directly across from the state park. Bluffs on this side of the river are steeper—about 1,000 feet.

White-tailed deer, wild turkey, squirrel, rabbit, quail, dove, duck and raccoon inhabit the thick hardwood and pine-hardwood forest. Because of the area's proximity to the state park, only bow hunting is allowed during deer season. Shotguns are legal for turkey and other small-game hunting.

Hunters should check general WMA regulations listed in the current "Hunting Seasons & Regulations" booklet (available at local stores and from the Georgia DNR). A Wildlife Management Area Stamp is required in addition to the regular hunting license and tags.

The Pigeon Creek Tract is open for foot traffic only. Visitors must leave their cars in the parking lot. Nichols Tract has limited vehicle access. Hiking is permitted throughout the hunting area during the off-season.

Facilities: *Primitive camping area with no facilities. Facilities are at Sprewell Bluff State Park (see page 71).* **Directions to Sprewell Bluff State Park**: *Upson County. From Thomaston, take GA 36 west 6 miles to Roland Road. Turn right and go to Alabama Road. Turn left and follow signs. You can pick up a map of the hunting areas at the ranger station.* **More Information**: *Georgia Department of Natural Resources, Wildlife Resources Division, 1014 Martin Luther King Jr. Boulevard, Fort Valley, GA 31030. 229/825-6354.*

BIKING

Thunder Scout Reservation Biking Trail

This biking trail, which is open to the public, winds throughout the 1,800-acre Thunder Scout Reservation, operated by the Flint River Council of the Boy Scouts of America. The trail follows the Flint River for 1.8 miles before ascending approximately 1,100 feet up Dripping Rocks mountain (see page 62).

Distance: An 8.5-mile loop trail. The portion of the trail that is along the river is a fairly easy ride, but once the trail turns up into the bluffs it is steep and much harder riding.

Palmetto

Palmetto is the common name given to several kinds of palm trees. The saw and the blue-stem are two palmettos that can be found in the Flint River Corridor.

Saw-palmetto *(Serenoa repens)* is a dwarf palm with stout, creeping underground stems that grows in hammocks and sandy Coastal Plain pinelands. An evergreen, it has green to yellowish-green, fan-shaped leaves that are one to three feet broad, and creamy-white, sweet-smelling flowers that bloom from May to July. Probably one of the most common native plants of Florida, the saw-palmetto gets its name from the saw-tooth edges on its slender leafstalks.

The blue-stem palmetto *(Sabal minor)* is similar to the saw-palmetto, but its leafstalks are smooth and fairly heavy and its leaves have a bluish-green cast. It grows in low woods or swamps, often along streams, in the Coastal Plain. In the Flint River Corridor, it can be found as far north as Sprewell Bluff (see page 78).

Trailhead Location: Thunder Scout Reservation (see page 73). Access the trail at the Gerald I. Lawhorn Canoe Base (see page next page) hanging canoe sign near the bulletin board.

Features: The course, which also serves as a hiking trail, starts on a rocky road along the Flint River, crosses Double Branch Creek and then switchbacks sharply up the mountain. Fast, singletrack lanes along ridges and fire roads and a steep downhill with numerous moguls makes it a competitive mountain bike track for the Thunderbolt Classic, a cross-country bike race held annually since 1994. Facilities for mountain bikers: bathroom, drinking water at campground spigots.

Days/Hours: *Trail open during daylight hours. During the summer or weekend training sessions, access to the trail may be limited.* **Fees**: *$2 requested donation for bikers and hikers, who must sign in and out, as well as sign a waiver located at the bulletin board at the trail head.*

OUTFITTERS

Gerald I. Lawhorn Canoe Base

Woods and river. Quiet and serene. A flat, wooded floodplain between Elkins Creek and the bluffs of Dripping Rocks. The Flint River silently flows in the background. It is a peaceful backdrop for a mission that is taken seriously—providing a wilderness experience along the Flint River.

A climber ascends the 50-foot climbing tower, Mt. OSMOSE, for the first time; bikers fasten their chin straps; rappellers harness up as they look down from the top of Dripping Rocks; two by two, canoeists carry green canoes and yellow oars to the put-in.

Owned and operated by the Flint River Council, Boy Scouts of America, the Canoe Base and Training Center is a full-fledged outfitter that can fully equip a group for a customized total wilderness experience. The key here, however, is that participants must be part of an organized group, but any group—Boy Scouts, Girl Scouts, youth groups, civic and corporate organizations—can take advantage of the facilities here.

Canoe Base rangers are qualified instructors who know the area well. They supervise summer camp programs and year-round high adventure activities, such as rock climbing, rappelling, kayaking, canoeing, whitewater rafting, spelunking, mountain biking, backpacking and hiking. Week-long programs include the Fifty Mile Afoot/Afloat—a combination of 23 miles on the Pine Mountain Trail and 27 miles on the Flint River, climbing and rappelling; tubing; and a three-hour conservation project. There are C.O.P.E./Rope courses; personal development programs for sports teams, work groups and youth groups; and the Outdoor School, a natural science environmental education program that involves individuals in the out-of-doors on a psychological as well as a physical level.

Salamander

Salamander is the common name for an order of tailed, usually four-legged amphibians. Timid and harmless, a salamander looks like a lizard but is related to the frog and toad.

Most salamanders are small and slender with long tails. They are cold-blooded animals with moist, slimy skins. Their bodies can replace lost parts, such as the tail and legs. They live in streams and ponds, on the land beneath stones and in caves or rotting logs where it is cool, dark and moist. Salamanders are somewhat sluggish and shy, feeding mostly at night on worms, slugs, snails and other small creatures.

Females may lay their eggs in water, where the larvae hatch with external gills that usually disappear during metamorphosis. Many salamanders, including those of the American tropics, lay eggs that hatch directly into small salamanders without passing through the free-living larval stage.

Eight of the nine salamander families occur in North America. The purple salamander can be found in the Pine Mountain area (see illustration on page 191).

Directions: *Upson County. From Woodbury, take GA 74 east about 6 miles. Turn south (right) at Thunder Scout Reservation sign. This is Thundering Springs Road. Go about 0.5 mile to Dripping Rocks Road and turn right. Follow road to Trading Post.* **More Information**: *Thunder Scout Reservation, 1166 Dripping Rocks Road, Molena, GA 30258. 706/646-2255; fax, 706/646-2120. Website: www.thunderbsa.org. Gerald I. Lawhorn Canoe Base, 706/647-6313. E-mail: canoe@thunderbsa.org.*

Flint River Outdoor Center

It's a Saturday afternoon in August. Cars and RVs fill the grassy parking lot. An Outdoor Center van, pulling a trailer loaded with large, orange rubber rafts and red and green canoes, rumbles in and stops in front of the boat house. River-weary canoeists haul their boats up the ramp between the lodge and boat house. "How was the river today?" asks Jim McDaniel, strolling up in his typical uniform of ball cap, shorts and T-shirt. Guests, with Tevas off and feet up, sip ice tea or beer on the gazebo while the Braves are up to bat on the lodge TV. Marge lights the candles on a cake. A McDaniel grandchild is having a birthday party at the pool.

This is the Flint River Outdoor Center. Relaxed, unpretentious and the only outfitter open to the public on the entire Flint River. A family business for more than 23 years, it is the McDaniel's home. A good place to come if you have never floated or canoed down the Flint. A good place to come if you have never floated or canoed down *any* river. A good place to return to time and time again.

In 1978, Jim and Marge McDaniel bought the little country store and realized they had found a strategically located spot for a river outfitter: next to the GA 36 Bridge over the Flint River—below some of the river's most scenic Class II stretches and less than a mile above the only Class III and IV, boat-eating, whitewater section on the entire Flint. They decided to add 12 rental canoes (and 24 paddles) to their inventory.

Today, the McDaniel's business extends from the original storefront where you can still buy snacks, white worms, alcoholic beverages and play video poker, to a two-story lodge with a rocking chair-filled wrap-around porch, swimming pool, boat house, decks, gazebos, outbuildings and RV campground. During the summer, the Outdoor Center offers five-, 10- and 20-mile canoe trips, as well as one-mile float trips for tubers, running shuttles from as far upriver as the GA 18 Bridge to the Po Biddy Bridge ramp on the downstream side.

Jim McDaniel, a self-described river rat who was born and raised in the area, is a good starting point for those wanting to learn more about recreation on the river and efforts to protect it.

Facilities: *Boat ramp (see map page 101); canoe, raft and tube rentals; shuttle service; convenience store with fishing supplies; lodge with private rooms and bunk rooms; campground (see page 74); game room and swimming pool; large, well-lighted parking area.* **Days/Hours**: *Outdoor Center – open daily,*

River Rapid Classifications

River rapids are classified according to their difficulty for canoeist. Most rapids on the upper Flint River can be confidently tackled by a beginning canoeist except those found below the GA 36 Bridge at Yellow Jacket Shoals. River rapids generally fit into one of the following classifications, but if the water temperature is below 50 degrees, or if the trip is an extended one in a wilderness area, the river should be considered one class more difficult than normal.

Class I – Moving water with a few riffles and small waves; few or no obstructions.

Class II – Easy rapids with waves up to three feet, and wide, clear channels that are obvious without scouting; some maneuvering is required.

Class III – Rapids with high, irregular waves often capable of swamping an open canoe; narrow passages that often require complex maneuvering; may require scouting from shore.

Class IV – Long, difficult rapids with constricted passages that often require precise maneuvering in very turbulent waters. Scouting from shore is often necessary, and conditions make rescue difficult. Ususally not possible for open canoes: boaters in covered canoes and kayaks should be able to Eskimo roll.

Class V – Extremely difficult, long, and very violent rapids with highly congested routes that nearly always must be scouted from shore. Rescue conditions are difficult and there is significant hazard to life in event of mishap. Ability to Eskimo roll is essential for kayaks and canoes.

Class VI – Difficulties of Class V carried to the extreme of navigability. Nearly impossible and very dangerous. For teams of experts only, after close study and with precautions taken.

year-round; sunrise to sunset. Canoe, raft and tube rentals and river shuttle service – open weekends, April through May and September through October; and daily, from Memorial Day to Labor Day. Any time during the year, rentals and shuttle service are available by reservation. **Fees***: Call for current rates on canoe, raft and tube rental and other equipment; river shuttle service; and guided canoe trips. For people running their own shuttle, boat ramp fee is $1 per boat and parking is $6 per day for buses and $3 per day for trailers and other vehicles. Single and double rooms are available at the lodge as well as suites with private bath. There is also a bunk room, which sleeps up to seven people. Prices include a continental breakfast. For camping rates, see page 74.* **Directions***: Upson County. From downtown Thomaston, take GA 36 west 8 miles. Cross over the bridge and the Outdoor Center is on the left.* **More Information***: Flint River Outdoor Center, 4429 Woodland Road, Thomaston, GA 30286-3235. 706/647-2633.*

BRIDGES

Double Bridges on GA 362

One bridge follows another at this river crossing known locally as "Double Bridges." The bridge furthest west actually crosses the river, while the other crosses floodplain. Access to the river is from an unpaved DOT right-of-way road on the west side of the river (see map page 67). **Location***: In Pike County where GA 362 crosses the Flint between the communities of Alvaton in Meriwether County and Hollonville in Pike County.*

David Knott Bridge on Flat Shoals Road

Built in 1958, this bridge is named for David Knott, a farmer who once lived in the area. The flat shoals across this wide stretch of the Flint have been a river crossing for thousands of years (see page 60). A washed-out, dirt boat ramp on the northeast side of the bridge provides river access (see map page 67). **Location***: On Meriwether and Pike County line where Flat Shoals Road crosses the Flint River between Gay and Concord.*

GA 18/74 Bridge

If you stand on this 1990 bridge and look upriver, you can see the 1887 pilings from the first railroad built through the town of Woodbury—the Georgia, Midland and Gulf Line. Later named Southern Railroad, the line ran from Columbus to Atlanta and marked the beginning of what would be a prosperous period for the town. A river gauge on the bridge indicates water levels up to 14 feet. During the 1994 flood, the water level was well past the 14-foot mark. Access to the river here is from a boat ramp on the west bank below the bridge (see map page 68). **Location***: On Meriwether and Pike County Line where Georgia 18/74 crosses the Flint between Woodbury and Molena.*

Talbot County

The Flint River enters Talbot County in its northeast corner, a couple of miles upstream from Sprewell Bluff, and continues downstream to form the county's eastern border.

"Talbot County, Georgia's 74th county, was created in 1827 from part of Muscogee County. The county and county seat, Talbotton, were named for Governor Matthew Talbot, who was serving as president of the Senate when Governor Rabun died. In addition to Talbotton, Talbot County has three other municipalities, Geneva, Junction City and Woodland. The first session of the Georgia Supreme Court was held on January 26, 1846 at the old Claiborne Hotel in Talbotton."

From *Georgia Snapshots*, Georgia Department of Community Affairs

For tourism information for towns in Talbot County, see Resources page 300.

GA 36 Bridge

A Town Lattice-design covered bridge, known as the Woodland-Thomaston Road Covered Bridge, once stretched across the Flint River just upstream from the present day GA 36 Bridge. Although beautiful and in good condition, the covered bridge was torn down, cut up, burned and replaced with this one—all in the name of progress. This concrete and steel extension, also called Wynn's Bridge, has an unofficial river gauge on a center piling which indicates water levels: seven feet is normal for summer; eight feet is optimal and normal for winter; and above nine feet the shoals below can be extremely dangerous for inexperienced paddlers. River access is from an unpaved road and washed-out boat ramp on the southeast side of the bridge (see map page 101). **Location**: *On Talbot and Upson County Line where GA 36 crosses the Flint between Woodland and Thomaston.*

Po Biddy Road Bridge

Built in 1956, this bridge is officially named the Chris Callier Bridge, but locals know it as Po Biddy, after the road, which leads from Thomaston to the community of Po Biddy Crossroads in Talbot County (see sidebar this page). An earlier Upson County map indicates that a Parker's Bridge once crossed the river at this site. Access to the river is from a boat ramp on the southeast side of the bridge (see map page 101). **Location**: *On Talbot and Upson County Line where Po Biddy Road (CR 419/172) crosses the Flint River about 7 miles south of Thomaston.*

How Po Biddy Got its Name

"The origin of the name of 'Po Biddy Crossroads' has been the subject of several tales. One is that as a group of people were eating a fried chicken picnic lunch at quarterly meeting at nearby Centerville Church, one of the ladies was heard to remark as her companion pickup up a drumstick, 'There goes the last of the po-biddy.'

"At any rate, sometime in the early 1930s Honorable Robert Harry Callier, long time clerk of Superior Court, operated a filling station at the crossroads and labeled it 'Po Biddy Filling Station.' It was a popular hanging out place in the long years of the depression and was headquarters for the Po Biddy baseball club which played its home games in the field south of the highway across from the station. It was later owned and operated by Hon. Maro Callier, later post-master at Talbotton for many years. It was visited by President Roosevelt in 1945 on one of his countryside trips a few days before his death in April at Warm Springs. The old building has been moved to a side yard and is no longer in use."

There Was a Land, A History of Talbot County, Georgia by Judge Robert H. Jordan

THE RIVER MARK

ON ONE OF HIS VISITS TO NORTH AMERICA A TRIBE OF NATIVE AMERICANS GAVE RIO **THE RIVER MARK**, A SWASH OF BLUE MADE FROM RIVER WATER, EARTH AND SUNLIGHT. HE HAS PROUDLY WORN IT EVER SINCE AND PASSES IT ON TO OTHERS WHO PRESERVE AND PROTECT RIVERS AND WETLANDS.

Section 3

Potato Creek to Lake Blackshear

WE FIND OUT how Rio got his River Mark and what it means. We learn about Benjamin Hawkins and the Indian Agency and how Andrew Jackson was responsible for moving Native Americans out of the region and making way for settlers.

Between Potato Creek and Lake Blackshear, use the Guidebook Section beginning on page 89 to explore: The Great Swamp, Montezuma Bluffs, where the Fall Line Meets the Great Divide, Oakbin Pond Preserve, Flint River Adventures, Auchumpkee Creek Covered Bridge, Musella, Whitewater Creek Park and the Flint River Wildlife Management Area.

SINCE **PREHISTORIC TIMES** THE PART OF THE FLINT WHERE THE HIGHWAY 128 BRIDGE NOW SPANS THE RIVER HAS BEEN USED AS A PLACE FOR RIVER CROSSING.

WILLIAM BARTRAM, THE AMERICAN EXPLORER AND NATURALIST, CROSSED THE FLINT HERE DURING HIS TRAVELS IN 1776.

I HOPE YOU REMEMBERED TO PACK THE IRON.

SETTLERS WITH FEW MEANS LOADED EVERYTHING IN BARRELS, CALLED HOGSHEADS, HAULED BY OX OR MULE.

EARLY STAGECOACHES PACKED WITH NINE PASSENGERS CROSSED THE RIVER HERE.

IN 1796 **GEORGE WASHINGTON** APPOINTED **BENJAMIN HAWKINS** INDIAN AGENT FOR ALL THE TERRITORY SOUTH OFTHE OHIO RIVER. HAWKINS SPOKE FLUENT FRENCH. HE HAD BEEN WASHINGTON'S TRANSLATOR DURING THE AMERICAN REVOLUTION.

BEN DID A GOOD JOB TRANSLATING FOR ME DURING THE RECENT CONFLICT WITH THE BRITISH. HE'LL BE A FRIEND TO THE INDIANS.

"I HEREBY APPOINT BENJAMIN HAWKINS PRINCIPAL AGENT FOR INDIAN AFFAIRS SOUTH OF THE OHIO RIVER."

HAWKINS CHOSE THE EAST BANK OF THE FLINT RIVER NEAR WHERE HIGHWAY 128 NOW CROSSES FOR THE SITE OF HIS **INDIAN AGENCY.**

THIS WILL BE A PERFECT SPOT. IT'S WELL LOCATED ON THE LOWER CREEK TRADING PATH. PLUS, I'LL HAVE A GOOD VIEW OF THE RIVER

THE AGENCY GREW TO INCLUDE AN OFFICE, TAVERN, BLACKSMITH SHOP, TANNING YARD, BEAR PEN, A GARDEN AND ORCHARDS. FOLLOWING THE ORIGINAL INDIAN TRADING PATH, THE **FEDERAL ROAD** CONNECTING WASHINGTON AND NEW ORLEANS PASSED THROUGH THE AGENCY. IN 1812 HAWKINS COUNTED 233 VEHICLES AND 3,726 TRAVELERS HEADED WEST ON THE ROAD.

ATTENTION: ALL INDIANS SOUTH OF THE OHIO RIVER. LAST CHANCE TO SIGN UP FOR COURSES BEFORE SPRING PLANTING SEASON. BEGINNING A PEACH ORCHARD IN GEORGIA HOW TO GROW STRAWBERRIES WINE MAKING FROM LOCAL GRAPES BOWS AND ARROWS TAKEN ON TRADE.

HAWKINS TRIED TO CONVINCE THE INDIANS TO GIVE UP HUNTING AND ADOPT THE AMERICAN AGRICULTURAL IDEAS.

HE EXPERIMENTED WITH DIFFERENT CROPS AND CORRESPONDED WITH **THOMAS JEFFERSON** ABOUT HIS SUCCESS.

"DEAR PRESIDENT JEFFERSON, I AM SENDING YOU A BOX OF GRAPE CUTTINGS. I HAVE BEEN EXPERIMENTING WITH THESE PLANTS HERE IN GEORGIA. I SUGGEST YOU PLANT THEM AT YOUR FARM IN VIRGINIA ON A HILL WITH SOUTHERN EXPOSURE SO THAT...

BUT MEANWHILE...
NEARBY, **ANDREW JACKSON** AND AN ARMY OF VOLUNTEERS FROM TENNESSEE WERE TEACHING THE INDIANS A DIFFERENT KIND OF LESSON ABOUT THEIR FUTURE IN AMERICA. TREATIES IN THE EARLY 1800S, AS A RESULT OF JACKSON'S BLOODY BATTLES WITH THE CREEKS, TURNED OVER MOST OF THE CREEK LAND IN THE FLINT AND CHATTAHOOCHEE RIVER VALLEY TO THE UNITED STATES AND OPENED UP THE REGION FOR SETTLEMENT.

CRACK!!

BLAM!!

Section 3

Potato Creek to Lake Blackshear

SIGNIFICANT NATURAL AREAS

The Great Swamp

Like most alluvial rivers draining the Piedmont, the Flint forms an extensive Fall Line swamp at its juncture with the Piedmont and Coastal Plain. For the Flint, this occurs three to four miles below the Colonel Benjamin Hawkins Bridge and continues for about 14 miles to the GA 96 Bridge. The swamp above the bridge is called Magnolia Swamp; the swamp below is known as Beechwood. Together, they are often referred to as the Great Swamp and form the largest swamp area on the Flint, second only to the Swamp of Toa (see page 129).

All of the silt, sand, clay and gravel that the river has been carrying through the Piedmont for miles now dumps out over the flat, wide Coastal Plain. Naturally, the Flint's floodplain, the flat area adjacent to the river that is frequently covered by water during flooding, widens and levels out. The river begins to meander. As the river curves back and forth, you'll notice how the water flows faster on the outside of the curve, causing the outside bank to erode. Deadfall and other debris also builds up in the outside curves as the water forces the obstructions against the bank. The effect is opposite on the inside of the curve. Here the water is moving much slower, allowing the silt and sand that it is carrying to drop out and build up into point bars—which happen to be great places to stop your boat and picnic or camp overnight. There are numerous such point bars between the Hawkins Bridge and Lake Blackshear.

Two other river phenomenon that are common in this stretch of river—but easier to distinguish on a map than by boating the river itself—are horseshoe bends and oxbows. A horseshoe bend is a meander that has become shaped like a very large horseshoe. An oxbow lake occurs as the neck of the horseshoe-shaped meander grows smaller and smaller, until it eventually cuts itself off from the rest of the river. Look at the river maps of this section on pages 135 and 136 and you will see horseshoe bends and oxbow lakes marked. For more information on point bars, meanders, horseshoe bends and oxbow lakes, see pages 274–277 in the "How Rivers Work" section of this book.

You'll also notice a change in the vegetation and an increase in the wildlife beginning in the Great Swamp area of the Flint. River cane is

The Coastal Plain

Once the Flint River leaves the Piedmont, it spreads out into the Coastal Plain, transforming itself into a wider, meandering river of swamps and sandy shores.

"The geologic formations in the southern half of the state are much simpler than those of the northern half, for the Coastal Plain section did not begin to appear until many millions of years after the formation of the mountains. At the time when the Appalachian Mountains were forming, the land now embraced by Georgia was tilted, so that its lower section was covered by the ocean and the erosion of the upper section was increased. During a long period of erosion vast quantities of debris were carried southward to the ocean, forming the layers of sands, clays and marls of the present Coast Plain.

"Beginning with the fall line hills, this southern section presents a slope gradually descending toward the seacoast with formations laid down in successive layers, of which the oldest is at the fall line and the youngest is at the coast. The deposits near the fall line hills are largely gravel, clays, and coarse light-colored sands, derived from the granites of the adjoining Piedmont Plateau. Red sands make up most of the southern part of these hills, although white limestone forms part of the surfaces of the Flint and Chattahoochee river valleys."

Georgia, the WPA Guide to its Towns and Countryside, compiled by workers of the 1940 Writers' Program of the Works Progress Administration in the State of Georgia

abundant here. Several species of cane indigenous to Georgia grow for miles along the river's edge between the Hawkins Bridge and the GA 127 Bridge. Spanish moss begins to appear more frequently below the GA 96 Bridge. You might also spot an occasional alligator sunning on the bank. Wild hogs, turkeys and white-tailed deer are numerous. On warm, sunny days turtles line themselves up single file on deadfall protruding from the water. But instantly, at the sound of a boat motor, like dominoes they fall into the water to hide.

To experience the Great Swamp, put in at the GA 96 Bridge boat ramp (see map page 135) and go either up or downstream.

Montezuma Bluffs

This 500-acre natural area, located on the east side of the Flint River two miles north of Montezuma, is part of the Fort Valley Plateau, a 150-foot escarpment overlooking the floodplain of the Flint River. Fifty to 75 million years ago, this section of Georgia was a seabed, compacted over time into the limestone now present. The Flint has worn away the younger layers of earth to expose fossilized oyster shells in the ancient limestone (see sidebar page 129).

Forested rocky-topped bluffs, deep ravines and a small percent of river-bottom floodplain make up the terrain. Because of the moist, steep slopes, these bluffs are largely undisturbed by agriculture and forestry, preserving the old growth forests of predominately beech and magnolia, as well as several unusual plant species. One of the state's best populations of relict trillium, an endangered trillium that grows mainly in undisturbed moist hardwood forests (see sidebar this page), grows above the floodplain in the limestone-enriched soil on the bluff's moist, shady slopes.

As in other parts of the upper Flint River watershed, plants from both the Piedmont and the Coastal Plain grow in close proximity at Montezuma Bluffs. A rare plant at home in the Cohutta Wilderness Area, mountain catchfly, stretches out on the limestone bluffs near the Coastal Plain's spruce pine; Spanish moss-draped white and chestnut oaks crisscross the shady ravines next to Southern magnolias and needle palms. In addition to the bluff forest, this site contains intact examples of bottomland hardwood forest and cypress-tupelo swamp.

Georgia acquired this land from the Nature Conservancy in 1993. There are no roads on Montezuma Bluffs and access to the area must be from the boat landing. All adjacent properties are privately owned and cannot be crossed to reach the area. The undeveloped bluffs and floodplain areas extend on both sides from the public boat ramp at the end of the paved country road. The Flint River cuts deep into the east bank during high water, flooding the boat ramp at least once a year. Deer hunting with bow and arrow is the only seasonal hunting allowed in the natural area.

Facilities: *Boat ramp (see map page 136) and parking.* **Directions**: *Macon County. From Montezuma, take GA 49 north about 2 miles. Turn*

Relict Trillium

Relict trillium (*Trillium reliquum*) grows in the hardwood forests of the Coastal Plain, among boulders or ledges with soft limestone, and in the Piedmont, in ravines and terraces with deep loamy soil. An endangered plant, it has been found in fewer than 30 sites, the majority of them in Georgia. It is believed that modern-day occurrences of the plant are relict—scattered remnants of a once more abundant plant.

Relict trillium grows low to the ground. Its leaves are elliptic to nearly round and have five shades of color, from green through blue-green to silver, with a central silvery streak on the upper surface. The flower, nestled between the three mottled leaves, blooms from March to April and emits an unpleasant, fetid odor. It's petals range in color from dark purple to yellow. Due to clear cutting of forest land for agriculture and pine plantations, the perennial herb has lost most of its habitat. Other threats to the trillium's existence are Japanese honeysuckle, Chinese privet, kudzu—and irresponsible individuals who remove the plant from its habitat.

Relict trillium can be found near the mouth of Auchumpkee Creek and in the Montezuma Bluffs Natural Area.

left onto CR 267 at the Wildlife Viewing sign. Go about 1 mile to boat ramp. **More Information**: *Georgia Department of Natural Resources, Wildlife Resources Division, 2024 Newton Road, Albany, GA 31701. 229/430-4254.*

The Fall Line Meets the Great Divide

The area between Musella and Roberta in Crawford County is one of the most remarkable physiographical areas of the state. It is where the Fall Line (see page 190), which runs mostly east and west across the state, intersects with US 341, which sits on the Eastern Continental Divide that runs north and south, or parallel, between the Ocmulgee and the Flint River watersheds. Water falling east of the ridge flows into the Ocmulgee and, eventually, into the Atlantic. Water falling west of the ridge flows into the Flint and then to the Gulf. Thus, a farmer in this area could have part of his farm in the Piedmont and part on the Coastal Plain. He could also have land that drained in both directions.

Oakbin Pond Preserve

Cypress pond habitats are common in the Coastal Plain of the Flint River Watershed. But growing amid the grasses and sedges of this open cypress pond in Dooly County, called Oakbin Pond, is one of the largest and healthiest populations of endangered Canby's dropwort found anywhere. A plant of the parsley family, Canby's dropwort is so rare that less than 20 populations have been documented in the world. These are distributed across four states—Maryland, North Carolina, South Carolina and Georgia.

The openness of Oakbin Pond is crucial to the continued vitality of Canby's dropwort, which flourishes in sunny areas. This exposure is maintained by a limited canopy cover and a water supply sufficient to flood the area annually. The deep, poorly drained soil traps water and maintains a shallow pool, while its high organic content provides a wealth of nutrients.

Approximately 80 percent of this 176-acre preserve, owned by the Nature Conservancy of Georgia, consists of cypress pond habitat. The remaining land is being restored to longleaf and shortleaf pine forest. The cypress-pond habitat supports various animals and birds, including night herons and wood ducks, snakes and cotton rats. The elusive bobcat may also frequent the area.

The Nature Conservancy allows visits to Oakbin Pond, with the request that visitors inform the Georgia Field Office in advance. The boardwalk provides some access to the wetland. American alligators and cottonmouth snakes have been observed at the preserve, and visitors are advised to exercise caution.

Facilities: *Trail and boardwalk.* **Directions**: *Dooly County. For directions and permissions, call the Nature Conservancy office.* **More Information**: *The Nature Conservancy of Georgia, 1401 Peachtree Street, NE, Suite 236, Atlanta, GA 30309. 404/873-6946.*

Cypress

Bald cypress (*Taxodium distichum (L.) Rich.*) occurs principally in swamps and ponds throughout most of the Coastal Plain. You'll see cypress in the swamps along the Flint River, particularly in the Great Swamp area (see page 89). It is a large, long-lived tree reaching heights of 150 feet with a gradually tapering trunk generally four to five feet in diameter above an abruptly enlarged base and terminating in a spreading, round crown. These cypress "knees" are usually what make cypress trees so distinguishable.

The Georgia Forestry Commission describes the tree's key characteristics as: "feather-like arrangement of the leaves, branches deciduous, cone small and round; bark fibrous, cinnamon-red; presence of cone-shaped knees around the base of the trunk." Its wood is "light, soft, not strong, very brittle, easily worked, straight-grained, varying in color from pale brown to nearly black with a somewhat pungent odor. Old growth heartwood very durable."

A somewhat smaller species, pond cypress, is 40 to 80 feet tall and one to two feet in diameter. The knees of bald cypress differ from those of pond cypress by being more narrowly conical and sharp pointed than the flattened, dome-shaped knees of pond cypress. Pond cypress occurs in shallow ponds, wet depressions in flatwoods and along stream banks throughout the Coastal Plain.

(continued on page 98)

Benjamin Hawkins
and the Creek Indian Agency

Upstream

US 19/80 Bridge

In 1796, George Washington appointed Colonel Benjamin Hawkins, his friend and translator during the American Revolution, "Principal Agent for Indian Affairs South of the Ohio River." From his appointment until his death in 1816, Hawkins was a part of, and helped shape, the history of the Flint River Corridor.

Flint River

Diary entry
"This is a rock ford and pretty good, the bank steep on the left side. Here the falls terminate and the flats begin to spread out."

The Federal Road in Georgia about 1813

Federal Road

Oconee R.

Ocmulgee R.

Altamaha R.

Chattahoochee R.

Flint R.

Colonel Benjamin Hawkins

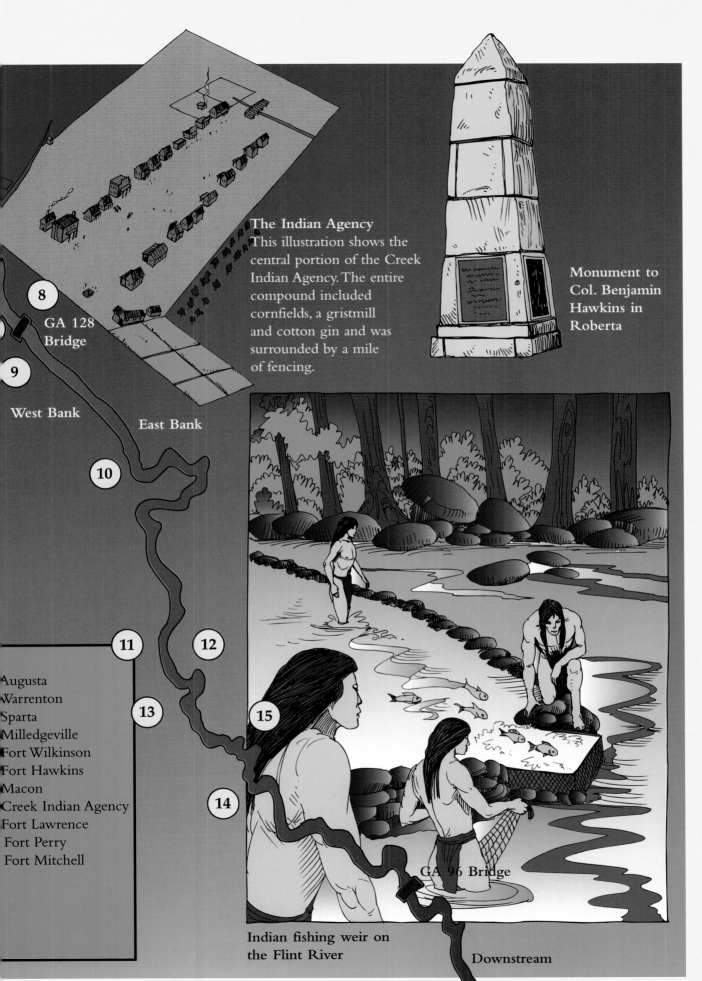

The Indian Agency
This illustration shows the central portion of the Creek Indian Agency. The entire compound included cornfields, a gristmill and cotton gin and was surrounded by a mile of fencing.

Monument to Col. Benjamin Hawkins in Roberta

8

GA 128 Bridge

9

West Bank

East Bank

10

11

12

13

14

15

Augusta
Warrenton
Sparta
Milledgeville
Fort Wilkinson
Fort Hawkins
Macon
Creek Indian Agency
Fort Lawrence
Fort Perry
Fort Mitchell

GA 96 Bridge

Indian fishing weir on the Flint River

Downstream

Benjamin Hawkins Territory

by Maxwell Duke

1. Benjamin Hawkins and the Creek Indian Agency

A few hundred yards south of the GA 128 Bridge is one of the most historic landmarks on the Flint River. It was here that one of Georgia's fascinating, but historically ignored, personalities made his home and served both his country and his Indian neighbors. His name was Benjamin Hawkins and on the gently rolling hill on the east bank overlooking the river is where he built the Creek Indian Agency.

Hawkins was a native of North Carolina. Fluent in French, he served as George Washington's interpreter during the American Revolution and was given the rank of colonel. After the war, the state of North Carolina elected him to the U.S. Senate for several terms. Then in 1796, Washington appointed Col. Hawkins "Principal Agent for Indian Affairs South of the Ohio River."

From the very beginning in his role as Indian Agent, Hawkins traveled extensively throughout the Creek Territory, keeping a journal that described the Indian towns he visited and the Indian culture he observed.

Around 1801, Hawkins selected an 8,000-acre site on the Flint River for his Indian Agency. It was located just below the Fall Line where the southern Piedmont meets the Coastal Plain. At that point, the river ended its rapid fall over hard, quartzite rocks and continued its journey to the sea at a slower, meandering pace over flatter, sandy terrain. This was also where a Creek Indian trail, known as the Lower Creek Trading Path, crossed the river. The path followed the Fall Line east to west, connecting Fort Augusta on the Savannah River with Creek Indian towns on the Chattahoochee River near the site that would eventually become Columbus.

Inside a rectangular-shaped compound about a mile around, Hawkins built 25 structures. These included his house, kitchen, an office, stables, a blacksmith shop, a tavern and a bear pen.

His peach orchard was the first commercial peach orchard in Georgia. He cultivated thousands of peach trees and distributed them to Indians up and down the river. Witnessing and recording the first killing frost of the peach industry, he sent a letter to his friend, President Thomas Jefferson, in March of 1809 saying, "The frost… has destroyed the most valuable of our fruit, peaches."

His huge strawberry patch was the envy of both the Indians and the white settlers. An 1812 newspaper account reported that Hawkins grew one plant that had 300 berries stemming from one root.

An avid promoter of grapes, Hawkins once sent President Jefferson a package containing 13 labeled varieties with complete instructions for planting and care.

Hawkins lived with his housekeeper Lavinia Downs for many years and they had six children. When a serious illness threatened to end his life, he and Lavinia married. Hawkins, however, recovered and lived another four years.

Honest, fair, well educated, hungry to learn and eager to share his experiences, Hawkins set out to educate Indians to use modern tools, technologies and agriculture. He tried to convince them to shift from an economy of commercial hunting to one that required less land. Hawkins realized that the Indians would have to integrate into the white culture if there was any chance of them continuing to live on their land. And they would have to learn to live on less land—no longer would they be able to roam the vast region that had been the Creek Nation. The Creeks would have to become a part of the civilization that was about to swallow them up or they would be pushed out. The older Indians understood the wisdom of this, but the younger Creek braves constantly resisted.

During his 20-year tenure Hawkins continuously found himself in an impossible situation—trying to balance the rights of Indians with the insatiable desire of American frontiersmen and settlers to move west and acquire new land.

Hawkins's method of dealing with the Indians was 180 degrees from the thinking of the popular military hero Andrew Jackson, who had little respect for Indian rights and wanted the land cleared for white settlers. Jackson fought decisive Indian battles in the region during Hawkins's tenure as Indian agent. Treaties after those battles took away huge portions of Creek territory under the Indian Agent's stewardship.

By the time Hawkins died in 1816, what he had feared during his lifetime was rapidly taking place—total eradication of the Creek Indians from the Flint River Corridor. Twenty years after Hawkins's death, his antagonist, Andrew Jackson, by then president, would order all Indians removed from the region during what would come to be called the Trail of Tears.

Hawkins's grave is located on the site of the Indian Agency and a monument to him is located a few miles east in Roberta.

2. Fishing Weir

The Indians of the Flint River were dedicated, resourceful fishermen. They used poison (obtained from crushed green walnuts); hooks (fashioned from bones); traps (woven together using cane); nets (sewn together using plant fiber); seines (constructed of small saplings woven together); spears; and bow and arrow.

On a grand scale they employed a fishing weir. The one at this site is consistent with others found at the Etowah River near Cartersville and on the Ocmulgee River just north of Hawkinsville.

The weir is constructed of rocks that were carried from nearby banks and the streambed. Using hundreds of boulders, some as large as three feet in diameter, two dams were built. Each dam, about 50 feet long, angled downriver, coming together to form a "V" with the apex facing downstream. A small passageway was left open in the crotch of the "V" near the center of the river so that the fish could be funneled into a corral.

Over the centuries, this weir has suffered some damage and deterioration but is still discernible. Aerial views of the site during low water periods are dramatic. Surface examination is more difficult because of extraneous rocks that have surfaced in and around the weir. However, considering its age, which could date back 6,000 years, the weir is in very good condition.

3. Indian Homestead

Before US 80 was widened to accommodate a new bridge, an archaeological excavation uncovered an Indian homestead on the site. Remains of a house and numerous artifacts were found dating back to the late 1700s. It is possible that the occupants of the homestead were associated with the historic town of Salenojuh a few miles south.

4. Indian Town of Salenojuh

On the west side of the river a couple of miles south of the present US 80 Bridge once stood the Indian town of Salenojuh. When Hawkins visited the town site, he learned that the town had had a significant population in 1787 just before it was abandoned. At that time, there were 70 males old enough to be considered warriors, or, as Hawkins called them, "gun-men."

The town's structures were built close together. It was apparently affluent and well-populated with a town square for political and religious gatherings and a hothouse, which was used much like a modern-day sauna.

The fields were well-fenced and extended three miles above the town, an ideal situation for raising hogs and cattle. Just above the fields were two curves in the river where the Indians cultivated 150 acres of rich farmland.

5. Indian Town of Chumcau

Chumcau was a historic Indian town located a couple of miles south of the Auchumpkee Creek confluence with the Flint. Although its exact location has escaped archaeological detection, it is nonetheless marked on a reliable map dated 1818.

Colonel Hawkins would have passed this exact location on his survey of Indian towns of the Flint River, but he does not mention the town. If Chumcau had been there on Hawkins's earlier visit or had it been remembered and reported by local Indians, he would certainly have mentioned it. It is possible that the town sprang into existence before Hawkins's death in 1816 but did not get listed in his initial report. In any event, by 1818 Chumcau had been established and was of significant size.

Such a spontaneous appearance of a town was not uncommon. Several instances have been documented whereby whole towns simply packed up and relocated almost overnight. Political unrest, trading advantages, soil exhaustion, hunting or crop failures, fuel shortages or perhaps even psychic events would have been reason enough for some towns to migrate.

6. Indian Town of Oleco

Located at the confluence of the first small creek south of Auchumpkee Creek on the east side of the river is the Indian town of Oleco. Like the Indian town of Chumcau, Oleco is not mentioned in Colonel Hawkins's original survey of the Flint River published in 1799—*A Sketch of the Creek Country in the Year 1798 and 1799*—but does make an appearance on the 1818 map that was printed only two years after his death.

7. Benjamin Hawkins Bridge

The GA 128 Bridge over the Flint is named the Benjamin Hawkins Bridge (see page 104).

8. Ecunhutkenene Indian Trail and the Federal Road

A few hundred yards south of the GA 128 Bridge at an outcropping of rock is Ecunhutkenene. In one of Colonel Hawkins's letters he named, described and told the significance of this place on the Flint River by writing:

"This [he is referring to Ecunhutkenene] also called Chelucconeneauhassee, the old horse path, the first path to the Creek nation. This is a rock ford and pretty good, the bank steep on the left (east) side. Here the falls terminate and the flats begin to spread out."

According to Hawkins, who spent much time collecting Indian words and learning to speak the Muscogee language, Chelucconeneauhassee meant "The Old Horse Path." The existence of this well-established trail and the "pretty good" ford made this a perfect place for him to establish his Creek Indian Agency.

The trail was part of an ancient Indian path that extended all the way from the Savannah River to the Chattahoochee River. It was also known as the Lower Creek Trading Path by European traders and as the Old Sandhill Path.

In 1803 during the administration of Thomas Jefferson, the federal government undertook the development of a road from Washington, D.C., to New Orleans that followed more or less the original Indian trading path. This route became known as the Federal Road (see page 23). It was also referred to as the Stage Coach Road.

In 1812 Hawkins recorded in his diary that 233 vehicles and 3,726 persons had headed west past his agency on the Flint in the six months between October 1811 and 1812.

In 1843 a telegraph line, connecting Washington and New Orleans, was constructed. The first telegraph line in Georgia, the wires followed the Federal Road between Macon and Columbus. People soon began calling this portion of the road the Federal Wire Road.

Today GA 128 between the Flint River and Macon follows much of the same route as the original Federal Road.

A somewhat undisturbed remnant of the Indian trail is still visible on the east bank of the river. It is probably wider now than it was originally because of extensive use by stagecoaches, wagons and horses, and because the dynamic action of floods and erosion has remodeled the final approach to the shoals. An outcropping of rock points to its location.

9. Fort Lawrence

Fort Lawrence was established in 1813 across the Flint River from Hawkins's Creek Indian Agency. It was situated within a five-mile area that was given over by the Creek Indians as a result of an earlier treaty. The fortification and the arrival of 600 soldiers were justified by the threat of a British invasion from the west related to the ongoing War of 1812. Hostile, war-like "Red Stick" Creek Indians led by Chief Tecumseh were in league with the British and posed an additional threat.

Such dangers distressed Hawkins. His plans and efforts were aimed at moving toward a peaceful coexistence between the whites and the Indians based on the modernization of the Indians' way of life, not by brute force of military intervention. However, he knew the Indian threat was something not be ignored and, therefore, welcomed the arrival of soldiers and the fortification across the river.

10. Neisler Mound

Several miles south of the Creek Indian Agency on the west bank of the river is the largest Indian mound on the Flint. It measures approximately 500 feet in circumference. It served as an earthen platform upon which a temple building was erected. The mound dates from the Mississippian Culture Period and was first occupied about A.D. 1200.

11. Hartley-Posey Indian Mound

Although similar to the Neisler Mound in almost all respects, the Hartley-Posey Mound is smaller and located on a steep, flat bluff that never floods, while the Neisler Mound is located in a low, flood-prone area. Why the Native Americans who occupied these two mounds chose such radically different sites for their mounds remains a mystery. Archaeologists have partially excavated the mound. It is of the Mississippian Culture period and was used sporadically from A.D. 1200 to sometime during the 1500s. Evidence suggests that this mound may have been abandoned from time to time in favor of the Neisler Mound. The shifting from one mound to the other was probably because the easily obtainable local firewood supply became exhausted.

12. Large Stand of River Cane

This is believed to be one of the largest stands of river cane in Georgia. Cane was one of the Indians' most valuable resources. It was used to make houses, arrows, scalping knives, rafts, mats, torches, drilling devices, shields, gaming devices, baskets, ceremonial fires and many other items employed in almost every aspect of their daily lives.

13. Indian Town of Coocohapofe

Coocohapofe was a town that had been abandoned by the time Hawkins surveyed the area in 1796. The translated name means "by Canes Ground." Its name was well-deserved. According to Hawkins, it was located on the western bank across from a swamp that was three miles deep. Today, that swamp and its adjacent lowlands still form the enormous canebrake that stretches for miles in all directions.

14. Indian Town of Patsiliga

This town takes its name from a nearby creek. Translated, the name identifies the creek as being a roosting area for the now-extinct passenger pigeon.

The site of this town has been archaeologically established and some preliminary work has been done. It is both a historically documented town as well as a site that was occupied by Indians in prehistoric times.

15. Magnolia Swamp and Beechwood Swamp

The gradient of the river here has leveled to only a drop of 1.8 feet per mile and the floodplain has expanded to as much as three miles in some places. This is a great swampland. Magnolia Swamp engulfs many square miles. It and Beechwood Swamp, further downstream, comprise the largest floodplain and swamp area of the river basin.

Magnolia Swamp is separated from Beechwood Swamp by name only. The landmark that divides them is the GA 96 Bridge that runs east and west, connecting Fort Valley and Reynolds. The southern end of the swamp joins hands with other swamps as far south as the GA 127 Bridge near Marshallville

Hammocks, slightly elevated areas in the floodplain, in both Beechwood and Magnolia swamps, provided living places for Woodland Period Indians from 1000 B.C. to about A.D. 800. These Indians had recently discovered the techniques of agriculture and found the hammocks particularly fertile and easy to work. The elevated zones also provided the Indians a place to build houses that had a better chance of staying above water during floods.

(continued from page 91)

NATURE-BASED EDUCATIONAL CENTERS

Flint River Adventures

Palmetto-roofed huts, clay cooking pots, totems, ceremonial carved snakes, the aroma of Southeastern Indian foods slowly cooking. This is the Flint River Adventures atmosphere—an atmosphere that imitates as authentically as possible that of a 1540 Uchee Indian village. Just five miles east of where Benjamin Hawkins built his Indian Agency on the banks of the Flint in 1801, costumed actors portray explorers, Indians and the Indian Agent himself at this living history camp.

Owner Maxwell Duke, a middle school teacher, turned his obsession with archaeology and Southeastern Indian history into a reality of sorts in 1990 when he bought 20 acres of land near the Flint River on Auchumpkee Creek. With the help of family, friends and students, he built the Indian village and turned to Benjamin Hawkins as the perfect historic figure to help him convey his knowledge of the Southeastern Indians.

Duke, as Hawkins, demonstrates Indian crafts, such as pottery making, flint knapping, blow gun manufacturing, Indian textile and basket manufacturing, seining, Indian cooking and mask making. He presents programs on artifact identification, discovering "undiscovered" archaeological sites and one for mature, adult audiences only called "The Adult Side of Indian Culture."

Duke also has a special mission of preserving the memory of Benjamin Hawkins, a frontiersman whom Duke believes is generally overlooked in history books. Several of Duke's programs focus on the agent, whom Duke portrays, as he reads from his diary and reminisces about his life among the Indians of middle Georgia.

Facilities: *Campgrounds with hot showers and restrooms; pavilion stage and auditorium; pavilion welcome porch with refrigerator, freezer, sink, outside gas stove, electricity and tables; picnic areas; fishing; hiking; swimming and boating.* **Days/Hours**: *Open by reservation only.* **Fees**: *Fees range from $10 per person per day to $400 to rent the entire campground for the weekend. Discounts are available for church groups, historical societies and educational institutions.* **Directions**: *Upson County. Entrance to the property is restricted to people who have made prior arrangements and have secured reservations.* **More Information**: *Flint River Adventures, 1471 Minor Road, Culloden, GA 31016. 229/836-2697. Website: www.hom.net/~stringer.*

HISTORIC SITES

Auchumpkee Creek Covered Bridge

Several covered bridges have spanned Auchumpkee Creek at this site, but the one that stands here today is a painstaking reproduction of the bridge that was destroyed during the flood of 1994. That bridge, built by the firm of J. Herring and W. Alford and completed in October 1892, was of Town Lattice design (see page 66), 120 feet

River Cane

River cane is a woody-stemmed, more or less evergreen, bamboo-like grass that commonly grows three to 15 feet or higher in low wet woods, stream bottoms, savannas and bogs. In primitive America, canebrakes were extensive from Virginia and Missouri southward.

"It is probable that like eighteenth-century Americans frontiersmen, the Indians judged the suitability of soils for corn cultivation in terms of stands of river cane (Arundinaria gigantea). Like corn, river cane is a grass, and the richer the soil the taller it grows. The rule of thumb for the eighteenth-century frontiersman was that if the cane grew five to ten feet, the soil was ordinary; if it grew twenty to thirty feet, the solid was excellent. In addition, river cane probably served the material needs of the Southeastern Indians in more ways than any other resource in their environment. Cane is a hard, flexible, water-resistant material that they used to manufacture a host of artifacts, including baskets, woven mats, knives, arrows, fish spears, blowguns, houses, and so on. Its leaves stay green the year around, and it therefore attracted herbivorous animals in winter, where they could be hunted. Likewise, bears often took up residence in canebrakes, as did carnivores such as red wolves and cougars. Canebrakes were superb places of refuge. They were very dense, and the dry leaves and stalks betrayed any intruding movement. When pursued, the Indians would head for the nearest canebrake. Some canebrakes were vast, covering thousands of acres. But over the centuries American farmers have eliminated them, and today few large stands of river cane survive."

Knights of Spain, Warriors of the Sun by Charles Hudson

long with a span of 96 feet. Although the bridge was closed to traffic in 1985, it had stood for more than 100 years before it collapsed under the pressure of the floodwaters. The raging water carried a huge tree limb down the creek—which knocked the covered bridge from its stacked stone moorings and smashed it against the overpass on Allen Road, 30 yards downstream.

Afterwards, preservationists labored to pull salvageable pieces of the bridge from the mud and then, with federal disaster relief money and privately raised funds, painstakingly recreated not only the design of the bridge but the manner in which it was built in 1892. They hired Arnold M. Graton of Ashton, New Hampshire, one of the country's premier covered-bridge craftsmen, to head up the re-construction. They employed traditional construction techniques, including wood pegs, or treenails, to hold the bridge together. Draft animals—including horses, mules and oxen—supplied the muscle to pull the structure across the creek by walking around a capstan to wind a rope that was attached to the bridge, thus moving it into place. The bridge was placed on temporary dunnage until the stone abutments supporting the ends of the bridge could be built up higher than future floods. Next, the bridge builders put on the roof, placed the weather boarding and constructed the approaches.

The area around the Auchumpkee Creek Covered Bridge was one of the earliest settled in Upson County. Named Hootenville for the Hooten family who ran a nearby ferry, it was once a thriving and lively community. During the 1830s, there was a hotel, bar rooms, grocery and dry goods stores, harness and blacksmith shops, a post office and relay station for stagecoaches and the Blountsville Academy.

On Allen Road just below the covered bridge is the site of an old gristmill, which has been known as McCord Mill, Respess Mill, Zorn's Mill and Wilmont's Mill, depending on the owner. Like the mill, Auchumpkee Creek Covered Bridge has had several names, including Zorn's Mill Bridge and Hootenville Bridge.

Directions: *Upson County. From Thomaston, take GA 19 south 12 miles to Allen Road. Turn left and go .7 miles to Auchumpkee Creek. Just before the concrete bridge over Auchumpkee Creek, turn left into a small parking area. The covered bridge, closed to traffic, stands just upstream from Allen Road and has a small picnic area.*

Musella

The little town of Musella in Crawford County is a living monument to Georgia's peach past. Just a block from the main highway on Old Highway 341 is the town, a handful of aging homes, farm sheds and warehouses where an old Atlanta & Fort Valley Railroad line once ran. On the east side of Old 341 stands the roadside outlet and packing plant of Dickey Farms. Established in 1890, it is the oldest peach packing operation in the state. The 1936 packing plant, a long, white shed shaded by a large awning, had the

Crawford County

The Flint River enters Crawford County on its western border and continues forming the county line until it leaves the county just downstream of the GA 96 Bridge.

"Crawford County, the 55th county formed in Georgia, was created in 1822 from Creek Indian lands and part of Houston County. Later, parts of Macon and Talbot counties were added. The county was named for William H. Crawford, who was U.S. Secretary of the Treasury when the county was created. A monument to Joanna Toutman, who designed and made the Lone Star Flag adopted by the State of Texas, can be found on the courthouse square. The flag was presented to a group of Georgia volunteers who were en route to help Texas fight in its war of independence in 1835. The county has one active municipality, Roberta. The county seat, Knoxville, received a charter in 1825, but it is no longer a functioning municipality. It was one of 187 inactive municipalities to lose their charters in 1995 as a result of a 1993 Act of the General Assembly. The county is located on the fall line and has traditionally been a leader in the state's peach production. There are 19 archaeological sites in the county that have been filed with the State Archeological Office. Of particular significance is the Creek habitation area along the Flint River. In Knoxville, there are several buildings listed on the National Register of Historic Places, including the Crawford County Courthouse (1831) and the Crawford County Jail (1882). The Roberta Historic District is also listed."

From *Georgia Snapshots*, Georgia Department of Community Affairs

For tourism information for towns in Crawford County, see Resources page 300.

first hydro-cooling system and brushing machine to remove peach fuzz. Open from mid-May to August, the outlet offers many kinds of peaches, including springgold, express, sunbrite, June gold, gold prince, candor, dixie red, sure crop, coronet, harvester, red haven, topaz, red globe and blake. To the left of the stands is the Musella Gin and Cotton Company. Established in 1913, then burned and re-built in 1930, it still gins more than 2,000 bales of cotton each year. Beyond the gin is the 200-acre peach orchard belonging to the Dickey family. On the west side of the road is the C. F. Hayes, Jr. building, a small general merchandise store, and the 1884 Musella Baptist Church, a picturesque, white New England-style structure with a steeple in the front and a steeply slanted roof.

Directions: *Crawford County. From Roberta, take US 341 about 6 miles north to Musella. Turn right onto Old Highway 341 and go a block to the old town.* **More Information**: *Roberta-Crawford County Chamber of Commerce, P.O. Box 417, Roberta, GA 31078. 478/836-3825.*

Flint River Ferry

From 1850 to 1988, a ferry crossed the Flint about four miles south of Marshallville and several hundred yards above the current GA 27 Bridge. Originally named Wannamaker's Ferry and later known as Holinshed's Ferry and Underwood's Ferry—after various owners and operators over the years—it has also been called the Marshallville Ferry, the Macon County Ferry, the Miona Ferry and the Flint River Ferry—it just depends on who you talk to. Nevertheless, the ferry that operated at this site was the last to operate in the state of Georgia, finally giving way to the concrete and steel bridge below.

The ferry itself, like others on the Flint and throughout Georgia, was initially a large wooden barge operated by a system of cables and pulleys and powered by the ferryman with a long pole, who would shift the ferry into the river's current to get additional power.

At some point, however, the wooden barge at this crossing was abandoned for a 55-foot metal barge with a plank floor. It was powered by a 1959 Chevrolet six-cylinder truck engine that wound two large cables, attached to trees on each side of the river, around a drum made from mowing machine blades. The crossing took a couple of minutes.

The ferry could carry one or two vehicles at a time, provided the weight was not more than two tons. To take the ferry in more modern times, all you had to do was drive down to the ferry landing, honk your horn and the ferry operator would come out of his house and take you across.

On days when river conditions were safe, the ferry was dependable, operating 24 hours a day. But river conditions, such as high water, low water and deadfall, unfortunately made the ferry inoperable about half the year. In 1985, the ferry was closed 187 days; in 1986 it was down 147 days. The ferry has been moved to Oglethorpe where it is being

Taylor County

The Flint River flows along the eastern border of Taylor County until it reaches the Macon County Line.

"Taylor County was created from Macon, Marion and Talbot counties in 1852, the 98th county organized. The county was named after Zachary Taylor, who won a victory at Buena Vista in the Mexican War and later became the 12th President of the United States. The county has two municipalities: Butler, the county seat, and Reynolds. Butler was named for General William Orlando Butler, another hero of the Mexican War. The Tuscaloosa Formation, located in the county, is a sand clay formation that represents the first prominent coastal plains deposits laid. The Wire Road, which ran through Taylor County, was named for the telegraph wire that stretched along it. The road was part of the stage highway from Richmond to New Orleans."

From *Georgia Snapshots*, Georgia Department of Community Affairs

For tourism information for towns in Taylor County, see Resources page 300.

 (continued on page 103)

Auchumpkee covered bridge

The Great Swamp

Like most alluvial rivers draining the Piedmont, the Flint forms an extensive Fall Line swamp at its juncture with the Piedmont and Coastal Plain. This occurs 3 to 4 miles below the Benjamin Hawkins Bridge and continues for 15 miles to the GA 96 Bridge. Magnolia Swamp is above the bridge. Beechwood Swamp is below the bridge. Together they form what is known as the Great Swamp and make up the largest such area in the river corridor. The level and often flooded landscape is marked by slow-moving water, meandering bends of the river, sandbars, oxbow lakes and yazoo streams. The area serves as a nursery for a wide variety of aquatic and animal life.

⑨

er Indian Mound

00 feet in circum-
this is the largest
ound on the Flint.
ciated with the
pian Period of
istory and was first
about A.D. 1200.

Griffin Branch

Canebrake

This is believed to be one the largest stands of river cane in Georgia.

Indian Town of Coocohapofe

⑩

10. Hartley-Posey Mound

From about the same period as the Neisler Mound, the Hartley-Posey mound is smaller and constructed on a steep flat bluff that never floods, while the Neisler mound is in a low, flood-prone area.

Indian Town
of Patsiliga

Magnolia Swamp

kins Gravesite

s is buried on a hillside
king the Flint on what was
e grounds of the Creek
Agency.

Patsiliga Creek

Reynolds

About 5 miles west of the river
via GA 96

Reynolds

Locator Map

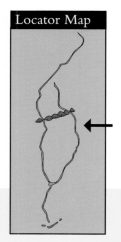

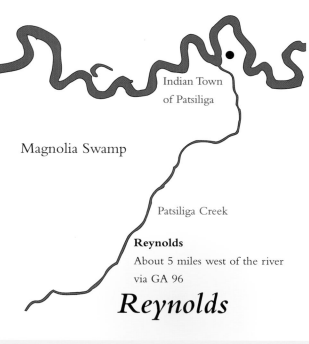

The Fall Line and Yellow Jacket Shoals

1. River Gauge

The GA 36 Bridge, also known as Wynn's Bridge, has an unofficial river gauge on a center piling which indicates water levels: 7 feet is normal for summer, 8 feet is optimal and normal for winter, above 9 to 10 feet the shoals below can be extremely dangerous for inexperienced paddlers.

2. GA 36 Boat Ramp

On east bank, just below the bridge. A much better and safer ramp is across the river at the Flint River Outdoor Center.

GA 36

Daniel Shoals

② ①
③

3. Flint River Outdoor Center Boat Ramp

On west bank, just below the GA 36 Bridge. Steep concrete ramp suitable for canoe, kayaks and rafts. Owned by the Flint River Outdoor Center and a small launch fee is charged. Shuttle services available up and down river.

Flint River Outdoor Center Campground

This is the only full-service campground open to the public between the headwaters and Lake Blackshear, 105 miles downstream.

Flint River Outdoor Center

Canoe and raft rental, shuttle service, lodge, camping and supplies. The perfect starting place for anyone to experience the Flint River.

Big Lazer Creek Wildlife Management Area (WMA)

Big Lazer Creek WMA encompasses 5,864 acres and includes 3 primitive camping areas, a fishing lake with boat ramp, fishing pier and restrooms, picnic area with tables and grills, hiking trails and 8-station shooting range for single projection ammunition.

4. Yellow Jacket Shoals

Once the river passes under the GA 36 Bridge, it begins its rapid descent through the Fall Line, the boundary that marks the edge of the ocean that once covered parts of Georgia, Alabama, South Carolina and Mississippi about 50 million years ago. Above the Fall Line is the red clay soil and hard rock of the Piedmont. Below the Fall Line is the flat, sandy Coastal Plain. Within 2.5 miles of the bridge, the river drops about 70 feet. A one-mile stretch of that, known as Yellow Jacket Shoals, drops about 40 feet, creating one of the most picturesque and unique sections of the entire river.

④ Yellow Jacket Shoals

Gibson Island

Hightower Shoals

⑤
⑥

Shoals

Big Lazer Creek

Woodland

5. Big Lazer Creek Access

This canoe and kayak put-in is located in the Big Lazer Creek WMA. The site offers a magnificent view of the Flint just below Hightower Shoals. On west bank, near mouth of Big Lazer Creek. A green sign with white letters marks the location of the creek.

Potato Creek

Hickman Island

Noel Island

Adams Island

Big Lazer Creek Public Fishing

A 195-acre public fishing lake in the WMA. Georgia Department of Natural Resources rangers stock the lake with largemouth bass, bream, bluegill, Redear sunfish, channel catfish and crappie.

Woodland

About 9 miles west of the river via GA 36

6. Big Lazer Creek Hil

A narrow path follows th from its confluence with to about 1 mile upstream

GA 36

River miles above mouth: 258.5
Counties: Talbot and Upson

Benjamin Hawkins Country

Auchumpkee Creek

Benjamin Hawkins

George Washington appointed Hawkins to oversee all Indian affairs south of the Ohio River. Hawkins spent his career trying to find a balance between opposing forces—Indians on one hand and land-hungry settlers and politicians on the other. Hawkins focused on teaching the Indians to use modern tools. He tried to convince them to shift from their lifestyle of commercial hunting to farming, which required less land.

1. Outcropping of Ice Age Pebbles

An outcropping of smooth pebbles, indicating that the river flowed over a different course in another geological era. The smooth pebbles in the riverbank were once on the surface. Today, they are buried under eight feet of soil that was deposited as a result of massive long-term erosion.

Auchumpkee Covered Bridge

After being swept away in the flood of 1994, this covered bridge was restored by local citizens.

2. Trillium Point

This point overlooks a beautiful set of shoals and is home to the relict trillium plant, an endangered plant. Relict trillium has lost most of its habitat due to clear-cutting of land for agriculture and pine plantations. It's found on the Coastal Plain among boulders or ledges with soft limestone and in the Piedmont in ravines and terraces with deep loamy soil.

● Indian Town of Chumcau

Shoal Bass

The native shoal bass inhabits the shallow shoals of Georgia, Alabama and the Florida Panhandle rivers. This relatively small member of the bass family is a favorite of fishermen. It's such an aggressive fighter, that some compare it to a largemouth bass of the same weight. Catches average around 2 pounds and a 4-to-5 pound shoalie is considered a whopper. The world record is an 8-pound, 12-ounce fish caught in the Apalachicola River by Carl W. Davis in 1995. The red pigment in the shoal bass eye causes some to confuse it with the redeye and Suwanee bass at first glance. But the shoal bass has recently been awarded its own species designation, *Micropterus cataractae* (the Latin word for shoal or shallow) to distinguish it from the redeye, *Micropterus coosae*. The shoal bass is generally olive green to nearly black along the back. Three diagonal black lines radiate along the side of the head. Ten to fifteen vertical blotches appear along the sides, with tiger stripes often appearing in between. The dorsal caudal and anal fins are dark olive green to grayish black.

Shoal Bass

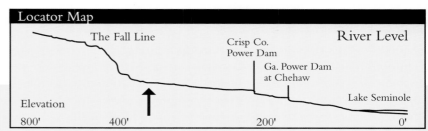

Locator Map

The Fall Line

Crisp Co. Power Dam

River Level

Ga. Power Dam at Chehaw

Lake Seminole

Elevation

800'   400'   200'   0'

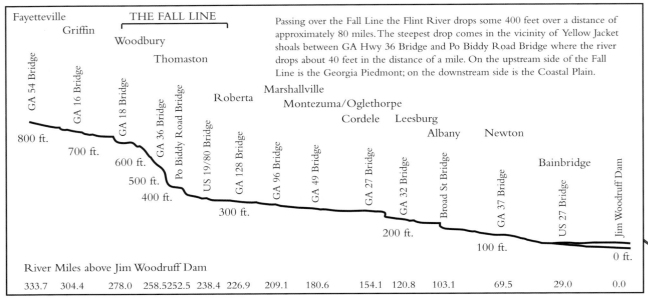

Passing over the Fall Line the Flint River drops some 400 feet over a distance of approximately 80 miles. The steepest drop comes in the vicinity of Yellow Jacket shoals between GA Hwy 36 Bridge and Po Biddy Road Bridge where the river drops about 40 feet in the distance of a mile. On the upstream side of the Fall Line is the Georgia Piedmont; on the downstream side is the Coastal Plain.

THE FALL LINE

Fayetteville
Griffin
Woodbury
Thomaston
Roberta
Marshallville
Montezuma/Oglethorpe
Cordele   Leesburg
Albany   Newton
Bainbridge

GA 54 Bridge
GA 16 Bridge
GA 18 Bridge
GA 36 Bridge
Po Biddy Road Bridge
US 19/80 Bridge
GA 128 Bridge
GA 96 Bridge
GA 49 Bridge
GA 27 Bridge
GA 32 Bridge
Broad St Bridge
GA 37 Bridge
US 27 Bridge
Jim Woodruff Dam

800 ft.
700 ft.
600 ft.
500 ft.
400 ft.
300 ft.
200 ft.
100 ft.
0 ft.

River Miles above Jim Woodruff Dam

| 333.7 | 304.4 | 278.0 | 258.5 | 252.5 | 238.4 | 226.9 | 209.1 | 180.6 | 154.1 | 120.8 | 103.1 | 69.5 | 29.0 | 0.0 |

River Profile

9. Indian Fishing Weir

Native Americans used hundreds of rocks to build a V-shaped dam with the point of the V heading downstream. They made each leg of the V about 50 feet long. They left an opening at the point so fish could pass out into a corral. This weir has suffered some damage but its outline is still clear, particularly in aerial photographs.

11. US 19/80 Boat Ramp

Steep, partially washed out concrete ramp with big drop off on west bank, just below the bridge

10. US 19/80 Bridge

Archaeological excavation here prior to the construction of the new bridge in 2000 uncovered the remains of an Indian homestead dating to the late 1700s.

12. Indian town of Salenojuh

The town was built in compact fashion with the structures close together. A town square was used for political and religious gatherings and a hot house was used much like a sauna. Seventy males old enough to be warriors or "gunmen" lived here, according to Indian Agent Benjamin Hawkins.

Swift Creek

Shoals

Fisherman at Big Lazer Creek

Locator Map

River Level

The Fall Line

Crisp Co. Power Dam

Ga. Power Dam at Chehaw

Lake Seminole

Elevation

| 800' | 400' | 200' | 0' |

US 19/80
River miles above mouth: 238.4
Counties: Taylor and Upson

See the Guidebook sections for additional information and directions to locations listed on this page.

Spider Lily

On the endangered species list in Georgia, the spider lily grows in colonies on the shoals of streams. It is found at just 11 locations in Georgia. Outside of Georgia it grows only in Alabama and Tennessee. Look for it at Yellow Jacket Shoals.

Spider Lily

Shoals

7. Po Biddy Road Bridge

Built in 1965, this bridge is officially named the Chris Callier Bridge, but locals know it as Po Biddy, after the road, which leads from Thomaston to the community of Po Biddy Crossroads in Talbot County.

⑦ ⑧

Po Biddy Road

Snipes Shoals

Shoals

Richland Creek

ing Trail

stream

he river

8. Po Biddy Road Boat Ramp

On east bank, just below bridge. Good for canoes and kayaks and for small jon boats that can handle shoals below. Past Po Biddy, the river slowly completes its transformation from a quick-flowing Piedmont river to a slower paced Coastal Plain river.

Talbotton

About 20 miles west of the river via US 80

Talbotton

Po Biddy Road

River miles above mouth: 252.5
Counties: Talbot and Upson

Locator Map

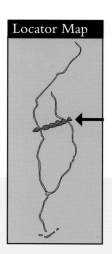

Roberta

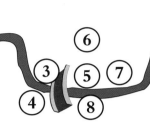

Roberta

About 6 miles east of the river via GA 128

3. Col. Benjamin Hawkins Bridge

Built in 1955, the bridge was named after the most important white man in the Creek Nation from 1796 until his death in 1816.

6. Federal Road

In 1805 Thomas Jefferson ordered a road built to connect Washington and New Orleans. It followed ancient Indian trading paths along Georgia's Fall Line, crossing the Flint just south of the present GA 128 Bridge. It served as the main route for traders, soldiers and pioneers who explored and settled this part of the United States.

GA 128 Bridge
(The Hawkins Bridge)

5. Creek Indian Agency

The Creek Indian Agency was the vehicle by which Hawkins hoped to obtain his goal of assimilating the Creeks into the white man's culture. The compound contained some 25 structures. Gardens, a peach orchard, strawberry patches, vineyards, a cornfield and a bear pen were outside the walls.

8. GA 128 Canoe Access

On west bank, just below the bridge

4. Fort Lawrence

The U.S. Government built Fort Lawrence in 1812 to defend against the British and their Indian allies in the War of 1812. At one time as many as 600 soldiers were garrisoned at the fort, located just across the river from Hawkins's Creek Indian Agency.

The Fall Line Meets the Great Divide

The area between Musella and Roberta in Crawford County is one of the most remarkable physiographic areas of the state. It is where the Fall Line, which runs mostly east and west across the state, intersects with US 341, which runs along the Eastern Continental Divide that runs north and South between the Ocmulgee and Flint watersheds. Water falling east of the ridge flows into the Ocmulgee and eventually into the Atlantic. Water falling west of the ridge flows into the Flint and then to the Gulf. Thus, a farmer in this area could have part of his farm in the Piedmont and part in the Coastal Plain. He could also have land that drained into the Gulf of Mexico and into the Atlantic.

9. Neis

About
ference
Indian
It is asse
Mississi
Indian
occupie

7. Ha

Hawki
overlo
once t
Indian

Neisler Mound

(continued from page 100)

restored and will one day be relocated to the northwest bank of the river between Oglethorpe and Montezuma.

More Information: *Macon County Chamber of Commerce, 316 South Dooly Street, Montezuma, GA 31063. 229/472-2391.*

PARKS

Whitewater Creek Park

This 482-acre park, which was once a state park, is now operated by Macon County. It lies 1.3 miles west of where Whitewater Creek empties into the Flint River. A dam on the creek forms the 175-acre lake, which is the focal point of the park.

Facilities: *Campground (see page 104); lake with beach area; screened pavilion with large fireplace, showers and restrooms; picnic shelter; playground and fishing.* **Days/Hours**: *Open daily, 7 a.m. to 10 p.m. Park Office – 8 a.m. to 5 p.m.* **Fees**: *For camping rates see page 104.* **Directions**: *Macon County. From Oglethorpe, take GA 128 north about 3.5 miles and follow the signs. Park is on the left.* **More Information**: *Whitewater Creek Park, GA 128 North, Oglethorpe, GA 31068. 229/472-8171.*

WILDLIFE MANAGEMENT AREAS

The Flint River Wildlife Management Area

These 2,300 acres of low, sandy uplands lie adjacent to the Flint River in Dooly County, just a couple of miles past its confluence with Hogcrawl Creek. Because access is mostly limited to four-wheel drive vehicles that can handle the wet terrain and steep ditches built by a former landowner to drain excess water, this public hunting area isn't really suitable for hiking or river access. The WMA is relatively small and best suited for foot travel when hunting as roads are narrow and boggy. Several roads were heavily damaged during the 1994 flood when nearly two thirds of the WMA was covered with water.

The habitats here are mostly pine and pine-hardwoods with scattered pockets of pure hardwoods found in old oxbows, bays and wet bottomlands near the river. Managed by the Georgia Department of Natural Resources, the WMA holds a good population of white-tailed deer (see sidebar this page) and a fair number of turkeys, rabbit and quail, with squirrels concentrated in the hardwood areas. In 1993, Dooly County became the first county in any state in the nation to request and receive a government regulation mandating that all young antlered white-tailed bucks be protected from hunters. This has allowed young bucks to get progressively older and therefore heavier with larger antlers. It has resulted in a 300 percent increase of mature bucks available to the hunting public. For general WMA regulations, license requirements and hunting seasons, hunters should obtain a current copy of the "Georgia Hunting Seasons & Regulations" booklet, available at local outdoors stores and the Georgia DNR.

White-tailed Deer

Few animals are hunted like the white-tailed deer. With an estimated population of 20 to 25 million in North America, white-tailed deer, also known as Virginia deer, are the most popular game in the United States. An estimated 11 million hunters track these animals each fall, many of them in the old fields and pine forests of south Georgia.

The size of the white-tailed deer's home range is dependent on a number of factors, including weather, food and human activity. They can be found in pine forests, which provide them food, shelter and soft bedding. White-tailed deer eat grass, leaves, bark, twigs, the tender sprouts of trees and other plants, moss, lichens, mushrooms and other types of fungi. The deer dig into the pine bedding for warmth, and fawns hide in thick bedding for protection from predators.

Whitetails are active at night, preferring to feed and mate in darkness. They remain active at dawn before bedding down at midday. Studies suggest that they rarely bed in the same spot twice, nor do they sleep for long periods of time in order to stay alert for predators. White-tailed deer are social animals found in herds, but the sexes largely stay separated. They communicate with grunting vocalizations and scents, primarily used during mating.

A white-tailed deer has a reddish-brown coat in summer, and a gray or bluish-gray coat in winter. It stands four to six feet tall. The tail, for which it is named, is seven to 11 inches long with brown hair on top and white underneath. If you come across a white-tailed deer in the forest, stand very still—deer have a hard time pinpointing a stationary object. Move a muscle, however, and the deer will be off into the woods—with tail straight up, the white side showing.

Facilities: 2 dove fields; no camping. **Days/Hours**: *Open daily, 24 hours. All visitors must check in at the check station.* **Directions**: *Dooly County. From Vienna, take GA 27 west 10 miles to GA 230. Turn right and go about 1 mile to the "Y" in the road. Take the road to the left, which is River Road. Go about 6 miles to Pleasant Hill Church. Turn left and follow the signs.* **More Information**: *Georgia Department of Natural Resources, Wildlife Resources Division, 2024 Newton Road, Albany, GA 31701. 229/430-4254.*

CAMPGROUNDS

Whitewater Creek Campground

This campground lies alongside Whitewater Pond, a 175-acre lake formed by a dam on Whitewater Creek, a tributary of the Flint just north of Oglethorpe.

Facilities: *16 RV sites with full hookups, including water, electricity and sewage; 56 regular hookups, including water and electricity; tent site. For other park facilities see page 103.* **Days/Hours**: *Open daily, 7 a.m. to 10 p.m. Park Office – 8 a.m. to 5 p.m.* **Fees**: *Full hookups, $12.50 per night; regular hookups, $10 per night; and tent sites, $7.50 per night.* **Directions**: *Macon County. From Oglethorpe, take GA 128 north about 3.5 miles and follow the signs. Park is on the left.* **More Information**: *Whitewater Creek Park, GA 128 North, Oglethorpe, GA 31068. 229/472-8171.*

BRIDGES

US 19/80 Bridge

Only vestiges of the Fall Line remain where this bridge crosses the Flint. The rugged, steep slopes are receding and a few rocky shoals protrude from the river channel. Before work began on the new bridge being constructed here, an archaeological excavation uncovered the remains of an Indian homestead dating to the late 1700s (see page 95). River access from boat ramp on west bank just below the bridge (see page map 101). **Location**: *On Taylor and Upson County line where US 19 and US 80 meet to cross the Flint south of Thomaston.*

Col. Benjamin Hawkins Bridge (GA 128)

This bridge spans the river at a location that has much historical and physical significance. Built in 1955, the bridge is commonly referred to as the Col. Benjamin Hawkins Bridge. Hawkins (see page 94) is buried here at the site of his Creek Indian Agency on the river's east bank just below the bridge. On the rocky ford just below this bridge was the very important Lower Creek Trading Path (see pages 22 and 96), which became a military road called the Federal Road (see page 23). In the 1830s, pioneers crossed the river here on a raft, on which the stagecoach and horses were drawn across by a rope. On the river's west bank stood Fort Lawrence (see page 96). Once the

De Soto's Second Crossing of the Flint

About 15 days after Hernando de Soto and his entourage crossed to the west side of the Flint near present-day Newton, it is believed they reached a shallow ford a few miles below today's GA 127 Bridge (see map page 135) and crossed back to the east again.

"By nightfall of the following day, they came to the River of Toa—again the Flint River. They spent the next three days traveling along a trail paralleling the western bank of this river. The trail probably skirted the edge of the floodplain forest that lay along the course of the river. Hence, as they traveled along, they would have had open longleaf pine-wiregrass forest on their left side, and dense floodplain forest on their right. There would have been few animals to be seen on their left, except perhaps occasional flocks of turkeys. Being a large and noisy army, they probably saw few to their right, either, but from this direction they were surely seen by floodplain forest fauna: deer, bear, panthers, cottontails, raccoons, squirrels, and by many kinds of birds.

"On March 21 they arrived at a place where they could cross to the eastern side of the Flint River. The most likely location is at an old fording place approximately five miles south of where Georgia State Road 127 crosses the river. . . .

"To span the Flint River, the Spaniards built a footbridge of pine poles lashed together. But the current in the river proved to be very strong, and two of their attempts at building a bridge were washed away. Finally, at the suggestion of Nuno do Tovar, they used crisscrossed timbers, and with this third attempt, the bridge held. By nightfall on March 22, they all got across to the eastern side of the river, and they camped in a pine woods."

Knights of Spain, Warriors of the Sun by Charles Hudson

Flint passes under this bridge, it departs the Piedmont and enters the Coastal Plain's wider, flatter terrain. River access is from a washed-out boat ramp on the southwest side of the bridge (see page 102). **Location**: *On the Crawford and Taylor County line where GA 128/137 crosses the Flint between Butler and Roberta.*

GA 96 Bridge

Built in 1993, this bridge crosses over a portion of the Flint that is surrounded by swamp—the Magnolia Swamp to the north of the bridge and the Beechwood Swamp to the south. Together they are known as the Great Swamp (see page 89). River access is from a concrete boat ramp on the southeast side of the bridge (see map page 135). **Location**: *On Taylor and Crawford County line where GA 96 crosses the Flint River between Reynolds and Fort Valley.*

GA 127 Bridge

This bridge, built in 1988, is named for Lewis H. "Bud" McKenzie, a former Georgia State Senator from the area. The bridge sits about a quarter of a mile below the site of the last river ferry crossing to operate in Georgia. There is no river access from the bridge but the old Flint River Ferry ramp is nearby (see map page 135). **Location**: *In Macon County where GA 127 crosses the Flint River near Marshallville.*

GA 49 Bridge

At least three other bridges have preceded the current structure, which was built in 1955 to link Oglethorpe and Montezuma: a one-lane 1889 bridge with wooden "turn outs" so buggies and other vehicles could pass—the clopping of horses and rattling boards could be heard in Montezuma on quiet nights; a steel and concrete bridge built in 1902 that would be underwater when the river was high; and in 1916 another steel and concrete bridge. In 1916 the floodplain between the two towns was filled in so that floodwaters wouldn't disrupt bridge traffic. An unofficial river gauge on the bridge's center pilings indicates the five-foot mark. River access from the George Hooks Boat Ramp is on the southwest side (see map page 136). **Location**: *In Macon County where GA 49 crosses the Flint River between Oglethorpe and Montezuma.*

GA 26 Bridge

Just a quarter mile below the GA 49 Bridge, this bridge was built in 1982 mainly so that logging trucks could detour around Montezuma's downtown. On the southwest bank is the area where Indian trader Timothy Barnard once had his trading post, Traveler Rest. **Location**: *In Macon County where GA 26 crosses the Flint River between Oglethorpe and Montezuma.*

Macon County

The Flint River runs right through the middle of Macon County and right between its two largest towns, Oglethorpe and Montezuma.

"Macon County is named in honor of General Nathaniel Macon, a North Carolina statesman and president pro tempore of the U.S. Senate. Macon County was carved from Houston and Marion counties in 1837. The county seat, Oglethorpe, takes its name from Georgia's founder. Other municipalities include Ideal, Marshallville, and Montezuma. Montezuma was named for the Aztec leader by soldiers returning from the Mexican War. Andersonville National Cemetery and Park is in the southwest tip of Macon County. Approximately 45,000 Union soldiers were imprisoned here during the Civil War, with 13,000 perishing from hunger and disease. Sam Henry Rumph of Macon County developed the Elberta Peach, the variety responsible for establishing Georgia as the peach state."

From *Georgia County Snapshots*, Georgia Department of Community Affairs

For tourism information for towns in Macon County, see Resources page 300.

Section 4

Lake Blackshear

W E LEARN THAT RIO has a weakness for high-priced river fashion. We put our flat-bottomed boat into the Flint at Turkey Creek Campground and motor *upstream* to explore the Great Swamp above and below Montezuma.

On and around Lake Blackshear, use the Guidebook Section beginning on page 112 to explore: Georgia Veterans Memorial State Park; the historic sites of Hugenin Ferry, Cork Ferry and Fort Early; the Georgia Cotton Museum; the Telephone Museum; Loren Williams Park; Rocky Point Park; Killebrew Park; Turkey Creek Campground; Lakeshore Marine Marina and Campground; Sonny's Campers Haven; Spring Creek Marina; the Crisp County Power Dam; the Cordele Fish Hatchery; and the Yucca Trace Trail.

SONNY'S AND TURKEY CREEK ARE DOWN-HOME CAMPGROUNDS FAVORED BY LOCAL RESIDENTS.

VETERANS STATE PARK, TURKEY CREEK OR SONNY'S ARE GOOD PLACES TO BEGIN AN EXPLORATION OF THE RIVER **UPSTREAM** FROM LAKE BLACKSHEAR.

I HOPE THAT BOOK OF YOURS...

YOU DON'T MIND IF WE CALL IT **"OUR" BOOK**, DO YOU?

AS I WAS SAYING, I HOPE THIS BOOK OF **OURS** WILL CONVINCE

ENVIRONMENTALISTS

TEACHERS

CHAMBERS OF COMMERCE

BIRD WATCHERS

FARMERS

PHOTOGRAPHERS

HIKERS

CANOEISTS

SEA KAYAKERS

MOTOR BOATERS

ARCHAEOLOGISTS

HISTORIANS

BICYCLE RIDERS

SWAMP EXPLORERS

ROCK CLIMBERS

LOCAL FISHERMEN AND HUNTERS

AND SUNDAY DRIVERS

THAT WE ALL HAVE A LOT IN COMMON WHEN IT COMES TO **ENJOYING AND PROTECTING** A RIVER. .

A Historic Creek Indian Town

Potato Creek

US 19/80 Bridge

1. Indian Fishing Weir
2. Indian Homestead—Dating from the late 1700s
3. Town of Salenojuh
4. Town of Chumcau
5. Town of Oleco
6. Creek Indian Agency—Established by Benjamin Hawkins in 1796
7. Neisler Indian Mound
8. Hartley-Posey Indian Mound
9. Town of Patsiliga

Po Biddy Road Bridge

Flint River

Prehistoric and historic Indian sites are located along the Flint River between Potato Creek in Upson County and Patsiliga Creek in Macon County, a distance of about 45 river miles.

North

Warriors, the color red

The layout of the square ground had religious, social and cultural meaning.

We

Sunset, death, the color

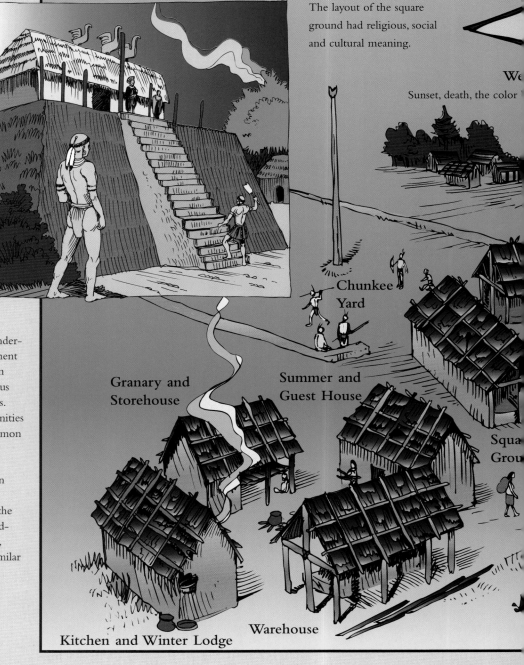

Chunkee Yard

Granary and Storehouse

Summer and Guest House

Squa
Grou

Warehouse

Kitchen and Winter Lodge

During the Mississippian period of Indian history (A.D. 900 to European contact in the mid-1500s), mound building, which had begun 1,500 years earlier during the Woodland period as a means of burial, took on more ceremonial and symbolic meanings.

Mississippian Mound sites were abandoned between 1300 and 1500 for reasons that have never been entirely under-stood. One theory is that the abandonment was due to the rapid spread of European diseases, such as smallpox, after Columbus and other explorers visited the Americas. The Mississippian people had no immunities to the explorers' diseases. Even the common cold was a killer. The spread of these diseases, as well as violent encounters, hastened the decline of the Mississippian culture.

The Creek Nation is believed to be the southeastern descendant of these mound-builders. After the Mississippian period, Creeks congregated in smaller towns similar to the one illustrated here.

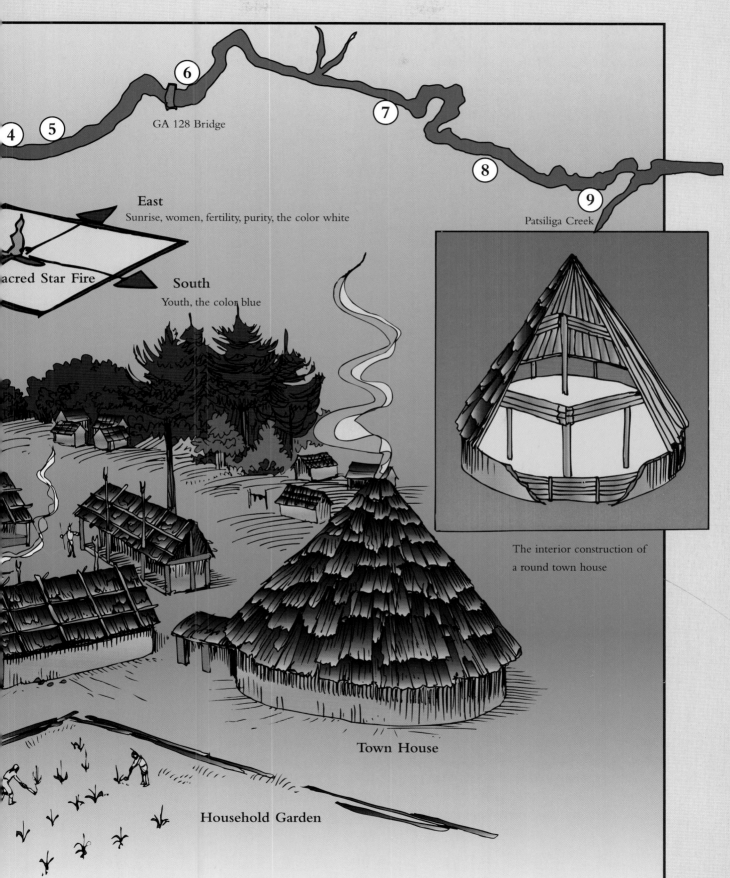

6

GA 128 Bridge

4 **5**

7

8

9

Patsiliga Creek

East
Sunrise, women, fertility, purity, the color white

Sacred Star Fire

South
Youth, the color blue

The interior construction of
a round town house

Town House

Household Garden

A Historic Creek Indian Town Flint River, late 1700s

THE MUSCOGULGES, or Muscogees, were a large group of Southeastern Indians sharing a common language. When Spanish, French and English explorers and traders came to this region, they found these Indian people living on creeks and rivers. The English referred to the Indians as "Creeks" and the name stuck.

Rivers provided the Creeks a plentiful source of food in the form of fish and mussels. River cane, which grew in the river corridor, was used for making arrows, spears and knives. With strips of river cane, Indian women wove watertight baskets and decorative mats used for flooring and wall coverings.

Rivers were trade and transportation corridors for the Creeks. Documented accounts report that Indians paddled dugout canoes down the Flint and Apalachicola Rivers, then continued down the west coast of Florida all the way to Cuba, and then returned.

Besides locating their towns on high ground alongside rivers, Creeks planted communal gardens in the floodplains, extending as far as three miles along the riverbank. Often these were located on the opposite bank from the town. Rich alluvial soil, washing down from the Piedmont, enriched the floodplain farmland. Here, the Indians grew corn, squash and beans.

By the time the first Europeans arrived in the Southeast, the Indian culture of the moundbuilding Mississippian culture was already in decline and the Indians of the region were living in smaller towns and villages. These Creek towns were cultural, religious and social centers, where about 200 to 300 people might live. A chief, known as a Mico, headed each town. While the most prominent individuals lived in the town, a family might "belong" to a town but live three miles downriver in their own little house.

When American naturalist and explorer William Bartram traveled through the Southeast in 1775, he described towns like the one on the preceding pages. Similar descriptions were recorded by other explorers and by Indian Agent Benjamin Hawkins, who served as Indian Agent in the region from 1796 to 1816.

The Town House or Chakofa

The town house or "chakofa" was the winter council house. It was the place where villagers gathered for ceremonies, dancing and socializing. It also provided shelter for the aged and homeless.

The shape of the town house might be round, square or rectangular. On the preceding page is a sketch of a round town house. A round town house had a diameter of 30 to 60 feet and was about 25 to 30 feet high. In large structures, there were tiers of raised platforms around the wall that could seat 500 people.

To build the town house, the Creeks dug a circular foundation about three feet deep and placed vertical

NATIVE AMERICAN TIMELINE

10,000 B.C.	8000 B.C.	1000 B.C.	A.D. 900	European Contact
Paleo Period	Archaic Period	Woodlands Period	Mississippian Period	Historic Period

Paleo Period (10,000 B.C. to 8000 B.C.)
The first humans in the Flint River Valley were hunter-gatherers who hunted giant mammoths, mastodons and ground sloth. Remains of these animals, as well as spear points used by the Indians, have been found in the river corridor.

Archaic Period (8000 B.C. to 1000 B.C.)
Flint River corridor Indians hunted smaller animals, such as deer. They relied more on gathering berries, nuts and roots. Many flaked arrowheads from this period have been found in the river corridor.

Woodlands Period (1000 B.C. to A.D. 900)
Indians began to use ceramic pottery to cook, serve and store food. They invented the bow and arrow and took an interest in death rituals. Their burial mounds dot river banks from the Fall Line to the Florida coast.

Mississippian Period (A.D. 900 to European Contact in the Mid-1500s)
Extensive maize cultivation along river floodplains gave the Indians an opportunity to develop a more settled existence. Two to three thousand Indians inhabited the large towns. Mound building became more than just a burial ceremony and took on greater religious and symbolic meanings.

The Historic Period (European Contact to Removal)
The Creek Indians abandoned the mound sites of the prehistoric Woodland and Mississippian periods and settled in smaller towns along creeks and rivers. European contact increased, soon followed by American pioneers settling the land. After a series of wars with the United States, most of the Creek Indians were removed to Oklahoma in 1836. Others fled to Florida to join the Seminoles for one last stand.

posts in the ground. They wove river cane in and out between the posts and applied clay mixed with grasses or Spanish moss to the woven surface, covering it completely. Sometimes, they applied whitewash made of crushed oyster shell and then painted religious symbols on the white surface.

Eight log columns on the inside of the circle supported a sloping log crib, which in turn held up the roof poles. Workers added a roof of cypress, elm or tulip popular bark.

Some town houses had no holes to let the smoke escape. European visitors often recorded in their journals how smoky the town houses were and even referred to them as "smoke houses."

Square Ground

The town house opened on to one corner of a quadrangle known as the square ground. This was the summer or "good weather" location of the sacred fire and the traditional center of a town's political and religious activities.

Four shelters, called clan beds, were situated around a square plaza. The number four was an important symbolic number for the Creeks, and the four sides of the square ground had specific meaning. The clan bed on the east side of the square, where the sun rose, was for women and symbolized fertility, birth, purity and the color white. The north clan bed was for warriors and symbolized the color red, which was associated with war. The west clan bed, where the sun set, was reserved for town elders and symbolized death and the color black. The south clan bed was for the youthful members of the town and the color associated with it was blue. A man's seating assignment reflected his change in age and role from infant to boy to warrior to old man. It suggested the male passage from the world of his mother to the world of men, and, finally, as an elder and the return to the female domain.

The clan beds varied in size but were often about 10 feet by 20 feet. The back wall of the clan beds was constructed in a manner similar to the town house. A space between the wall and the roof allowed air to circulate under the shelter. Inside the shelter were a series of elevated benches where participants sat.

The Chunkee Yard

The chunkee yard was a ball court about 600 to 900 feet long. Spectators sat on an earthen ridge around the edge. Chunkee players rolled a six-inch

diameter stone across the yard. Competitors threw spears at the spot where they expected the chunkee stone to stop rolling. The closest to the spot won.

Creeks also played a form of stickball using two sticks with hand-sized nets at one end. A ball was carried or tossed using the sticks. The pole in the center of the ground was the target for a stickball game. An object fastened to the top of the pole served as a target for archery or spear-throwing practice. The two poles at the end of the field were usually decorated with scalps, skulls or other trophies of war.

Family Housing

The well-to-do in a town set up family housing similar to that of the square ground. The family compound consisted of a summer and guest house, a kitchen and winter lodge, a warehouse for hides and furs and a two-story storehouse for crops and grains. Male members of the family controlled the guest quarters, while women held sway over the domestic space. On the upper floor of the storehouse was a council house and open loft reserved for the senior member of the family. A family compound may have also included granaries, corncribs and animal pens.

Each family had a household garden for its own use, in addition to the town garden, which was located in the creek or river floodplain. All adults helped tend the common garden, which restocked town granaries supervised by town officials.

LAKE BLACKSHEAR ARCHAEOLOGY

When Lake Blackshear was built in the 1930s, tree stumps were left in the lake. Later, as outboard motors became popular, the stumps became hazardous for boaters. In the early 1970s, the lake was lowered 11 feet so the most dangerous stumps could be removed. During this process, the state invited archaeologists to survey the lake for sites of interest. The archaeologists found 212 Indian sites in the lake area, uncovering everything from campsites to small villages. They concluded that the lake must have been a major population center, dating back some 800 years.

Archaeologists collected stone tools and broken pieces of pottery. In one burial site they discovered a large, elaborate shell bead necklace, a headdress made of deer antler, a turtle shell rattle and huge pits of mussels shell—the remains of thousands of Indian meals. The survey showed that over the years the lake's currents had destroyed all but the most durable artifacts, but even so, the inventory from the survey was measured in wheelbarrow loads rather than individual pieces.

Section 4

Lake Blackshear

NATURE-BASED EDUCATIONAL CENTERS

Georgia Veterans Memorial State Park

Interpreting the natural environments found in the park is the focus of the nature classes given at Georgia Veterans Memorial State Park. Two nature trails—the Yucca Trace Trail, which interprets the sand hill environment associated with the area, and the Lake Shore Trail, which interprets the wetland environment—form the basis of the nature programs. Park staff conduct guided tours of both trails; each lasts about 45 minutes. The Yucca Trace Trail has 14 different stations where hikers can see specific trees and plants and are likely to see various area wildlife. This trail is also open to self-guided tours (see page 122), and the staff has printed information for those hikers who prefer to experience the trail on their own. The Lake Shore Trail tour explores wetlands around the park. Park staff take visitors in a hay wagon to three different areas: the swamps, the marshes and the wetlands. Along the way, visitors get out for a close-up view of the different environments. Through these types of hands-on activities, students learn the characteristics of the environments and how they are important to wildlife and humans. Twilight nature hikes, nature trail tours and nature discovery hunts are just a few of the programs offered on weekends and during the summer.

Besides nature studies, the park, which is dedicated to the men and women who have fought for this country, offers programs that interpret lessons of U.S. history. This is done through tours of the two park museums. The park's indoor museum covers the Revolutionary War through the Gulf War, and the outdoor museum features aircraft, armored vehicles and guns from World War I through Vietnam. Audio-visual and classroom programs are also available. Groups should make reservations at least two weeks prior to a visit.

Facilities: *Georgia Veterans Memorial State Park (see page 116).* **Days/Hours**: *Open daily, year-round. Park — 7 a.m. to 10 p.m. Visitor Center — 8 a.m. to 5 p.m.* **Fees**: *Parking, $2; school vehicles free. Program rates vary.* **Directions**: *Crisp County. From Cordele, take US 280 west about 9 miles to GA 230. Park entrance is on the left.* **More Information**: *Georgia Veterans Memorial State Park, 2459-A US Hwy 280 West, Cordele, GA 31015. 229/276-2371. Website: www.gastateparks.org.*

The Yucca Plant

The Yucca is a somewhat woody-stemmed, evergreen plant with alternate, crowded, swordlike or dagger-like leaves. The showy white or creamy-white flowers are sometimes tinted purple or green and have a six-parted, bell-shaped perianth and six stamens. They are pollinated by a small moth, the larvae of which feed upon the seeds. The fruits are elliptical, more or less six-sided capsules containing a number of seeds. The Native Americans used the leaves to make mats, rope, sandals and baskets and ate the fruit and flowers.

Spanish bayonet *(Yucca aloifolia* L.) is a type of yucca, a group in the agave (ah-gah-vay) family. Spanish bayonet is a yucca plant with a stem to about 15 feet high, commonly covered with downward-pointing old leaves, and with a dense cluster of spreading ones at the ends of branches. It ranges throughout the Coastal Plain and from North Carolina south to Florida, growing in sandy woods and among coastal sand dunes. You can see Spanish bayonet as you walk the Yucca Trail at Georgia Veterans Memorial State Park (see page 122).

HISTORIC SITES

Hugenin Ferry

The Hugenin Ferry was one of two different ferries known to have operated across the Flint in the Lake Blackshear area. The Hugenin Ferry probably came into existence between 1828 and 1845 and ended operation around 1937 when the US 280 Bridge was built over the Flint, seven years after the dam was constructed. It was known by several different names, Hugenin being the first, and the Cox Ferry being the last, after a family who owned the ferry until its final run.

The ferry was located just south of where Gum Creek enters the Flint. During the 19th century, there were numerous settlers around here, as well as a post office known as Gum Creek.

The ferry was guided by a cable stretched across the river and anchored in concrete in the ground on each bank. The boat's cable and pulley system was designed to work much the same as a sail. A pulley could be let out at either end of the vessel so that one end of the boat could swing out to allow the water current to help push it across the river. Whichever direction the boat was headed, the rear of it was allowed to swing out to help propel it forward.

The road that led to the ferry went westward from the Cordele area to Americus. Known as the Columbus–St. Mary's Road, it followed, in part, what is today's US 280 and was possibly the first road built through this area. Today, the road is known in Crisp County as Ferry Landing Road, although the section of road that actually led to the ferry is now completely inundated with Lake Blackshear.

On a map of Lake Blackshear, you can see how the road goes to the lake and then picks up on the other side. After the 1994 flood broke the Crisp County Dam (see page 123), the river pretty much returned to its channel and employees of the Crisp County Power Commission located the old ferry road bed and documented their findings in a booklet, *Hugenin, Yesteryear's Ferry on the Flint*. The book is loaded with historical photos, as well as photos taken during the survey.

Cork Ferry

The Cork Ferry crossed the Flint south of Hugenin Ferry, between Cedar and Swift Creeks near the northern portion of Land Lot 33 in the 15th Land District. Although much is unknown about this ferry, it is believed to have been the first ferry to operate in Crisp County and to have ended operation by 1916. There were no families by the name of Cork recorded as property owners at the time, so the ferry possibly got its name from the cork trees that have been found planted in the general area.

A cable guided the wooden ferry across the river. The ferry was powered manually, probably by using a wooden tool with a groove

Canada Goose

Of the 13 kinds of wild geese that live in the United States and Canada, the Canada goose is the best-known. Its nesting ground extends from arctic Canada to the prairie states of the United States. The Canada goose has grayish plumage, a black neck and head and a broad white band across its throat and cheeks. It ranges in length from 25 to 45 inches.

Geese are migratory birds, flying north in the summer and south in the winter. By the late 1970s, the geese had gradually stopped flying as far south as Georgia, so the Department of Natural Resources decided to release Canada geese in the state for two reasons: to merely reintroduce a bird that had disappeared in the state and to provide a valued migratory species for hunting. From 1978 to 1982, the DNR released 500 Canada geese in northeast Georgia. Today, thousands of the birds range all along the length of the Flint and other Georgia rivers. You'll see hundreds of them as you travel around and on Lake Blackshear.

which clutched the cable. When the ferryman pulled the tool, it propelled the boat forward, aided by the river's current. More than likely, the ferry carried one vehicle at a time.

The access roads to the ferry are under water at Lake Blackshear, but one part of the road that led to the ferry ran along a ridge that was six feet or more above the river. From there, travelers would have had a nice view of the Flint and the area that is now Lake Blackshear.

Fort Early

Fort Early was a frontier fort that was built in 1812 by General David Blackshear on a bluff overlooking the Flint River about five miles below Cedar Creek. Named for Peter Early, governor of Georgia at that time, Fort Early was constructed to protect settlers in the area during the War of 1812. Nothing remains of the fort, but it is believed to have been a stockade like many others that were used in Indian warfare. General Blackshear, a noted Indian fighter who also cut the old Blackshear Trail through the area, headquartered his troops at Fort Early during the War of 1812. On February 13, 1818, General Andrew Jackson and his army arrived at the fort and used it in the campaign against the Seminole Indians of Florida and Creek Indians of Georgia.

A monument to Fort Early, constructed by the Fort Early Chapter of the Daughters of the American Revolution, is located on the banks of the Flint River in the vicinity of where the fort once stood.

Directions: *Crisp County. From Cordele, take GA 300 south about 11.5 miles to Lakeshore Drive. Turn right and go about 1 mile. The monument is on the right just past the intersection with Lakeshore Way.*

MUSEUMS

Georgia Cotton Museum

Historically and culturally cotton has been significant to the growth of the Flint River Valley. Exhibits at this cotton museum in Dooly County outline the history of cotton—explaining how farmers planted, cultivated and harvested the crop; and how slavery was the backbone of the cotton economy.

Days/Hours: *Open Monday through Saturday, 9:15 a.m. to 4 p.m.* **Admission**: *Free; tours, $2 per person.* **Directions**: *Dooly County. From I-75, take Exit 109 and turn west onto GA 215. Go about 0.5 mile. The museum is on the right, directly in front of the hospital.* **More Information**: *Georgia Cotton Museum, 1321 East Union Street, Vienna, GA 31092. 229/268-2045.*

Georgia Rural Telephone Museum

Housed in a 1920s cotton warehouse, this is one of the largest collections of antique telephones and telephone memorabilia in the world. The collection, which dates from 1876 to the present, includes

Dooly County

The Flint River enters Dooly County on its western border.

"Dooly County, the 48th county formed in Georgia, was created in 1821. It was one of the original landlot counties and was later divided to make Crisp and parts of Macon, Pulaski, Turner, Wilcox, and Worth counties. The county was named for Colonel John Dooly, a revolutionary war hero who helped prosecute Tories in 1779 and was murdered by them the following year. Vienna (pronounced vye-enna locally), the county seat, was named after the capital of Austria."

From *Georgia Snapshots*, Georgia Department of Community Affairs

For tourism information for towns in Dooly County, see Resources page 300.

a 1876 liquid transmitter, the first transmitter through which speech was transmitted; an 1882 50-line switch board; an 1880 operator headset; and early pay phones, including the rare silver dollar pay phones. The nearly 2,000 pieces of vintage phone equipment, everything from hand-cranked wooden voice boxes to life-size displays of switchboard operators in period costumes, occupy 18,000 square feet.

Days/Hours: *Monday through Friday, 9 a.m. to 5 p.m. Open Saturday by special arrangement. Tours take about an hour, so visitors should arrive no later than 4 p.m.* **Admission**: *Adults, $5; seniors, $4; students, $2.* **Directions**: *Crisp County. From I-75 in Cordele, take Exit 101 and turn west onto US 280. Go about 20 miles to Leslie. Turn left onto Bailey Avenue (GA 195). The museum is on the left.* **More Information**: *Georgia Rural Telephone Museum, 134 Bailey Avenue, P.O. Box 187, Leslie, GA 31764. 229/874-4786.*

LAKES

Lake Blackshear

In 1930 the Crisp County hydroelectric dam impounded the Flint River, creating this 8,700-acre lake 10 miles west of Cordele. Since then the lake has become a popular Central Georgia recreation area, with lake homes dotting the banks; weekend boaters and skiers churning up the water; fishermen working the creeks and backwater near Spanish moss-draped cypress trees; and campers enjoying the facilities at the 1,322-acre Georgia Veterans Memorial State Park. On the west side of the lake, tree farms and private hunting lands still rule; the University of Georgia operates 4,000 acres for its forestry program here. In 1973, the southern stretch of the lake from the US 280 Bridge was cleared of stumps and undergrowth to provide a better playground for boaters and swimmers. The swampy, northern backwaters—with its islands, cypress trees, stumps and snags—was left behind as a natural habitat for wildlife. Over the last 20 years, traditional fish camps have evolved into convenience stores with dockside gas, from Sonny's Campers Haven on the north side of the lake to Lakeshore Marine on the south.

The Georgia Department of Natural Resources and the Crisp County Power Commission share responsibility for the lake. DNR stocks the lake with largemouth bass, white bass, hybrid bass (a cross between the white bass and the striped bass), sunfish, perch, crappie and catfish. The utility company operates seven boat ramps and parking areas, mostly on the southeast side of the lake. Crisp Power also maintains an herbicide spraying program to control algae growth during the warm months—although sunlight doesn't penetrate the dark waters enough to cause a problem with excessive growth. In 1984, members of local industry, academia and government formed The Lake Blackshear Watershed Association to protect the long-term health of the Flint River, the lake and its tributaries.

Catfish

Catfish is the name of a large group of fish, most of which have two to four pairs of whiskers. These whiskers, called barbels, resemble the whiskers of a cat—thus the name. Many of the more than 2,000 species of catfish also have sharp spines on the back fins and on the fins near the gills. The spines of some kinds of catfish give off a poison when they pierce another animal. Unlike most fish, catfish have no scales over their skin.

The smallest kinds of catfish measure only one to one and a half inches long and weigh about one tenth ounce. The largest species may grow more than 10 feet long and weigh 400 pounds.

Catfish are found in most parts of the world. Some kinds live in freshwater, and others in saltwater. Catfish are mostly nocturnal scavengers, living near the bottom in quiet, shallow waters feeding on tiny animals and bits of animal flesh near the bottom of a pond or slow-moving river. A few species of catfish, including the channel catfish which can be found in the Flint, live in swift streams. The channel catfish with its slender body and a forked tail can be found in the Flint River as well as in Lake Blackshear and Lake Seminole. Many fish hatcheries, such as the Cordele Fish Hatchery (see page 121) and the Warm Springs Regional Fisheries Center (see page 222), raise channel catfish for southwest Georgia waters.

Directions: *Crisp County. From Cordele, take US 280 west approxi-mately 10 miles.* **More Information**: *Crisp County Power Commission, Office of Resource Management, 1611 North 2nd Street, P.O. Box 1218, Cordele, GA 31010. 229/273-3820.*

PARKS

Georgia Veterans Memorial State Park

This 1,322-acre Georgia state park lies on the east bank of Lake Blackshear, practically halfway between the lake's beginnings at the Crisp County Power Dam and its backwaters near the US 27 Bridge. It is one of the most visited state parks in Georgia.

When returning World War II veterans purchased the land for the park in 1945, they intended to build a permanent memorial to U.S. veterans—the blueprints even called for an airplane landing strip and lakeside homes. In keeping with that wish, the park's visitor center houses a small military museum, with indoor exhibits covering events from the Revolutionary War through the Gulf War, while an outdoor exhibit includes tanks, armored vehicles, guns and aircraft, including a B-29 bomber manufactured in Marietta.

Surrounding three sides of the park, the main attraction is the 7,000-acre Lake Blackshear. The park has a sand swimming beach and bath house as well as boat ramps, docks and fishing piers located all around its shoreline. Two nature trails provide numerous chances to see unusual plant life and wildlife. Birding enthusiasts will find dozens of viewing opportunities. Year-round residents at the park include great blue heron (see sidebar this page), Canada goose (see sidebar page 113), bald eagle, red-headed woodpecker, cooper's hawk, barred owl, mourning dove and wild turkey. Residents during breeding season include wood duck (see sidebar page 119), egret (see sidebar page 121) and osprey (see page 257); a detailed bird list is available at the information center.

Annual events include Artifact Identification Day, usually the third Saturday of October, in which archaeologists and trained staff persons examine Indian and war artifacts brought by visitors. Besides special activities for Easter, Memorial Day, Independence Day and Veterans Day, bird dog field trials are held in the spring and fall. Spectators travel in wagons pulled by tractors and follow the field judges to get an up-close view of the dogs' performance. A year-round park specialty is model airplane flying. Flyers should register at the visitor center and show proof of insurance before taking off from the model plane strips located near the outdoor ordnance exhibit.

Facilities: *Cottages and campsites (see page 119); 4 boat ramps, 2 with docks (see map page 169); enclosed and open group and picnic shelters with tables, grills, water and electricity; 18-hole golf course; 15,000-square-foot conference center; visitor center with souvenirs and snacks; picnic areas with tables and grills; sand swimming beach; swimming pool with lifeguards; two*

Great Blue Heron

It stands silent, still—searching the dark waters with telescopic eyes, waiting for an unsuspecting school of fish. Long, pencil-thin legs stand motionless on the shallow banks of the pond. An extended, s-shaped neck strikes swiftly as the fish encroach. With a great scooping motion, it casually flips the fish into the air and ducks underneath to swallow it whole. Satisfied, the great blue heron stretches its long wings and gracefully launches itself into the air.

These enormous yet elegant birds grow to a height of four feet. They live high in the trees, in colonies of 50 to a thousand nests. Sharing trees with other cormorants, ibises and egrets, they nest together for protection. Upon inspection of the herons' nesting trees, one should be aware of a particular defense system the birds use against intruders. The great blue heron has a tendency to regurgitate or defecate their last meal upon unwelcome guests below. The bottom of the tree takes such abuse, that over a course of time the nesting trees eventually lose their bark and die—forcing the great blue heron to move on.

nature trails — The Yucca Trace Trail (see page 122) through a sand hill environment and the Lake Shore Trail through a wetlands area; playground; butterfly garden; fish cleaning area; restrooms and drinking water. **Days/Hours**: *Open daily, year-round. Park — 7 a.m. to 10 p.m. Visitor Center — 8 a.m. to 5 p.m. Swimming pool — Tuesday through Sunday, mid-June through Labor Day; weekends only from Memorial Day weekend until mid-June.* **Fees**: *Swimming pool, $2, free for registered cottage guests. $2 park pass required daily for vehicles under 13 persons. All other facilities subject to user fees. Contact the state park office for the latest information on fees and reservations.* **Directions**: *Crisp County. From Cordele, take US 280 west about 9 miles to GA 230. Park entrance is on the left.* **More Information**: *Georgia Veterans Memorial State Park, 2459-A US Hwy 280 West, Cordele, GA 31015. 229/276-2371 (park), 229/276-2377 (golf course), 800/459-1230 (conference retreat). Website: www.gastateparks.org.*

Loron Williams County Park

This small park, in a Lake Blackshear residential neighborhood, offers the only public swimming area on the lake besides the state park. The flat, sandy lake bottom, the views of the wooded shoreline across the lake and the power dam to the south make this a popular place for swimming or picnicking. Dr. Loron Williams (1889-1964), a well-known Crisp County doctor, donated the land for this park.

Facilities: *Boat ramp (see map page 170), grass beach, sea wall, swimming area, covered shelter with 3 picnic tables and grills, small playground, drinking water, restrooms and changing area.* **Days/Hours**: *Daily, from daylight until dark.* **Directions**: *Crisp County. From Cordele, take GA 300 south about 11.5 miles to Lakeshore Drive. Turn right and go about 1.5 miles to the park and follow signs.* **More Information**: *Crisp County Power Commission, Office of Resource Management, 1611 North 2nd Street, P.O. Box 1218, Cordele, GA 31010. 229/273-3820.*

Rocky Point Park

This little park is tucked away in a residential neighborhood that borders Swift Creek. With its cypress trees dotting the water, the creek resembles the more natural areas of Lake Blackshear's northern backwaters. An unpaved boat ramp, located to the left of the park sign, provides access to the creek.

Facilities: *Boat ramp (see map page 170) and covered picnic shelter with 4 concrete picnic tables.* **Days/Hours**: *Open daily, from daylight until dark.* **Directions**: *Crisp County. From Cordele, take GA 300 south about 12 miles to Arabi-Warwick Road. Turn left and go 1.5 miles to Barry Road. Turn right and go .25 mile to Swift Creek Road. Turn right and follow signs.* **More Information**: *Crisp County Power Commission, Office of Resource Management, 1611 North 2nd Street, P.O. Box 1218, Cordele, GA 31010. 229/273-3820.*

Crisp County

The Flint River and Lake Blackshear create the western border of Crisp County.

"Crisp County was created in 1905 from territory formerly belonging to Dooly County. It was named for Charles Frederick Crisp, a jurist, and Speaker of the U. S. House of Representatives between 1891 and 1893. Arabi and Cordele are the only two incorporated municipalities in the county. Cordele, the county seat, was a 'child of the railroad' having built up at a junction of the Savannah, Americus, and Montgomery Railroads. It was named for the daughter of the railroad's president. Crisp County became the first county in the nation to own and operate its own electrical power plant. It was started in 1930, with Lake Blackshear on the Flint River providing its power source… Georgia Veterans Memorial State Park [see page 116], a park on the banks of Lake Blackshear, was established as a permanent memorial to the U. S. Veterans who served, fought, and died for freedom."

From *Georgia Snapshots*, Georgia Department of Community Affairs

For tourism information for towns in Crisp County, see Resources page 300.

Killebrew Park

Named after Emmett Killebrew, the engineer who designed the Crisp Power Dam, this is the first park and boat ramp on the Flint River below the dam. From here, you have a good view of the dam and the high bluffs where the river re-enters its natural course. Just before entering the park, on the shoulder of Power Dam Road, lies a four-blade steel turbine from the dam's early days in the late 1920s; today's turbines consist of five stainless-steel blades.

Always pay close attention to sirens at this park: an intermittent blast means a generator is being turned on; a steady blast announces that spillway gates are releasing large volumes of water. If the latter occurs, you should leave the area, and boaters, within hearing range of the siren, should take their boats out of the water at the boat ramp. Further downstream, the gradual rise of the water should be hardly noticeable; but close to the dam, the rising water can create hazardous currents.

Facilities: *Boat ramp (see map page 170), picnic tables, drinking water and restrooms, located up steep flight of stairs at the power dam.* **Directions**: *Worth County. From Cordele, take GA 300 south about 13.5 miles to Power Dam Road. Turn right and follow signs.* **More Information**: *Crisp County Power Commission, Office of Resource Management, 1611 North 2nd Street, P.O. Box 1218, Cordele, GA 31010. 229/273-3820.*

CAMPGROUNDS

Turkey Creek Campground

This six-acre, privately owned campground lies on the banks of Turkey Creek, approximately a half mile from the Flint River and close enough to the Luther Storey Bridge on GA 27 to hear the rumble of semitrailers. Some older residents still refer to the creek winding past the campground as the Big Pennahatchee Creek, which is joined upstream by Little Pennahatchee Creek and Turkey Creek. In 1996, the current proprietor, Raymond Hobbs, bought the former home site and carved out a campground, complete with boat ramp and a 3,200-square-foot metal shed across from the campsites. The camping area combines the looks of a rural trailer park—rental RV units are available by the week and month—with the functionality of a campground for hunters at the nearby Flint River Wildlife Management Area, about six miles north (see page 103). When Georgia Veterans Memorial State Park runs out of vacancies, rangers refer campers here. Swimming is not permitted along the 600-foot waterfront or from the small island that holds four campsites. A campground manager lives full time on the premises.

Facilities: *9 on-site campers available for rent by the day, week and month; 35 RV and tent camping sites with water and electrical hookups, 18 with sewage hookups, as well as grills and picnic tables; 15 primitive camping sites on the small island; more primitive sites are available if necessary; boat ramp*

Worth County

Just below the Crisp Power Dam, the Flint River enters Worth County to form part of its western border.

"Worth County obtained its territory from Dooly and Irwin counties in 1853. The county was named for Major General William J. Worth who served in the Mexican War. The Flint River forms a part of the county's western boundary. A dam on the river at the north county line creates Lake Blackshear. Pindertown [see map page 170], an Indian village of note in pioneer days, was located on the Flint River in Worth County. For years it had the only post office in that section of the state. In addition to the county seat of Sylvester, Worth County has three other municipalities: Poulan, Sumner, and Warwick. Sylvester was originally known as 'Isabella Station,' but in 1894 the name was changed to honor a prominent local family."

From *Georgia Snapshots*, Georgia Department of Community Affairs

For tourism information for towns in Worth County, see Resources page 300.

(see map page 169); drinking water; dump station; fish cleaning station; restrooms with showers; soft drink machine; ice machine; propane and live bait for sale. **Days/Hours**: *Open daily.* **Fees**: *Campsites, $15 for 2 persons, $2 for each extra person. Rental fee for RVs, $70-$80 per week. Boat ramp fee for non-campers, $2.* **Directions**: *Dooly County. From Vienna, take GA 27 9.5 miles to Drayton Lane. Turn right and follow signs.* **More Information**: *Turkey Creek Campground, 156 Pat's Camp Road, Vienna, GA 31092. 229/268-6475 (office); 229/273-8738 (home).*

Lakeshore Marine Campground

This RV campground along the waterfront at Lake Blackshear is part of the Lakeshore Marine facility and is located on the northern portion of the lake between the US 280 Bridge and the Seaboard Coastline Bridge.

Facilities: *30 waterfront RV sites with electrical, water, sewer and cable TV hookups. For marina facilities, see page 120.* **Days/Hours**: *Open daily.* **Fees**: *Campsites, $20 per night; $125 per week. Call about monthly rates. Boat ramp, $2.* **Directions**: *Sumter County. From Americus, take US 280 east for 20 miles. Turn right into Lakeshore Marine just before the US 280 Bridge across Lake Blackshear.* **More Information**: *Lakeshore Marine, Hwy 280 – Flint River Bridge, Leslie, GA 31764. 229/853-2275.*

Georgia Veterans Memorial Park Campground

The original park plans included lakefront home sites for veterans. Instead, the waterfront property adjacent to Boy Scout Slough has been developed for campers, so the rows of pine trees that were planted to separate property lines, now provide shade for RV and tent sites.

Facilities: *Campsites — 77 tent and trailer campsites with water, electrical and cable TV hookups, picnic tables, fire rings or grills; 3 comfort stations with hot showers; 2 wastewater dump stations and laundry facilities. Two pioneer camping areas for organized groups, with cleared tent areas and primitive privies. Cottages — 10 2-bedroom, 1-bath, each with 4 double beds, fireplace, screened porch, kitchen supplies and linen. Maximum occupancy is 8 persons.* **Fees**: *Waterfront sites — $18 per night for a 2-night minimum Friday and Saturday stay; non-waterfront sites, $15 per night. Pioneer campsites — $15 per night (no minimum stay). Campsites can be rented for one night on a "walk in" basis if available. Cottages — $70 weekdays and $80 Fridays and Saturdays with a five-night minimum stay from Memorial Day weekend through Labor Day. $65 weekdays and $75 Fridays and Saturdays with a two-night minimum stay during the rest of the year. Summer rates apply to Thanksgiving weekend with a three-night minimum stay. Campsites and cottages can be rented for one night on a "walk-in" basis, if available.* **Directions**: *Crisp County. From Cordele, take US 280 west about 9 miles to GA 230. Park entrance is on the left. Follow the signs to the park office and campground.* **More Information**: *Georgia Veterans Memorial State Park, 2459-A US Hwy 280 West, Cordele, GA 31015. 229/276-2371*

Wood Duck

The wood duck is a bird that lives in the woods of southern Canada and throughout the United States. The male is the most colorful of North American ducks. Its upper feathers glitter with green, blue and purple. Underneath, it is red, yellow and white. Females are brown above and yellowish below. Both males and females have large crests. The birds measure about 20 inches long and have short necks and long tails.

Wood ducks are at home on water, land or air. Their feet, able to propel them through water, also have sharp claws and strong hind toes to help them perch on tree limbs.

Wood ducks spend much time in ponds and streams near woods, going into the woods to feed on seeds, acorns, berries, nuts and insects. They use the flooded trees and deadfall in the river for protection from predators. They nest in hollow trees, sometimes 40 feet from the ground and usually in the woods away from the water. Female wood ducks lay eight to 15 creamy-white eggs.

In late summer, look for males that are molting their old feathers and growing new ones for the migration flight. The plumage at this time, called eclipse plumage, is drab. It allows the duck to be inconspicuous at a time when it is without flight feathers.

(park); 229/276-2377 (golf course); 800/459-1230 (conference retreat). Website: www.gastateparks.org.

MARINAS AND FISH CAMPS

Sonny's Campers Haven

Located on Lake Blackshear below the GA 27 Bridge, Sonny's Campers Haven is nearly impossible to miss in the early evening. That's when the jukebox cranks up and the place is, in the words of its owner Sonny Carr, "lit up like Cordele at night." The name "Campers Haven" evokes a time when live bait was sold from concrete fish wells in the back of the little fish camp. These days the wells are dry, but the beer flows outside on the patio, which faces the boat dock and the five-acre island where Sonny's goats and chickens freerange.

Facilities: *Boat ramp (see map page 169), gas dock but fuel may not be available during the summer's busiest weekends, restaurant and bar, snacks and restrooms.* **Directions**: *Dooly County. From Vienna, take GA 27 west about 9 miles to GA 230 (Cannon Road). Turn left and go 1.25 miles to Campers Haven Road. Turn right and follow signs.* **Location on lake**: *On east bank, below the GA 27 Bridge (see map page 169). Turn at DNR sign indicating Gum Pond and go about .25 mile into the inlet.* **More Information**: *Sonny's Campers Haven, Route 1, Vienna, GA 31092. 229/268-9076.*

Spring Creek Marina

Spring Creek Marina operates a boat dock with gas in a natural setting of cypress trees. On the opposite side of Lamar Road from the marina, the picturesque but long closed Spring Creek Bait & Tackle still maintains a boat ramp.

Facilities: *Gas dock (as elsewhere on Lake Blackshear, boaters are advised to check on fuel availability in advance during busy weekends), snacks and beverages, boat ramp across road (see map page 169).* **Directions**: *Sumter County. From Americus, take US 280 east about 19 miles to Lamar Road. Turn left and go 1.5 miles. Marina is on your right just before you get to the bridge over Spring Creek.* **Location on lake**: *On west bank, about 1.5 miles north of the GA 280 Bridge (see map page 169). Turn up Spring Creek. The boat dock is on your left just before the bridge over Lamar Road.* **More Information**: *Spring Creek Tavern, 3077 Lamar Road, Cobb, GA 31735. 229/853-5395.*

Lakeshore Marine

One of only two businesses that caters to boaters on the west side of Lake Blackshear, this privately operated marina sits directly across the lake from Georgia Veterans Memorial State Park. When the state park posts a no-vacancy sign for campsites, they send campers here.

Fishing Lake Blackshear

Throughout the shallow, swampy areas of Lake Blackshear, cypress trees rise from the water, providing the perfect place for bass to hide.

"Several types of structures in Lake Blackshear hold bass, but the main one is the abundant cypress trees standing in shallow water in many areas of the lake. As is often the case, the single tree or clump of two or three trees that are separated from the rest of the stand usually hold more and bigger bass. The most successful pattern for taking bass from the stands of cypress consists of tossing topwater jerkbait to the base of the trees early or late in the day. In between these times, a dark-colored, Texas-rigged plastic worm is the best bait to cast to these same areas. On sunny days place the lure to the shady side of the tree and tight to the trunk. If the sky is overcast, work the worm a little farther from the base. This pattern works throughout the year on Blackshear.

"The very best area for fishing the cypress trees on the reservoir is in Gum Creek, just in front of the boat ramp at Veterans State Park. In fact, many local anglers never bother to fish any of the other stands of cypress on the lake, preferring to spend their time casting to these trees. Other good but smaller stands of cypress are found in Swift and Cedar Creeks, as well as dotted along both shores of the main body of the lake."

Bass Fishing in Georgia by Jimmy Jacobs

Facilities: *25 covered wet slips; 25 covered dry slips; permanent storage available; gas dock (as elsewhere on Lake Blackshear, boaters are advised to check on fuel availability in advance during busy weekends); boat ramp (see map page 169); camping (see page 119); fully-equipped ski shop with swimwear and boating accessories; convenience store with snacks, soft drinks, beer and ice; small grass beach with a sea wall, picnic tables and restroom facilities; banquet room; mini-storage.* **Days/Hours**: *Open daily, 24 hours with honor box. Ski Shop – open April to Sept., Monday through Saturday, 10 a.m. to 5 p.m.; Sunday, 1 p.m. to 5 p.m.; call for hours during off-season.* **Fees**: *Boat ramp, $2.* **Directions**: *Sumter County. From Americus, take US 280 east for 20 miles. Turn right into Lakeshore Marina just before the US 280 Bridge across Lake Blackshear.* **Location on lake**: *On west bank, just below the US 280 Bridge (see map page 169).* **More Information**: *Lakeshore Marine, Hwy 280—Flint River Bridge, Leslie, GA 31764. 229/853-2275.*

FISHING

Cordele Fish Hatchery

Although the focus of the hatchery is raising channel catfish, hybrid bass and shoal bass for southwest Georgia waters, the Department of Natural Resources staff welcome the public to stroll along the grounds. Twenty-seven earthen ponds, ranging from .2-2.5 acres, dot the hatchery's 160 acres. One-lane access roads also serve as grassy dikes between the rows of ponds.

Shoal bass, which are native to the Flint, are raised here, but only stocked on the river below Lake Blackshear to Seminole—the shoals upriver have a large enough shoal bass population without the hatchery's help. The ponds attract many species of birds: wood storks in late summer; ospreys in fall and winter; purple martins in early summer; red-tailed and red-shouldered hawks, great blue herons, cormorants, egrets (snowy, cattle, and common) and Canada geese.

Before entering the pond area, check in with fishery employees. The busiest time of year is during harvest in the fall and hatching in the spring. During the school year, children tour the hatchery and round off their visit with a chance to hook a 2-3 pound catfish stocked especially for them. Due to plankton blooms and summer algae, water visibility is usually limited. Tour groups with a minimum of 10 wishing to visit the hatchery should call ahead for an appointment.

Facilities: *3 picnic tables and restrooms.* **Days/Hours**: *Monday through Friday, 8 a.m. to 4:30 p.m.* **Directions**: *Crisp County. From Cordele, take US 280 west about 1.5 miles to Fish Hatchery Road. Turn right and go 1.5 miles to Williams Lake Road. Turn right and then left into the hatchery entrance.* **More Information**: *Cordele Fish Hatchery, 392 Fish Hatchery Road, Cordele, GA 31015. 229/276-2362.*

Egret

Egret is the snow-white heron—the bird that grows the long plumes prized by hat makers, or milliners, who call the plumes, aigrettes. The valuable plumes grow between the shoulder blades of the birds and extend over and beyond the tail. But plumes appear only on the adults—and during the nesting season. This means that when the parent birds are killed for their plumage, the young are helpless and starve to death. At one time, all American egrets were nearly exterminated due to hunting, but today, protective legislation and bird sanctuaries ensure their survival.

Several species of egret live in America, mostly in the southern states. Snowy egret, great egret and cattle egret take up residence at Lake Blackshear during the breeding season. The great egret, about 40 inches long, is the only species native to both America and Eurasia. The tall, handsome American egret and the snowy egret have the finest plumage. The cattle egret is a small white bird with pink eyes and yellow bill. It feeds on insects stirred up by grazing cattle. Originally from Asia, it was first seen in Florida in 1942. It is now fairly common in many parts of the United States.

HIKES AND WALKS

The Yucca Trace Trail

The trail, which opened in the spring of 1995 as part of the Olympic Signature Event, interprets the sand hill environment associated with this area. The park staff at Georgia Veterans Memorial State Park produces a guide to the nature trail that you can pick up at the park office. Park staff also conduct guided trail tours. Check with the park office for schedules.

Distance: This is a flat, easy to walk, 0.5-mile nature trail and hiking trail loop.

Trailhead: Georgia Veterans Memorial State Park (see page 116). Pick up a park map at the visitor center. The trailhead is to the right of the fitness center.

Features: Ancient cork oak trees, the largest of their kind in Georgia, line the entrance to this nature trail at Georgia Veterans Memorial State Park. Cork oak trees live to be 300-400 years old, and these were supposedly planted by members of the Hernando de Soto expedition, who crossed the Flint River twice in 1540 during their quest for gold.

Fourteen different stations along the trail interpret different plants that can be seen, as well as wildlife that live there. Longleaf, shortleaf and loblolly pine, persimmon and water oak are some of the trees you will see, while prickly pear, huckleberry, blackberries, sassafras and Spanish bayonet (see sidebar page 112) grow abundantly. Look for the tracks of squirrel, deer, opossum and rabbit and the nests of songbirds, such as bluebirds, cardinals, brown thrashers, mockingbirds and catbirds.

BRIDGES

GA 27 Bridge

Built in 1959, this bridge is commonly referred to as the "Luther Storey Bridge." A bronze marker honors Luther Storey, and other veterans from Sumter and Dooly Counties, all of whom gave their lives in World War II or the Korean War. **Location**: *On Sumter and Dooly County line where GA 27 crosses the Flint River between Americus and Vienna.*

US 280 Bridge

This 0.4-mile-long bridge, built in 1984, replaced a 1938 structure, which was left standing on the downstream and is used as a fishing bridge. The bridge is commonly called the US 280 or the Cobb Memorial Bridge, being named after war veterans Gen. Howell Cobb and Capt. John A. Cobb. South of this bridge marks the most active portion of Lake Blackshear. **Location**: *On Sumter and Crisp County line where US 280 crosses the Flint between Cordele and DeSoto.*

Sumter County

The Flint River enters Sumter County near the town of Andersonville and forms the county's western border.

"Sumter County was created in 1831 from a portion of Lee County and was named for General Thomas Sumter of South Carolina, a soldier of the French and Indian Wars as well as the American Revolution. The county has five municipalities including Americus, the county seat. The others include Andersonville, DeSoto, Leslie, and Plains. Americus—the masculine version of America—was the name pulled from a hat. The town of Andersonville has won a Phoenix Award for Preservation, Conservation and Beautification. The site of the infamous Civil War prison camp that bore the community's name is in nearby Macon County. Pennington St. James, a log church built in 1927 of cypress logs and native fieldstone, was designed by the same architects who designed the Cathedral of St. John the Divine in New York City. Americus is home to Habitat for Humanity International, a non-profit organization dedicated to eliminating substandard housing around the world. It is now one of the top ten homebuilders in the country. Jimmy Carter, former President of the United States and former Governor of Georgia, is from Plains. Charles Lindbergh learned to fly in Sumter County. Mr. Lindbergh bought a military surplus 'Jenny' aircraft in the county and had it assembled at Souther Field. Mechanics there gave him flying lessons and saw him off on his first solo flight."

From *Georgia Snapshots*, Georgia Department of Community Affairs

For tourism information for towns in Sumter County, see Resources page 299.

DAMS

Crisp County Power Dam

A group of Crisp County citizens—not a utility company, as is usually the case—proposed the 1930 dam that was built on the Flint River near Swift Creek. After much opposition and political hurdles that included passing an amendment to the state constitution to permit a bond-issue election, construction began on the first county-owned and county-operated hydroelectric power project in the United States.

Currently, Plant Crisp maintains four hydroelectric units that provide an annual average of 47 million kilowatt hours, along with 15 million kilowatts from coal-fired steam units and 5 million kilowatts from a gas turbine unit. The 1,500-foot-long concrete slab-and-buttress dam stands 30 feet high from the lake elevation to the downstream water level. The 3,000-foot-long earthen dike was partially washed away during the 1994 flood; when it was repaired a year later, the dike was built with a concrete cap and its height was lowered by a foot so that it would provide an emergency spillway for future flood waters. Paddlers wishing to portage the dam should plan ahead. The last boat ramp north of the dam, the Plant Crisp ramp (see map page 170) is located 1.5 miles from the first ramp below the dam, Killebrew Park ramp (see map page 170).

Directions: *Crisp County. From Cordele, take GA 300 south about 13 miles to Power Dam Road. Turn right and go 2 miles to the dam.* **More Information**: *Crisp County Power Commission, Office of Resource Management, 1611 North 2nd Street, P.O. Box 1218, Cordele, GA 31010. 229/273-3820.*

Schley County

Schley County lies west of the river within the Flint River Watershed.

"Schley County was created in 1857 from parts of Marion, Macon, and Sumter counties. Georgia's 122nd county was named for Georgia Governor William Schley. The name of the county is pronounced 'sly.' Ellaville, the county seat, is the only municipality in Schley County. The city was named for Ella Burton, the daughter of the man who sold the land for the town site. Built in 1899, the county courthouse is on the National Register of Historic Places. The City of Ellaville's water system is one of only two in the state which use duckweed [see sidebar page 43] as a natural water filter instead of chemicals."

From *Georgia Snapshots*, Georgia Department of Community Affairs

For tourism information for towns in Schley County, see Resources page 300.

Section 5

Lake Blackshear to Bainbridge

RIO TELLS US how the Flint River got its name. We travel along the part of the river that runs through the Floridian aquifer. We see relic hunters, finding Indian arrowheads in the river channels's potholes, and discover fossils imbedded in a limestone creekbed.

Between Lake Blackshear and Bainbridge, use the Guidebook Section beginning on page 129 to explore: The Swamp of Toa, considered to be, after the Okefenokee, the most significant swamp and wetland in Georgia; Dry Creek Swamp Preserve; Creekside Education Center; the site of Old Herod Town; Parott; Thronateeska Heritage Center; Lake Chehaw and The Parks at Chehaw; Turner Field Park; Georgia Power Dam Park; Albany Veterans Park; Albany Nursery Wildlife Management Area; Chickasawhatchee Wildlife Management Area; and Elmodel Wildlife Management Area.

ATTENTION BOATERS:
YOU ARE ENTERING THE KARST TOPOGRAPHY * OF SOUTHWEST GEORGIA WATCH FOR SINKHOLES

THE SPRINGS AND AQUIFER SYSTEM YOU'LL SEE ON THIS SECTION OF THE RIVER HAVE ALWAYS BEEN AS FASCINATING AND BEAUTIFUL TO ME AS MY WATERFALLS IN YOUR NORTH GEORGIA MOUNTAINS.

*KARST TOPOGRAPHY
A LANDSCAPE CHARACTERIZED BY SINKS, SOLUTION VALLEYS, AND OTHER FEATURES PRODUCED BY GROUND WATER ACTIVITY.

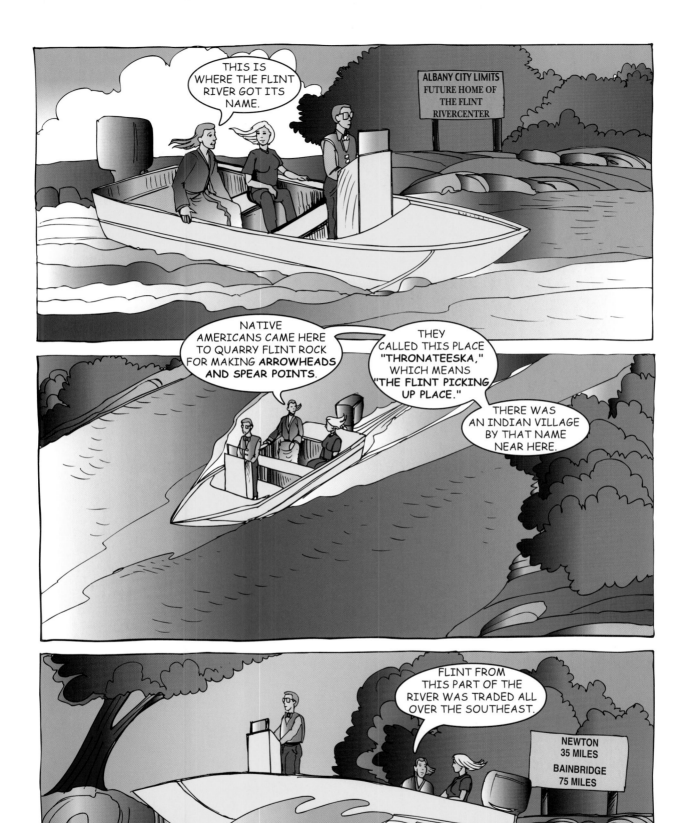

RELIC HUNTERS IN THE FLINT USE HOMEMADE AND STORE-BOUGHT RIGS TO SEARCH THE POTHOLES IN THE LIMESTONE BOTTOM FOR PREHISTORIC ANIMAL TEETH, BONES AND TUSKS AND INDIAN RELICS, SUCH AS ARROWHEADS, SPEAR POINTS AND PIECES OF POTTERY.

Section 5

Lake Blackshear to Bainbridge

SIGNIFICANT NATURAL AREAS

Radium Springs

Discharging 70,000 gallons of water a minute, Georgia's largest natural spring pours out of the Ocala aquifer, whose rain-filled limestone caverns and tunnels lie underneath the Flint River here. A natural flow of water from the ground at a single point or within a restricted area, a spring can have hot, warm or cold water. At an even 68 degrees year round, Radium Springs falls within the "warm" springs range of 66 to 98 degrees Fahrenheit.

A water analysis of the springs back in the early 1900s revealed traces of radium isotopes. At the time, European spas boasted of the curative effects of radium. Since Radium Springs had more radium than the springs at Hot Springs, Arkansas; Saratoga, California; or the most famous of the European spas, it—like many other warm and hot spring areas—was developed as a health resort (see page 132).

The beauty of Radium Springs, however, is what is most memorable. Known as Skywater by the Creek Indians and Blue Springs in the early days of Albany, the spring's sparkling waters appear sapphire-blue in color as they issue from the deep recesses of the Earth to form a huge pool of water. From the Radium Springs pool area—located behind the former casino building and set amid 1920s-era flourishes of concrete walkways, terraces and gazebos—the illusion of blue continues as the water meanders along a shallow creek, past private residences and through wetlands of Spanish moss-draped oaks, pine and cypress's. After flowing a half mile and passing over a small concrete dam, the spring waters reach the Flint River, about four miles south of Albany.

Radium Springs is currently closed to the public. The state of Georgia, which owns the springs along with 84 adjacent acres, hopes to incoporate the springs into their striped bass management program, using it as a cool-water refuge for striped bass (see map page 204).

Swamp of Toa

The Swamp of Toa, a hardwood swamp in Southwest Georgia, is the most extensive limesink area in Georgia—limesinks being depressional wetlands formed by the dissolution or collapse of underlying limestone. Many of these limesinks are connected to the ground water

Fossils

A fossil is a rock containing the preserved remains of once-living animals or plants. Fossils are formed when an animal or plant is buried in sediment. Usually, the soft parts rot away, but the hardest parts remain. This is why most fossils consist of the bones or shells of animals, or the leaves or woody parts of plants. In some marine fossils, shells my be replaced by other minerals, or an impression of the insides or outside may be preserved.

Fossils are found in sedimentary rocks, especially limestone and shale. Many fossils are of plants and animals now extinct, such as dinosaurs. Fossils reveal details about the animals and plants that existed millions of years ago, and enable scientists to date the rocks in which they appear. Fossils showing footprints or burrows rather than remains are called trace fossils.

Fossils can be easily found in the limestone riverbed and banks of the Flint in the Coastal Plain area.

aquifers, making the Swamp of Toa the primary recharge area for the entire Floridam aquifer (see page 156), which provides drinking water to Florida, South Georgia and the Georgia coast.

The swamp is one of the largest remaining freshwater swamps in the Southeast United States and one of the South's most productive ecosystems, providing four basic functions: it holds water and mitigates flooding; its biotic system nourishes wildlife; it recharges underground aquifers; and it cleans waters. Encompassing parts of Dougherty, Baker and Calhoun Counties, it is a haven for plants and wildlife. Three hundred-year-old cypress trees grow in wonder, as do oaks, beech, gum and magnolia. Wild turkeys, bald eagles, rare amphibians (including the blind cave salamander), fish and birds, (including the endangered marshland stork), roam throughout.

Some people call the swamp Chickasawhatchee, a Creek word that loosely translates into "Council House Creek," while others know it as the Swamp of Toa, taken from the name of a 19th century Creek Indian Chief. The swamp was the site of one of the hardest-fought battles of the Creek War of 1836 (see sidebar this page).

In 2000, the Nature Conservancy purchased a 15,100-acre tract of the Swamp of Toa from the St. Joe Company, based in Jacksonville and Florida's largest real estate operating company, for $30 million. Their intention is to transfer the tract to the Georgia Department of Natural Resources to be used as a wildlife management area. The Swamp of Toa has more uplands than the Okefenokee Swamp, so people can actually walk much of these marshes. The best way to experience the Swamp of Toa is to go to the Chickasawhatchee Wildlife Management Area—the swamp is all around you.

Directions: *Dougherty, Baker and Calhoun Counties. From Albany, take GA 62 west about 23 miles to the small of town of Leary and look for Jordan's General Store and the Chickasawhatchee WMA check-in post for hunters (see page 148).*

Dry Creek Swamp Preserve

Flatwoods and cypress-gum swamps make up this small preserve just south of Albany, which harbors a little roadside population of the endangered species, Cooley meadowrue. There are only nine recorded populations of the plant in existence, and Dry Creek Swamp Preserve houses the only known occurrence of the Cooley meadowrue in Georgia. This tall and spindly, white-flowered perennial grows along the edges of intermittent drainage areas. The plant, which has separate male and female plants, requires open space in order to propagate because it depends upon wind to transport pollen from the male to the female. Historically, frequent fires probably helped to eliminate competing vegetation and maintain clearings in which the meadowrue could thrive.

Two other plants that you can see at Dry Creek Swamp Preserve are the unusual Turk's-cap lily and the rare woods poppy-mallow.

Battle of Chickasawhatchee

Creek Indians, who continued to resist their removal into Indian Territory, fought one of their last battles in Georgia during the Creek Indian War of 1836 in what is now the Chickasawhatchee Wildlife Management Area.

"In today's Baker County, one of the hardest battles of the Creek War was fought in 1836. In the latter part of June 1836, the Creek Indians, after burning Roanoke in Stewart County, departed for Florida to join the Seminoles. On their way they passed through today's Baker County with a group of white militia after them. The group of Indians, some 300 warriors, took possession of an island in the Chickasawhatchee Swamp and prepared to defend themselves. By that time the Georgia militia, having grown to about 500 men, surrounded the swamp and moved in to give battle to the Indians. The Creeks were defeated with a large number killed and wounded, before they retreated southward toward Florida. The whites had one killed and nine wounded in the struggle.

"After the battle, the Creek Indians fled into Florida to escape the Georgians. The Indians left behind many supplies, including 36 tents, and an incredible quantity of beef, bacon, horses, saddles, bridles, and many cooking utensils....

"Modern maps show the only island in the Chickasawhatchee Creek and Swamp to be immediately west of Elmodel along GA 37. Another possibility is north of that place in the lower part of the present-day Chickasaw-hatchee Wildlife Management Area. That possible spot is just east of GA 27 and north of Clear Lake Road, some three miles north of Elmodel. The swamp is much larger at the upper site."

Indian Heritage of Georgia by Marion R. Hemperley

Native Americans once made soup from the bulbs of the red-orange Turk's-cap lily, which is one of the most striking of all native lilies. Growing along the roadside, the poppy-mallow has deep pink flowers that bloom in summer.

Owned by the Nature Conservancy of Georgia, the 20-acre site has been adapted by the staff of the Miller Brewing Company, who help with the hands-on management of the property. The Georgia Department of Transportation and the Mitchell Electrical Membership Corporation both maintain rights-of-way along this section of the highway, and have kept the site fairly open, ensuring that the plants get the direct sunlight and breezes they require for survival.

Visitors are welcome at the preserve, but are asked to inform The Nature Conservancy of Georgia beforehand. You should have a clear idea of what the Cooley meadowrue looks like and where it occurs on the site (most are on the wettest portion of the right-of-way) to avoid damaging the plants accidentally.

More Information: *The Nature Conservancy of Georgia, 1401 Peachtree Street, NE, Suite 236, Atlanta, GA 30309. 404/873-6946.*

NATURE-BASED EDUCATIONAL CENTERS

Jones Ecological Center

Located around and including a 15-mile stretch of Ichaway-nochaway Creek—a tributary of the Flint—Joseph W. Jones Ecological Research Center at Ichauway is a research site that uses the creek as part of its outdoor laboratory.

The 29,000-acre property was established originally as a traditional quail hunting reserve in the 1920s by Robert W. Woodruff, longtime chairman of The Coca-Cola Company. An avid outdoorsman, Mr. Woodruff recognized the natural characteristics of his Ichauway plantation—one of the most extensive tracts of longleaf pine and wiregrass in the United States. Upon his death, the Robert W. Woodruff Foundation established the Jones Ecological Research Center at Ichauway, naming it in honor of Joseph W. Jones, an associate of Mr. Woodruff's and chairman of the Woodruff Foundation.

The center's mission is to provide a program of excellence in ecology and natural resource management that includes integrated research, education and conservation goals. The center conducts both short- and long-term multidisciplinary research, using experimental and descriptive studies of managed and less disturbed regional ecosystems. While not open to the public, new information is transferred to targeted conservation and natural resource constituencies through the center's education program. In addition to its use as an outdoor laboratory, Ichauway is used as a site for conserving and restoring regional ecosystems, and as an education demonstration for ecology and natural resource management.

The Flood of 1994

On July 4, 1994, Tropical Storm Alberto moved from the Gulf of Mexico and stalled out over Georgia. For 11 days, rain relentlessly fell across the state as tributary floodwaters combined and moved downstream in the Flint River. With every day that passed, it became more and more apparent that this was the worst natural disaster to ever occur in the state and, in the end, 55 counties in Georgia were declared Federal disaster areas.

Facts of the flood:

Thirteen inches of rainfall in areas most effected, although the greatest total rainfall of 27.6 inches (21.1 inches in 24 hours) was recorded in Americus.

Thirty-three fatalities, mostly due to vehicles being swept from flooded roadways.

Montezuma exceeded 100-year flood stage by 3.7 feet; Albany by 5.1 feet; Newton by 3.9 feet and Bainbridge by 2.2 feet.

18,000 homes flooded with total flood damages to public and private property estimated at over 1 billion dollars.

Over 130 million dollars in road and bridge damage in Georgia.

Contaminants in floodwaters included industrial chemicals, untreated sewage and agricultural chemicals.

Deposits of sediment and contaminants in floodplains and estuaries, impaired crop production, aquatic habitats and fisheries.

The Crisp County dam at Lake Blackshear breached.

Sinkholes formed in Albany area, with its cavernous limestone formations under the ground. Homes destroyed or condemned.

Nearly 500,000 acres of cropland impacted by flood, causing estimated 100 millions in damage.

Directions: *Baker County. From Newton, take GA 91 southwest 10.5 miles to Ichawaynochaway Creek. Cross the creek; the center is on the right.* **More Information**: *Joseph W. Jones Ecological Research Center, Route 2, Box 2324, Newton, GA 31770. 229/734-4706; fax, 229/734-4707.*

Creekside Education Center

Surrounded by the rich vegetation around Muckalee Creek, the Creekside Education Center is the nexus of educational activities at the Parks at Chehaw. Housed in this 10,000-square-foot facility are volunteer and staff offices, conference areas that include state-of-the-art videoconferencing and a large atrium for traveling exhibits and overnight indoor camping experiences.

Directions: *Dougherty County. From Leesburg, take US 19/82 south about 5 miles to GA 133. Bear left and go 3.5 miles to GA 91/Philema Road. Turn left and go 1 mile. The park is on the left.* **More Information**: *The Parks at Chehaw, 105 Chehaw Park Road, Albany, GA 31701. 229/430-3012. Website: www.parksatchehaw.org.*

HISTORIC SITES

Radium Springs

The white-stucco casino with its columns and cupola at Radium Springs is probably one of Albany's most recognizable sites. A nostalgic reminder of days gone by, the springs is a place dear to the heart of longtime Albany residents.

But Radium Springs has been a favorite spot for humans for centuries. Indian artifacts and relics, such as arrowheads and other projectiles, dating from 100 B.C., have been found in the area. In 1921, two large pottery shards were discovered at Radium Springs that, when put together, became a three-legged pot with two handles, resembling a human face. The pot is on display at Thronateeska Heritage Foundation. Native Americans also have left traces behind of their fishing camps and tool manufacturing sites in the area. The earliest recorded inhabitants were the Hitchiti and the Ososchi, two sub-tribes of the Lower Creek Indians. They believed the translucent blue waters possessed magical and curative powers. Their name for Radium Springs, "Skywater," reflected their belief that the sapphire-blue color had dropped from the sky and into the waters of the spring. The Ososchi deserted Skywater by 1794. The Hitchiti, who lived on both sides of the Flint at Radium Springs, were a small village of industrious people, who fenced their town and raised cattle, horses and hogs. However, in 1818, just four years after white settlers entered the area, a smallpox epidemic decimated the Hitchiti people.

The first white landowner of Skywater was Captain Erasmus Gay. Gay and other early white settlers began calling "Skywater," "Blue Springs." In the years leading up to and after the Civil War, Blue Springs ownership changed hands several times and became a popular

Lee County

The Flint River flows along the western border of Lee County.

"Lee County was one of the original landlot counties acquired from the Creek Indians in 1826. Georgia's 68th county, it was named for Richard Henry Lee who had proposed in the Continental Congress that the colonies declare themselves free and independent. He was noted for capturing Augusta from the British in 1781, and was the father of Robert E. Lee. The first county courthouse in Lee County was in Starkville, but fire destroyed it in 1856. The courthouse in Leesburg, the present county seat, was also hit by fire in 1872."

From *Georgia County Snapshots*, Gerogia Department of Community Affairs

For tourism information for towns in Lee County, see Resources page 300.

place for local people to swim and picnic. But it was not until 1916, when W. E. Hickey purchased the springs, that an effort was made to turn the springs into a commercial recreational area. He built a restaurant, bowling alley, country store with slot machines and dance hall. The springs owner enhanced the pool by removing rocks, widening the creek banks and erecting a small dam to deepen its waters.

In 1925, during the height of the Roaring '20s, wealthy New York financier Barron G. Collier acquired the property with the intention of building a first-class tourist attraction. It is Collier's faded handiwork that remains today. The white, stucco-finished casino, with columns and cupola, is an Albany landmark that survives thanks to major renovations after a disastrous 1982 fire and the 1994 flood. The grounds of the pool area resemble a scene from a faded 1920s postcard—grand flourishes of concrete walkways, terraces and gazebos surround the ethereal, sapphire-blue springs. Collier almost changed the resort's name back to Skywater but then a water analysis revealed traces of radium isotopes in the water. Collier decided to name the resort Radium Springs to take advantage of the current popular health fad involving the metallic element.

In addition to the casino and pool, Collier built an 18-hole golf course beside the Flint and offered amenities like scenic drives along the river, bridle paths through pine forests, tennis courts, fishing, canoeing and trap-shooting. But as a business venture, Radium Springs quickly lost out to bigger, flashier Florida resorts. Still, the resort had its heyday as a prime location for Southwest Georgia conventions, high school dances, political rallies, holiday celebrations and debutante balls. During World War II the casino saw action as an Air Force Officer's Club, and through the 1980s enjoyed success at different times as a restaurant and social club.

The Radium Springs Hotel and other buildings are presently under private ownership and closed to the public.

Old Herod Town

The old town of Herod was one of the last Indian villages to remain in the area after the white settlers moved in. It was settled by Noah Herod, who was either an Indian or a white who lived in the Creek Indian Nation. Because it was located across the line from the huge 1814 land cession, in which all Georgia lands to the south, including nearly all of the Swamp of Toa, was stripped away from friendly Indians, Old Herod was said to have the air of a teeming refugee camp. Legend has it that when General Andrew Jackson and his command of 900 Georgia Militia and friendly Creek Indians entered the village on their way to Florida to fight the Seminoles in 1818, they were joined by Chief Herod and his warriors, who declared himself a "firm friend of the white settlers."

A granite boulder monument erected in 1913 and a state historical marker stands near the site of the old settlement. The monument

Steamboat Navigation

The Flint River connected Albany and southwest Georgia with the Gulf of Mexico port of Apalachicola, but steamboating was never an easy business on smaller tributaries like the Flint.

"According to one reckoning, over one hundred commercial watercraft operated on this river system between 1840 and 1860. These vessels adapted their girth to the dimensions of the river. Their average size was between one hundred and two hundred tons. Most could carry their own weight in cargo while only drawing two and a half feet of water when fully loaded.

"The Flint and Chipola rivers, being smaller tributaries than the main stream, required even smaller boats. During the cotton season, light draft barges or 'boxes' were regularly poled between Albany and Apalachicola. The Albany commission merchants who owned one line claimed that their vessels had the capacity of holding 1,500 bales 'on any stage of the river, if necessary.' One of the largest of these barges, the Rebecca, measured one hundred and three feet long, over seventeen feet wide, and three feet deep. It drew only two feet when heavily loaded. Cotton boxes transported cotton along the upper Chattahoochee above Eufaula, as well."

Fair to Middlin'—The Antebellum Cotton Trade of the Apalachicola/Chattahoochee River Valley by Lynn Willoughby commemorates the fact that Jackson and his troops came through the town while the marker is more a memorial to the Indians.

Directions: *Terrell County. From Dawson, take GA 55 south about 5.5 miles to Doveral-Herod Road in the middle of Herod. The monument and historical marker are on the right.*

Battle of Ichawaynochaway Swamp

On July 25, 1838, during the Second Creek Indian War, the Creek engaged the Georgia Militia twice in what has become known as the Battle of Ichawaynochaway Swamp. In the first battle, the Indians won and the Georgians retreated, carrying their wounded and expecting the Indians to attack again. However, when the Indians did not, the militia troops quickly found the Indians' trail and followed them. Overtaking and surrounding them where Ichawaynochaway, Chenubee and Turkey Creeks come together in Terrell County, the militia completely routed the Creek Indians from their encampment. Three militia were killed and 13 wounded. But it was never known how many Indians died. A monument to the battle stands near the junction of the three creeks.

Directions: *Terrell County. From Dawson, take Cherry Cola Road northwest about 7.5 miles to Old Sandfill Road. Just past the road on the right is the monument.*

Parrott

In the 1980s, when a movie company was looking for a location to shoot *The Long Riders*, a film about the Jesse James gang, it chose Parrott—mainly because nothing had changed there since John Lawson Parrott, a Confederate veteran, planter and businessman founded the town in 1889. Tin-roofed red brick buildings, raised sidewalks, a wooden train depot, dirt streets—the town had looked the same for 100 years.

Today, much has changed—in the name of restoration only. Spruced up and painted, the turn-of-the-century cotton warehouses, drugstores, banks and other buildings are now 17 antique shops, restaurants and art galleries. The old train depot is the Pottery Depot. And the streets are paved.

Directions: *Terrell County. From Dawson, take GA 520 north about 9 miles to the main street of Parrott.* **More Information**: *Terrell County Chamber of Commerce, 127 West Lee Street, P.O. Box 405, Dawson, GA 31742. 229/995-2011.*

Terrell County

Terrell County lies west of the river within the Flint River Watershed.

"Terrell County was carved from portions of Randolph and Lee counties in 1856. Georgia's 113th county was named for Dr. William Terrell of Sparta, who had served in both the state legislature and Congress. Dawson, the county seat, was named for William C. Dawson, jurist, congressman, and U.S. Senator. Terrell County has three other municipalities: Bronwood, Parrott and Sasser. Shortly after Atlanta's capture in the Civil War, Governor Joseph E. Brown arranged for a refugee camp at Dawson to shelter some 300 women and children who had fled the city. The 'Exile Camp' was later used to house a detachment of 50 Union soldiers assigned to keep order in the area. Their kind behavior toward local citizens was long noted by the community. Parrott is a picturesque little town that has been used for several western movies including 'The Long Riders.' There are two sites listed on the National Register of Historic Places. These are the Terrell County courthouse and the Garden Club House. Another interesting building is the Chickasawhatchee Primitive Baptist Church which was built in 1858. It is the oldest church still standing on its original site in Terrell County."

From *Georgia County Snapshots*, Georgia Department of Community Affairs

For tourism information for towns in Terrell County, see Resources page 300.

 (continued on page 137)

Alligator in the Great Swamp

Hogcrawl Creek

Flint River Wildlife Management Area

2,300 acres of low, sandy uplands. The habitats here are mostly pine and pine-hardwoods with scattered pickets of pure hardwoods found in old oxbows, bays and wet bottomlands near the river. Accessible by 4-wheel drive vehicles and foot.

Sweetwater Creek

Duck hunters

The Great Swamp

The Great Swamp

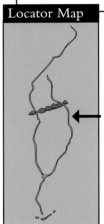

Locator Map

1. GA 96 Boat Ramp
On east bank, just below
the bridge

GA 96 Bridge

Beechwood Swamp

Magnolia Swamp

Dead River

Beechwood Swamp
Part of the Great Swamp. Below
GA 96 Bridge, it is known as the
Beechwood Swamp; above the
bridge, it is called Magnolia Swamp.

Sandbars below GA 96 Bridge

GA 96
River miles above mouth: 209.1
Counties: Taylor and Crawford

Montezuma to the Flint River Wildlife Management Area

Spring Creek

Montezuma
Just east of the river

Montezuma

GA 49 Bridge   GA 26 Bridge

1. Montezuma Bluffs Boat Ramp
Two-lane concrete ramp with easy grade on east bank, approximately 12 miles below the GA 127 Bridge and 3 miles above GA 49 Bridge

Buck Creek

Timothy Barnard's Place
Timothy Barnard, the first white man to settle in the region, operated a trading post on this site from about 1770 until 1820. He influenced the flow of trade goods up and down the Flint River and worked with Benjamin Hawkins as an interpreter, assistant and confidant.

Oglethorpe
Just west of the river

Oglethorpe

Locator Map

2. George Hooks Boat Ramp
Wide concrete ramp with easy grade on west bank, just below the GA 49 Bridge

Locator Map

The Fall Line

Elevation
800'   400'

GA 49
River miles above mouth: 180.6
County: Macon

GA 26
River miles above mouth: 180
County: Macon

See the Guidebook sections for additional information and directions to locations listed on this page.

Canoe outfitter in the Great Swamp

De Soto's Route

Hernando de Soto's route through Georgia and the Southeast has been long disputed among historians and archaeologists. One theory holds that he crossed the Flint River here, 5 miles south of the GA 127 Bridge in the spring of 1540 with 600 soldiers, 213 horses, about 200 hogs, a number of mules, scores of slaves, a pack of large attack dogs, tons of equipment and a few priests.

Montezuma Bluffs

This 500-acre natural area on the east side of the river is part of the Fort Valley Plateau, a 150-foot escarpment overlooking the river floodplain. Fifty to 75 million years ago, this section of Georgia was a seabed. It compacted over time into the limestone now present. The river has worn away the younger layers of earth to expose fossilized oyster shells in the ancient limestone.

Swamp Boardwalk

Whitewater Creek Park

48-acre park operated by Macon County

Whitewater Creek

Locator Map

The Fall Line

Crisp Co.
Power Dam

River Level

Ga. Power Dam
at Chehaw

Lake Seminole

Elevation

800'   400'   200'   0'

See the Guidebook sections for additional information and directions to locations listed on this page.   135

Marshallville

Anhinga in Magnolia Swamp

Gin Creek

Marshallville
About 6 miles east of the river
via GA 127

2. Flint River Ferry
Site of the last working ferry in
Georgia, the ferry ran from 1850 to
1988. Known by various names over
the years, including Wannamaker's,
Underwood's, the Marshallville,
Miona and the Macon County Ferry.

GA 127 Bridge

3. Flint River Ferry Boat Ramp
Unpaved ramp a 0.25 north of the
bridge

Miona Springs
The use of Miona Springs as a place for
healing and as an important meeting place
reaches back into Indian history. The
Indians believed the waters of these springs
to have healing properties, making it a
popular Indian gathering place.

GA 127
River miles above mouth: 196.1
County: Macon

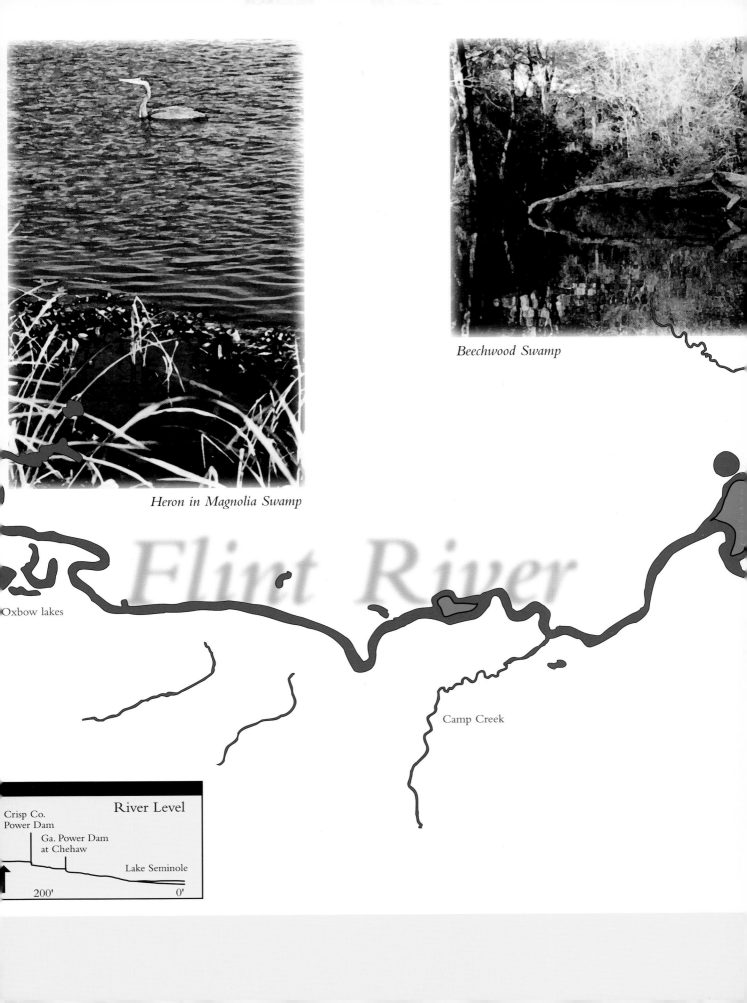

Heron in Magnolia Swamp

Beechwood Swamp

Flint River

Oxbow lakes

Camp Creek

River Level

Crisp Co.
Power Dam

Ga. Power Dam
at Chehaw

Lake Seminole

200'   0'

(continued from page 134)

MUSEUMS

Thronateeska Heritage Center

The Central of Georgia. Atlantic Coast Line. Georgia Northern. Albany & Northern. Seaboard Air Line. At one time, these five different railroads served the city of Albany with seven rail lines and as many as 55 trains converging daily at the city's Union Station just one block from the Flint River. Today, that 1912 brick passenger terminal is called Discovery Depot and houses a local and regional history and heritage museum that is part of the Thronateeska Heritage Center. Established in 1974, Thronateeska's mission is to tell the story of Southwest Georgia, including that of Native Americans, steamboats on the Flint, the emergence of railroads and automobiles and the Albany Civil Rights Movement.

The non-profit center, located on a wide, brick street in downtown Albany, includes several structures in addition to the Discovery Depot. The REA building houses the Wetherbee Planetarium, the only planetarium in Southwest Georgia open to the public, and the Discovery Center, a hands-on museum where you can learn about light and electricity, magnetism and sound, nature and history. The Fryer-Merrit House, an 1880s home, is used for Thronateeska's administrative offices. And a Southern Railway baggage car boasts a model train exhibit that depicts a train journey from the city to the country. A Georgia Northern steam locomotive and several other railcars sit nearby, awaiting restoration.

Facilities: *Discovery Depot, Wetherbee Planetarium, Discovery Center, model railroad display, steam locomotive and meeting room facilities.* **Days/Hours**: *Administrative Office – Monday through Friday, 9 a.m. to 5 p.m. Discovery Depot – Wednesday through Saturday, noon to 4 p.m. Model Train Exhibit – Saturday, 1 p.m. to 4 p.m.* **Fees**: *Discovery Depot – $4; Discovery Center and Wetherbee Planetarium – $4. The model railroad display, sponsored and maintained by the Flint River Model Railroad Club, accepts donations.* **Directions**: *Dougherty County. In Albany, take Oglethorpe Boulevard to Washington (a one-way street). Turn north and go 1 block to Roosevelt. Turn right.* **More Information**: *Thronateeska Heritage Center, 100 W. Roosevelt Avenue, Albany, GA 31701. 229/432-6955; fax: 229/435-1572.*

LAKES

Lake Chehaw

In 1921 as part of the Flint River Project, Georgia Power Company impounded this reservoir at the junction of the Flint River and Muckalee and Kinchafoonee Creeks. Older maps may still refer to the entire body of water as "Lake Worth," but Worth was actually created by the backwater of the Muckafoonee dam (Muckalee + Kinchafoonee = Muckafoonee), which was built in 1906, retired in

Dougherty County

The Flint River flows through Dougherty County and right through the middle of Albany, the county seat.

"Dougherty County was created in 1853 from part of Baker County. Georgia's 102nd county was named for Charles Dougherty of Athens, a judge of the Western Circuit and a popular advocate of state rights. The only incorporated community in the county is the county seat of Albany. The city is named for the New York State capital. Radium Springs is located within the county just south of Albany. The springs are the largest in Georgia, discharging 70,000 gallons of 68 degree water each minute. The springs received its current name in 1925 when the spring water tested was found to contain traces of radium isotopes. During the 1920s a club casino was operated on the banks of the springs [see page 132]...Dougherty County, which has more pecan trees than any other county in the nation, is a strong contributor to south Georgia's claim as the pecan capital of the world."

From *Georgia County Snapshots*, Georgia Department of Community Affairs

For tourism information for towns in Dougherty County, see Resources page 300.

(continued on page 145)

River to Rails

A Walking Tour of Historic Albany

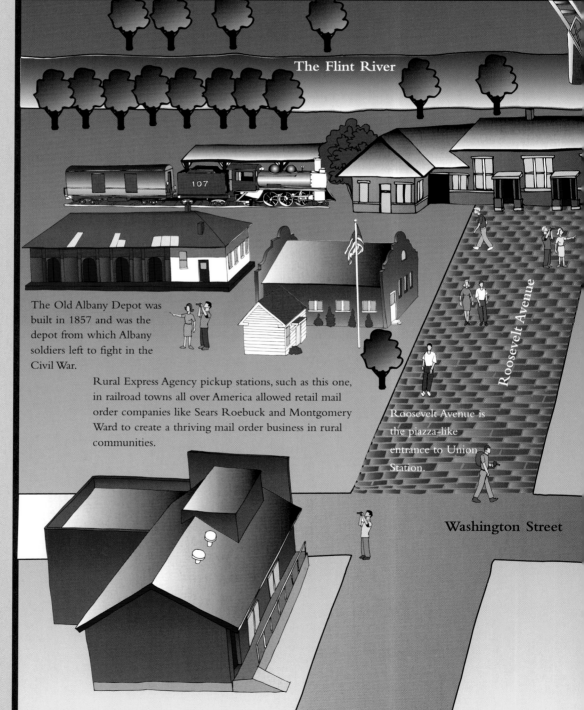

This 1911 steam locomotive originally traveled a route between New York and Key West, Florida.

The Old Albany Depot was built in 1857 and was the depot from which Albany soldiers left to fight in the Civil War.

Rural Express Agency pickup stations, such as this one, in railroad towns all over America allowed retail mail order companies like Sears Roebuck and Montgomery Ward to create a thriving mail order business in rural communities.

This is the Pecan Exchange for a region known as the "Pecan Capital of the World." Farmers brought pecans to this warehouse to sell. From here they were shipped all over the country.

The Flint River

Roosevelt Avenue

Roosevelt Avenue is the piazza-like entrance to Union Station.

Washington Street

The Flint River connected Albany and southwest Georgia with the Gulf of Mexico port of Apalachicola, which—up until the Civil War—was the third-busiest port on the Gulf behind New Orleans and Mobile.

Nelson Tift founded Albany as a port on the Flint River to transport cotton and other farm products to market.

Between 1828 and 1861 some 130 river-boats of all shapes and sizes traveled the Apalachicola-Flint-Chattahoochee River System.

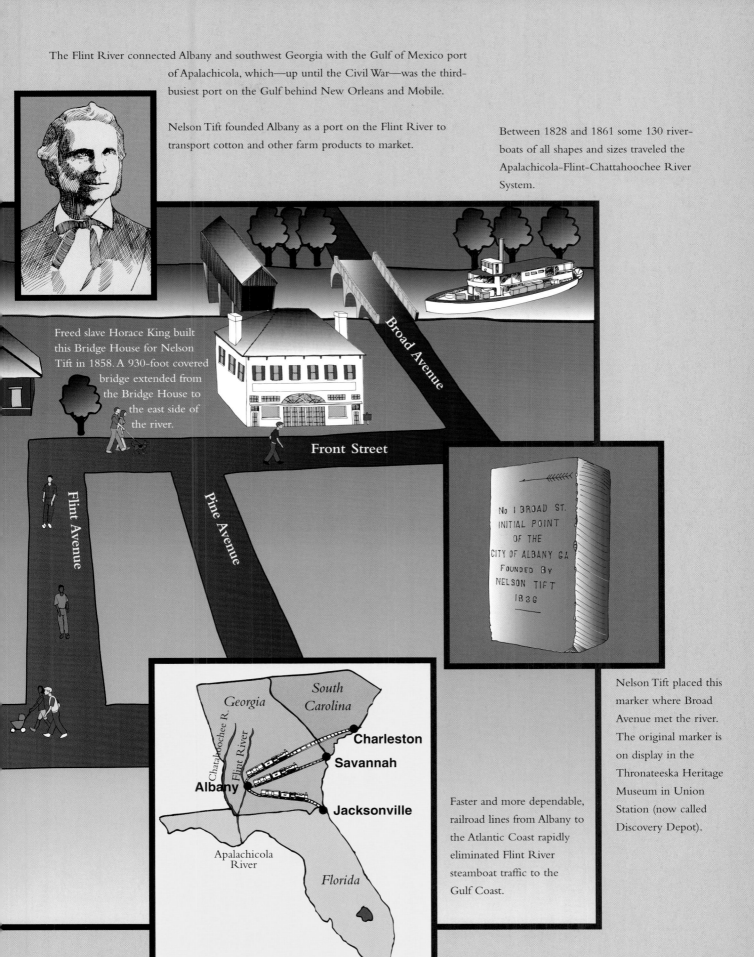

Freed slave Horace King built this Bridge House for Nelson Tift in 1858. A 930-foot covered bridge extended from the Bridge House to the east side of the river.

Broad Avenue

Front Street

Flint Avenue

Pine Avenue

No I BROAD ST.
INITIAL POINT
OF THE
CITY OF ALBANY GA
FOUNDED BY
NELSON TIFT
1836

Nelson Tift placed this marker where Broad Avenue met the river. The original marker is on display in the Thronateeska Heritage Museum in Union Station (now called Discovery Depot).

Georgia

South Carolina

Chattahoochee R.

Flint River

Charleston

Savannah

Albany

Jacksonville

Apalachicola River

Florida

Faster and more dependable, railroad lines from Albany to the Atlantic Coast rapidly eliminated Flint River steamboat traffic to the Gulf Coast.

River to Rails, A Walking Tour of Historic Albany

I
N THE BEGINNING, the Apalachicola–Flint-Chattahoochee River System was the main thoroughfare for transporting goods in and out of southwest Georgia to market. The new land owners found outlets for their cotton, hides, lumber, sugar, corn and tobacco through the Gulf of Mexico. Cotton was the principal commodity shipped, exceeding a value of $7 million in the year ending August 1860. For much of the antebellum period, Apalachicola was the third-leading port on the Gulf behind Mobile and New Orleans, suggesting the productiveness of these agricultural lands of which Albany was an important collection point.

Nelson Tift and the Founding of Albany

Nelson Tift, born in Croton, Connecticut, on July 23, 1810, was to find his destiny on the Flint River in Albany, Georgia. As a young man he worked in the mercantile business with his father for a while in Key West, Florida, before moving on to do business in Augusta, Georgia. In March 1836, he accepted a job offer in Hawkinsville, Georgia, buying cotton and selling groceries at an establishment there.

That September, he formed a company with a group of men headed by John Rawls, president of a Hawkinsville bank. Their purpose was to found a town on the west bank of the Flint River in what was then Baker County "for the purpose of merchandising, boating, traffic and c."

Interest in Rawls, Tift & Company was divided into 18 shares, with Tift receiving three whole shares and an equal interest in three other common stock shares. He also assumed the job of running the business for one year. The property of the company was listed as "one Steamboat in complete order intended for the navigation of the Flint River and two lots of land situated on the West bank of the Flint River in Baker County, intended for the location of a town." So from the beginning, the founding of Albany was a deliberate commercial venture managed by Nelson Tift.

When Tift arrived at the site on October 13, 1836, he found a virgin territory except for a few scattered settlements. Most of the Creek Indians had been forced westward by then, except for a few who had fled to Florida to join the Seminoles.

The land held great promise. Cotton prices were soaring and planters in the eastern part of Georgia and the Carolinas, who had depleted the soil on their plantations from too much cotton cultivating, were buying up land in this newly opened region of southwest Georgia to establish new plantations. The land here was good, rich river bottom land. Land that was perfect for growing cotton. All it took was property, slaves and a way to get the cotton to market.

Tift, who was an entrepreneur rather than a cotton planter, made his business of "getting the cotton to market" the impetus in building a town. He immediately laid out Albany in lots. On his own two lots on the banks of the Flint, he laid the cornerstone of the town. He built a cotton warehouse, a store and a boat landing. He owned the ferry rights and established a ferry. By the end of 1836, a few lots had been sold at $200 for a corner lot and $150 for middle lots.

In his diary 30 years later, Tift described the founding of Albany:

"Albany, the present capitol of Dougherty County, was commenced in October, 1836, in an unbroken pine forest by the construction of two log houses, store and dwelling on lot number 1, Broad Street, and a cotton shed, east, across the street. A steam boat, built for the purpose by the Watts family of Fort Gaines—the 'Mary Emeline' and a barge bought from the estate of Lewis Bond, brought the first goods from Apalachicola to Albany… A steam saw and grist mill established, other houses built, stores, dwellings, hotel, churches school houses &c. Some log and some plank —and we were gradually re-enforced by doctors, lawyers, preachers, schoolteachers, some gamblers and rowdies, and all other sorts which go to make up a frontier town."

The Flint River, and later the railroads, were lifelines to the markets of the outside world. Early on, Nelson Tift regarded the Flint as the principal asset of the region. He wrote in his diary in 1876:

"Emptying into the Gulf of Mexico through Apalachicola, was the natural and common outlet for the exportation of the produce of the country, and the introduction of goods for consumption. Steamboats, barges, and boxes, were used for these purposes. Flint River is largely supplied with springs and underground streams through the limestone foundation, and, by actual measurement made by James R. Butt, Esq., it furnishes in the dry seasons a much larger supply of water than either the Ocmulgee or the Chattahoochee Rivers."

But Tift soon found that steamboats transporting cotton down the river could not always be relied upon. In January 1837, the *Mary Emeline*, the steamboat owned by Rawls, Tift & Company, made its first trip up the Flint River from Apalachicola toward Albany. For some reason, it was unable to reach the settlement and the goods had to be unloaded at Hell's Gate Shoal and sent up by barge.

Tift then purchased two barges for shipping cotton to market at Apalachicola and bringing back provisions on the return trip. Later in January, he took the *Mary Emeline* back to Apalachicola and purchased about $8,000 worth of goods. On the return trip, the steamboat frequently ran aground on the shoals. Sometimes a week or more would pass before it could resume the trip upriver. In early March 1837, the *Mary Emeline* reached Albany for the first time. The freight was unloaded and 220 bales of cotton loaded for the return trip to Apalachicola. In addition, the steamboat stopped at Bainbridge to pick up another 40 bales. Once in Apalachicola, Tift shipped his bales to a cotton factor at Charleston, South Carolina. Thus began Tift's river trade business. It was never easy, but without a way to transport cotton, the surrounding county could not have been opened so early to its extensive cultivation and Albany's emergence as a shipping center would have been dubious.

Despite Tift's vision and leadership, the Albany venture was not an immediate financial success. Rawls, Tift & Company stockholders became discouraged and sold their interest to Tift, who never doubted that this region of Southwest Georgia would become an important part of the state. And for 55 years, Tift would continue to be one of the most important men in the region. He took an active interest in developing nearly any type of

industry in Albany: steamboating, saw milling, flour milling, patent pharmaceuticals, meat packing for the Confederate Navy, shipbuilding in New Orleans under Confederate commission. He published a weekly newspaper, the *Albany Patriot*, and held public office. His toll bridge, built in 1858, was the first bridge over the Flint at Albany, replacing the ferry he had owned. And always remembering that getting the cotton to market and transporting goods into Albany was all important to its growth, he was a prime promoter of railroads to the town. When the first train of cars over the Georgia and Florida Railroad reached Albany in 1857, Nelson Tift was the railroad's president.

The outbreak of the Civil War interrupted railroad construction as well as cotton cultivation, but both resumed and expanded in the years after the war. As the railroads and lumber companies cleared the piney woods east of the Flint River, cotton production spread rapidly into the wiregrass counties. In the 40 years between 1859 and 1899, cotton production increased all over Southwest Georgia.

Nelson Tift survived the war as the second-richest planter in Southwest Georgia, even though about one-third of his wealth was lost because of the war and the emancipation of his slaves. As energetic as ever, he continued to be a key motivating factor in extending a network of rail lines out of Albany. These rail connections made Albany the focus of ginning, pressing and shipping the new bonanza in cotton, ensuring the town's post-Civil War future as a transportation and shipping center.

From his first look at the Flint River until his death on November 18, 1891, Nelson Tift was a man who shaped his own destiny, as well as that of the town he founded.

Broad Avenue Bridge

When Nelson Tift first laid out Albany, Broad Street ran through the center of town and continued down to the west bank of the Flint to meet the river. This was Albany's zero-mile post. Tift put a stone marker at the spot which read, "No. 1 Broad St. Initial Point of the City of Albany, GA, Founded by Nelson Tift, 1836." From here, cargo—mostly cotton—was loaded on steamboats and barges for the voyage downriver to Apalachicola.

In 1920 the bridge that presently spans the river at

Broad Street was constructed. Four concrete benches built into the bridge bear bronze markers dedicating the bridge as a memorial to Dougherty County World War I veterans and commemorating the people involved in the bridge's construction.

The northeast marker reads: "As the enduring expression of a community's pride and gratitude this bridge was erected A.D. 1920 as a memorial to those who went from Dougherty County to serve their country in the World War 1917–1919."

The southeast marker reads: "We hold in grateful remembrance those who stepped from the pursuits of peace in response to the call of their country and of civilization, and in the World War 1917–119 offered themselves for the maintenance of American rights, for the preservation of American ideals and for the realization of Humanity's Hopes."

Riverboats

Between 1828 and 1861, about 130 steamboats plied the waters of the river system. Typically, these were side-wheelers—flat-bottomed boats with shallow draft and no holds. Cotton bales, hogsheads of sugar and stacked lumber were shipped on deck. Most of these were built in shipyards along the Ohio and Mississippi Rivers, but several steamboats were built and launched near Albany during the late 1840s. On January 17, 1846, the new steamboat *Albany* was launched from the boatyard above the city, and by March was making regular trips to Apalachicola. In April 1846, the *Flint* was launched from the same boatyard.

To some extent, barges towed by steamboats were used for shipping, but "cotton boxes," square, barge-like vessels that were cheap to build, were found to be the most practical method of shipping cotton down the river. A cotton box built in 1838 at Danville, above Albany, was probably the first one used on the Flint. This box reportedly carried 360 bales of cotton to Apalachicola at an average charge of $2.50 per bale.

River trade was important to the economic life of Southwest Georgia people, but it was a hazardous business. The river system was usually navigable as far north as Bainbridge year round. But toward Columbus on the Chattahoochee and toward Albany on the Flint, it was subject to the restrictions and dangers of low water or low bridges in high-water

times. During dry months, light cotton boxes capable of carrying 150 to 200 bales could be used; but the larger boxes, carrying from 400 to 700 bales, had to wait until water levels were high enough to make the trip to Apalachicola.

Boats coming up the river from Apalachicola, a journey that took more than a week, seemed to have the most difficulty. When fuel ran low or food was needed, the boat would stop and the crew would chop wood, hunt and fish. Frequently, boats and barges would run aground, boilers would burst or overhanging trees would knock over the smoke stack. Fires triggered by boilers allowed to go dry or sparks from the smokestack meant disaster. In 1845 alone, boats were lost in three catastrophes. One, the *Viola*, struck a rock just below Albany and sank. In 1854 the steamer *Florence* struck a jutting rock and sank a mile below Albany with 345 bales of cotton on board.

Appeals were made to the state legislature for appropriations to improve the Flint's navigability. An 80-foot wide channel was cut at Hell's Gate, the most dangerous shoal on the river; but overall, the state did little to improve the river for navigation.

The coming of the railroads to the region in the 1850s sounded the death knell of steamboating. In 1850 about 80 percent of the region's produce reached Apalachicola. A decade later it had fallen by half. The same decade saw a decline in water levels because of a down cycle in rainfall. Afterwards, the fortunes made in railroad construction, operation and speculation dominated Georgia politics, as indeed it dominated those of the nation.

Toll Bridge and Bridge House

Historically, this was the site of the ferry that Nelson Tift ran at Albany from its founding in 1836 until he built a toll bridge on the site in 1858. Tift, who owned both ferry and bridge rights here, let the contract for the bridge in June 1858 to Dr. A. J. Robinson of Columbus, Georgia, who brought in Horace King (see sidebar page 66), the freed slave and celebrated bridge builder, to supervise the work.

For a cost of $30,000, King built a covered bridge that sat on three piers of stone and had an overall length of 930 feet. He also constructed a large, two-story brick building, known as the Bridge House, on the Albany side of the river. The entrance to the bridge on the Albany side was through an archway in the center of the building. The bridge keeper occupied one side of the ground floor; Tift's office the other. The second floor extended over the archway and was a theater, known as Tift's Hall. Decorated by New York artists, it was considered the most beautiful theater in the state. The walls were painted with frescoes and it was decorated with stage scenery. Leading actors and actresses of the day appeared on the stage here. The Bridge House was a popular Albany site for social events, such as dances and masked balls.

During the Civil War, the great cellars of the Bridge House were converted into packing houses and the back yard became a slaughter pen. Thousands of cattle, hogs and sheep were barreled in pickle for the use of the Confederate Navy.

Roosevelt Avenue

The 75-foot wide, piazza-like entrance way to Union Station is paved with red bricks put down at the same time the passenger terminal was built in 1913 and polished smooth by more than a half-century of foot, mule, horse and car traffic. The remnants of an old city trolley line run down the center of Roosevelt Union Station. Originally called North Avenue, the street's name was changed to Roosevelt in the 1930s in honor of President Franklin Delano Roosevelt.

The Pecan Exchange

In the 1920s the growth of pecan farming in the region made it an alternative to cotton as a money crop for Albany area farmers. Albany soon became known as the "Pecan Capital of the World." There are still more pecan trees in the Albany area than anywhere else in the country. Regional growers brought their harvested crops to this brick building on the corner of Roosevelt and Washington, known as the Pecan Exchange. Traders purchased the crop and from here the pecans were loaded on trains and shipped to markets all over the country.

Rural Express Agency

The small red brick building with the South-western style curved roof line standing in front of Union Station housed the Rural Express Agency, the

UPS or Federal Express service of the 1930s and '40s. REA pickup stations like this in railroad towns all over America allowed retail mail-order companies, such as Sears Roebuck and Montgomery Ward, to create a thriving mail-order business. Residents from Albany and surrounding areas came here to pick up merchandise ordered from other parts of the country.

Now a part of the Thronateeska Heritage Center, it houses the Discovery Center and Weatherbee Planetarium.

Railroads

Where the hazards and inconsistencies of river traffic were a challenge, the finances and politics involved in railroad building were just as hazardous. Several attempts to bring a railroad to Albany by planters, as well as by Nelson Tift, failed before the first train of cars over the Georgia and Florida Railroad arrived at the Albany Depot from Americus in September of 1857, just a few years before the Civil War.

The importance of the railroad to the city was seen almost immediately. According to the *Albany Patriot*, five brickyards were busy supplying brick for new buildings, including warehouses, a passenger depot, stores, offices, and residences. Nelson Tift was replacing his ferry with a toll bridge across the Flint and a brick Bridge House.

At first, rail lines were intended primarily as a means of shipping cotton and other produce to market; but with the addition of passenger cars, railroads soon opened a whole new world to travelers, making trips to Macon, Savannah and Augusta and all points in between easier and safer.

The brick building with a tin roof to the north of Union Station is the original Albany freight depot built in 1857, three years before the Civil War. Each side of the building has four arched doorways where cargo—mostly cotton—was loaded and unloaded. The southern end of the building, painted white, was for passengers; the larger northern end was a warehouse, where 500-pound cotton bales were stored before being loaded onto trains.

In April 1861, the Albany Guards, escorted to the depot by the Dougherty Hussars and Albany Independents, left from this station to join other Confederate troops at Augusta while a band played

"The Girl I Left Behind Me." The Guards became Company E of the Fourth Georgia Infantry. On May 3 at Augusta the company was mustered into the Confederate service and the following day en route to Richmond. By the end of the year, the Guards were in the thick of the fighting around Norfolk. The company saw service in important battles under Lee's command, including Malvern Hill, Chancellorsville, Sharpsburg, Gettysburg, and at the end, were present at Appomattox. Some were killed in battle, others died from disease, many were injured and the fate of others was unknown.

The Civil War was but an interruption in the growth of railroads in Southwest Georgia. As soon as the war was over, there was an immediate revival of interest in extending a network of rail lines out of Albany.

By the turn of the century Albany had become a rail center. At its peak, five railroads—the Central of Georgia, the Atlantic Coast Line, Georgia Northern, the Seaboard Air Line, and the Albany and Northern —had seven rail lines operating from the city and as many as 55 passenger trains passed through the city every day.

But just as the railroad tracks had replaced the river in economic importance, the railroad would eventually give way to highways, and the Albany region would come to rely on gasoline-powered trucks for its economic prosperity.

In the 1930s descendants of Nelson Tift operated a grocery company in part of the old depot building. Water damage from the 1994 flood is evident along the base.

1911 Steam Locomotive

An outdoor train museum—consisting of a 1911 steam engine, a 1920s Southern Railway baggage car, an Atlantic Coast Line 1910 railway post office, two cabooses and four boxcars—sits between Union Station and the Old Albany Depot. The locomotive, Number 107, originally traveled a route between New York and Key West, Florida, until a hurricane wiped out the rail line. It was purchased by Georgia Northern—the name now painted on its side—and donated to the city in the 1950s. One caboose is a Southern Railway 1969 model while the other is a Chesapeake and Ohio built in 1971. Originally

owned by Atlantic Coast Line, the four 40-foot boxcars were built in 1951 and then rebuilt by Seaboard Coastline in 1971.

Plans for the museum include building a train shed, stabilizing 500 to 600 feet of track, cosmetically restoring the steam engine and painting the baggage car and the railway post office car. Currently, the baggage car houses a model railroad.

Union Station

By 1910 Albany was the railroad hub of Southwest Georgia. The red brick Union Railroad Station, capped with an impressive tile roof and set off by twin portecocheres, was built in 1913, replacing a wooden Victorian building. The station was constructed in the "Prairie Style" design popularized by Frank Lloyd Wright, where horizontal lines have the effect of appearing to connect the building to the landscape. The section of the building at the far left was the baggage handling area. The middle section was the ticketing booth and the waiting area, built to reflect the segregation laws at the time with a wall dividing the area into separate "White" and "Colored" sections. The station is one of just a few remaining stations built in this manner that remain standing today. On the right was a restaurant frequented by Albanians for weekday lunch and on weekends to observe the coming and going of passenger trains and their well-heeled passengers on their way from New York and other northern cities to the heavily advertised state of Florida.

When a 1940 tornado hit Albany, winds blew off most of the station's clay tile roof, its north portecochere and the two original dormers. The dormers were never replaced and the portecocheres were rebuilt with only half their original overhang.

The last passenger train pulled out of Union Station in 1971. Today, it's name has been changed to Discovery Depot and it houses the Thronateeska Heritage Museum.

(continued from 137)

1938 and is used today as a free-crested spillway near the current power dam. When the Flint River Project impounded the main river channel in 1921, that backwater was known as "Georgia Power Lake."

These days, the entire 1,400-acre reservoir, which straddles Albany's city limits and Lee and Dougherty Counties goes by the name of Lake Chehaw, after the Indian tribe whose village on the Flint was mistakenly destroyed by the Georgia Militia in 1818.

Around Lake Chehaw's 36 miles of shoreline are residential neighborhoods and several recreational areas. Georgia Power, the largest non-government provider of recreation facilities in the state, maintains a heavily wooded day-use area near the power dam (see page 146) for boating, fishing, hiking and biking. The Parks at Chehaw (see page 146) provides a fishing dock and hiking trails along the banks of the impounded Muckalee Creek. Albany's Recreation Department operates two boat ramps on Lake Chehaw: Cleve Cox Landing on Muckafoonee Creek and Cromartie Beach Landing on the lake's main body, about one and a half miles from the dam. Its Turner Field Ramp serves boaters a little further up river, about four miles north of the dam. For boat ramp locations, see map page 203.

The Georgia Department of Natural Resources annually stocks around 10,000 hybrid bass in the lake; fishing for largemouth bass, crappie, bluegill and shellcracker is considered to be fair. Anglers can usually be found below the dam in the tailrace area of the lake trying to catch a trophy-size striped bass or 10–15 pound flathead catfish. Georgia Power Company provides free lake maps at area bait shops.

More Information: *Georgia Power Company, Bartlett's Ferry Land Management Office, 1516 Bartlett's Ferry Road, Fortson, GA 31808. 1-888-GPC-LAKE or 706/322-0228.*

PARKS

Turner Field Park

This former navy base, located along the upper stretches of the Flint River as it approaches Albany, is now a unique riverfront recreational area. Maintained by the Albany Recreation Department, the park is centered around an 18-hole golf course and fronts about two miles of shoreline. The red barn by the boat ramp was once a naval boat house and has recently been renovated into an enclosed picnic pavilion.

Facilities: *Boat ramp (see map page 203), 18-hole golf course and clubhouse, picnic pavilion, picnic tables, playground, gymnasium, racquetball courts, softball fields, restrooms and drinking water.* **Days/Hours**: *Open daily, sunrise until 9 p.m. from May through October, until 6 p.m. from November through April.* **Fees**: *All facilities are subject to user fees.* **Directions**: *Doughterty County. In Albany, take US 19/82 north to Turner Field Exit. Turn right onto Clark Avenue and then left onto Turner Field Road. Go to McAdams Road, turn left and follow the signs.* **More Information**: *City of Albany Recreation Department, 1301 N. Monroe, Albany, GA 31701.*

Chehaw Town

"The Chehaw Indians had settlements in the Creek Confederacy on both the Flint and Chattahoochee Rivers. The village on the former stream was located immediately north of Leesburg....

"The Chehaw Town was very friendly to the whites and furnished supplies and warriors to the U.S. and Georgia troops in their war with the Lower Creeks and Seminoles, 1814–1818. Governor Rabin of Georgia ordered Captain Obediah Wright to leave Hartford (across the Ocmulgee River from today's Hawkinsville) and go to the Flint River to take action against two Indian chiefs, Hopaunee and Felemma, who were very unfriendly to the whites. Both chiefs lived on the Flint (but not in Chehaw Town).

"Captain Wright and 270 men marched southward to attack the two towns of Hopaunee and Felemma. However, he received word that Chief Hopaunee had taken refuge in the Chehaw Town. On April 30, 1818, completely disregarding orders, Wright moved against the Chehaw Town, and ordered his men to destroy the village but not to injure women or children. Within two hours the town was in flames, as no resistance was encountered since all the warriors were away helping General Andrew Jackson in Florida. Accounts differ as to how many Indians were killed, but one report stated seven men, one woman, and two children.

"Immediately Captain Wright was in deep trouble, as the incident was reported and discussed all the way to the halls of Congress in Washington. Everyone agreed that Captain Wright was very much in error and he was ordered arrested, and on May 29 he was placed in jail. However, Wright became alarmed at what his fate might be and somehow escaped from jail never to be heard from again."

Indian Heritage in Georgia by Marion R. Hemperley

229/430-5222. Turner Field Golf Course, 200 McAdais Road, Albany, GA 31701. 229/430-5267.

Georgia Power Dam Park

Within earshot of traffic on the US 19/82 Bypass, hikers can pick up pieces of flint near the limestone banks of the river just below the Georgia Power Dam on Lake Chehaw. Hiking, along with fishing, boating and biking, are all available at this heavily wooded day-use area maintained by Georgia Power Company.

Facilities: *Ramp for canoe portage above the dam, picnic shelter and picnic tables with grills located in day-use area on west side of dam; below the dam a boat ramp for portage and boat trailers (see map page 203). Bank fishing, tailrace fishing pier and hiking and biking on unpaved roads that border the Flint River and Muckafoonee Creek.* **Days/Hours**: *Open daily, daylight hours.* **Directions**: *Dougherty County. In Albany, take GA 91 (Philema Road) north to Jewel Street and turn right; at the end of the street turn left. Travel past the Georgia Power office and follow signs.* **More Information**: *Georgia Power Company, Bartlett's Ferry Land Management Office, 1516 Bartlett's Ferry Road, Fortson, GA 31808. 1-888-GPC-LAKE or 706/322-0228.*

The Parks at Chehaw

On a late autumn afternoon, dozens of deer peacefully roam the acreage at the Parks at Chehaw. White-tailed deer, fox, alligators, tortoises, beavers, squirrels, bobcats, gopher, numerous species of birds—they all make their home at this 800-acre recreational area that stretches along Muckalee Creek at its confluence with Kinchafoonee Creek in Albany.

Named after one of three villages of Creek Indians that once inhabited the area here, the Parks at Chehaw offers a wide range of outdoor activities for the people who enter its gates. Within this one recreational area are several "parks," featuring uniquely different activities: Creekside Park with its nature trails, picnic areas, fishing ponds and a 15 X 24-foot floating dock on the creek; Play Park with Playscape, a 15,000-square-foot, community-built play park that includes a jungle fortress, a rocket, a ship, a tree house and an elephant trunk slide; RV Park for campers; and BMX Bicycle Track and a Bike Park for recreational and mountain bikers.

Perhaps the most unique park within a park is the 150-acre Wild Animal Park. Created with design input from naturalist Jim Fowler of television's *Wild Kingdom*, Chehaw's Wild Animal Park was dedicated in 1977, replacing the concrete and cage zoo that had been in Albany since 1910. You can walk on elevated boardwalks and paths through more than 100 acres of Georgia's piney woods and cypress swamps to get view both native and exotic animals roaming in their natural habitats. The Park's main theme is African Trails and features animals and habitats specific to the African savanna and forests.

The Flat Lands of South Georgia

"Below the fall line hills, near the central part of the state, the topography changes abruptly into the flat lands of south Georgia, where longleaf pines tower above an undergrowth of wire grass, wild leguminous plants, or gallberry bushes. Also plentiful in this region is the slash pine of great potential value for paper making. The trunks of many of these pines are gashed for turpentine, and the air is sharp with its clean and pungent odor. Throughout south Georgia and on the coastal islands grows the mighty live oak, its gnarled trunk supporting thickly foliaged branches hung with waving streamers of gray Spanish moss."

Georgia, the WPA Guide to its Towns and Countryside compiled by workers of the 1940 Writers' Program of the Works Progress Administration in the State of Georgia

Near the Wild Animal Park, you can catch the Wiregrass Express for a 20-minute train ride through Chehaw's longleaf pine and wiregrass restoration area. And at the park's southern end situated along the Muckalee Creek is the 10,000-square-foot Creekside Education Center (see page 132), which offers school and community-based nature programming.

Facilities: *Wild Animal Park, Creekside Education Center; campsites (see page 149), screened pavilion with indoor grill, kitchen facilities, tables and chairs and restrooms; 10 picnic shelters; fishing dock; hiking trails (see page 149); BMX track; biking trail; playground; miniature train; concessions and restrooms.* **Days/Hours**: *Park – open daily, 9 a.m. to 5 p.m. Wild Animal Park – open daily, 9:30 a.m. to 5 p.m. Closed New Year's Day, Thanksgiving and Christmas.* **Fees**: *Park – $2 per car and $10 per bus. Wild Animal Park – additional $2 per adult (12 years of age and up) and $1 each for children, seniors and military. Wiregrass Express – $2 per person.* **Directions**: *Dougherty County. From Leesburg, take US 19/82 south about 5 miles to GA 133. Bear left and go 3.5 miles to GA 91/Philema Road. Turn left and go 1 mile. The park is on the left.* **More Information**: *Parks at Chehaw, 105 Chehaw Park Road, Albany, GA 31701. 229/430-5275. Website: www.parksatchehaw.org.*

Albany Veterans Park

This seven-acre scenic park rests along the banks of the Flint River adjacent to Oglethorpe Bridge and the Albany Civic Center. A walking path winds around water oaks and sycamores and out to a wooden overlook that extends over the river. Besides the footpath, the park—which only promotes passive outdoor activities—features a Vietnam War memorial carved from a 24,000-pound block of Georgia granite. The memorial lists the names of the 42 men from Dougherty and Lee Counties who died in that conflict. There is also a 2,500-seat outdoor amphitheater where people can sit on grass and concrete terraces to enjoy music and theatrical performances.

This area was well under water during the 1994 flood. A monument paying tribute to the thousands of volunteers who helped rebuild Albany after the flood's devastation sits at a crosswalk lined with Bradford pears between Veterans Park and the Civic Center.

Facilities: *Amphitheater and walking trail.* **Days/Hours**: *Open daily, 8 a.m. until dark, except during reserved events.* **Directions**: *Dougherty County. In Albany, take Oglethorpe Boulevard east to the Oglethorpe Bridge (see page 151). Park is on the right just before you cross the bridge.* **More Information**: *Veterans Park, Albany Civic Center, 100 West Oglethorpe Boulevard, Albany, GA 31701. 229/430-5200.*

WILDLIFE MANAGEMENT AREAS

Albany Nursery Wildlife Management Area
This small, 300-acre wildlife management area is a favored spot for

Longleaf Pine

When the first Europeans stepped foot in the southeast, the most dominant forest ecosystem was that of the longleaf pine. Stretching from what is now east Texas through the lower Coastal Plain to Virginia, an estimated 60 to 90 million acres of longleaf pine existed. Among the most biodiverse of all forest ecosystems, it supported hundreds of plant and animal species specifically adapted to conditions created in that forest.

Distinguished by dark green, 10 to 18-inch needles, occurring in bundles of threes, the 150-foot longleaf pine grows best on well-drained sandy soils. Its slightly curved cones are usually six to 10 inches long. Many consider the longleaf superior to other southern pines; the quality of its wood products are the most valuable, the most aesthetically pleasing and the most resistant to insects, disease and fire.

In fact, fire helps longleaf pine to flourish (see sidebar page 246). Fires lit by Native Americans to facilitate hunting and travel and as a way of managing game—kept the forest healthy. Today, due to fire suppression, land development and conversion to other types of pine forests, only about 3 million acres of longleaf pine remain, Many species, including the red-cockaded woodpecker (see sidebar page 262) and the gopher tortoise, who depend directly on the longleaf ecosystem have become endangered or threatened as the tree gradually disappears. With so many animals relying on the gopher tortoise's existence alone (see sidebar page 160), you can immediately realize the domino effect that takes place.

disabled hunters. It is in the headwaters of the Swamp of Toa, the second-largest swamp system in the state. Hunting and bird watching activities are promoted here. An interpretive wildlife trail makes a two-mile loop through the hardwood forests and wetlands of the property where atamasco lily, trillium and buckeye grow. Wildlife that make their home here include white-tailed deer, wild turkey, bobcat, fox, raccoon and gray squirrel. Bird watchers will find wood ducks, barred owls, hawks, songbirds, great blue herons and common egret.

Deer and turkey hunts, organized exclusively for the physically disabled, take place at the Albany Nursery. Hunters must apply by letter to the Wildlife Resources Division. For general WMA regulations, license requirements and hunting seasons, hunters should obtain a current copy of "Georgia Hunting Seasons & Regulations" available at local outdoors stores and from the Georgia DNR.

Facilities: *None. Camping is not allowed.* **Days/Hours**: *Open daily, 24 hours.* **Directions**: *Dougherty County. From Albany, take GA 234 (Gillionville Highway) west 11 miles. Turn right on Tallahassee Road. Go 1.2 miles to entrance marked by Wildlife Resources Division sign.* **More Information**: *Georgia Department of Natural Resources, Wildlife Resources Division, 2024 Newton Road, Albany, GA 31701-3576. 229/430-4254.*

Chickasawhatchee Wildlife Management Area

Chickasawhatchee Creek runs through or borders a major portion of this wildlife management area, which covers 9,836 acres in southeastern Calhoun and northern Baker Counties. It is a part of the vast area known as the Swamp of Toa (see page 129) and currently provides the only reliable public access to that area.

Chickasawhatchee is operated for hunting only. Managed by the Georgia Department of Natural Resources, the area maintains good populations of deer, turkey and squirrel; fair populations of quail and dove; and a low population of waterfowl, mainly wood ducks.

Pine plantations and natural pine stands of varying ages comprise the upland habitats here. These bisect the numerous small hardwood tributaries that drain eastward into the Chickasawhatchee, which drains into the Ichawaynochaway about five miles downstream of the WMA's southern border. Relatively small and isolated gum ponds and cypress domes are scattered across the pine uplands.

Hunters must check-in or sign-in once before each hunt. The check-in station is at Jordan's Grocery on GA 62. For general WMA regulations, license requirements and hunting seasons, hunters should obtain a current copy of "Georgia Hunting Seasons & Regulations," available at local outdoors stores and from the Georgia DNR.

There are much more uplands in this swamp area than in the Okefenokee Swamp, for example, so you can walk through much of the area. All roads can be used throughout the WMA. A map is available at the check station.

Facilities: *None. Camping is not allowed in the WMA.* **Days/Hours**:

Slash Pine

A pine found commonly on the tree plantations of south Georgia, the slash pine *(Pinus elliottii* Engelm.*)* is confined principally to the lower Coastal Plain. Its habitat is mostly low, moist sandy sites, but it can often be found thriving on the drier ridges common to its range.

Key characteristics, according to the Georgia Forestry Commission, are "leaves or needles 8 to 12 inches long in clusters of two or three to the sheath" and "cones 3 to 6 inches long, brown, glossy."

The slash and longleaf pine are the two species which produce gum turpentine and rosin. The slash pine has a "heavy, hard, strong, coarse-grained, rich, dark orange-colored heartwood and white sapwood."

Open daily, 24 hours. **Directions**: *Calhoun and Baker Counties. From Newton, take Pretoria Road north about 13.5 miles to its junction with GA 62. Turn left and go 11.5 miles to check station at Jordan's Grocery.* **More Information**: *Georgia Department of Natural Resources, Wildlife Resources Division, 2024 Newton Road, Albany, GA 31701-3576. 229/430-4254.*

Elmodel Wildlife Management Area

This 1,576-acre wildlife management area in the Upper Coastal Plain caters to dove and small game hunting. There are five dove fields and two ponds located on the property. Dove, fox, bobcat, raccoon, opossum and all small game can be hunted at Elmodel. For general WMA regulations, license requirements and hunting seasons, hunters should obtain a current copy of "Georgia Hunting Seasons & Regulations," available at local outdoors stores and from the DNR.

Facilities: *None. Camping is not allowed in the WMA.* **Days/Hours**: *Open daily, 24 hours.* **Directions**: *Baker County. From Newton, take GA 37 north 8 miles. Turn left on Power Dam Road. Area is on the right.* **More Information**: *Georgia Department of Natural Resources, Wildlife Resources Division, 2024 Newton Road, Albany, GA 31701-3576. 229/430-4254.*

CAMPGROUNDS

The Parks at Chehaw Campground

At the Parks at Chehaw, you can pitch a tent or pull up your RV to a site surrounded by a BMX track, a play park and a Wild Animal Park. There is something for the entire family at this campground near Muckalee Creek and Lake Chehaw in Albany.

Facilities: *50 RV and trailer campsites with water and electrical hookups, central bath house, laundry facilities, drink machine and dump station; 25 tent sites with water and centrally located covered picnic area and adjacent bath house; and some primitive campsites available.* **Days/Hours**: *Open daily, 9 a.m. to 5 p.m. Closed Thanksgiving, Christmas and New Year's Day.* **Fees**: *RV and trailers, $12 per day; senior citizens, $10 per day; tent campsites, $6 per day; primitive campsites, call for group rates.* **Directions**: *Dougherty County. From Leesburg, take US 19/82 south about 5 miles to GA 133. Bear left and go 3.5 miles to GA 91/Philema Road. Turn left and go 1 mile. The park is on the left.* **More Information**: *The Parks at Chehaw, 105 Chehaw Park Road, Albany, Georgia 31701. 229/430-5275. Website: www.parksatchehaw.org.*

HIKES AND WALKS

The Parks at Chehaw Hiking Trails

The primary hiking trails in the Parks at Chehaw are in the Creekside Park section, beginning near the boat dock and ponds and running parallel partway to Muckalee Creek. Although hikers must defer to bikers, hiking is allowed on the park's mountain bike trail.

Baker County

The Flint River flows down the eastern border of and through the county seat of Newton.

"Baker County was created from Early County in 1825. Georgia's 61st county was named for Colonel John Baker, a Puritan and noted patriot of the Revolutionary War. Newton is the county seat and the only incorporated community in the county. The Baker County Courthouse has been damaged by floods three times-in 1925, 1929, and 1994. Newton was named for Sergeant John Newton of South Carolina, a soldier in the Revolutionary War. Primarily an agricultural community, Baker County produces peanuts, cotton, canola, poultry, and beef. The last battle of the Creek Indian War of 1836 [see sidebar page 130] was fought in Baker County at Chickasawhatchee Swamp near Red Bluff. Indian villages were first recorded in the Baker County area by Spanish explorer Hernando DeSoto in 1540. Baker County is home to several plantations, ranging in size from 5,000 to 28,000 acres. The largest is Ichauway Plantation, once owned by Coca-Cola magnate Robert Woodruff. The plantation now houses the Joseph W. Jones Ecological Research Center [see page 131], one of the largest outdoor research centers in the world. Scientists study local vegetation, water systems, and wildlife, including 32 species of endangered plants and animals found on the plantation."

From *Georgia County Snapshots*, Georgia Department of Community Affairs

For tourism information for towns in Baker County, see Resources page 300.

Distance: Creekside Park – 2 to 3 miles of easy walking nature trails, which are well-marked and self-interpretive. Bike Park – about 2 miles of old logging roads over fairly flat terrain.

Trailhead location: The Parks at Chehaw (see page 146). Pick up a map at the main office. Creekside Trails – trailhead near the boat dock. Bike Park - trailhead at Bike Park parking area.

Features: Because of their proximity to the creek, the vegetation and wildlife at the Creekside trails differ from that along the logging roads in the Bike Park. Together the hiking and bike trails present an excellent overview of the plant and animal life unique to this area. Look for bobcat, deer, red fox and armadillo tracks along the trails; while deer and armadillo sightings are common. Along the creek and the wetlands, there are wood storks, beaver, otter, egrets and little and great blue herons as well as green herons. All of these animals live among the park's diverse vegetation, which includes southern wax myrtle, bayberry, crabapple, native wild iris and American beautyberry at the park's northern end. Cypress knees, silver bells, native azaleas, hollow water oak, wild amaryllis and jack-in-the-pulpit can be seen along the paths on the park's southern end.

BRIDGES

GA 32 Bridge

On the east bank just above this bridge once stood the Indian village of Pindertown, which later became a steamboat landing. The bridge, built in 1955, is now surrounded by the private hunting plantations that are so common to this portion of the Flint River Valley. River access is from a boat ramp on the southwest side of the bridge (see map page 170). **Location**: *On Lee and Worth County line where GA 32 crosses the Flint River, 9 miles east of Leesburg.*

US 19/82 Bypass Bridge

Built in 1967, this is the first bridge south of the Albany power dam. If you look upstream from the bridge, you can see where Muckafoonee Creek enters the river on the left, about halfway between the bridge and the power dam in the distance, about 0.5 mile upstream. About 0.25 mile below the bridge is the Norfolk Southern Railway Bridge. Wetlands surround the bridge. **Location**: *In Dougherty County where US 19/82 Bypass crosses the Flint in Albany.*

Broad Avenue Bridge

Built in 1920, this bridge, which runs through the heart of Albany, is the grand dame of bridges still in use over the Flint River. Just upstream from the Broad Avenue Bridge are the arched spans of the Norfolk Southern Railway Bridge, while just downstream is the Oglethorpe Boulevard Bridge. **Location**: *In Dougherty County where Broad Avenue crosses the Flint River in Albany.*

Oglethorpe Boulevard Bridge

Sitting just below the Broad Avenue Bridge and running through the center of Albany is this bridge, built in 1953. Albany's Veterans Park and Amphitheater (see page 147) is located on the southeast side of the bridge. **Location**: *In Dougherty County where Oglethorpe Boulevard (US 19, US 82, GA 3, GA 50) crosses the Flint River in Albany.*

Oakridge Drive (GA 234/133)

This 1976 bridge on the south side of Albany is the last bridge over the Flint until you get to Newton, 30.8 miles south. **Location**: *In Dougherty County where Oakridge Drive (GA 234/133) crosses the Flint River in Albany.*

GA 37 Bridge

This bridge, officially named the "James Henderson Hall, Sr. Bridge" was built in 1971. During the 1994 flood, the Flint River rose 21 feet above flood level, covering the bridge as well as most of the town square at Newton. River access on the east side about 0.5 mile north of bridge from an unpaved parking lot and concrete boat ramp (see map page 237) on Rivertrace Road. **Location**: *On the Baker and Mitchell County line where GA 37 crosses the Flint River, just east of Newton.*

DAMS

Georgia Power Dam

Holding back the waters of the Flint River at Lake Chehaw is what is known simply as the Georgia Power Dam. Built in 1921 as part of the power company's Flint River Project, this concrete slab and buttress power dam measures 464 feet long, with a structural height of 46 feet. Its three units generate an annual average of 34,400 megawatt hours. Located in the day-use area just west of the power dam, the similarly constructed Muckafoonee dam, built in 1906 and retired in 1938, now serves as an overflow for Lake Chehaw's rising waters. Engineers monitor the lake's water levels from a remote site at Plant Mitchell, located approximately 12 miles south on the Flint River.

More Information: *Georgia Power Company, Bartlett's Ferry Land Management Office, 1516 Bartlett's Ferry Road, Fortson, GA 31808. 1-888-GPC-LAKE or 706/322-0228.*

Mitchell County

The Flint River creates the western border of Mitchell County.

"Mitchell County was created from Baker County in 1857. The Act creating the county noted that it was named after General Henry Mitchell. He had been a state senator from Warren County, president of the Senate, a presidential elector, and commander of the Georgia troops after the Revolutionary War. The widely held view among historians, however, was that the county was named for General David B. Mitchell, who was twice governor of Georgia. There are four incorporated municipalities in the county: Baconton, Camilla, Pelham, and Sale City. Camilla, the county seat, is named for General David Mitchell's daughter. Pelham was named for Major John Pelham, the 'boy artillerist' who was mortally wounded at the Battle of Kelly's Ford in 1863. The western border of the county is defined by the Flint River."

From *Georgia County Snapshots*, Georgia Department of Community Affairs

For tourism information for towns in Mitchell County, see Resources page 300.

Section 6

Bainbridge and Lake Seminole

W E RETURN TO LAKE SEMINOLE, where we first met Rio. We find out that the Flint River, along with the Chattahoochee and Apalachicola, had a rich history of paddle boat travel. We listen to Jack Wingate, who spins tales about the history of the region, as well as the fishing and hunting adventures to be discovered there.

In Bainbridge and on Lake Seminole, use the Guidebook Section beginning on page 160 to explore: Bainbridge via a guided walking tour, Lake Seminole with all of its parks and Corps of Engineers day use areas and boat ramps, Seminole State Park and its system of hiking trails, Jim Woodruff Dam Fishing Area, Chattahoochee Park, Cheney Griffin Park, Earl May Boat Basin, Spring Creek Park, Harvel Pond, Apalachee Wildlife Management Area, Lake Seminole Wildlife Management Area, Lunker Lodge, Big Jim's Landing and Lodge, Seminole Sportsman's Lodge and Marina, Trails End Marina and Campground and Seminole Lodge Marina.

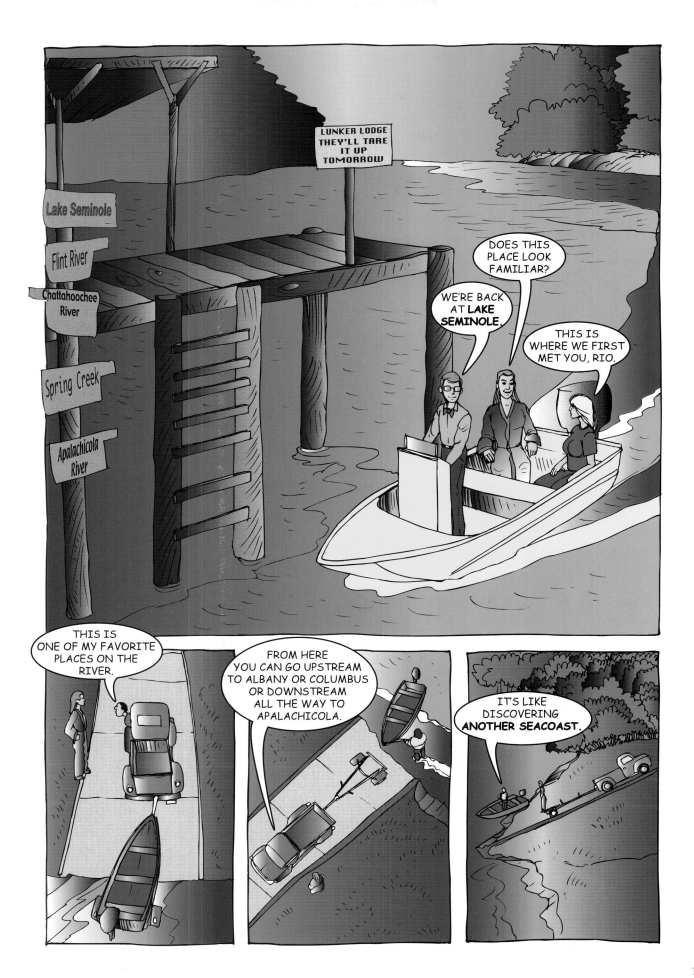

153

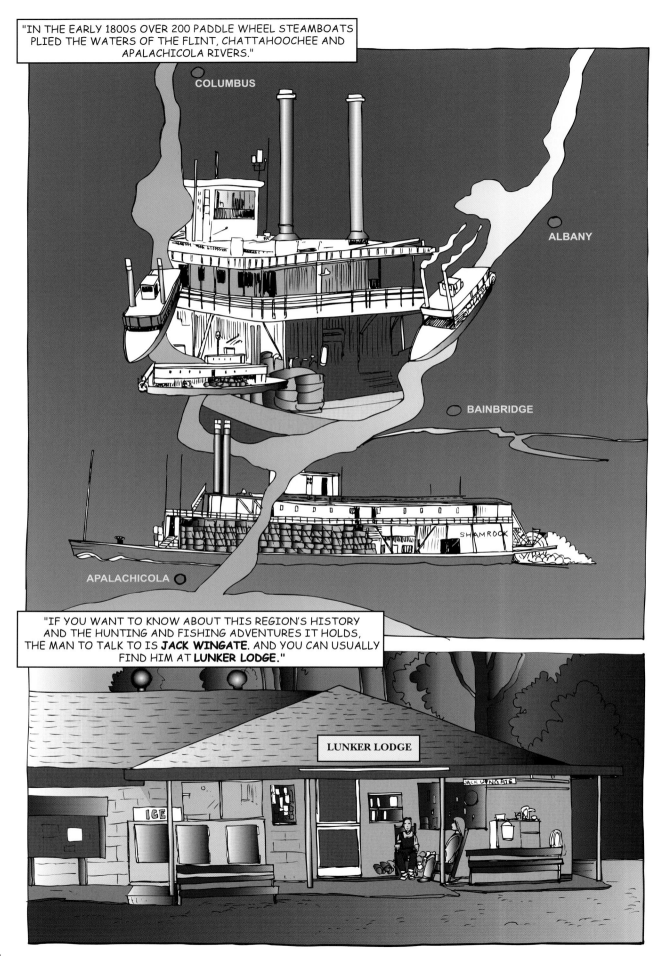

"IN THE EARLY 1800S OVER 200 PADDLE WHEEL STEAMBOATS PLIED THE WATERS OF THE FLINT, CHATTAHOOCHEE AND APALACHICOLA RIVERS."

"IF YOU WANT TO KNOW ABOUT THIS REGION'S HISTORY AND THE HUNTING AND FISHING ADVENTURES IT HOLDS, THE MAN TO TALK TO IS **JACK WINGATE**. AND YOU CAN USUALLY FIND HIM AT **LUNKER LODGE**."

The Flint and the Floridan Aquifer

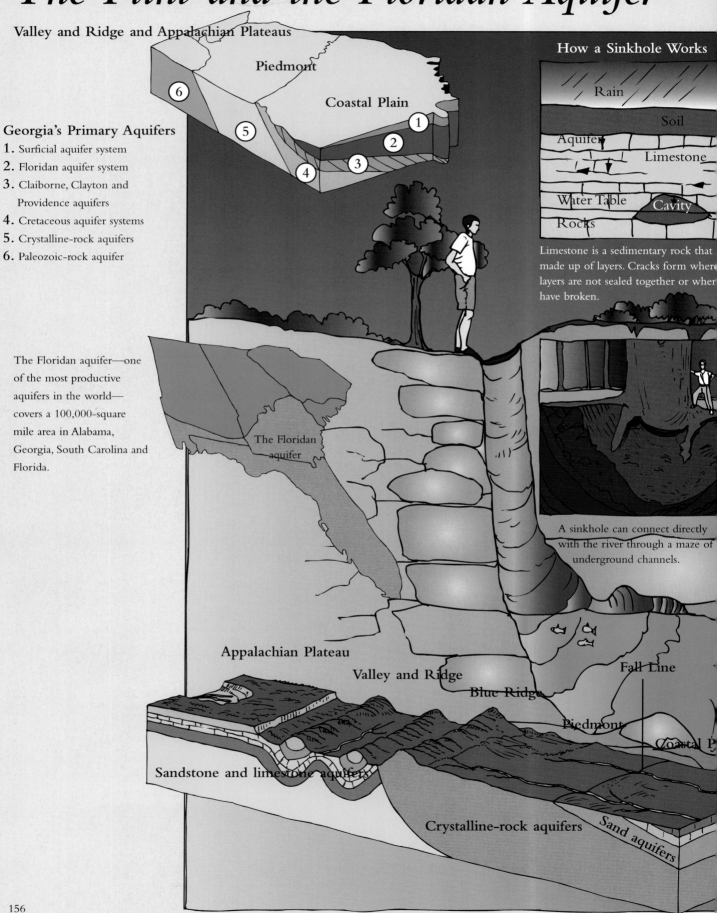

Valley and Ridge and Appalachian Plateaus

Piedmont

Coastal Plain

Georgia's Primary Aquifers

1. Surficial aquifer system

2. Floridan aquifer system

3. Claiborne, Clayton and Providence aquifers

4. Cretaceous aquifer systems

5. Crystalline-rock aquifers

6. Paleozoic-rock aquifer

The Floridan aquifer—one of the most productive aquifers in the world—covers a 100,000-square mile area in Alabama, Georgia, South Carolina and Florida.

The Floridan aquifer

Appalachian Plateau

Valley and Ridge

Blue Ridge

Fall Line

Piedmont

Coastal P

Sandstone and limestone aquifers

Crystalline-rock aquifers

Sand aquifers

How a Sinkhole Works

Rain

Soil

Aquifer

Limestone

Water Table

Cavity

Rocks

Limestone is a sedimentary rock that made up of layers. Cracks form where layers are not sealed together or wher have broken.

A sinkhole can connect directly with the river through a maze of underground channels.

...mestone dissolves in water the way a sugar cube ...es, only much slower. As water trickles through ...e rock, it forms a "solution cavity," or cave, at a ...ak area at the water table.

Eventually, the roof of the cavity collapses to form a sinkhole. The undercutting of the cave continues.

Soil washes into the sinkhole. The cave roof is cemented by recrystallized limestone.

...experienced divers have explored the caverns of ...e Floridan aquifer beneath the Flint River.

A city worker inspects a relatively dry portion of the Floridan aquifer beneath Mills Stadium in Albany.

Springs from the aquifer flow directly into the Flint River.

...imestone aquifers

Ten large springs and numerous small ones flow from the Floridan aquifer into the Flint River.

An Aquifer Primer

AN AQUIFER is an underground layer of rock that collects and holds water. The water in an aquifer is always moving, always flowing. In fact, an aquifer is like an underground river flowing downhill to the ocean. An aquifer fills up as rainwater filters down through the sand and soil particles. Eventually, this water, cleansed by the sand, reaches a confining layer of limestone. There it is held in pockets, or hollow spaces, in the rock until a well is drilled to bring the water to the surface, or until it bubbles up through a natural hole and becomes a spring.

An aquifer system consists of two or more aquifers that are hydraulically connected—that is, their flow systems function similarly and a change in the condition of one aquifer affects the other.

Georgia Aquifers

Georgia has six different aquifers or aquifer systems stacked on top of each other like layers of a ham and cheese sandwich on whole wheat bread with lettuce, tomato and mayonnaise. Each layer is different, but they all work together. Each aquifer layer is composed of a different material. Water flows through each of these layers at a different rate. The aquifers in Georgia are the Surficial aquifer system; the Floridan aquifer system; the Claiborne, Clayton and Providence aquifers; the Cretaceous aquifer systems; the Crystalline-rock aquifers and the Paleozoic-rock aquifer.

Cities and towns draw water from the aquifers. Industries, farmers and individuals drill wells into the aquifer and pump water from it. Farmers use water from the aquifer to irrigate their crops.

The Floridan Aquifer

The Floridan aquifer system is one of the most productive aquifers in the world. This aquifer system lies underneath an area of about 100,000 square miles in southern Alabama, southern Georgia, southern South Carolina and all of Florida. It is composed of easily dissolved limestone and is riddled with holes like a giant Swiss cheese.

The Floridan aquifer provides water for several large cities, including Albany, Savannah and Brunswick in Georgia and Tallahassee, Jacksonville, Orlando and St. Petersburg in Florida. In addition, the Floridan aquifer system provides water for hundreds of thousands of people in smaller communities and rural areas.

Boating through the Floridan Aquifer

If you are boating on the Flint River, you will begin to see signs of the Floridan aquifer below Lake Blackshear. Above Blackshear, the river bottom is mostly sand and mud. But below Blackshear, the currents have mostly washed the silt away, exposing the beautiful white, limestone bottom.

Below the Georgia Power Dam at Lake Chehaw, the presence of the Floridan aquifer becomes even more obvious. In addition to the limestone river bottom, rugged limestone banks are more and more common. Unlike the river bottom, which has been worked smooth by the current, the banks are jagged, shot through with cracks and holes, some as tiny as a pencil point, while some are as big as a basketball.

In a corridor 50 to 100 feet wide, the river cuts down through the Floridan aquifer. The banks are increasingly interesting and often spectacular. Limestone overhangs jut out over the water 10 to 20 feet above the surface. Dark, narrow caves cut into the bank far enough for a canoe or small jon boat to disappear into them. Large aqua-blue springs and small seeps flow out of the aquifer and into the river.

On the dark, moist banks roots from large cypress and sycamore trees intertwine with the limestone passages, giving the banks a mystic, otherworldly appearance. In some places, hundreds of cypress knees stand at attention where river meets limestone.

In the drier months of summer and fall, the river water is very clear and you can look over the side of your boat to see the white limestone river bed. Over the centuries, the relics of prehistoric animals and Native Americans who inhabited this region have sunk into the deep potholes in the limestone floor of the river. Local divers frequent this part of the river to collect arrowheads and prehistoric stone tools, as well as the bones and teeth of mastodons and giant sloth.

During the riverboat era on the Flint, Chattahoochee and Apalachicola Rivers, workers dredged the river channel to create a safe passageway for cotton barges. In places along the river, great pieces of limestone the size of minivans, called dredge spoils, are stacked against the riverbanks.

Between Albany and where the river begins to back up for Lake Seminole, the water volume in the Flint doubles. Most of this increased flow comes from the springs of the Floridan aquifer.

Karst Topography

A karst is an area of irregular limestone in which the flow of groundwater has eroded the underground terrain, producing fissures, sinkholes, underground streams and caverns. People refer to this as karst topography; this is the kind of topography found in the Flint River Basin below Lake Blackshear.

In contrast to a landscape formed by surface streams, which is characterized by an intricate network of stream valleys, karst topography lacks a well-integrated drainage system. Rainwater flows through the ground rather than flowing over it. In limestone areas like that found in the Flint River Basin, rainwater filters down through the rock, dissolving the calcium carbonate and gradually, carving out underground passages. The water moves slowly through a system of caverns and caves. Eventually, underground rivers form, which may emerge as springs.

Sinkholes are numerous, and in many karst regions they dominate the landscape. Other well-known karst topography regions in the United States are in Florida, Kentucky and southern Indiana. Noted karst areas in the world include the former Yugoslavia and China.

Sinkholes

Sinkholes can occur anytime and anywhere in a karst region for a number of reasons. One way is when the water level in the aquifer drops, leaving the solution cavity, or cave, without water to support its roof. The water level can drop for a number of reasons, such as too little rainfall or too much water pumped out of the aquifer.

Once the cavity is dry, a crack begins to grow in the clay that lies under the sandy soil and above the limestone. This is perhaps caused by water seepage wearing away the clay and eroding the limestone beneath it. Eventually, the sand runs through the crack—like sand in an hourglass—and into the cavity in the limestone. When heavy rains add too much weight to the sandy soil above, the roof of the limestone cave may crash in, causing the ground above and everything on it—trees and sometimes even roads and houses—to fall into the hole.

When John Sperry, now retired, was chief engineer for the city of Albany in 1993, he wrote a letter about sinkholes in the Albany area and what could be done about them. What Mr. Sperry describes here is illustrated by the drawing (which was adapted from his original) on the previous pages:

"The word 'limesink' pertains to the natural occurrence of the collapse of the residuum or surface soils into cavities or caverns in the underlying limestone. An area such as this is known as karst.

"The process generally begins with a solution channel in the top of the limestone, which allows soils to drop into the caverns from the bottom. This is accelerated by a fluctuating water table such as we have in this area. The final plug of surface soil falls suddenly and dramatically and a hole appears, usually three to six feet in diameter and six to eight feet deep, but sometimes as much as 20 feet deep.

"It must be understood that a limesink may occur anywhere in Dougherty County. Some areas such as Radium Springs, Hilsman Park or Mills Stadium are more prone to have sinkholes than others, but they can happen anywhere.

"If a limesink is left alone, the overhanging sides will collapse inward and the side slopes reverse themselves. After a very long time, natural erosion makes a gentle slope and the depression may begin to hold water and become a pond. Many times people have tried to deepen a pond and in so doing would remove enough of the plug to cause the pond to drain suddenly and fail to hold water in the future."

Section 6

Bainbridge and Lake Seminole

NATURE-BASED EDUCATIONAL CENTERS

Seminole State Park

The state park hires a park naturalist each summer to conduct its summer nature programs. Classes are offered according to the strengths of the naturalist, as well as the interests and ages of various groups visiting the park. Past summer nature programs have included classes on Native Americans and on wildlife, such as snakes, alligators and the rare gopher tortoise.

Guided hikes on the 2.2-mile Gopher Tortoise Trail (see page 184) are available year-round to large groups by appointment only. Park guides interpret the wiregrass habitat of the gopher tortoise community that lives in the trail area. On Friday and Saturday nights during the summer, the park naturalist conducts a Night Hike of the trail. With flashlights in hand, hikers explore the trail, looking for tortoise, deer, raccoon and other wildlife that might be out and about at night.

Days/Hours: *Park – 7 a.m. to 10 p.m.; office – 8 a.m. to 5 p.m.* **Fees**: *Rates quoted individually; parking, $2; school buses free.* **Directions**: *Seminole County. From Donalsonville, take GA 39 south for 16 miles. Turn left onto GA 253. The well-marked park gate is about 0.25 mile on the right side of the road.* **More Information**: *Seminole State Park, Route 2, Donalsonville, GA 31745. 229/861-3137. Georgia State Parks and Historic Sites, 205 Butler Street, Suite 1352 East, Atlanta, GA 30334. Website: www.gastateparks.org. Central Reservations Center, 800/864-7275. Monday through Friday, 8 a.m. to 5 p.m.*

LAKES

Lake Seminole

For eons the Flint came tumbling through an area of steep-walled forested ravines to meet up with the Chattahoochee, where they joined forces to form the Apalachicola—rolling on through the Florida Panhandle to the Apalachicola Bay.

Today, where those three rivers meet is Lake Seminole, named for the renegade Creek Indians who sought freedom from Andrew Jackson and his army. It is a wild and beautiful lake—37,500 acres with 376 miles of shoreline—formed by the Jim Woodruff Lock and

Gopher Tortoise

One of the oldest living species native to Georgia, the gopher tortoise was designated the state reptile in 1989. Descended from a group of tortoises that originated in North America 60 million years ago, it is known for digging deep, gopher-like burrows up to 40 feet wide and 10 feet deep. The tortoise is considered a keystone species in its wiregrass habitat because the burrows provide shelter for numerous animals, including snake, opossum, fox, bobcat and armadillo.

Weighing in at about nine pounds, its front limbs are flattened for digging and are heavily scaled. The domed brown shell averages up to 12 inches long. Found throughout the southeast United States as well as coastal islands off Georgia and Florida, the gopher tortoise's home range is dependent on herbaceous grass cover. Reclusive by nature, it spends about 50 to 70 percent of its time in the tunnels. Coming out every few days—usually in the morning before it gets too hot—it forages for low growing vegetation, such as wiregrass and broadleaf grasses, or on fruits, such as gopher apples, pawpaws, blackberries, prickly pears and saw palmetto berries.

Adult gopher tortoises can live 40 years or longer, but reproduction potential is low. Several weeks after mating in early spring, females usually lay four to seven eggs in a sand mound near their burrows. About three months later, the eggs hatch. Predators, however, sabotage many of these nests, making it 10 years sometimes before a female has a successful clutch.

Scientists fear the tortoises have declined in numbers by 80 percent over the past century due to loss of habitat. Today, they are protected by state and federal laws throughout their range. Georgia may be the last stronghold for them in the world.

Dam, the second dam to impede the Flint and the 16th dam to impede the Chattahoochee (and, hopefully, the last).

For about 200 million years, a shallow sea covered the Lake Seminole area. Over the ages, rivers deposited a 7,000-foot thick layer of sediment over the ancient African bedrock. Compressed until they hardened into rock, these older sediments are made of sands and clays washed from the North American continent, and the shells of countless generations of sea creatures.

Approximately 20 million years ago, this area became part of a shallow marine bank when a 500-foot thick sequence of limestone, made up of tiny sea creature shells, was deposited. Although there are a few places where the limestone is visible due to an unusual dome-like uplift, most of it is covered by river-borne continental sands from erosion of the once-lofty Appalachian Mountains. Look for sections of this ancient sea floor and fossil sea shells along the Jim Woodruff Dam entrance road and in the park on the west bank of the river, south of the dam.

More sediment poured in during the "Ice Ages" when huge glaciers advanced across North America. The sea gradually withdrew from previously high levels, leaving the land to be ultimately shaped by surface streams.

Today, Lake Seminole flows through a diverse terrain, which includes limesinks, cypress ponds, hardwood and pine forests and shady steep ravines formed by the Apalachicola River Bluffs. These bluffs originate in Southwest Georgia and extend along the Flint River, from about 10 miles above the dam downstream along the east bank of the Apalachicola River for a distance of about 25 miles into Florida. Ravines and small valleys cut into the bluffs, terminating into a natural amphitheater. Tampa Limestone underlies much of the remainder of the area. Here, numerous sloughs, lime sinks and flat pinelands dominate the surface topography.

The varied topography, with its unique variety of plant and animal species, is an idyllic spot for hikers, bird watchers, photographers and plant enthusiasts. Rivers, streams, sloughs and sinkholes support a variety of aquatic plants. A moderate climate and the sandy, light-colored soil of the lime sink plains at Lake Seminole support a distinctive Coastal Plain vegetation dominated by pine, oak, gum and cypress. Upland areas are given to pine and wiregrass, a grass with tough, wiry roots. Separated from the lime sink plains area by an escarpment, or long cliff, the Tifton Upland region of Lake Seminole is dominated by longleaf pine, although other conifers, evergreen and deciduous trees are also found here. The ravines dissecting the bluffs along the banks, above and below the dam, contain a wide variety of plant life, including conifers and broadleaf deciduous trees. The Florida Torreya (see page 255), a coniferous tree, and its extremely rare cousin, the Florida yew, are two endangered trees found only in the Apalachicola Bluffs.

The Wiregrass Habitat

One of the most characteristic plant species associated with the longleaf pine forest is wiregrass—any of various grasses, such as Bermuda grass, having tough wiry roots or root stocks. Wiregrass provides habitat for many animals, including the gopher tortoise, the threatened reptile who digs large burrows in these sandy areas. These tunnels, in turn, are home not only to the tortoise but also to an estimated 80 vertebrate species and 200 invertebrate species who use them as shelter against bad weather and predators.

The longleaf pine understory—the shrub and grass layer growing beneath the forest canopy—includes many berry-producing plants such as saw palmetto, gallberry, dwarf huckleberry, wax myrtle, gopher apple and fetter-bush. All are important wildlife foods. Grasses and herbs on the forest floor include broom-sedge, Indian grass, Beggarweed, deer tongue, partidge pea, rabbit tobacco and wiregrass.

Botantist and wildlife ecologists have recognized that natural longleaf pine forests and wiregrass habitats require fire in order to flourish. Fire, every five to ten years, burns the pine needles and leaves so that seeds have bare soil in which to sprout. Saw palmetto fronds and other plants of the understory burn back, and young oak trees that have begun to grow are killed. If the oaks continue to grow in the absence of fire, pine seedlings are shaded out, wiregrass and other wildflowers fail to bloom and pine flatwoods can become oak hammocks—and animals, like the gopher tortoise, loose their habitat.

This flora diversity fosters a vast abundance of mammal, reptile, amphibian, bird and fish species, both game and nongame. The lake and its surrounding areas provide an ideal location for nature lovers to observe wildlife. Some of the most common wildlife seen around the lake are whitetail deer, fox, squirrel, rabbit, opossum, skunk, armadillo, mink, gray fox, bobcat and turkey. Lake Seminole also hosts a variety of unique species: the black swamp snake, the map turtle and the gopher tortoise. The bald eagle and peregrine falcon are migratory visitors. Ospreys are a common sight and can be seen nesting atop dead trees in the lake (see sidebar page 257).

The Lake Seminole region is historically rich, having been occupied and used by man for at least 10,000 years. The Paleo-Indians in the Lake Seminole area hunted with wooden thrusting spears or javelins. The lanceolate points from these weapons are still found beside swampy places or near springs and streams where the animals came to drink. Divers have found a good number in the rivers. Numerous Native American villages flourished on the banks of the Chattahoochee and the Flint in prehistoric times. Evidence of that prehistoric occupation is found on all high points along the banks. Many sites are revealed by ancient piles of shells exposed on eroded river banks. Later, these native peoples developed highly complex societies based on corn agriculture. They survived well into the period of the European colonization until their eventual decline and removal from the area.

Spanish explorer Hernando de Soto led the first European expedition into the area in 1542. But it was one hundred years later before there would be any Spanish settlements established. In 1633 three missions were founded in the present-day Lake Seminole area—San Carlos, San Nicolas and Santa Cruz de Sabacola. All three sites are now under the waters of Lake Seminole.

Fishing, hiking, swimming, hunting, water skiing, camping, bird watching, nature photography—Lake Seminole's moderate climate allows you to experience a variety of recreational activities year round. There are numerous day use areas and campgrounds around the lake, all of which are listed in this guidebook section. Some are state-, county-, or city-maintained, but most are operated by the U.S. Army Corps of Engineers at Lake Seminole. Park Rangers patrol recreation areas by land and water, and corps campgrounds have attendants who live on-site and are available to help with registering and finding campsites.

The Lake Seminole Visitor Center is a good place to learn more about the lake's recreational activities as well as the physical, biological and cultural characteristics of the Lake Seminole area. There is an interactive relief map of the area and displays on the area's history, including Native American habitation and dam construction. The visitor center is located in the U.S. Army Corps of Engineers Resource Management Office just one mile north of Chattahoochee,

Santa Cruz de Sabacola El Menor Mission

"Located in Seminole County near the forks of the Chattahoochee and Flint Rivers was a town of Hitchiti-speaking Lower Creek Indians. A Spanish Mission, Santa Cruz de Sabacola El Menor, was established there in 1675. By 1685, English traders from Charles Town [Charleston, S.C.] had contact with the Lower Creeks. The English in Carolina and the Spanish in Florida were both seeking the alliance of the tribe. Spanish efforts to establish missions further up the Chattahoochee were unsuccessful and the Christianized portion of the Indians moved south to Sabacola. In 1717, the pro-Spanish Indian leader, Cherokeeleche (Cherokee killer) built a stockade on the site. The town was abandoned after a raid by pro-English Indians in 1724. The site of Sabacola is now under the waters of Lake Seminole."

Historic Chattahoochee Commission Historic Marker at bath house in swimming area of Seminole State Park

Florida, and is open five days a week, Monday through Friday, from 8 a.m. to 4:30 p.m.

Directions: *From Chattahoochee, Florida, take US 90 west toward the Victory Bridge. Turn right on Booster Club Road and follow the signs.* **More Information**: *U.S. Army Corps of Engineers, Lake Seminole Resource Management, P.O. Box 96, Chattahoochee, FL 32324. 229/662-2001; fax, 229/662-2903; 24-hour lake information, 229/662-2814. Website: www.sam.usace.army.mil/sam/op/rec/seminole.*

PARKS

Jim Woodruff Dam Fishing Area

Located below the dam on the east bank of the Apalachicola River, the dam's tailrace is a good place to fish. If you're lucky, you might see a boat or barge lock through the Jim Woodruff Lock and Dam.

Facilities: *Fishing pier. Restroom facilities are available in the Powerhouse or the Resource Manager's Office.* **Days/Hours**: *Open daily, 8 a.m. to 10 p.m.* **Directions**: *Gadsden County, Florida. Off US 90, just east of Victory Bridge in Chattahoochee, FL. Look for the signs.* **More Information**: *See Resource Management Office, above.*

Chattahoochee Park

Chattahoochee Park sits on one of Lake Seminole's highest points— bluffs that are a part of the Pelham escarpment that extends along a portion of the lake's southeastern shore. At an elevation of about 200 feet, the park's Turkey Flight Overlook is a good place to view the lake, and the Turkey Flight Nature Area is a good place to see the many plants and animals that live in this type of environment.

Facilities: *Boat ramp (see map page 239), swimming beach and bath house, one 150-person covered picnic shelter with 10 tables and two 100-person covered picnic shelters with eight tables, picnic area, the Turkey Flight Nature Area (see page 185), playground, drinking water and restrooms. Each picnic shelter includes a grill and electrical outlets; the larger and one of the smaller shelters also include lights.* **Days/Hours**: *Open daily, 8 a.m. to 10 p.m.* **Fees**: *Boat ramp, $2; swimming, $1 per person; picnic shelters, $30 to reserve. Picnic shelters are available on a first-come basis without charge or may be reserved by contacting the Resource Management Office.* **Directions**: *Decatur County. From Chattahoochee, Florida, take GA 192 (Booster Club Road) east about 2 miles. The park is on the left.* **More Information**: *See Resource Management Office, above.*

River Junction Landing

River Junction Landing Road, which leads to this Corps of Engineers day use area, cuts through some of the steep Torreya ravines that lie in this area of the Pelham escarpment.

Facilities: *Boat ramp with courtesy dock (see map page 239), primitive campgrounds (see page 174); picnic area, restrooms and drinking water.*

Jim Woodruff

James Waldo Woodruff was born in Columbus, Georgia, in 1879. An engineer with a wide variety of business interests, he spent the greater part of his life working toward the goal of providing a navigable Apalachicola, Flint and Chattahoochee River System. In recognition of Woodruff's support for the lock and dam project and distinguished public service, the project was named for him in 1957.

Days/Hours: *Open daily, 8 a.m. to 10 p.m.* **Fees**: *Boat ramp, $2; camping, see page 174.* **Directions**: *Decatur County. From Chattahoochee, Florida, take GA 192 east (Booster Club Road) about 4 miles. Turn left onto River Junction Landing Road and follow the signs.* **More Information**: *See Resource Management Office on page 163.*

Faceville Landing Park

The Corps-operated park is located on a small inlet on the eastern shore of the Flint River section of the lake. It, as well as the town of Faceville, are named after William Face, a master carpenter who came to the area in the early 1830s to build the federal arsenal at Chattahoochee, which still stands. He also built a trading post at the intersection of two Indian trails, which grew into the community of Faceville. A historical marker on GA 97 marks the site.

Facilities: *Boat ramp with courtesy dock (see map page 239), campground (see page 175), a 100-person capacity picnic shelter with 6 tables and electric grill, picnic tables with grills and pit toilets.* **Days/Hours**: *Open daily, 8 a.m. to 10 p.m.* **Fees**: *Boat ramp, $2; picnic shelter, $30. Picnic shelters are available on a first-come basis without charge or may be reserved by contacting the Resource Management Office.* **Directions**: *Decatur County. From Bainbridge, take GA 97 south about 12 miles. Turn right onto Faceville Landing Road and go 3 miles to the park.* **More Information**: *See Resource Management Office on page 163.*

Earl May Boat Basin Park

The Boat Basin in Bainbridge is a good place to enjoy the river and all it has to offer—and a particularly beautiful place to be at sunset. The historic McKenzie-Reynolds Home, now home to the Bainbridge-Decatur County Chamber of Commerce, stands sentinel along the river. Motor boats cruise up and down the gray-green Flint, which is about 75 to 100 yards wide at this point. Across the river is a silent landscape of wetlands and woods. Follow the paved road that begins in the Boat Basin and continues north under the old railroad bridge and on to Cheney Griffin Park, meandering with the curve of the river all the way. Or stop and join the locals who fish and picnic under the Spanish moss-draped live oak, cypress, sweetgum and hickory that line the river's banks.

Facilities: *Boat ramp (see map page 239), campsites (see page 175), picnic shelters with grills, picnic tables, playground, fishing ponds stocked with fish, steam-powered sawmill, historic steam-powered train engine, baseball and softball fields, restrooms and drinking water.* **Days/Hours**: *Open daily, 6 a.m. to 11 p.m.* **Fees**: *For camping rates, see page 175.* **Directions**: *Decatur County. From Bainbridge, take College Street north to the Flint River.* **More Information**: *Bainbridge-Decatur County Chamber of Commerce, P.O. Box 736, Bainbridge, GA 31717. 229/246-4774; fax 229/243-7633.*

Corps of Engineers

Although the U.S. Army Corps of Engineers may work closely with other federal, state and local agencies, the Corps is the major agency in charge of managing the lakeshore and lake at Seminole. Its duties include managing most of the park areas and campgrounds around the lake and ensuring public safety and protection of the lake environment by enforcing the rules and regulations that govern how the public can use the lake. In conjunction with the Department of Natural Resources (DNR), the Corps monitors water quality by routinely testing the lake's waters. The Corps also works with the DNR and the U.S. Fish and Wildlife Service to protect and enhance fish, wildlife and plant populations around the lake. The Corps presents water safety and environmental awareness programs to thousands of schoolchildren.

Cheney Griffin Park

Spanish moss-covered live oaks grace the 50-foot boardwalk that overlooks a bend in the Flint River at this Bainbridge municipal park. When Bainbridge was a busy steamboat landing, this was a lively section of the river. Now, it is merely peaceful and a good place to spend a quiet day on the Flint. From this strategic location, all four bridges that cross the river in Bainbridge are visible: the GA 27 Business Bridge and a CSX Railroad Bridge upstream, and the GA 27/82 Bypass Bridge and another CSX Railroad Bridge downstream. A paved road connects this park with the Earl May Boat Basin Park just downstream (see page 164).

Facilities: *Boat ramp (see map page 239), picnic shelters with grills, picnic tables, playground, boardwalk and fishing pier along the river, 4 lighted tennis courts, restrooms and drinking water. The Flint River Seafood Restaurant faces the river, 200 yards away (open Monday through Saturday, 11 a.m. to 8:45 p.m.).* **Days/Hours**: *Open daily, 6 a.m. to 11 p.m.* **Directions**: *Decatur County. From the Bainbridge city square, take Waters Street west 4 blocks to Cheney Griffin Park.* **More Information**: *Bainbridge-Decatur County Chamber of Commerce, P.O. Box 736, Bainbridge, GA 31717. 229/246-4774; fax 229/243-7633.*

Hales Landing Park

This recently renovated park is the first Corps of Engineers park south of Bainbridge. It lies along a picturesque inlet on the west bank of the river.

Facilities: *Boat ramp with courtesy dock (see map page 239); campgrounds (see page 175); a 100-person capacity picnic shelter with eight tables, electric grill, electrical outlets and lights; picnic area; restrooms and drinking water.* **Days/Hours**: *Open daily, 8 a.m. to 10 p.m.* **Fees**: *Boat ramp, $2. Picnic shelters are available on a first-come basis without charge or may be reserved for $30 by contacting the Resource Management Office.* **Directions**: *Decatur County. From Bainbridge, take GA 253 south about 3 miles to where Ten Mile Still Road branches to the left. Stay on Ten Mile Still Road about 2 miles to Hales Landing Road. Turn left. The park is at the end of the road.* **More Information**: *See Resource Management Office on page 163.*

Reynoldsville Park

This Corps park is located on the Spring Creek portion of Lake Seminole. It got its name from the town of Reynoldsville, which was named after Reuben Arthur Reynolds, the town's first postmaster. Reynolds, whose family moved to the area in 1850 when he was two years old, built the post office across the road from his own home.

Facilities: *Boat ramp (see map page 239), picnic tables with grills, pit toilet and paved parking. Knights Restaurant is on the grounds and serves steaks and fish platters, sells bait and tackle and has a shower room.* **Days/Hours**: *Park – open daily, 8 a.m. to 10 p.m. Knight's Restaurant – Open Sunday, 7 a.m. to 8 p.m.; Monday, Tuesday and Thursday, 7 a.m. to 9 p.m.; and*

Live Oak

These are the trees that you always think of as being covered with Spanish moss. The live oak (*Quercus virginiana* Mill.) is Georgia's official state tree and is found growing along the Georgia coast as well as westward in the lower Coastal Plain. Live oaks grow more and more common as you progress along the Flint River from Albany heading south.

The Georgia Forestry Commission describes the tree's chief characteristics: "leaves evergreen, thick, leathery and hairy below, margins slightly rolled; acorn enclosed in a cup for 1/3 to 1/2 its length. Tree has a distinct spreading appearance, although an upright form occurs in some areas." The wood is "a red oak. Very heavy, hard, strong, tough, close-grained, light brown or yellow. Hardest and heaviest of Georgia's oaks."

Live oaks are used as ornamental shade trees, but at one time they were used for shipbuilding because of their large size and great strength.

Friday and Saturday, 7 a.m. to 10 p.m. The restaurant is closed on Wednesdays. **Fees**: *Boat ramp, $2.* **Directions**: *Seminole County. From Reynoldsville, take GA 253 south about 2.5 miles. Turn left onto Rhodes Ferry Road, which dead ends into Spring Creek and Reynoldsville Park.* **More Information**: *See Resource Management Office on page 163.*

Spring Creek Park

This Corps–maintained site looks out over a wide expanse of the Spring Creek portion of the lake.

Facilities: *Boat ramp (see map page 239); 100-person picnic shelter with eight tables, grill and electric outlet; picnic area and toilets. The park is adjacent to the restaurant and facilities at Big Jim's Landing and Lodging (see page 178).* **Days/Hours**: *Open daily, 8 a.m. to 10 p.m.* **Fees**: *Boat ramp, $2. Picnic shelters are available on a first-come basis without charge or may be reserved for $30 by contacting the Resource Management Office.* **Directions**: *Seminole County. From Reynoldsville, take GA 253 south about 3 miles. Turn left at the park sign and go about 1 mile. The park is at the end of the road.* **More Information**: *See Resource Management Office on page 163.*

Sealy Point

This park, maintained by Seminole County, is located between Fish Pond Drain and Spring Creek on what is known as Sealy's Island.

Facilities: *Boat ramp (see map page 239), picnic areas, bathrooms and drinking water.* **Days/Hours**: *Open daily, 24 hours.* **Directions**: *Seminole County. From Reynoldsville, take GA 253 south about 5.5 miles to GA 374. Turn left and go about 3 miles. The park is on the left.* **More Information**: *Seminole County Recreation Department, 229/524-6112.*

Harvel Pond

Although there is no access to Harvel Pond through Seminole State Park, the park manages this recreation area. The self-contained pond is used only for fishing.

Facilities: *Boat ramp (see map page 239), picnic tables and paved parking. No toilets or drinking water.* **Days/Hours**: *Open daily, 7 a.m. to 10 p.m.* **Fees**: *$2 park pass is required daily to cover parking for vehicles under 13 persons; an annual park pass can be purchased at the Park Office for $25 and is valid at all Georgia State Parks. All other facilities are subject to user fees. Contact the state park office for the latest information on fees and reservations.* **Directions**: *Seminole County. From Reynoldsville, take GA 253 south about 5.5 miles to GA 374. Turn left and go about 1.5 miles, following the signs.* **More Information**: *Seminole State Park, Route 2, Donalsonville, GA 31745. 229/861-3137. Georgia State Parks and Historic Sites, 205 Butler Street, Suite 1352 East, Atlanta, GA 30334. Website: www.gastateparks.org. Central Reservations Center, 800/864-7275. Monday through Friday, 8 a.m. to 5 p.m.*

Steamboats on Spring Creek

Steamboats worked the entire Apalachicola-Flint-Chattahoochee River System during the 1800s—even the shallow, spring-fed Spring Creek.

"This was steamboat country indeed. Their sights were impressive, whether going or coming around the bend or idling at the landing where they seemed to fill the whole stream more so than on the wide Mississippi. As a matter of fact their shallow draft of only a few inches and the skill of their pilots made it possible to navigate the adjacent creeks as well as the rivers. Many, many times I have seen a steamer leave the Flint, go up Spring Creek not much wider than the boat four miles to Oil Still Springs, load turpentine products and go back out at night. The roustabouts sang and yelled to produce the helpful rhythms as they rolled and guided the heavy kegs down a steep hill, across the highly seasoned and resilient gang planks and then spun them around upright in the proper place on the deck. Unbelievably impressive to a young boy! They all had big boilers to generate steam from fat pin wood that sent great quantities of the very blackest smoke, usually from the tall twin stacks on the fore."

Prologue by Maston O'Neal

Seminole State Park

From its lakeside setting of longleaf pine and wiregrass prairie on Fish Pond Drain to its marshy habitats surrounding Harvel Pond, Seminole State Park displays much of Lake Seminole's diversity in both wildlife and natural areas. The threatened gopher tortoise, the only tortoise native to Georgia, burrows into the sandy soils of its wiregrass habitat along the park's nature trail. Egret, heron and hawk circle above the pine forests of this 604–acre Georgia State Park on the upper reaches of Lake Seminole. Each summer the park hires a staff naturalist to conduct programs that interpret the many wildlife and natural environments (see page 160).

Facilities: *14 two-and-three bedroom rental cottages, a 50-site campground (see page 176), four boat ramps (see map page 239, including Harvel Pond, see page 166), two fishing piers, a swimming beach, an enclosed group shelter with adjacent volleyball court, five picnic shelters, playgrounds, the Gopher Tortoise Nature Trail (see page 184), canoe and paddle boat rentals, bicycle rentals and an 18-hole miniature golf course. The group shelter seats 75 and comes with stove, sink, refrigerator, folding chairs and tables and heating and air-conditioning. It must be rented through the park office. The picnic shelters seat about 30 people and include four tables, grills, water and lights; they can be reserved.* **Days/Hours**: *Park – open daily, 7 a.m. to 10 p.m.; office – 8 a.m. to 5 p.m.* **Fees**: *$2 park pass is required daily to cover parking for vehicles under 13 persons; an annual park pass can be purchased at the Park Office for $25 and is valid at all Georgia State Parks. All other facilities are subject to user fees. Contact the state park office for the latest information on fees and reservations.* **Directions**: *Seminole County. From Donalsonville, take GA 39 south for 16 miles. Turn left onto GA 253. The well-marked park gate is about 0.25 mile on the right side of the road.* **More Information**: *Seminole State Park, Route 2, Donalsonville, GA 31745. 229/861-3137. Georgia State Parks and Historic Sites, 205 Butler Street, Suite 1352 East, Atlanta, GA 30334. Website: www.gastateparks.org. Central Reservations Center, 800/864-7275. Monday through Friday, 8 a.m. to 5 p.m.*

Rays Lake Park

This Corps of Engineers park is the northernmost park on Fish Pond Drain.

Facilities: *Boat ramp (see map page 239), 100-person covered picnic shelter with six tables and grill, picnic tables, grills, pit toilets and paved parking.* **Days/Hours**: *Open daily, 8 a.m. to 10 p.m.* **Fees**: *Boat ramp, $2. Picnic shelters are available on a first-come basis without charge, or may be reserved for $20 by contacting the Resource Management Office.* **Directions**: *Seminole County. From Reynoldsville, take GA 253 south about 1.0 mile to FDR Road. Turn right and go about 4 miles to GA 374. Turn left and go about 1 mile. The access road to Rays Lake is on the left after you cross the bridge. Follow the signs.* **More Information**: *See Resource Management Office on page 163.*

Seminole County

Seminole County lies between the Flint and Chattahoochee arms of Lake Seminole in extreme southeast Georgia.

"Seminole County was created in 1920 from portions of Decatur and Early counties. It was named for the Seminole Indians who, faced with re-settlement, left their lands in the Chattahoochee River Valley and moved to the Florida Everglades. Led by their chief, Osceola, they fought two bloody frontier wars with the U.S. Army. The county has two incorporated municipalities, Iron City and Donalsonville, the largest and the county seat. Donalsonville was named for Jonathan E. Donalson, a member of a prominent family who had pioneered Decatur County. The creation of Lake Seminole behind the Jim Woodruff Lock and Dam inundated many acres in the southern portion of the county. What had largely been swampland was turned into a water recreation resource. Fairchild State Park [now Fairchild Landing Park, see page 168], Reynoldsville State Park [now Reynoldsville Park, see page 165] and Seminole State Park [see page 167] are all on the Seminole County side of the lake."

From *Georgia County Snapshots*, Georgia Department of Community Affairs

For tourism information on towns in Seminole County, see Resources page 300.

Cummings Landing Park

This park is named for the Cummings family, who first settled in the area in 1890. Peter Sidney Cummings Sr. acquired property and built a large sawmill around which the long-gone community of Lela, named for his wife, sprang up.

Facilities: *Boat ramp (see map page 239), picnic tables, grills, restrooms and drinking water.* **Days/Hours**: *Open daily, 8 a.m. to 10 p.m.* **Fees**: *Boat ramp, $2.* **Directions**: *Seminole County. From Reynoldsville, take GA 253 south about 7.5 miles to GA 39. Turn left and go about 1.5 miles and follow the signs.* **More Information**: *See Resource Management Office on page 163.*

Fairchilds Park

This Corps of Engineers park was once the site of a large cotton plantation owned by the Fairchild family, who first settled in this area around 1825. Steamboats would stop at the Fairchild Landing on the Chattahoochee to pick up bales of cotton from the plantation and other products from the surrounding farms and businesses and unload seafood shipped from Apalachicola. The old Fairchild plantation house still stands on River Road near the park.

Facilities: *Boat ramp (see map page 239), fishing pier, picnic tables, grills, pit toilet and dirt parking lot.* **Days/Hours**: *Open daily, 8 a.m. to 10 p.m.* **Fees**: *Boat ramp, $2.* **Directions**: *Seminole County. From Donalsonville, take GA 91 south about 6.5 miles to GA 221. Turn left and go 12 miles. Look for the signs. The park will be on the right.* **More Information**: *See Resource Management Office on page 163.*

Desser Landing

This Corps-operated recreation area takes its name from an old steamboat landing that once stood nearby. The landing and the town of Desser, four miles east of here, were named in honor of the oldest daughter of Isaac K. Horn. Horn moved to the community when it was known as simply the Salem Community, after the nearby Salem Church. Horn, who was the town postmaster, and his family ran the general store, which housed the Desser Post Office, a cotton gin and a gristmill.

Facilities: *Boat ramp (see map page 239), picnic tables and pit toilet.* **Days/Hours**: *Open daily, 8 a.m. to 10 p.m.* **Fees**: *Boat ramp, $2.* **Directions**: *Seminole County. From Donalsonville, take GA 91 south for 6.5 miles to GA 221. Turn left and go 7 miles. Turn right onto Desser Landing Road. Road dead ends into park.* **More Information**: *See Resource Management Office on page 163.*

Neals Landing Park

The park is the northernmost Corps of Engineers park on the Chattahoochee River channel of what is Lake Seminole. The old Neals Landing Road, which is now GA 91, once crossed the river

Steamboat Landings

During the steamboat era of 1828 to 1928, the Apalachicola-Flint-Chattahoochee River System boasted dozens of boat landings, named for the families, plantations or towns that operated them. While the steamboat landings are long gone, many of these sites still bear their old names.

"In the lonely pine forests of Georgia, Alabama and north Florida, these wharves served as gathering places for farmers and planters, travelers, and occasionally the idle daughters of nearby plantations. The sporadic arrival of a steamboat, announced by the blast of a whistle or the firing of a gun, brought people scurrying toward the landing to watch the slaves load and unload the steamboat. Since many of these landings were located on steep bluffs, this process was quite interesting to observe. Long wooden slides, which extended from the top of the bluff to the river's edge, were used to conduct the cargo down the hill. Bale after bale of cotton, as well as other heavy freight (even pigs), were sent tumbling down the steep incline and into the bowels of the boat. When at last the freight was stored and the shouting had stopped, the steamer noisily pulled away from the dock and disappeared around the bend in a cloud of smoke, leaving the onlookers to return to the relative quiet and isolation of their work until the next steamer announced itself."

Fair to Middlin'—The Antebellum Cotton Trade of the Apalachicola/Chattahoochee River Valley by Lynn Willoughby

 (continued on page 171)

Abrams Creek

8. Pindertown

On the east bank above this bridge once stood the Indian Village of Pindertown, which later became a steamboat landing.

9. GA 32 Boat Ramp

On west bank, just below the bridge

GA 32 Bridge

8

9

Negro Head Branch

River

Philema Branch

mestone Bottom

f Lake Blackshear, the river bed is mostly sand.
Blackshear, it is mostly limestone. Sand covers
stone in some places. In others, the swift
sweep the bottom clean, revealing the white
e. Pockets in the limestone are natural collect-
s for the artifacts of Native Americans who
ng the riverbanks and for the teeth and bones
s that roamed the area in prehistoric times.

Leesburg

About 10 miles west of
the river via GA 32

Leesburg

GA 32

River miles above mouth: 120.8
Counties: Lee and Worth

Lake Blackshear and Georgia Veterans Memorial State Park

Fisherman's shack on Turk

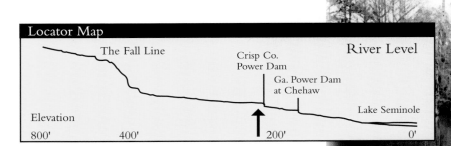

Locator Map

The Fall Line

Crisp Co.
Power Dam

Ga. Power Dam
at Chehaw

River Level

Lake Seminole

Elevation

800'   400'   200'   0'

Flint River

Pennys Bluff

2. Turkey Creek Campground

6-acre privately owned campground

Turkey Creek Campground
Boat Ramp

Grass Patch

3. Sonny's Campe

Sonny's Campers
Haven Boat Ran
Gum P

GA 27 Bridge

Groves Landing

1. Reeves Landing Boat Ramp

HONOR
BOX

GA 27 Bridge

Built in 1959, the GA 27 Bridge
is also called the Luther Storey
Bridge. A bronze marker honors
Luther Story and other veterans
from Sumter and Dooly
Counties who died in WWII or
the Korean War.

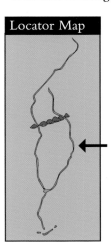

Locator Map

Americus

About 19 miles west of the river via
GA 27

Americus

GA 27

River miles above mouth: 154.1
Counties: Sumter and Dooly

Lake Blackshear to GA 32 Bridge

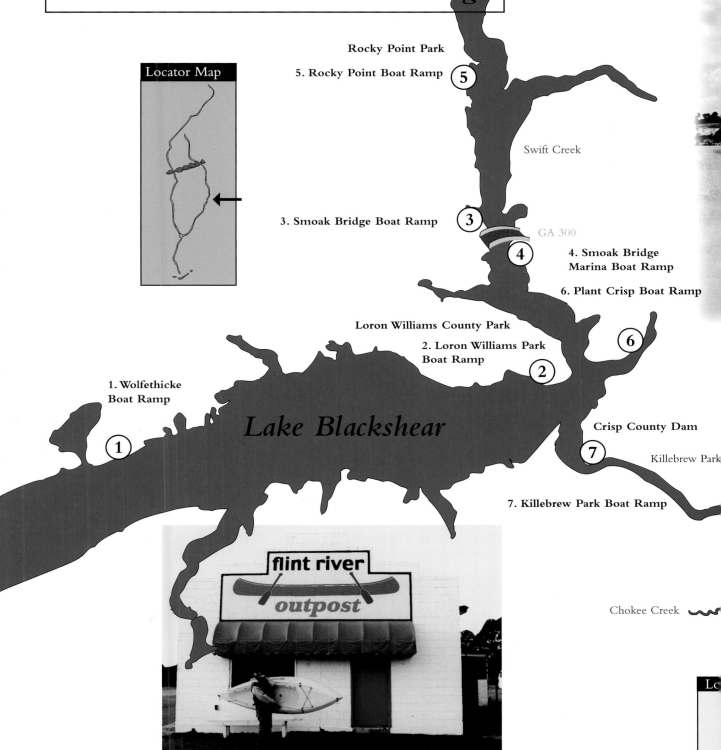

Locator Map

Rocky Point Park

5. Rocky Point Boat Ramp ⑤

Swift Creek

3. Smoak Bridge Boat Ramp ③

GA 300

④

4. Smoak Bridge Marina Boat Ramp

6. Plant Crisp Boat Ramp

Loron Williams County Park

2. Loron Williams Park Boat Ramp ②

1. Wolfethicke Boat Ramp

Lake Blackshear

①

⑥

Crisp County Dam

⑦

Killebrew Park

7. Killebrew Park Boat Ramp

flint river outpost

Chokee Creek

John Singletary at his Flint River Outpost

Cordele
About 9 miles east of the
river via GA Hwy 280

Cordele

Boat Trip

Use a jon boat and small outboard engine to boat between Veterans State Park on Lake Blackshear or Turkey Creek Campground up river to Montezuma. A winding river course, sandbars and extensive swamplands characterize the journey. About 37 miles from Veterans State Park and about 29 miles from Turkey Creek Campground to Montezuma.

Cordele Fish Hatchery

The public is welcome to tour the grounds where 27 earthen ponds dot the hatchery's 160 acres. Shoal bass, native to the Flint River, are raised here.

Georgia Veterans Memorial State Park

A 1,322-acre state park with cottages and campsites, 4 boat ramps, picnic shelters, 18-hole golf course, swimming pool, beach, conference center, nature trails and military museum

7. Veterans Memorial State Park

Gum Creek Boat Ramps at Georgia Veterans Memorial State Park

US 280 Bridge

ear

Gum Creek

Gully Creek

⑧

Cedar Creek

8. Boy Scout Slough Boat Ramp

Boy Scout Slough

⑦

9. Cedar Creek Boat Ramp

⑨

⑥ ⑤

5. Lakeshore Marine

Marina with wet and dry slips, gas, convenience store and restroom facilities

Lakeshore Marine Campground

Pecan Slough

6. Lakeshore Marine Boat Ramp

Egrets at Georgia Veterans Memorial State Park

y Creek

Tony Walker at the Cordele Fish Hatchery

s **Haven**

3

Lake Blacks

Spring Creek

4

Buzzards Roost

Dock on Spring Creek

Spring Creek
Boat Ramp

4. Spring Creek Marina
Boat dock with gas in a
natural setting of cypress trees

Fisherman below the Crisp County Power Dam on Lake Blackshear

Canoe Trips

Paddle from the boat ramp in Killebrew Park below
Crisp County Power Dam to the GA 32 Bridge. A
combination of flat water and Class I Shoals. About
12 miles.

Flint

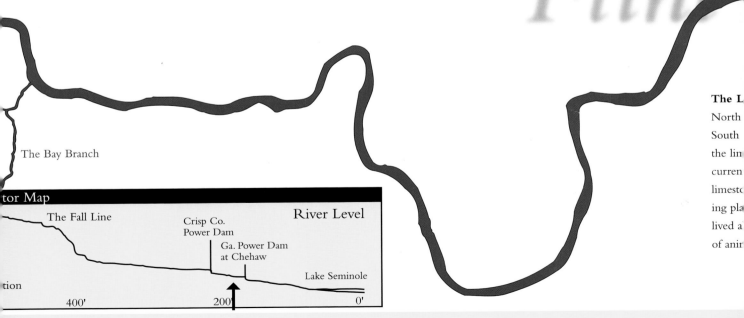

The Bay Branch

The L

North

South

the lin

curren

limesto

ing pla

lived a

of anir

tor Map

River Level

The Fall Line

Crisp Co.
Power Dam

Ga. Power Dam
at Chehaw

Lake Seminole

tion

400'   200'   0'

(continued from page 168)

here at Neals Ferry, connecting this part of Southwest Georgia to Florida. Neals Landing and Ferry operated until 1927, when it was replaced by a toll-collecting suspension, or swinging, bridge, the only such bridge south of the Mason-Dixon line. With a center span high enough for steamboats to pass under it, the bridge was a harrowing experience for cars traveling over it. It was condemned in 1953, torn down in 1955 and replaced in 1956 with a concrete and steel bridge named in honor of Georgia Governor Herman Talmadge.

Facilities: *Boat ramp (see map page 239), campground (see page 176), picnic area, restrooms and drinking water.* **Days/Hours**: *Open daily, 8 a.m. to 10 p.m.* **Directions**: *Jackson County, Florida. From Donalsonville, take GA 91 south 9 miles to the river. As soon as you cross the river (and the state line into Florida), GA 91 turns into FL 2 and the park is on the left.* **More Information**: *See Resource Management Office on page 163.*

Buena Vista Park

Woods and marsh surround this park, operated by Jackson County, Florida. Here the waters of the Chattahoochee River are just beginning to back up and show signs of becoming Lake Seminole.

Facilities: *Boat ramp (see map page 239) and picnic tables. Neither drinking water nor toilets are available here.* **Days/Hours**: *Open daily, 24 hours.* **Directions**: *Jackson County, Florida. From Sneads, Florida, take SR 271 north for 15 miles. Sign for access road to park is on the left.*

Parramore Landing Park

Operated by the Corps of Engineers, this park is located near the site of an old steamboat landing once owned by the Parramore family of Seminole County.

Facilities: *Boat ramp (see map page 239), picnic area, restrooms and drinking water. Adjacent to privately owned restaurant, bait and tackle store and campground (see page 180).* **Days/Hours**: *Open daily, 8 a.m. to 10 p.m.* **Fees**: *Boat ramp, $2.* **Directions**: *Jackson County, Florida. From Sneads, FL, take SR 271 north about 11 miles to Parramore Road. Turn right and follow the signs.* **More Information**: *See Resource Management Office on page 163.*

Three Rivers State Recreation Area

Appropriately named, Three Rivers State Recreation Area sits on high ground near where the Flint and Chattahoochee Rivers converge to form the Apalachicola—an event more visible in the days before the Woodruff Dam was built. This 682-acre Florida state park occupies two miles of shoreline on Lake Seminole's southwestern lake shore. Its terrain of high hills and steep ravines, consisting of hardwood hammock and high pine land communities, resembles that of the Appalachian Mountains. Here, gray fox and white-tailed deer roam the woods while alligators and snapping turtles sun on the lake's banks.

Fowltown

"In extreme southwestern Georgia, in Seminole County, the Creek Indians had at least two settlements named Fowltown. The first was located in today's Chason Park in Bainbridge. That Fowltown was completely destroyed by the U.S. Army on January 4, 1818. When the troops attacked the settlement, they found it abandoned because all the inhabitants had fled eastward across the Ochlockonee River. The latter area would have been near today's Monticello, Jefferson County, Florida.

"The Creek Indians had another settlement named Fowltown located in land lot 196, district 14, on the eastern bank of the Chattahoochee River in western Seminole County. Little is known of that old town but it is shown on the original 1820 state surveys of that area. An early trail once ran there and in later years a whiteman's highway crossed at that place. The approach to the eastern side of the river was known as Smart Landing and on the western, or Alabama, side it was called Fairchild Landing. That area is immediately north of today's Fairchilds Park (on the Georgia side) [see page 168]."

Indian Heritage of Georgia by Marion R. Hemperely

Facilities: *Boat ramp (see map page 239), 2 campgrounds (see page 177), 100-foot fishing pier, a covered picnic shelter, picnic areas, playground, hiking trails (see page 184) and canoe rentals.* **Days/Hours**: *Open daily, 8 a.m. until sunset.* **Fees**: *$2 per car or $1 per person. All other facilities are subject to user fees. Contact the state park office for the latest information on fees and reservations.* **Directions**: *Jackson County, Florida. From Sneads, Florida, take SR 271 north 2 miles. Park entrance on right.* **More Information**: *Three Rivers State Recreation Area, 7908 Three Rivers Park Road, Sneads, FL 32460. 850/482-9006. Florida Parks website: www.dep.state.fl.us/parks.*

Sneads Park

On the southwest shore of the lake, this Corps of Engineers park is well-equipped for family fun.

Facilities: *Boat ramp (see map page 239); swimming beach; 150-person covered picnic shelters with 14 tables, grill and electrical outlets and 100-person covered picnic shelter with eight tables, grill and electrical outlets; picnic area; playground; volleyball and horseshoe courts; bath houses; restrooms and drinking water.* **Days/Hours**: *Open daily, 8 a.m. to 10 p.m.* **Fees**: *Boat ramp, $2; swimming, $1. Picnic shelters are available on a first-come basis without charge, or may be reserved for $30 by contacting the Resource Management Office.* **Directions**: *Jackson County, Florida. Off US 90, just east of Sneads.* **More Information**: *See Resource Management Office on page 163.*

Westbank Overlook

Strictly a sightseeing spot, this Corps–maintained overlook on the southwest shore of Lake Seminole provides an excellent vantage of lake and the Jim Woodruff Lock and Dam.

Facilities: *Well-manicured area with ample concrete parking on two tiers. No other facilities.* **Directions**: *Jackson County, Florida. From Chattahoochee, Florida take US 90 west across the Victory Bridge and follow the signs.* **More Information**: *See Resource Management Office on page 163.*

WILDLIFE MANAGEMENT AREAS

Apalachee Wildlife Management Area

This public wildlife and recreational area makes a definite contribution to the wildness that defines Lake Seminole. The Apalachee WMA covers 7,952 acres of land in Jackson County, Florida, and more than five miles along the lake's western shoreline. There are three zones for hunting: the larger area, Zone A, is a favorite of dove, quail and deer hunters; Zones B and C cover roughly 2,000 acres of swampy terrain along the Chattahoochee River and are mostly used by deer hunters. Deer, rabbit, squirrel, turkey, raccoon, opossum, skunk, coyote, beaver, nutria, armadillo, bobcat, mink and otter—all can be found here. Migratory birds in the area include woodcock, rails, common moorhens, snipe, crows, coot and duck. Most hunters in these areas use a boat for getting around.

The Battle of Fowltown

At the end of 1817 and on into 1818, the U.S. army, in a conflict labeled the First Seminole War, fought the Seminole Indians in what was, in many ways, a continuation of the Creek Indian War of 1813–1814.

"The spark that touched off what many historians refer to as The First Seminole War was the Battle of Fowltown, actually two battles about a week apart. This occurred on the east side of the Flint opposite Fort Scott about four miles south of present day Bainbridge. The chief whose name was really E-ne-me-haut-by, sent word to Colonel David Twiggs, then the commandant of Fort Scott, 'not to cross, nor cut a stick of wood on the east side of the Flint. That land is mine,' he said. 'I am directed by the powers above and the powers below to protect and defend it. I shall do so.'

"A few days later when General Gaines arrived at Fort Scott, he sent Colonel Twiggs and 250 soldiers to the Fowltown to bring the chief to Fort Scott to 'ascertain whether his hostile temper had abated.' The approach of so many soldiers started the shooting which resulted in the death of a few Indians, but no Americans. A week later, however, another detachment under Lieutenant Colonel Matthew Arbuckle made a second raid on the village at which time more Indians were killed and this time the American musician named Aaron Hughes. In some dispatches he was called a bugler and in others a fifer. In going to and from the Fowltown the U.S. troops crossed at the present site of Bainbridge, which is upstream from the shortest route. In returning the last time, they erected a small picket fort on a high bluff at the crossing and named it for their popular comrade [Aaron Hughes]."

Prologue by Masten O'Neal

The U.S. Army Corps of Engineers and the Florida Game and Freshwater Fish Commission, who cooperatively manage Apalachee, plan to increase the diversity of wildlife found here even more through a program to restore and enhance approximately 3,700 acres of this hardwood-pine habitat to a more natural longleaf pine-wiregrass habitat. When the first Europeans settled in what would become the Southeast United States, there were about 60 million acres of longleaf pine and wiregrass. But excessive logging of virgin stands and poor replanting methods have caused these communities to dwindle to little more than 4 million acres today. Restoring this habitat should restore the species associated with it, namely the gopher tortoise, the bobwhite quail, the Eastern indigo snake and the fox squirrel.

Wildlife observation, fishing and controlled and seasonal hunting are all allowed within Apalachee. Camping is prohibited in the WMA but is available nearby at Three Rivers State Park (see page 177) and at Neals Landing (see page 176). Be sure to check on local regulations before hunting. Hunting permits, state licenses and migratory water-fowl stamps may be required. Fishing and hunting regulation booklets are available free of charge at the Resource Management Office and area stores.

Facilities: *Boat ramps in and near the WMA are Arnold Landing, Neals Landing, Buena Vista Landing and Parramore Landing (see map page 239).* **Days/Hours**: *Check station open 5 a.m. through one hour after sunset.* **Directions**: *Jackson County, Florida. From Sneads, Florida, take SR 271 north 3 miles and follow the signs.* **More Information**: *Florida Fish and Wildlife Conservation Commission, Northwest Region, 1911 Highway 2321, Panama City, FL 32409-1658. 850/265-3677. Website: www.state.fl.us/fwc.*

Lake Seminole Wildlife Management Area

This wildlife management area consists of 16,895 acres, stretching across both Seminole and Decatur Counties and bordering much of Lake Seminole. Hunting, fishing, hiking, bird watching and boating can all be enjoyed within the WMA boundaries.

Deer, fox, bobcat, raccoon, opossum and feral hog are some of the wildlife that inhabit the area. Seventy-nine species of fish have been recorded in the lake, with sizeable populations of catfish, crappie and bream. Lunker largemouth (see sidebar page 177), hybrid and striped bass (see map page 204) are abundant.

There are numerous park areas around the lake and no hunting is allowed within 300 yards of a house, dock, building or other struc-ture, or a developed recreation area, such as a beach, campground or boat ramp. For general WMA regulations, license requirements and hunting seasons, hunters should obtain a current copy of the "Georgia Hunting Seasons & Regulations" booklet, available at local outdoors stores and from the Georgia DNR.

Coot

Coot is a common name for members of a genus of birds of the rail family, also called mud hens or swamphens, because they inhabit the marshy borders of streams and lakes throughout the world.

Ducklike birds, coots have a short, straight bill that extends up the fore-head to form a horny shield. Instead of webbed feet, coots have flaps on each toe. The American coot, found in bays, lakes and ponds throughout central North America and flying over the waters of Lake Seminole, is about 16 inches long. A dark slate color, the coot has a white bill crossed by a dark band near the tip, with a reddish spot on the forehead shield.

A coot runs over the water before taking flight. It swims well, dives for protection and eats a variety of plants and small animals. Its nest is a hollow heap of broken, dead reeds.

Facilities: *Boat ramps into the WMA are located at Hales Landing, Ten Mile Landing, Hutchinsons Ferry Landing, Spring Creek Landing, Reynolds Landing and Butlers Ferry Landing (see map page 239).* **Days/Hours**: *Open daily, 24 hours.* **Directions**: *Seminole and Decatur Counties. From Bainbridge, take GA 253 south about 3 miles to Ten Mile Still Road. Turn left and go about 2 miles to Hales Landing on the left. There is a map there of each of the WMA tracts.* **More Information**: *Georgia Department of Natural Resources, Wildlife Resources Division, 2024 Newton Road, Albany, GA 31701-3576. 229/430-4254.*

CAMPGROUNDS

East Bank Campground

Family recreation and comfort are all part of the camping experience at this Corps campground on the east bank of Lake Seminole near the dam. Some of the sites sit directly along the waterfront, while most are shaded by the mixed hardwood forest that covers the banks.

Facilities: *69 campsites with electrical and water hookups; two tent sites and one site designed specifically for handicap access; boat ramp with courtesy dock (see map page 239); two bathhouses with showers; coin laundry; dump station; pay phone; drinking water; 30-person covered picnic shelter with grill and electrical outlet; picnic tables and grills; nature trail; playground; and shuffleboard, horseshoe, tetherball and volleyball courts.* **Days/Hours**: *Open daily. Campground gate is locked from 10 p.m. to 7 a.m.* **Fees**: *full hookup, $12 per night; tent sites, $8 per night; visitors, $2 per day. Corps-operated campgrounds are available on a first-come basis. Park attendants or hosts live on the site and will assist you with registering and finding a campsite. Picnic shelters are available on a first-come basis without charge, or may be reserved for $20 by contacting the Resource Management Office.* **Directions**: *Decatur County. From US 90 in Chattahoochee, Florida, turn north onto Booster Club Road and go 1 mile to East Bank Road. Turn left and follow the signs.* **More Information**: *See Resource Management Office on page 163. East Bank Campground, 229/662-9273.*

River Junction Landing Campground

This small campground sits at the end of a ravine in the bluffs along Lake Seminole's southeast bank. The area is a perfect example of the steeper Torreya ravines that cut through the Apalachicola River Bluffs in the Pelham escarpment.

Facilities: *16 campsites, bathhouse with showers, drinking water and pay phone; boat ramp (see map page 239) and picnic area available to campers at adjoining day use park (see page 163).* **Days/Hours**: *Open daily. Campground gate is locked from 10 p.m. to 7 a.m.* **Fees**: *tents, $5 per tent, per night. Corps-operated campgrounds are available on a first-come basis. Park attendants or hosts live on the site and will assist you with registering and finding a campsite.* **Directions**: *Decatur County. From US 90 in*

Mayflies

A mayfly is a delicate, soft-bodied insect with gauzy wings held vertically when they are at rest. The aquatic mayfly nymphs feed on small plants and animals and on organic debris. They live from a few months to three years in the water, depending on the species. In the adult stage, a mayfly lives only hours or a few days. Adult mayflies take in no food; their nonfunctional mouthparts are greatly reduced in size. Adults mate in flight, countless millions sometimes involved in a nuptial swarming that often takes place near water. After her eggs are laid in the water, the female dies. Both nymphs and adults are an important food of fishes.

Harmless but abundant, mayflies are native to the Lake Seminole area. Their presence is an indicator of good water quality. They do not bite, but swarms can be so thick that they can impede breathing.

One night the Corps of Engineers got a call from a campground where mayflies were clustering around an electric light. Campers complained that the odor from dead flies was bothersome. When Corps workers got to the site, they found a three-foot pile of expired flies that had to be hauled away with a front loader.

Chattahoochee, Florida, turn north onto Booster Club Road and go about 4 miles to River Junction Landing Road. Turn left and follow the signs. **More Information***: See Resource Management Office on page 163.*

Faceville Landing Campground

Campsites here at Faceville are primitive, but lie along the banks of a quiet inlet. The area is in the lower part of the Pelham escarpment, where steep Torreya ravines run between the bluffs.

Facilities*: Primitive campsites with no facilities within campground area. Day use facilities available at Faceville Landing Park (see page 164) adjoining the campground.* **Days/Hours***: Open daily. Campground gate is locked from 10 p.m. to 7 a.m.* **Fees***: No fees for camping here. Corps-operated campgrounds are available on a first-come basis. Park attendants or hosts live on the site and will assist you with registering and finding a campsite.* **Directions***: Decatur County. From Bainbridge, take GA 97 southwest about 12 miles. Turn right onto Faceville Landing Road and go 3 miles to the park.* **More Information***: See Resource Management Office on page 163.*

Earl May Boat Basin Campground

Sitting along the Flint River in Albany under the Spanish-moss covered live oaks and cypress trees is this campground in a park known as the Boat Basin.

Facilities*: 10 campsites with water and electrical hookups, picnic tables and grills, dump station, bathhouses and restrooms.* **Days/Hours***: Open daily, 24 hours. Bainbridge city police patrol park area and campground.* **Fees***: $9 per night. Honor system box is located at campground. Campsites are on a first-come, first-serve basis.* **Directions***: Decatur County. From Bainbridge, take College Street north to the Flint River.* **More Information***: Bainbridge City Leisure Services, 223 Donalson Street, Bainbridge, GA 31717. 229/248-2010.*

Hales Landing Campground

This primitive but recently renovated Corps campground faces a picturesque inlet along the west bank of the Flint River arm of Lake Seminole.

Facilities*: 14 campsites and one site designed specifically for handicap access; boat ramp with courtesy dock (see map page 239); bathhouse with showers; pay phone; drinking water; 100-person picnic shelter with eight tables, electric grill, electrical outlet and lights. A day use area adjoins the campground.* **Days/Hours***: Open daily. Campground gate is locked from 10 p.m. to 7 a.m.* **Fees***: Camping, $5 per night. Corps-operated campgrounds are available on a first-come basis. Park attendants or hosts live on the site and will assist you with registering and finding a campsite. Picnic shelters are available on a first-come basis without charge, or may be reserved for $30 by contacting the Resource Management Office.* **Directions***: Decatur County. From Bainbridge, take GA 253 south for 3 miles to where Ten Mile Still Road branches to the left. Stay on Ten Mile Still Road about 2 miles to*

The Sinking of the Viola

The Apalachicola-Flint-Chattahoochee River System was the highway for moving cotton to market during the 1800s, but transporting cotton on a steamboat could be a very hazardous venture.

"This was a year of steamboat disasters and the Viola, *[owned by] Captain H. W. Van Vechten, was snagged and sunk in the Flint River a few miles below Bainbridge. She had 1,030 bales of cotton aboard. The* Viola *was reported as a total loss. This was especially hard to bear for Captain Van Vechten as he had also owned one half of the recently lost* Siren.

"However, much of the Viola's *cargo of cotton was saved in a damaged condition. Captain Van Vechten had just brought the vessel from New Orleans for the river trade. The* Viola *of 156 tons, was built in 1834 in Brownsville, Pennsylvania. However, she was raised and ran for several years."*

Perilous Journeys: A History of Steamboating on the Chattahoochee, Apalachicola, and Flint Rivers, 1828–1928 by Edward A. Mueller

Hales Landing Road. Turn left and follow the signs. Park is at the end of the road. **More Information**: *See Resource Management Office on page 163.*

Seminole State Park Campground

Shaded by longleaf pines amid wildflowers and wiregrass, families can pitch their tents or hook up their RVs in a quiet setting along the banks of Fish Pond Drain at Lake Seminole State Park (see page 167). In an adjacent area surrounded by the park's Gopher Tortoise Trail (see page 184), the state park also provides a pioneer camping area for organized groups only.

Facilities: *50 campsites each with water and electrical hookups, picnic table and fire ring or grill; 2 comfort stations with hot showers, flush toilets, laundry facilities and electrical outlets; playground; dump station and a covered chapel area with Sunday services.* **Days/Hours**: *Park – open daily, 7 a.m. to 10 p.m.; office – 8 a.m. to 5 p.m.* **Fees**: *Campsite with hookups, $15 plus park pass; tent sites and vehicles without hookups, $13 plus park pass: waterfront sites, add $2 to above rates; pioneer camping, $1 per person, per night with a minimum of $20 plus Park Pass for each vehicle. The $2 park pass is required daily to cover parking for vehicles under 13 persons; an annual park pass can be purchased at the Park Office for $25 and is valid at all Georgia State Parks. Discounts for senior citizens and disabled Georgia veterans are available. Fees are subject to change without notice so campers should contact Seminole State Park for the latest information.* **Directions**: *Seminole County. From Donalsonville, take GA 39 south for 16 miles. Turn left onto GA 253. The well-marked park gate is about 0.25 mile on the right side of the road.* **More Information**: *Seminole State Park, Route 2, Donalsonville, GA 31745. 229/861-3137. Georgia State Parks and Historic Sites, 205 Butler Street, Suite 1352 East, Atlanta, GA 30334. Website: www.gastateparks.org. Central Reservations Center, 800/864-7275. Monday through Friday, 8 a.m. to 5 p.m.*

Neals Landing Campground

This wooded campground is on the Florida side of the Chattahoochee River at the site of the old Neals Landing and Ferry, which operated until 1927. It is adjacent to Neals Landing Park.

Facilities: *11 campsites without hookups, bathhouse with showers, dump station, pay phone and drinking water. Boat ramp (see map page 239) and picnic area located in Neals Landing day use area (see page 168).* **Days/Hours**: *Open daily. Campground gate is locked from 10 p.m. to 7 a.m.* **Fees**: *Camping, $5 per night. Corps-operated campgrounds are available on a first- come basis. Park attendants or hosts live on the site and will assist you with registering and finding a campsite.* **Directions**: *Jackson County, Florida. From Donalsonville, take GA 91 south 9 miles to the river. As soon as you cross the river (and the state line into Florida), GA 91 turns into FL 2 and the campground is on the left.* **More Information**: *See Resource Management Office on page 163.*

Bald Eagle

When adopted as the American national symbol in 1782, wildlife experts estimate there were between 25,000 to 75,000 nesting bald eagles in the lower 48 states. By the early 1960s however, there were fewer than 450 nesting pairs. Habitat destruction, illegal shooting and pesticides—notably DDT, were the major causes of the bald eagle's decline. While habitat loss remains a threat, huge efforts have helped to raise the population to an estimated 4,000 nesting pairs today.

Bald eagles require a quiet, isolated environment with tall trees and clean bodies of water. They are most likely to be found near large rivers, lakes, marshes and other wetland areas. Bald eagles build enormous nests, or aeries, reaching as much as 10 feet across and weighing as much as 2,000 pounds. As the aeries are reused and added to each year, they may become so big that they are susceptible to blowing down during a storm.

Fish make up 60 to 90 percent of a bald eagle's diet. They'll also feed on waterfowl, small mammals and carrion. They are known to pirate fish from ospreys and harass vultures into disgorging their food. They are an important part of the food chain, cleaning up carcasses and hunting the weaker members of smaller animal species.

Bald eagles usually mate for life. Their courtship displays are impressive—aerial displays of free-falling, mid-air somersaults with interlocked talons, chases, dives and siderolls. They establish and defend territories together and, generally, return to the same breeding territory each year.

Bald eagles can often be seen soaring over the waters of the Flint as it flows through the Coastal Plain.

Three Rivers State Recreation Area

Campers have their choice of two campgrounds at Three Rivers State Recreation Area: Lakeside Campground for family camping and Highlands Youth Campground for Scout groups and other organized youth and adult group camping.

Facilities: *Lakeside Campground – campsites with and without water and electrical hookups, boat ramp, fishing pier, playground area, showers, restrooms and public phones. Access to the Lakeside Nature Trail is on the east side of the campground. Highlands Youth Campground – sites with and without water, two fire circles, showers and restrooms. This campground is also used as a backup for tent campers who don't need electricity. A dump station is located near the Highlands area.* **Fees**: *Camping, $8 per night; electricity, additional $2.* **Directions**: *Jackson County, Florida. From Sneads, Florida, take SR 271 north for 2 miles. Park entrance on right.* **More Information**: *Three Rivers State Recreation Area, 7908 Three Rivers Park Road, Sneads, FL 32460. 850/482-9006. Florida Parks website: www.dep.state.fl.us/parks.*

MARINAS AND FISH CAMPS

Wingate's Lunker Lodge

It's the granddaddy of fish camps, and Jack Wingate is the grand-daddy of bass fishermen. If you hang around long enough, you're sure to find Jack, rocking on the front porch or drinking ice tea at one of the red-and white-checked clothed tables in the dining room. But if you don't get to see him, you can read the framed articles about his honors and exploits that hang from the dining room's walls. Indian artifacts, pottery, flint arrowheads, deer antlers and even a stuffed alligator—all from the surrounding area—fill the display cases that line the room. Consider yourself lucky if you can get a driving tour of the area or a guided boat trip on Lake Seminole with Jack. But whether you eat lunch at Wingate's Restaurant, camp at Bass Island Campgrounds or just sit a spell on the front porch or dock, a trip to Wingate's Lunker Lodge is a genuine Lake Seminole experience.

Facilities: *62 covered slips, gas, boat rentals, fishing guides, tackle shop with all necessary provisions. Lunker Lodge – 16 rooms, each with air conditioning and color TV; stag retreat (men only), sleeps 18. Bass Island Campground – 48 RV sites, each with water and electric hookups; some sites with sewer connections and/or cable TV; showers; laundry; picnic tables; restrooms; playground and dump station. Primitive camping area – 34 tent sites with electricity and water. Known for its barbecue and house dressing, Wingate's Restaurant serves breakfast, lunch and dinner country style–eggs, grits, meat and three, fried chicken, catfish, seafood and steak dinners. Wingate's Fish Camp for Boys offers sessions each June through August.* **Days/Hours**: *Open daily. Sunday through Thursday, 6:30 a.m. to 8 p.m.; Friday and Saturday, 6 a.m. to 9 p.m. Closed on Christmas Day.* **Fees**: *Boat ramp, $2 but free to guests.* **Directions**: *Decatur County. From Bainbridge, take GA 97 south about 15 miles to GA 97 Spur. Turn right and go 3 miles. You'll*

Largemouth Bass

The largemouth bass, or lunker largemouth as it is called, is one of the most sought-after and respected fresh-water gamefish in America. Known as a fierce competitor when hooked, fishermen often dream of reeling in a 20-pounder for the record books. The average size of these fish is three pounds in the North and eight to 10 in the South—but 20-pound catches are not uncommon. Lake Seminole is one of the prime largemouth bass fishing lakes in the United States.

The largemouth bass is a species of elongated, predatory sunfish that prefer shallow, quiet ponds, lakes and slow-moving rivers or streams. When viewing the fish from the side, the fish's mouth extends just beyond the eye. The sides of the fish are an olive-green and black color, while its belly is a light mixture of gold, yellow and white. A dark, horizontal band, which fades and breaks up with age, runs along the middle of the fish.

The bass will eat just about anything that is alive, moves and fits in its mouth. As the largemouth bass has an exceptionally large mouth, it can swallow its prey whole. If the prey struggles, the bass will simply hold it in its powerful jaws, swim around with it and shake it into submission.

Each spring, the male largemouth bass digs a nest and the female lays up to 25,000 eggs. Within three to six days the eggs become fingerlings. The male largemouth bass guards over the offspring until they reach a size of about one inch. The fish remain in schools as they grow, but become more independent as they mature. During the spawning season of spring and early summer, both sexes become extremely aggressive.

see the signs. Wingate's is on the left. **Location on Water**: *Located on the east bank of the main body of Lake Seminole. Turn toward east bank at mile marker 10.4.* **More Information**: *Troy Barfield, owner, Wingate's Lunker Lodge, 139 Wingate Road, Bainbridge, GA 31717. 229/246-0658.*

Big Jim's Landing & Lodging

On Friday and Saturday afternoons, the oyster shucking begins behind the party pavilion at Big Jim's Oyster Bar. By 5 p.m. the hot wings are frying, the shrimp is boiling and the beer is starting to flow as the jukebox cranks up some country tunes by Garth and Shania. It's the weekend at Big Jim's, and the fishermen, duck hunters, campers and locals start to gather after a day of cruising Lake Seminole. It's an adult crowd that drifts in, sitting down on pink vinyl and steel-rimmed chairs at the linoleum tables, enjoying oysters on the half shell, fried cheese sticks, stuffed peppers with crab. In good weather, the crowd spills out to the tent and picnic tables that sit along the inlet. You can tie your boat up to the weathered-looking dock and join the fun, or walk over from the motel units and campground. This is a fish camp with a laid-back party atmosphere. Owners Jim and Linda Snell extend their Southern hospitality to the very end, with a sign that reads, "Thanks, y'all come back."

Facilities: *10 covered boat slips and courtesy dock, motel with 4 single units and 4 kitchenette units, 16 RV campsites with electrical and water hookups and showers, tent campsites, boat ramp, Big Jim's Oyster Bar and party pavilion, Lulu's Restaurant and bait and tackle store. There is no gas.* **Days/Hours**: *Big Jim's Landing & Lodging – open daily. Lulu's Restaurant – open Sunday through Wednesday, 6 a.m. to 2 p.m. for breakfast and lunch; Thursday through Saturday, 6 a.m. to 10 a.m. for breakfast, 11 a.m. to 2 p.m. for lunch and 5 p.m. to 9 p.m. for dinner. Big Jim's Oyster Bar – open Friday and Saturday, 5 p.m. to 11 p.m.* **Rates**: *Covered boat slips, $20 per month. Boat slips are free to campers and lodgers. Motel – single (sleeps two), $32 per night; unit with kitchenette (sleeps six), $46 per night; each additional person, $10. RV storage, $45 per month; RV space, $225 per month or $12 per day, including full hookup and public showers; tent camping, $8 per day.* **Directions**: *Seminole County. From Reynoldsville, take GA 253 south for 3 miles to Reynolds Landing Road. Turn left and go about 1 mile. Big Jim's is at the end of the road.* **Location on the Water**: *Near mouth of Spring Creek, next to Spring Creek Park.* **More Information**: *Jimmy and Linda Snell, owners. Big Jim's Landing and Lodging, Route 5, Box 1105D, Donalsonville, GA 31745. 229/861-3247.*

Seminole Sportsman's Lodge & Marina

Located near the geographic center of Lake Seminole, this fish camp claims to be "at the heart of the Lake's best fishing." Both fishing and duck hunting regulars—and their families—return here year after year, as do the bass clubs and fishing tournament participants keeping the facilities booked ahead for several months.

Jack Wingate's Spanish Mission Story

Fishing guide and storyteller, Jack Wingate knows a lot about Lake Seminole—its wildlife, Indian battles, forts, and, in this story, the Spanish missions that are now under its waters.

"There was in 1685, the time that the Explorer [Hernando de Soto] came through, a Spanish Mission, in what is now the southern part of Seminole County. This mission was engaged by the Spanish at St. Augustine to furnish corn for the Fort. This corn was transported 200 miles to the Fort on the backs of the little Indian Boys. The boys had baskets made to fit their backs and held above a bushel of corn. The kids were well treated by the Spanish so long as they moved the corn with care not to spill any. When they emptied the baskets at St. Augustine, they took a short rest, then filled the baskets with sea shells and brought them back to lower Seminole County. This might account for the numerous salt water sea shells that are found in that area near Burial Sites.

"This Mission was the last of three missions that were in the area and the only one in Seminole County. Its name was Santa Cruz de Sabacola El Menor. The Mission before that was San Carlos, located in Jackson County, Florida. The one before that was San Nichols located in Decatur County, Georgia. The Spanish first occupied this area sometime in the 16th century."

"The Indians Thereabouts" by Jack Wingate from *Cornerstone of Georgia— Seminole County*

Facilities: *12 large slips; 15 small slips; open storage and twenty storage sheds; gas dock and oil and battery charging; sand boat ramp; jon boats and pontoon boat rentals; store with groceries, licenses, bait and tackle. No maintenance. Campground — 22 campsites with and without water and electrical hookups, some with sewers, dump station, showers and restrooms. Primitive campsites for tent camping in the pine woods. Motel and cabins — 1, 2, and 3 bedrooms; air-conditioned; some with kitchenette.* **Days/Hours**: *Open daily. Weekdays, 7 a.m. to 5 p.m.; weekends, 7 a.m. to 7 p.m. Emergency service available after hours.* **Directions**: *Seminole County. From Donalsonville, take GA 39 south for 16 miles. A few yards south of its intersection with GA 253, turn left and follow the signs.* **Location on Water**: *This marina is located approximately 3 miles up Fish Pond Drain across from Seminole State Park.* **More Information**: *Seminole Sportsman's Lodge & Marina, Route 3, Box 215-A, Donalsonville, GA 31745. 229/861-3862.*

Trails End Marina & Campground

This family-owned and operated marina stands on a site that was once owned by a family who were pioneer settlers of Seminole County. The Turnage family farmed surrounding land, established a ferry that was a major crossing point and later established a steamboat landing that became a major center from which farmers shipped their cotton and agricultural goods to market. In 1923, Daniel Turnage sold Turnage Ferry and Landing to L. C. Butler, who then called it Butler's Ferry and Landing.

Facilities: *23 covered boat slips; 15 uncovered boat slips; covered and uncovered dry storage; gas; professional guides; boat repairs; boat rentals; courtesy car; boat ramp (see map page 239); ship's store with live bait, tackle, souvenirs, fishing and camping supplies, ice and cold drinks. A hot food bar serves hamburgers, hot dogs, chili, barbeque, grilled fish and chicken sandwiches and "the best cold-weather, crock-pot lunches around." Campground — 13 campsites with electrical, water and sewer hookups; bathhouses and restrooms. Eleven acres of property has been cleared for primitive tent camping. Motel units — 5 units, each sleeps eight, fully-equipped kitchen.* **Days/Hours**: *Open daily, 6:30 a.m. to 5:30 p.m. Gas is available 24 hours a day.* **Fees**: *Primitive camping for organized youth groups is available at no charge. Call for reservations and all other rates, including group and extended stay rates.* **Directions**: *Seminole County. From Reynoldsville, take GA 253 south about 9 miles to its end and follow the signs.* **Location on water**: *This marina is located at mile marker 8.2 on the east bank, approximately 0.25 miles off the main channel of the Chattahoochee River portion of Lake Seminole.* **More Information**: *Trails End Marina and Campground, Rt. 3, Box 188, Donalsonville, GA 31745. 229/861-2060 or 800/322-5916; fax 229/861-2383. Website: www.trailsendmarina.com.*

Southern Magnolia

Perhaps one of the most symbolically southern of all trees, the Southern Magnolia *(Magnolia grandiflora L.)* is a large beautiful, spreading evergreen tree, native to the Coastal Plain, but planted throughout the state of Georgia.

The Southern Magnolia grows 60 to 80 feet high with a trunk two to three feet in diameter, terminating in a spreading, pyramidal head. The Georgia Forestry Commission gives its key characteristics as "leaves evergreen, 5 to 10 inches long, 2 to 3 inches wide; flower large, fragrant; fruit a reddish bur."

The tree occurs in swamp forests, alluvial floodplains, maritime forests and low woods of the Coastal Plain. It is widely planted as a specimen tree for its showy, fragrant, creamy-white flowers, which appear in late spring and early summer, and its large, shiny leaves. It is fast growing and hardy throughout most of the Southeast. The wood is used for furniture, paneling, veneer and cabinet work. Numerous species of birds and small mammals consume its seeds.

Parramore Landing

This small campground and bait shop is located adjacent to the Corps-operated Parramore Landing Park.

Facilities: *10 covered boat slips, eight campsites with electrical and water hookups, five with sewer; boat dock, restaurant with bait and tackle shop. Other facilities at the adjacent Parramore Landing Park (see page 171).* **Days/Hours**: *Bait Shop — 6 a.m. to 4:30 p.m.* **Location of the Water**: *On the west bank of the main channel of the Chattahoochee River portion of the lake at mile marker 13.* **Directions**: *Jackson County, Florida. From Sneads, FL, take SR 271 north about 11 miles to Parramore Road. Turn right and follow the signs.* **More Information**: *Operators, Ralph and Diane Cox, Parramore Landing, 7768 Parramore Road, Sneads, FL 32460. 850/592-2091.*

Seminole Lodge Marina, Motel and Campground

Monte and Becky Anderson's establishment here just 2.5 miles north of the Woodruff Dam can be a welcome sight if you're boating upriver from Apalachicola. And if you're headed downriver to that same port, you should think about stopping here first. This is your last chance for gas for about 105 miles. The Andersons, who live on the premises, have gone to great lengths to renovate and improve the services at this 43-acre lodge and marina, which they acquired just a few years ago. Their hard work and friendliness to guests make this a good place to stop or stay.

Facilities: *Covered and extra-wide boat slips; full-service fuel dock; store with hunting and fishing licenses, groceries, ice, bait, tackle, lake maps and payphone. Motel — single, double and kitchenette units on waterfront with bath/shower and TV; air-conditioned. Campsite with electric, water and sewer hookups; showers and use of boat ramp. Camper rentals and storage available.* **Days/Hours**: *Open daily, 6 a.m. to 8 p.m.* **Fees**: *Boat slips, $5 per day or $45 per month; RVs with electric and water, $11 per night; RVs with electric, water and sewer, $12.50 per night; tent sites, $8 per night; boat ramp, $2 per day.* **Directions**: *Jackson County, Florida. From Sneads, Florida on US 90, turn north on Legion Road at the Dairy Queen. Go 2 miles to the dirt road on the right and follow signs.* **Location on water**: *On main body of lake on the west bank at mile marker 2.5. Turn left into the inlet.* **More Information**: *Becky and Monte Anderson, owners, Seminole Lodge, 2360 Legion Road, Sneads, FL 32460. 850/593-6886 or 800/410-5209.*

FISHING

Leaping eight-pound bass, skeleton cypress protruding from the dark, clear water and the white blooms of lily pads have attracted fishermen to Lake Seminole from all over the world. The Flint and Chattahoochee Rivers and their spring-fed tributaries all lend to the excellent fishing at Seminole.

Lake Seminole is ranked as one of the top largemouth bass fishing

---

Fishing Lake Seminole

"Since its impoundment, Lake Seminole has consistently been rated among the best bass-fishing destinations in the region and has often been listed among the top five or six nationally. That reputation has been based on Seminole's regular yield of large num-bers of bass weighing over five pounds each, including a good many in the eight- to 10-pound range. Needless to say, these large fish have drawn a steady stream of anglers to the lake. Over the years surveys have found that up to 73 percent of the fishing pressure on the reservoir is directed at large-mouth bass.

"Largemouths are by far the dominant black bass in Lake Seminole. However, shoal bass are present in all the lake's feeder streams, particularly far up the Chattahoochee and Flint Rivers. Also, since spotted bass have shown up in the Apalachicola River below the reservoir, there is at least a remote possibility of hooking one in Lake Seminole."

Bass Fishing in Georgia by Jimmy Jacobs

lakes in the United States. Other species of fish, including striped and hybrid bass, bream, crappie, bluegills, red ear sunfishes, mullet and catfish, also abound in this sportsman's paradise.

Seminole is shallow with a maximum depth of 35 feet and an average depth of nine feet. The hot spots on Lake Seminole have adjacent deep water where the predators gather, waiting for the shad to swim around the point. Some of the better areas are the old Fort Scott area, the Hutchinson Ferry Bank, Coots Landing and Stones Landing. The latter two are good locations to find hybrids, stripers and white bass.

Prime bass fishing is in the spring. Best baits include spinner-baits and plastic worms as the bass move into the shallows. Good topwater fishing for bass is later in the summer. Bluegill and shellcracker are caught in the spring, using crickets and earthworms. Fly-fishing is excellent for bream when the mayflies hatch and fall into the lake. Some large strings of speckled perch are caught in January and February using live minnows.

Lake Seminole, just as other lakes, has its own particular bank topography, underwater structure, stream currents and fish population. Professional guides know all the peculiarities of their lake. Inexperienced fishermen or families looking for an enjoyable day's outing will increase their pleasure ten-fold by taking advantage of the experience of a professional guide. Even the most experienced fishermen find that one or two days of guide fees is a good investment before launching out on their own. The best guides not only make sure their customers fish, but provide insights into the fishing habits of different species, lake ecology, weather lore and other aspects that will enhance a fishing experience.

When booking a fishing guide always check to make sure who is responsible for all tackle (rods, reels, lures); boat and gasoline; all live bait; life jackets; lunch, drinks snacks and ice; and rain gear. Be sure to understand exactly what is included in the guide fees.

HIKES AND WALKS

Bainbridge Walking Tour
On a 75-foot bluff above the Flint River and 10 miles from its confluence with the Chattahoochee, Indian trader, express rider and general Indian-country politician James Burgess established a trading post at the site of a Creek Indian village called Puckanawhitla. Little is known about Puckanawhitla, except that by 1778 the Indians were mostly driven out and the village was being called Burgess Town.

By 1817, when U.S. soldiers came to build a federal outpost, Burgess Town was disappearing, too. The soldiers named their outpost, Fort Hughes in honor of a young bugler killed by renegade Indians at the site. A temporary satellite station of Fort Scott, the small lonely picket works was abandoned after three years, but the name lingered.

Decatur County
The Flint River flows through Decatur County and through the county seat of Bainbridge as well.

"Decatur County was created in 1823 from portions of Early County. The county was named in honor of Commodore Stephen Decatur who defeated the Barbary Coast pirates at Tripoli in 1815. Bainbridge, the county seat, was named for Commodore William Bainbridge, commander of the U.S. Constitution, 'Old Ironsides.' The Decatur County area was the site of several battles between Indians and early settlers. In the early 1700s, both the Spanish and English fought with Creek Indians. In 1818, General Andrew Jackson led troops from Tennessee, Kentucky, and Georgia to victory over the Seminole Indians."

From *Georgia County Snapshots*, Georgia Department of Community Affairs

For tourism information for towns in Decatur County, see Resources page 299.

When the army withdrew, a man named Moody, who had been a soldier under the command of General Andrew Jackson in the Seminole War of 1818, built a cabin near the fort and started a ferry.

Once the Seminoles were defeated in 1824, Fort Hughes was re-named Bainbridge for Commodore William Bainbridge, commander of "Old Ironsides" during the War of 1812. On December 8, 1823, the Georgia Legislature created Decatur County. Land for a county seat was purchased in 1826, and the city of Bainbridge was incorporated in 1829.

The Flint, with its connection to the Chattahoochee and the Apalachicola, was part of a large ready-made water system; and Bainbridge from its earliest days was a river town, shipping products from surrounding farms and forests down the Flint to Apalachicola Bay. Indian villages, de Soto explorations, Spanish missions, Colonial trading, Andrew Jackson's Indian-fighting army—a lot has gone on up and down this valley. This is an area rich in American history, and Bainbridge is right in the heart of it.

The following tour of this historic area begins at the Bainbridge town square, which was originally the Court House Square, but is now called Willis Park. This town square is characteristic of the south's personality and reveals more about its town than any other town square in the south. There are monuments to World Wars I and II and the Korean and Vietnam Wars. There's a bell from the steamboat *John W. Callahan, Jr.* There are historical markers for El Cameo Real, an Indian trail that connected St. Augustine and Pensacola and crossed the Flint near present day Bainbridge, and de Soto's discovery of the Flint. There are monuments to former mayors, to former Georgia Governor Marvin Griffin and to a local teacher and her students who died in the Winecoff Hotel fire in Atlanta on December 7, 1946. Magnolia, live oak and crape myrtle grace the lawn. Baskets of pink impatiens hang from the lightposts. The centerpiece of it all is a Confederate monument honoring the Bainbridge volunteers, later called the Bainbridge Independents. A white Victorian-style gazebo completes the setting. This square merits a leisurely walk, with time to read the inscriptions and reflect on the architecture, as well as the very "southernness" of the setting.

From the square, go north on Broad Street and stop by the Bainbridge Hardware Company. Lofton Willis has assembled a large variety of products that reflect rural Southwest Georgia life—catfish baskets, cotton baskets, iron skillets, tack for farm animals. His main line of business, however, is supplying big tools for the economic bedrock of this community—the farms, peanut processing factories and feed mills that line US 27. He's also got two mint-condition Model-T Fords in the store's attic.

Go back to Water Street and head west toward the Flint River. The first block of Water Street boasts some interesting historic structures. On the right corner is the Decatur County Courthouse, built in

Fort Scott

Today, the site of Fort Scott is surrounded by the waters of Lake Seminole.

"Fort Scott was erected in late 1816 on the first high ground, or bluff, above the confluence of Spring Creek and Flint River in today's Seminole County. That site later became part of land lot 224, district 21, and it was almost due east of Sealy Plantation, and about 16 miles southwest of Bainbridge. The fort was maintained by the U.S. Army during the First Creek War as protection from the Creeks of Alabama moving across the southwestern tip of Georgia on their way to Florida. Fort Scott was garrisoned until 1821, by which time the Indian troubles were over. A cannon monument was erected on the old fort site in 1883, but immediately prior to the creation of the lake, was moved to Chason Park, Bainbridge."

Indian Heritage of Georgia by Marion R. Hemperley

1903. The original clock, weighing one and a half tons, is still in use. There's a historical marker on the creation of Decatur County and a huge magnolia that's protected through a city ordinance to preserve landmark trees. Next is the courthouse annex, formerly the county jail. On the left side of the street is the Conger Building, built in the late 1800s by an old, established Bainbridge family; the 1890 Mitchell Willis Building and the 1914 City Hall and Firehouse, reflecting the Mission-style architecture popular in the early 1900s. This building, now known as the Firehouse Center and Gallery, is home to the Bainbridge-Decatur County Council for the Arts and the Decatur County Historical Society Museum, which has on exhibit a dugout canoe found on the east bank of the Flint River about five miles north of Bainbridge. The canoe, which is made of a single cypress tree, is 12 feet, 11 inches long; 24 inches wide; and 14 inches deep. It appears to have been made by European tools and probably dates from the late 1700s or early 1800s.

Continue on Water Street to Donalson Street and turn right. This street will curve to the right and turn into Jackson Street. At 330 Jackson is Chason Park, a very historic piece of property in Bainbridge. Some historians believe de Soto and his men crossed the Flint at this site more than four centuries ago. This site on the bluffs overlooking the Flint is also the location of Fort Hughes and the founding of Bainbridge.

Go back to Water Street and continue a little further until it ends at Cheney Griffin Park (see page 165). This park affords a wonderful view of the river as it flows under the US 27 Business Bridge upstream and an old railroad bridge downstream. Live oak adorned with Spanish moss, small cypress tress, sweetgum and hickory line the curves of the riverbank. Picnickers sit at tables under the trees, facing the river as boats cruise up and down. This is a particularly beautiful place to be at sunset. There's a wooden walkway for strolling along the river, and docks and boat ramps for boating. Smells from the Flint River Seafood Restaurant fill the air.

Continue left around the park to a road that begins under the old railroad bridge and follows the curve of the river, providing one of the most scenic river experiences in Georgia. This is a natural, rural riverbank environment. Moss-covered live oaks line both sides of the road right down to the riverbank. Motorboats cruise up and down the grey-green Flint, which is about 75 to 100 yards wide at this point. Locals fish and picnic under the trees in the evening. The west bank of the river is lined with wetlands and woods.

Cross under the US 27/84 Bypass Bridge. The road continues along the riverbank and connects with the Earl May Boat Basin and its boat ramps, picnic areas, campsites and stocked fishing ponds (see page 164). There is a historic steam-powered train engine at the park, and it's worth the time to stop and take a look at this massive structure that overtook riverboats as a transportation preference.

Fort Recovery

"The small town of Recovery on GA 97 in extreme southwestern Decatur County, retains the name of a Creek Indian War fortification once located in that area. In June 1816, the U.S. Army established Fort Scott on the Flint River just above the Florida line. There was much fighting nearby during that period, and the Army built two additional stations to help house the soldiers. Fort Recovery was established as a hospital or recovery area for troops wounded in the fighting in that section. Fort Scott and probably Fort Recovery were abandoned in September 1821, as the war had ended by that time and the need for protection from the Indians had ended. Camp (as it was sometimes known) Recovery was located southeast of today's Recovery about 4/10 mile down that highway, thence southwestward across a field for 1/10 mile."

Indian Heritage of Georgia by Marion R. Hemperely

Also in the park is the Bainbridge-Decatur County Chamber of Commerce, located in the historic 1921 McKenzie-Reynolds Home. An interesting photo in the house shows it surrounded by water during the July 1994 flood. At the chamber of commerce you can pick up a free "Bainbridge Heritage Tour" brochure for a self-guided driving and walking tour of more than 50 historic homes, churches and other structures in Bainbridge.

More Information: *Bainbridge-Decatur County Chamber of Commerce, P.O. Box 736, Bainbridge, GA 31717. 229/246-4774 or 800/243-4774; fax 229/243-7633. Website: www.bainbridgega.com/chamber*

Gopher Tortoise Trail

This system of nature trails at Seminole State Park gets its name from the threatened gopher tortoise. While native to the America, the wiregrass region is one of the few remaining habitats for this threatened reptiles.

Distance: The full loop route is 2.2 miles. Several access points allow hikers to walk just a portion of the trail.

Trailhead Location: Seminole State Park (see page 167). The trail, which is located on the southeast side of the park, can be accessed from several marked locations near the cottages or beside the chapel in the campground area. Parking is available near both ends of the trail, but cars must display the $2 park pass.

Features: The trail loops its way through pine, swamp and wiregrass natural areas. Fairly level, sandy and hard, the easily walked trail would be possible to traverse in a wheelchair. The resident gopher tortoises, which burrow deep into the ground, leave their marks all along the trail—large, easy to spot holes in the sandy ground. Signs along the trail, many rusted or partially removed, identify the flora and fauna native to the area. The park offers guided trail hikes by appointment.

Half Dry Creek Trail

This trail, which crosses a creek bed that runs dry unless there's a rain, is one of two hiking trails located in Three Rivers State Recreation Area.

Distance: This 0.75-mile loop trail is of a moderate grade.

Trailhead Location: Three Rivers State Recreation Area (see page 171). The trail can be accessed at the east end of the picnic area.

Features: The trail traverses the hilly terrain and steep ravines of this mixed hardwood forest. There's plenty of opportunity to see the wildlife that live in this type of natural area—white-tailed deer, raccoon, fox squirrel and grey fox. Even a bobcat could appear.

Lakeside Trail

This nature trail, which partly lies along Lake Seminole's shoreline within Three Rivers State Recreation Area, is a good place to observe the park's wildlife and natural areas. It's a particularly good trail for

Cypress

Bald cypress *(Taxodium distichum (L.) Rich.)* occurs principally in swamps and ponds throughout most of the Coastal Plain. You'll see cypress all along the Flint River, particularly from the Great Swamp area (see page 89) to Lake Seminole. It is a large, long-lived tree reaching heights of 150 feet with a gradually tapering trunk generally four to five feet in diameter above an abruptly enlarged base and terminating in a spreading, round crown. These cypress "knees" are usually what make cypress trees so distinguishable.

The Georgia Forestry Commission describes the tree's key characteristics as: "feather-like arrangement of the leaves, branches deciduous, cone small and round; bark fibrous, cinnamon-red; presence of cone-shaped knees around the base of the trunk." Its wood is "light, soft, not strong, very brittle, easily worked, straight-grained, varying in color from pale brown to nearly black with a somewhat pungent color. Old growth heartwood very durable."

A somewhat smaller species, pond cypress, is 40 to 80 feet tall and one to two feet in diameter. The knees of bald cypress differ from those of pond cypress by being more narrowly conical and sharp pointed than the flattened, dome-shaped knees of pond cypress. Pond cypress occurs in shallow ponds, wet depressions in flatwoods and along stream banks throughout the Coastal Plain.

birding, especially during the winter months when migrating water-fowl, such as geese and duck, are at their peak on the lake and the bare trees provide maximum viewing of ospreys and eagles.

Distance: This 1.75-mile loop is advertised as a leisurely one-hour walk, but it can be completed in half an hour at a brisk pace.

Trailhead Location: Three Rivers State Recreation Area (see page 171). Lakeside Trail begins and ends between sites three and four at the Lakeside Campground.

Features: During the first half of the loop, the trail winds along the water—sometimes within 15 feet—providing close-up views of the lake. The return loop circles back through the pine and hardwood forest. The trail is strewn with roots and is of moderate grade and is wide enough for two people to walk abreast easily. Magnolia and Spanish moss abound, as do spider and duck. Even an armadillo or two can be spotted. Be on the lookout for white-tailed deer, fox, snapping turtle and alligator.

Turkey Flight Overlook Trail

The bluffs that border the southeastern side of Lake Seminole and the Torreya ravines that dissect them are part of the lower Pelham escarpment. Here, within the steep-walled forested ravines, live a wide variety of plant life, including conifers and broadleaf deciduous trees. This plant life supports an abundance of wildlife, many of which can be seen by walking through the Turkey Flight Nature Area in Chattahoochee Park. From the Overlook, which is off the nature trail but directly across the road, you can look out over the lake from one of its highest vantage points.

Distance: This nature trail is an easy 0.3 mile walk on a wide, well-marked trail.

Trailhead Location: Chattahoochee Park (see page 163). The trail can be accessed from three different locations off the paved walking lane that runs beside the one-way paved road leading into the area. Parking is available near both ends of the trail, but the trail also loops so you can return to your car without taking the walking lane.

Features: The trail cuts through woods laden with Spanish moss and populated with magnolia, maple, beech and elm trees. Look out for deer and fox tracks—fresh tracks are easy to spot. Wild turkey, bald eagle, bobwhite quail, pileated woodpecker, gopher tortoise and alligator all inhabit the area and are commonly seen. A trail map, which includes information about some of the wildlife living in the area, is available at the park and at the Resource Management Office.

The Birth of an Alligator

A female alligator builds her nest above ground. She forms leaves, branches and mud into a mound about three-feet high and seven-feet across. She scoops out a hole in the center and lays 20 to 70 eggs in it, then covers it over. As the leaves and branches rot, they give off enough heat to keep the eggs warm.

The eggs are white, hard-shelled and slightly larger than a hen's eggs. The mother stays near the nest, protecting it against predators. After about nine weeks, the young emerge from the eggs. When they hatch, they make a high-pitched yelp and the mother comes to scratch open the nest. When hatched, the baby alligator is about nine inches long and grows about a foot a year for the first six years. Alligators are more protective of their young than most reptiles. The mother guards her young for a year or more.

Alligators probably live to be 50 or 60 years old. A male, 11- to 12-feet long, may weigh 450 to 550 pounds.

HUNTING

Lake Seminole

Much of the Lake Seminole area is open to hunting for duck, deer, rabbit, squirrel, quail, dove and turkey. The Apalachee Game Management Area in Florida and various tracts in Georgia (see page 172) are managed by the respective states as game management areas. Hunting is allowed on all Corps-managed lands and waters if they are not expressly closed. Examples of areas closed are developed recreation areas, marinas and operations areas. Numerous public launching ramps provide easy access to the water for waterfowl hunters. Rental boats are also available at local marinas.

Hunters should use caution while hunting in areas immediately adjacent to private development. A valid state hunting license is required when hunting on Lake Seminole, and in game management areas a stamp is also required. Fishing and hunting regulation booklets are available free of charge at the Resource Management Office and at area stores.

BRIDGES

US 27 Business Bridge

This 1959 bridge that leads into downtown Bainbridge is one of four bridges that cross the Flint within a one-mile stretch of river. Upstream from this bridge stands a CSX Railroad Bridge. Downstream you can see Cheney Griffin Park on the east bank, another CSX Railroad Bridge and below that the US 27/82 Bypass Bridge. River access below the bridge from a ramp at Cheney Griffin Park (see map page 239). **Location**: *In Decatur County where US 27 Business crosses the Flint River in Bainbridge.*

US 27/84 Bypass Bridge

This bridge, built in 1976, is officially known as the Emmett Culbreth and Myrvin Culbreth Bridge. A sign designates the Flint River here as an "Inland Waterway." A paved road the goes under a portion of this bridge connects Cheney Griffin Park upstream with the Earl May Boat Basin downstream. River access is from Cheney Griffin Park or the Boat Basin (see map page 239). **Location**: *In Decatur County where US 27/84 Bypass Bridge crosses the Flint River on the outskirts of Bainbridge.*

Locking Through

Navigation locks allow recreational and commercial boats to travel from lake level to river level and back. Most people are a little anxious the first time they approach a dam, but locking through is a relatively simple and fun experience.

1. Signal the lockmaster as you approach by calling on VHF radio Channel 16 or cell phone (Woodruff Lockmaster, 850/663-4692), or by pulling the ropes at the upstream or downstream sides of the dam to sound a horn. Ropes are sometimes difficult to reach in choppy water, so it is good to have a VHF radio or cell phone when going through locks, just in case.

2. The lockmaster will signal you into the lock via traffic lights or horn blasts. A flashing red light means "do not enter," a flashing amber light means "approach slowly" and a flashing green light means "enter." A long horn blast means "enter the lock" and a short horn blast means "leave the lock."

3. Pay attention to instructions and signals from lock attendants as you enter the lock; they will direct you to one of the floating locks. Be particularly cautious if you are entering with a lot of other boats or a very large vessel.

4. Have at least one 150-foot mooring line ready. On the Jim Woodruff lock, boat passengers do the mooring. These passengers should wear PFDs. Tie the line to the floating lock and shut off the motor.

5. The lowering and lifting process is fairly slow. But the noises of the floating locks as they do their job is eerie—as the locks are large and very hollow.

6. When the process is completed, the lock gates will open. You are now on the same level as the river (or the lake). Release your lines and proceed slowly from the lock.

DAMS

Jim Woodruff Lock and Dam

The southernmost dam on the Chattahoochee, Flint and Apalachicola River System, the Jim Woodruff Lock and Dam is located on the downstream end of Lake Seminole. Completed in 1957 by the U.S. Army Corps of Engineers, the dam was the first of three locks and dams constructed to improve navigation on the river and provide a source for generating electricity. The lock is 82 feet wide by 450 feet high with a maximum lift of 33 feet. It operates 24 hours a day, seven days a week.

Before construction of the project, the Chattahoochee and Flint Rivers were only three feet deep in this area. Now a channel nine feet deep and 100 feet wide is maintained to allow commercial traffic from the Gulf Intercoastal Waterway to Bainbridge on the Flint, and to Columbus on the Chattahoochee. Three power plant units, each with a capacity of 10,000 kilowatts, put out an average annual energy output of 220 million kilowatts. The impoundment, Lake Seminole, is operated at a relatively constant level, at an elevation of 77.5 feet above mean sea level. Although there is some fluctuating for power production, no storage for flood control is provided.

For boaters wishing to lock through the Jim Woodruff Lock and Dam, refer to the sidebar on this page. The lock is open daily, 24 hours a day, and the Lockmaster can be reached at 850/663-4692.

The best places to view the dam are from the West Bank Overlook (see page 172) and the Jim Woodruff Dam Fishing Deck and Powerhouse Area (see page 163) on the east bank. You can arrange a group tour of the powerhouse by calling the powerhouse superintendent at 229/663-2291.

Below the dam, the mighty Flint and Chattahoochee become the mighty Apalachicola.

Directions: *Jackson and Gadsden Counties, Florida. The West Bank Overlook is off US 90, just west of Victory Bridge in Sneads, Florida. To get to the east bank, continue east on US 90, crossing the river to Chattahoochee, Florida.*

Navigation Window

In the drier months of the summer, the Apalachicola River dribbles down in some places to a depth of four feet, too low for large barge traffic. During such droughts the U.S. Army Corps of Engineers periodically unleashes an extra measure of water from its dams to boost the water level to eight or nine feet so commercial vessels can steam up the river. The release is coordinated among all the Corps dams, from Buford on Lake Lanier to Jim Woodruff on Lake Seminole.

Releases happen about four times a year and take place according to a schedule set in advance by the Corps. For two days the river slowly rises, remains navigable for up to 14 days, then goes down to its former level within a day or two after the water is shut off. Commercial towing boats, having gathered near the mouth of the Apalachicola River, race up the temporarily invigorated river during the two-week period, better known as a navigation window. According to the Corps, barges haul 33,000 tons of cargo up the river during each window and 637,000 total tons during each year.

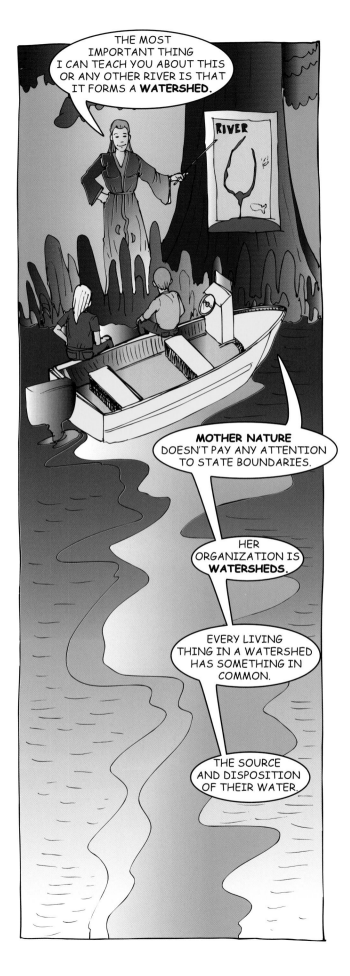

Section 7

The Land Between the Rivers

THANKS TO RIO we begin to understand the importance of a watershed and how much everyone in a watershed has in common. We go exploring in the Flint-Chattahoochee Watershed, the "Land Between the Rivers," and identify an amazingly diverse mixture of natural and cultural attractions that tell the story of the region.

In the Land Between the Rivers, use the Guidebook Section beginning on page 198 to explore Warm Springs, Franklin Roosevelt's Little White House and Franklin D. Roosevelt State Park; Pine Mountain Trail; Oxbow Meadows Environmental Learning Center; the Columbus Museum; Andersonville National Historic Site and Andersonville Village; Coheelee Creek Covered Bridge; Jimmy Carter National Historic Site; Kolomoki Mounds; Rood Creek Indian Mounds; the Bluff at Fort Gaines; Florence Marina State Park with its Kirbo Interpretive Center; Westville; George T. Bagby State Park; Providence Canyon State Conservation Park and its hiking trails; Smith Landing Park; Spring Creek Park; Eufaula National Wildlife Refuge; Hannahatchee Creek Wildlife Management Area; Lake Walter F. George Wildlife Management Area; Steve Cocke Fish Hatchery; and Warm Springs Regional Fisheries Center.

Pine Mountain
Gateway to the Land Between the Rivers

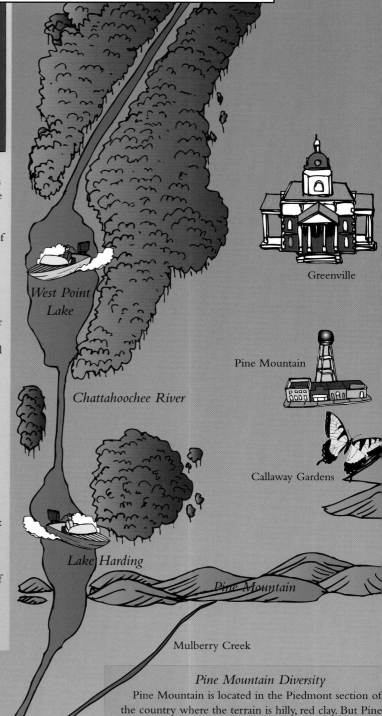

Appalachian Mountains

Pine Mountain

Southeastern Perspective

The Fall Line

A few miles south of Pine Mountain is the "Fall Line." This rocky boundary, which today separates the Piedmont from the Coastal Plain, is the geological remains of what was once a seacoast. Eons ago, everything south of the Fall Line was ocean. Then 50 million years ago, during the tertiary period of geologic history, this ocean water began to recede. Slowly. Over hundreds of thousands of years. Until it finally formed the eastern and southeastern shoreline as we know it today.

Dramatic changes in elevation occur near the Fall Line. These elevation changes produce rapids and shoals in rivers and streams that cross the Fall Line border. On the Flint River these occur around Yellow Jacket Shoals.

Above the Fall Line is the Piedmont, below it is the Coastal Plain. Piedmont terrain is characterized by rolling hills and red, clay soil, while the Coastal Plain terrain is characterized by soft, sandy sediments and limestone.

Pine Mountain Geology

Pine Mountain is the southernmost of the Appalachian Mountain chain, which extends down the East Coast of the United States. These mountains are ancient—250 million years old. Originally, Pine Mountain was 3,000 feet high—much higher than today's elevation of 900 to 1,400 feet. But for millions of years, water has continually flowed over the mountain, eroding the mountain's quartzite rock into the tiniest of particles. On the east side of Pine Mountain, the Flint River found its path through the softest part of the rocks. And like other waterways through the mountain, the Flint carried these particles, along with other sediment, downstream. The white sand beaches of the Gulf Coast, the fertile flood plains of the Flint and Chattahoochee River Valleys, the rich soil of the Dougherty Plain—all are the result of this erosion process. As for Pine Mountain itself, the mountains that remain are hard Hollis quartzite and very resistant to erosion.

West Point Lake

Greenville

Chattahoochee River

Pine Mountain

Callaway Gardens

Lake Harding

Pine Mountain

Mulberry Creek

Columbus

Pine Mountain Diversity

Pine Mountain is located in the Piedmont section of the country where the terrain is hilly, red clay. But Pine Mountain, as its name suggests, seems more like an Appalachian mountain environment. Its highest peak is nearly 1,400 feet. It is rugged with quartzite outcrops, rocks, and waterfalls. There are old woods of shortleaf p hickory and oak. Because of its mountain-like environment, mountain plants and animals have found a home here. On the other hand, its nearness to the Coastal Pla where temperatures are mild, make it a place where warmer weather plants and animals like to live, too.

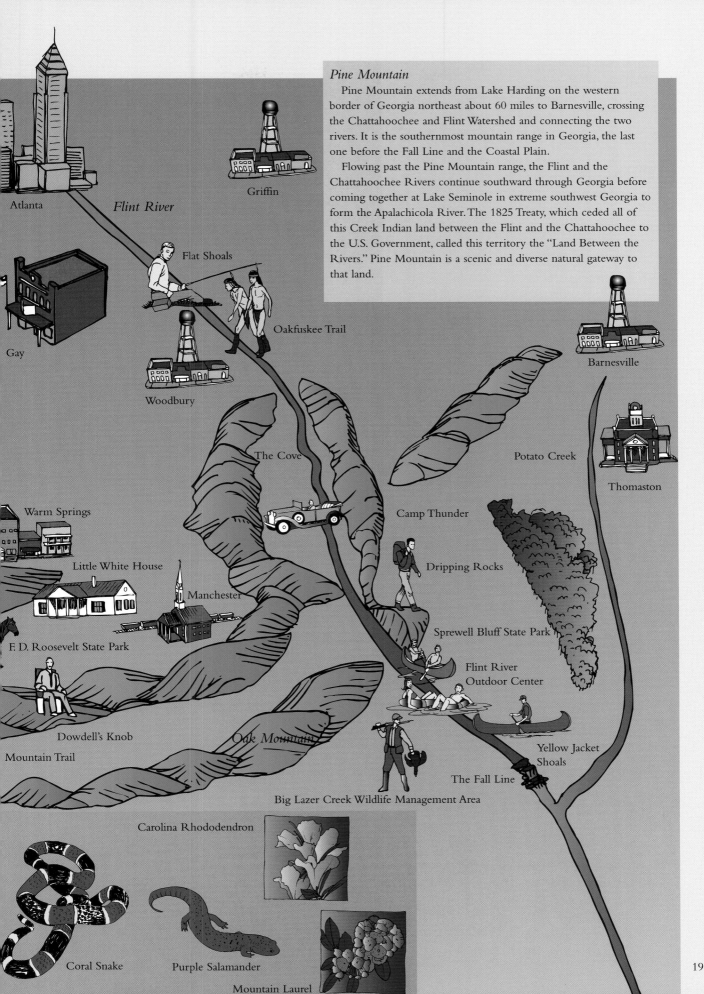

Pine Mountain

Pine Mountain extends from Lake Harding on the western border of Georgia northeast about 60 miles to Barnesville, crossing the Chattahoochee and Flint Watershed and connecting the two rivers. It is the southernmost mountain range in Georgia, the last one before the Fall Line and the Coastal Plain.

Flowing past the Pine Mountain range, the Flint and the Chattahoochee Rivers continue southward through Georgia before coming together at Lake Seminole in extreme southwest Georgia to form the Apalachicola River. The 1825 Treaty, which ceded all of this Creek Indian land between the Flint and the Chattahoochee to the U.S. Government, called this territory the "Land Between the Rivers." Pine Mountain is a scenic and diverse natural gateway to that land.

Atlanta

Flint River

Griffin

Flat Shoals

Gay

Oakfuskee Trail

Woodbury

Barnesville

The Cove

Potato Creek

Thomaston

Warm Springs

Camp Thunder

Little White House

Dripping Rocks

Manchester

Sprewell Bluff State Park

F. D. Roosevelt State Park

Flint River
Outdoor Center

Dowdell's Knob

Oak Mountain

Mountain Trail

Yellow Jacket
Shoals

The Fall Line

Big Lazer Creek Wildlife Management Area

Carolina Rhododendron

Coral Snake

Purple Salamander

Mountain Laurel

Pine Mountain

Gateway to the Land Between the Rivers

FLAT SHOALS is an area rich with history. The flat shoals across here have made this a river crossing for hundreds of years (see the Oakfuskee Trail, below). If you stand on the David Knott Bridge and look downstream, the abutments of the former wooden bridge still loom directly in front of you. The ruins of an old mill with its granite stones, hewn square and stacked without mortar, are on the right bank. A little further downstream on the right bank is a very large, flat outcrop. This was a favorite place to fish for President Franklin D. Roosevelt when he stayed at Warm Springs in the 1930s and '40s.

For more information, see pages 60 and 65.

Oakfuskee Trail

The Oakfuskee Trail was an old Indian path that entered the Land between the Rivers at Flat Shoals. It was the main branch of the famous Upper Creek Trading Route—one of the main east-west paths used by Indians since prehistoric times—and went from the Savannah River to the Tallapoosa in Alabama. The Oakfuskee Trail traversed Georgia through Warrenton, Eatonton, Indian Springs and Griffin, then through Meriwether and Troup Counties to the Chattahoochee, where it crossed into Alabama a few miles above West Point, continued through Dadeville and ended at Oakfuskee Town, a Creek settlement on the Tallapoosa River.

White traders began using the trail in the early 1700s. In time, it became a noted pioneer trace and, eventually, a leading stagecoach road, which was called the Greenville Stage Road.

To follow the trail a short distance, leave Flat Shoals, heading west into Meriwether County on Flat Shoals Road. About 1 mile from the river, bear left onto Magnolia Road, a dirt road that is marked the Greenville-Flat Shoals Road on older county maps. Stay on this about 2 miles, until it dead ends into GA 74. A historical marker for the Oakfuskee Trail will be on your right. At one time, the trail continued due west to Red Oak Creek, crossed the creek and continued west, merging into what is now GA Spur 109. The trail roughly follows this highway southwest to Greenville and then west to Odessadale. Just beyond Odessadale, the Oakfuskee Trail leaves GA Spur 109 to go southwest into Troup County.

Woodbury

The oldest town in Meriwether County, Woodbury had its beginning when a few houses were built between 1828 and 1830 at the crossroads of two well-traveled roads about 10 miles southeast of Greenville and about 3 miles west of the Flint River. Because the land there was "surfaced with perfectly white sand," according to one source, the community became known as Sandtown. When the first post office opened in 1845, the town's name was changed to Woodberry, and then in 1854 changed again to Woodbury.

Like many other small towns in the Land between the Rivers, Woodbury's real growth began when it got its first railroad. In 1887 the Georgia, Midland and Gulf (later named the Southern Railway Company) line from Columbus to Atlanta put a rail through town; the Macon and Birmingham Railroad line came around 1890. A third line came through town in 1907 when the Atlanta, Birmingham and Atlantic (later named the Seaboard Coastline Railroad Company) began extending their line from Manchester to Atlanta, making Woodbury a busy railroad center. A cotton market was established and warehouses, mercantile stores and a hotel were built.

The Cove

At the Flint River, the ridges of Pine Mountain form a near-perfect circle that encloses a fertile basin known simply as the Cove. This is one of the most beautiful and geologically interesting parts of the region (see page 63).

Within the confines of the Cove, Indians farmed, as did the pioneers who settled the Cove in the 1830s. It is believed that the Creek Indians cleared land in the upper end of the Cove and spent the summers growing their annual corn crop. The first road in the Cove was laid out in a circle and the people built their homes around it. There has never been a railroad or a post office in the Cove and although there are paved roads through the area, it is still a quite isolated community. Franklin Roosevelt loved to visit the Cove whenever he came to Warm Springs. He enjoyed talking politics with Charlie Gilbert at his community store, or stopping at the home of Bun and Sallie Wright to hear Mr. Wright play folk music on his fiddle or watch him clog dance. In spite of innovations and modernization, the Cove remains unique, both in its isolation and in the scenic beauty of its natural surroundings.

To drive through the Cove, go to the intersection of GA 74/85 and GA 109 in Woodbury. Go south on GA 85 about 0.5 mile to Cove Road. Turn left and go 3 miles to Upper Cove Road on your right. There is a rusted historical marker on the left that is hard to see. This is the beginning of the loop road. Stay left on Cove Road until you come to the other end of Upper Cove Road on your right. Turn right and follow it back to Cove Road and the historical marker. Turn left to head back out of the Cove the way you came. If you have a map (which you should), take a different road out for a diversion.

Thomaston

Established as the county seat of Upson County, Thomaston's growth has been dependent upon the mills established along the Fall Line creeks that enter the Flint in this area. Potato and Tobler Creeks. in particular, saw rise to some of the most prosperous textile mills in Middle Georgia. This was good cotton-growing land, and it was only smart to use the natural resources of the area for cotton manufacturing. Spinning, weaving and shipping cotton became just as important to the cotton culture as planting, cultivation, harvesting and marketing the crop.

With four water-powered textile mills operating by the Civil War, the area around Thomaston was considered the center of Middle Georgia's textile industry and during the War, it was the textile manufacturing center for the Confederacy. In April 1865, General James Wilson and his Union forces entered Upson County via the old Double Bridges across the Flint River, completely destroying all four textile plants, several gristmills, the Upson County Railroad and most of the area's plantations.

The textile industry, however, emerged from the Civil War as practically the only manufacturing industry of any size. New textile operations went up in Thomaston, producing an amazing variety of products, including yarn, osnaburg cloth, duck, raw sheeting and fine sheets, thread, rope, apparel fabrics, tire cord, seat covers, towels and denim, as well as providing services for bleaching, dyeing, sanforizing and hemming. The Thomaston Cotton Mills, founded in 1899, became the area's largest, building four plants and constructing extensive mill villages along the northern edge of Thomaston by 1926.

For more information, see Resources, page 300.

Potato Creek

This stream enters the Flint River 7 miles south of Thomaston. It is particularly noted for the steep drop that occurs between Thomaston and the Flint as the stream tumbles through the Fall Line on the eastern edge of the Pine Mountain range.

Dripping Rocks

Just east of Woodbury, the Flint River begins to wind through the Pine Mountain range, making its way to an area known as Dripping Rocks. Here, within a mile, the river's elevation drops about 10 feet as the bluffs on both sides rise to more than 1,100 feet—the highest along the Flint. The ravine between Moss Fall at Dripping Rocks and the Flint is a good place to see plants and animals common to northern and to southern environments.

For more information, see page 62. The best way to explore Dripping Rocks is to walk the trail (see page 77) that follows the river.

Thunder Scout Reservation (Camp Thunder)

This area, near the mouth of Elkins Creek and the Flint River, has been a campsite for hundreds of years. But since 1938, it has been the Boy Scouts of America who have camped, fished, canoed and hiked in this scenic area that they call Camp Thunder.

For more information, see page 73.

Sprewell Bluff State Park

Opened in 1994, this is the only state park on the Flint River. It sits on the east bank of one of the river's most beautiful natural areas—Sprewell Bluff. Here, rocky shoals stretch the width of the river, and bluffs tower on both banks.

For more information, see pages 64 and 70.

Flint River Outdoor Center

This is the only outfitter open to the public on the entire Flint River. During the summer, the Outdoor Center offers five-, 10- and 20-mile canoe trips as well as one-mile float trips for tubers, running shuttles from as far upriver as the GA 18 Bridge to the Po Biddy Bridge ramp on the downstream side.

For more information, see page 81.

Yellow Jacket Shoals

Once the Flint River passes under the GA 36 Bridge between Talbot and Upson Counties, it begins its rapid descent through the Fall Line. A one-mile stretch, known as Yellow Jacket Shoals, drops about 40 feet, creating one of the most picturesque and unique sections of the Flint. Summer months are particularly beautiful with rare and endangered plants, such as the spider lily and blue flag, blooming on the small rock islands.

For more information, see page 64.

Big Lazer Creek Wildlife Management Area

Big Lazer Creek WMA encompasses 5,864 acres of land between Big Lazer Creek, the Flint River and Po Biddy Road in Talbot County. Like other wildlife management areas, Big Lazer is designed for hunting and fishing, but nearly any other outdoor recreational activity can be enjoyed—hiking, picnicking, swimming, camping, canoeing, bird watching, biking and horseback riding.

For more information, see page 71.

Dowdell's Knob

Dowdell's Knob faces south, a flat rock outcrop that juts out over Pine Mountain Valley at an elevation of 1,395 feet. From here, the Land Between the Rivers is as far as the eye can see. Oak Mountain to the south. Manchester to the east and Shiloh to the west. The greenness of a deciduous forest of black and chestnut oak, hickories and shortleaf pine and the vastness of a starry night.

The knob is named for the Dowdell family, cotton planters who once owned much of Pine Mountain Valley. But Franklin D. Roosevelt gave it prominence. It was one of his favorite spots. He came here often with friends, hosting elaborate catered picnics where martinis flowed and servants served steak on china and linens. At times he came here just to sit, as he did in the early spring of 1945—right before he died at Warm Springs. A historical marker is at the site, as well as the concrete grill that FDR had built for his picnics.

Directions: *From Warm Springs, take GA 85 west 3.5 miles to GA 190 and turn right. Go 3 miles and bear left on the mile-long spur which leads up to Dowdell's Knob.*

Oak Mountain

From Dowdell's Knob, you can look south out over Pine Mountain Valley toward a mountain ridge that runs parallel to Pine Mountain. This is Oak Mountain, the southernmost ridge of the Pine Mountain range and the very last ridge of the Appalachians. The mountain, which is very similar to Pine Mountain in terms of physical makeup and vegetation, begins near Hamilton and ends at the Flint River to form part of Sprewell Bluff at the Fall Line.

The Warm Springs

Warm Springs is the most famous of Georgia's seven-known warm springs. It is the largest, with a flow of up to 914 gallons per minute, and the warmest, with an average temperature of 88 degrees Fahrenheit. These warm waters, which emerge at the base of a hill at the Warm Springs Pools Complex, is what first brought Franklin D. Roosevelt to the area in 1924.

To learn more about the geology of the Warm Springs, see page 198.

Little White House State Historic Site

The Little White House sits on the north slope of Pine Mountain, overlooking a deep, wooded ravine of pines, oaks, hickories, magnolias, mountain laurel and wild azalea. This is where one of the greatest U.S. presidents, Franklin Delano Roosevelt, spent many of his happier moments.

Slipping away from his Secret Service men in a specially designed car, he could drive around the countryside to visit the people of his rural Georgia neighborhood. Manchester, Greenville, the Cove. He enjoyed their friendship and learned their problems, which were typical of rural communities all over the nation—lack of jobs, lack of money or financial security, poor roads, high electricity rates or no service at all, farm lands exhausted from poor agricultural practices, depleted natural resources. From here he formulated many of the New Deal policies read about in history books—policies that led the nation out of its worst depression.

For more information about FDR and the Little White House, see page 202.

Warm Springs Pools Complex

About a mile from the Little White House are the spring-fed pools that attracted Franklin D. Roosevelt to the Warm Springs area in 1924. Now drained, except for during an annual hydrotherapy session, these pools are part of the Little White House State Historic Site. You can walk down into the pools where a basin-type fountain pumps water from the 11 springs beneath the concrete—just enough for you to dip in your hands and feel the water's 88-degree warmth.

For more information, see page 207.

Town of Warm Springs

During the Roosevelt years at the Little White House, the president was a common sight on the streets of Warm Springs. He often drove his hand-controlled convertible into town, parked in front of the Tuscawilla Soda Company, and ordered an ice cream soda. Throngs of foreign dignitaries, secret service agents, Hollywood celebrities and press descended upon the little town, milling around the lobby of the Hotel Tuscawilla, dining at the Meriwether Inn or walking the short distance down the dusty road to the president's residence. From Roosevelt's first visit in 1924 to his last in 1945, Warm Springs, Georgia, was in the limelight.

You can still buy a soda at the Tuscawilla Soda Company and stay at the 1907 Hotel Tuscawilla, renamed the Hotel Warm Springs. Now it's tourists who walk the streets—more than 300,000 a year—of this thriving shopping community. More than 60 specialty shops, featuring crafts, collectibles, antiques and furniture, and numerous restaurants can be found in the restored late-19th and early-20th century buildings that line the streets of the one-mile-square town that was once a president's neighborhood.

For more information, see Resources page 300.

Manchester

From his favorite spot on Dowdell's Knob, Franklin D. Roosevelt would have been aware of the town of Manchester on the other side of Pine Mountain. He would have been interested in the conditions of the blue-collar workers who sweated at the rail yards and mills of this Pine Mountain industrial town, which from the beginning was intended to be an industrial center for the surrounding area.

Named for the industrial town of Manchester, England, it was laid out in 1908 after the Atlanta, Birmingham and Atlantic chose the site for the junction of three main railroad lines and built extensive repair and assembly yards and shops there.

In 1909, Callaway Cotton Mills located a drapery mill here for the manufacture of industrial fabrics. About 350 people were initially employed, but soon the mill was employing about 1,000 people and operating three shifts a day. Some 200 acres of the large tract of land purchased by Fuller E. Callaway, owner of the mill, was divided into building lots and sold for $75 each to prospective residents.

Planned by the Manchester Land Development Company, Manchester's older sections are laid out in squares with streets running east to west and avenues running north to south. The streets of the original mill area are named for persons and trees. By 1912, Manchester was the largest town in the area.

Today, Manchester is still very much like the Manchester of those early years. Each year, the town holds a Manchester Railroad Days to celebrate the history of railroads as well as its heritage.

For more information, see Resources page 300.

Gay

When stagecoaches, traveling the Greenville Stage Road on their route between Griffin and LaGrange, entered Meriwether County at Flat Shoals on the Flint River, their first stop was at Sasserville, about three miles from the Shoals. The community, named after William Sasser, who settled here in 1829, changed its name to Gay in 1882 when Sasser's grandson, William F. Gay, opened a small store and secured a post office for the town and became the town's first postmaster and mayor.

Growth for Gay did not occur until 1908, however, when the Atlanta, Birmingham and Atlantic (AB&A) railroad, now the Seaboard Coastline Railroad Company, brought their line from Birmingham to Atlanta straight through the little town. During the following years, Gay was the largest cotton shipping point in Meriwether County as well as the largest shipping point on the new railroad between Atlanta and Fitzgerald. Cotton had been the chief money crop in the area, but when several large landowners began to grow peaches in the 1930s, Gay became an important peach-packing center, with about eight to 10 sheds operating and on peak days shipping 40 to 50 cars a day.

When Roosevelt became president, the town witnessed the passing of dignitaries, celebrities, the press and the president along those same tracks, all making there way to Warm Springs and the Little White House. In 1939 Gay got its first paved road connecting it with Greenville (Spur 109). This was the first road in the United States to be built by WPA labor under the Roosevelt Administration— possibly to assure the president a better ride to one of his favorite fishing spots at Flat Shoals.

Today, Gay is a sleepy little town except for two times a year, the first full weekends in May and October, when it hosts the Cotton Pickin' Antique, Art and Craft Fair on the same site where both William Sasser and William Gay built their homes. The 1891 Gay home still stands, and you can see it along with the cotton warehouse, cotton gin and other buildings that were part of the town's history.

For more information, see Resources page 300.

Greenville

When President Roosevelt took his Model-T Ford with the special hand controls out for a ramble in the countryside, Greenville was one the towns he traveled to. At that time, the paved road from Atlanta ended here in Greenville, the county seat of Meriwether County. Today, Greenville is a pleasant town centered around a town square dominated by an imposing red-brick and white-columned Classical Revival county courthouse. Originally built in 1832, the courthouse was rebuilt in 1903 after it was damaged by the tornado of 1893, and restored again in 1976 after a fire.

Many antebellum homes in Greenville now have Victorian or "Gingerbread" fronts as a result of that same tornado. After the tornado tore away the southern colonial facades from the old houses, they were rebuilt in the "modern" Victorian style of the 1890s and early 1900s. Other buildings of architectural note: the Italian Villa style 1896 old Meriwether County Jail, with its three-story hanging tower with open arches at the scaffold level (located just off the square and northeast of the courthouse); the red brick, Country French, Park-Culpepper-Kennedy Law Office, with arched windows and four-cornered pointed roof with ornamental iron work, which now houses the Meriwether Historical Society (located on the east side of the square); the circa 1835 Pinkston-Moss House, one of the few antebellum homes unscathed by the tornado (located on LaGrange Road); and the Gables, a Gothic-Revival home built shortly after the Civil War (located on LaGrange Road).

For more information, see Resources page 300.

F. D. Roosevelt State Park

Using picks, shovels, and wheelbarrows—not machinery—the Civilian Conservation Corps (CCC) dug the 15-acre Lake Delano and 25-acre Lake Franklin. The less machinery used, the more hands needed—all part of Roosevelt's plan to create more jobs for young men left unemployed by the Great Depression. Trees cleared for building the lakes became the wood for building the group camp dining halls, kitchens and barracks and log cabins along Lake Delano. Stone blasted from the mountain was used to construct the Roosevelt Inn (which is now the park's information center), the Liberty Bell Pool and the Roosevelt Memorial Bridge, which crosses King's Gap.

For more information, see page 211.

Pine Mountain Trail

Unusual rock outcroppings, waterfalls, beaver dams, historic sites, mountain vegetation—all can be seen along this trail. Hard Hollis quartzite makes up most of Pine Mountain, and any time rock is exposed, look for the whitish crystals of quartz. Vegetation along the summit and hillsides of the mountain is more typical of an Appalachian mixed hardwood forest than the Georgia Piedmont.

For more information about hiking the Pine Mountain Trail, see page 224.

The Town of Pine Mountain

In the beginning it was called Chipley and like many other "boom" towns, it sprang up because it was the terminus of a railroad line. Incorporated in 1882, Chipley grew up around both sides of the railroad tracks and became a hub for the transport of cotton and other farm products and the importation of fertilizer and manufactured goods.

Like many railroad towns, Chipley was a little rough around the edges. When a tornado nearly destroyed the town in 1908, many town fathers believed it to be divine punishment. Between the Depression and the toll cotton took on the area's soil, the once-booming town declined. The thing that would change the history of Chipley forever was its proximity to a farm owned by a man named Cason Callaway and another owned by President Franklin D. Roosevelt.

At the urging of Callaway, who, with his Callaway Gardens, became the largest employer and the greatest factor in the local economy, the name Chipley was changed to Pine Mountain in 1958. Today, the former railroad town of Chipley in Harris County is a village of restaurants, inns, craft galleries, artists' studios, and antique shops all adjacent to one of the most-visited resorts in Georgia.

For more information, see Resources page 300.

Callaway Gardens

When Cason Callaway, leading Georgia businessman and personal friend of President Franklin D. Roosevelt, stepped down as leader of the family mill empire, the LaGrange textile magnate decided to pursue a longtime dream to farm. His dream first took shape when his wife Virginia and he, while exploring Pine Mountain in the 1920s, spotted the deep, clear pool of Blue Springs underneath a granite cliff. Enchanted, they visited frequently; and on one summer picnic, they found a rare Plumleaf azalea. Upon investigation, they discovered that the July-blooming azalea was native only within a 100-mile radius of Blue Springs. The flower inspired them to purchase the land in Harris County adjacent to Blue

Springs and later to build Callaway Gardens.

Today, Callaway Gardens is a 14,000-acre man-made landscape in a natural setting with gardens, woodlands, lakes, wildlife and recreation facilities. The Plumleaf, or Prunifolia, azalea today serves as the Gardens' floral emblem.

A variety of educational programs are available for all ages, featuring topics from butterfly gardening to ecology hikes. Numerous special events, such as the Spring Celebration, Autumn Adventure and Fantasy in Lights, take place throughout the year.

Directions: *Harris County. From Atlanta, take I-85 south about 70 miles to I-185 (Exit 21). Continue south on I-185 to US 27 (Exit 42). Turn left and go 11 miles to Callaway Gardens.* **More Information**: *Callaway Gardens, P.O. Box 2000, Pine Mountain, GA 31822-2000. 800/225-5292. Website: www.callawaygardens.com.*

Mulberry Creek

Mulberry and mountain laurel cover the banks of this wilderness stream as it flows west off Pine Mountain, emptying into the Chattahoochee River about 26 miles north of Columbus. For most of its length, it is a placid stream, but once it reaches the Fall Line, it makes an unexpected drop over a four-foot rock ledge and plunges toward a tortuous 40-foot fall, all within two miles of the river.

Columbus

Founded on the banks of the Chattahoochee River in 1828, Columbus is where the river meets the Fall Line, separating the Piedmont and the Coastal Plain, and plunges down a series of cascades for a 35-mile stretch of the river. This is where settlers came and built their mills—mills that ground flour and corn meal and processed the cotton of surrounding plantations sent up to Columbus on barges and steamboats navigating the river. Mills built next to the falls that man had harnessed for power.

Today, Columbus is a landscape of red brick—the red brick of huge, cotton warehouses that line the river's edge, reminding everyone of the role that cotton, textiles, mills, falls and the river have played in its history.

For more information, see Resources, page 300.

Section 7

The Land Between the Rivers

SIGNIFICANT NATURAL AREAS

The Warm Springs

Flowing from beneath the north slope of Pine Mountain several miles away, Warm Springs is the most famous of Georgia's seven known warm springs. Emerging at a rate of 844 to 914 gallons of water per minute and at a temperature of 88 degrees, it has the highest temperature and largest discharge of the seven springs, after completing a journey that has taken it from rain cloud to rocks 3,800 feet below ground.

First, the rain falls on the crest of Pine Mountain, then seeps down a crack, or fault trace, between the underlying Woodland gneiss and the Hollis quartzite, an immense layer of rock that lies beneath the 200- to 500-foot ridges lifting Pine Mountain above the surrounding upland. This groundwater travels down the quartzite, where it is heated by geothermal energy estimated to range from 95 to 120 degrees Fahrenheit, until it meets a solid wall of rock. Pressure from more rainfall forces the water to flow up another fault trace until it discharges at 844 to 914 gallons a minute at the base of a low knoll. This process takes about eight weeks to complete.

The Warm Springs water flows out of the ground in several places on the grounds of the Warm Springs Pool Complex (see page 207), but the pools and bath house were built at the base of the hill nearest the most productive source of water. At the southern end of the pool, masonry chambers form a cistern that controls the water's discharge. The mineral-rich water, which supplies the Little White House historic site and Roosevelt Institute, includes bicarbonate, silica, calcium, magnesium, sulfate, potassium, sodium and chloride.

NATURE-BASED EDUCATIONAL CENTERS

Oxbow Meadows Environmental Learning Center

Oxbow Meadows clearly demonstrates what it teaches—that the environment shapes our lives and that we can shape, for better or for worse, the environment. The site itself is an example of how damaged land can be reclaimed and maintained using environmentally sound practices. This land, which was once a Native American burial ground, was farmed in the early 1900s, mined for sand and clay to

Warm Springs in Georgia

A spring is a natural flow of water within a restricted area. Springs can be either warm, hot or cold. A warm spring is where the water is from 66 to 98 degrees Fahrenheit. Below 66 degrees is a cold spring, above 98 degrees is a hot spring.

Georgia has seven warm springs, which all rise along a belt that stretches from Warm Springs to Barnesville.

Warm Springs produces 844 to 914 gallons of water per minute at 87.6 to 99.2 degrees Fahrenheit.

Parkman Springs produces 50 to 100 gallons of water per minute at 76.6 degrees Fahrenheit.

Brown's Spring produces 15 to 30 gallons of water per minute at 68.1 to 69 degrees Fahrenheit.

Thundering Spring produces 380 gallons of water per minute at 73.9 to 74.2 degrees Fahrenheit.

Barker Spring produces 30 gallons of water per minute at 74.2 degrees Fahrenheit.

Lifsey Spring produces 83 gallons of water per minute at 78.5 degrees Fahrenheit.

Taylor Spring produces 385 gallons of water per minute at 74.8 degrees Fahrenheit.

make bricks in the 1940s and 1950s, and then turned into a city landfill in the 1970s. But in 1996, the citizens of Columbus took action. The city capped the landfill with three feet of compacted dirt, sank monitoring wells and opened an environmental learning center on the reclaimed land. The pits are now wetland ponds and a 300-year old natural oxbow lake gives the area its name.

At Oxbow, nature is a classroom, where the focus is on the wetlands and woodlands of the Chattahoochee River floodplain. It is a good place for bird watching or for seeing river wildlife, such as beavers, turtles, snakes and fish. Oxbow takes a hands-on approach to environmental education, offering programs for all ages as well as teacher workshops and annual events, like the "Help the Hooch" cleanup day in October.

Facilities: *Learning center with lecture/presentation room, wet lab and nature exhibits; wetland areas; and two educational trails, the Riparian Woodlands Loop and the Trail of Measurements.* **Days/Hours**: *Open daily. Monday through Friday, 11 a.m. to 5 p.m.; Saturday, noon to 3 p.m.; Sunday, 11 a.m. to 3 p.m.* **Directions**: *Muscogee County. From Columbus, take I-185 south to the Custer Road exit at Fort Benning. Turn right (west) off the exit and follow Custer Road about 1.5 miles to where it ends at South Lumpkin Road. Turn right and go about 0.5 mile. The entrance to Oxbow Meadows is on the left.* **More Information**: *Oxbow Meadows Environmental Learning Center, 3491 South Lumpkin Road, Columbus, GA 31901. 706/687-4090; fax 706/687-3020. Website: www.oxbow.colstate.edu.*

HISTORIC SITES

Andersonville National Historic Site

Where the small stream named Stockade Branch merges with Sweetwater Creek, just six miles west of the Flint River, once stood the most notorious war prison in the Confederacy—Andersonville. From 1864 to 1865, Confederate guards interred 45,000 Union prisoners of war (POW) over a period of 14 months. Of these, 12,914 died from disease, poor sanitation, malnutrition, overcrowding or exposure to the elements. Stockade Branch ran through this 26.5-acre area, surrounded by a 15-foot high stockade of hewed pine logs. When it entered the pen, it carried fresh water; when it exited, it carried the human filth and suffering of men living an extremely harsh and miserable existence.

Andersonville, or Camp Sumter as it was officially known, was one of the largest of the many Confederate military prisons established during the Civil War. Today, it is one of the most moving Civil War shrines in all of the South. The white cross Union graves lie in rows in the Andersonville National Cemetery, and the prison site itself stands as a stark reminder of the horrors of that war.

The National Prisoner of War Museum is the best place to begin your tour of the 475-acre park. Since 1970 the National Park Service,

Muscogee County

Muscogee County's western border, as well as its county seat of Columbus, lies along the Chattahoochee River in the Land Between the Rivers.

"Muscogee County was acquired from Creek Indian territory in 1826 and was the 69th county established. The county is named for the Muscogee Indians, whose family included the Creek and Seminoles."

From *Georgia County Snapshots*, Georgia Department of Community Affairs

For tourism information for towns in Muscogee County, see Resources page 300.

which administers the site, has expanded its mission to honor American POWs of all wars. A 27-minute audio-visual program entitled *Echoes of Captivity* relates the overall prisoner of war story. Museum exhibits pertain to themes common to all POWs. Photographs, drawings and maps in the museum illustrate what a tortured existence life in Andersonville was for the Union soldiers confined there. After exploring the museum, drive and walk the self-guided tour of the prison site and cemetery.

Facilities: *Museum, picnic area and restrooms.* **Days/Hours**: *Open daily. Park grounds – 8 a.m. to 5 p.m. National Prisoner of War Museum – 8:30 a.m. to 5 p.m., except New Year's Day and Christmas.* **Fees**: *Taped driving tour rental, $1.* **Directions**: *Sumter County. From Americus, take GA 49 northeast for 10 miles. The entrance to the park is on the right.* **More Information**: *Andersonville National Historic Site, National Park Service, U.S. Department of Interior, Route 1, Box 800, Andersonville, GA 31711. 229/924-0343.*

Coheelee Creek Covered Bridge

The covered bridge that spans Coheelee Creek at McDonald's Ford is not only historically significant—it is the southernmost original covered bridge in the United States—but its picturesque setting of waterfalls and forests mimics a mountain environment, allowing mountain plants to grow in abundance.

Constructed in 1891 by J. W. Baughman, the Coheelee Creek Covered Bridge has a 96-foot span and is of a queen post truss design (or modified king post truss) rather than the more popular Town Lattice design. The king post truss was formed by one vertical post in the center with two diagonals and a horizontal post across the bottom, known as a bottom chord. The queen post truss design replaced the peak of the king post triangle with a horizontal cross-piece, or upper chord. This design strengthened the bridge, allowing it to span a greater length, but it was still not as strong as the Town Lattice, which could support spans well over 100 feet.

The bridge is found on River Road, one of the oldest Indian trails in Early County. The covered bridge served travelers until the mid-1900s, when a concrete bridge was built upstream to accommodate taller, wider and heavier vehicles. Eventually, the road through the bridge was reduced to foot traffic only. In 1959, John Williams donated property around the bridge to the county to be used as a park, which was later named after his wife, Fannie Askew Williams.

Coheelee Creek, which enters the Chattahoochee about a half mile below the covered bridge, has a hard limestone bed underlain by softer clays that has produced three waterfalls on the creek. (See "How Rivers Work" on page 272.) Plants growing in the environment include Alabama azalea and Piedmont azalea, Florida maple and red maple, dogwood, false indigo, American beech, croton, titi, wax myrtle, numerous ferns, Spanish moss, wild ginger, wild Easter lily and spider lily. Bobcat, deer, wild turkey, coyote and armadillo make there

The Land de Soto Saw

In 1540, Hernando de Soto and his men moved slowly, following the Flint upstream and cutting a path through the wilderness.

"What lay before De Soto and his army was a considerable expanse of pine barrens and sandy soils, the same longleaf pine-wiregrass vegetation they had already seen in north Florida. All of the 18th-century and early 19th-century travelers who described the pine barrens spoke of the depressingly monotonous stands of widely spaced, immense pine trees, with very little foliage except wiregrass growing underneath. Deer, turkey, and bear shunned the pine barrens, and even smaller animals—cottontails, squirrels, opossum, and raccoons—were scarce. The pine barrens were home to animals with unusual adaptations, such as the gopher tortoise and the red-cockaded woodpecker....

"The pine barrens were also shunned by the native people. No large Mississippian sites occur in areas once dominated by pine barrens. The monotony of the pine barrens was only relieved by the floodplain forests, which grew adjacent to the rivers cutting through the coastal plain, particularly the larger rivers whose headwaters lay in the higher, geologically older interior. In these moist floodplains the partnership between fire, longleaf pines, and wiregrass was broken. In contrast to the open forest of the pine barrens, the floodplain forests were ribbons of dense forest consisting of bald cypress, tupelo gum, sweetgum, willow oak, and water hickory, as well as luxuriant shrubs. These were overgrown by peppervine, rattan vine, cowitch vine, and smilax vine, growing so thick in places they choked out small trees. Likewise, large stands of cane grew in floodplain forests so densely they excluded all competition from other plants."

Knights of Spain, Warriors of the Sun by Charles Hudson

home here; the river corridor in which the park lies is a main migratory route for many birds.

Facilities: *Park with picnic tables.* **Directions**: *Early County. From Blakely, take GA 62 southwest about 1 mile to Chancey Mill Road. Turn right and go about 7 miles to Covered Bridge Road. Turn left and go 3 miles to the bridge. Park is on the right, just before the bridge.*

Jimmy Carter National Historic Site

One town in the land between the rivers greatly influenced the character, ideas and policies of a president of the United States. That town is Plains, and the president, of course, is Jimmy Carter. Today, the president's residence, the farm he grew up on, the school he attended from first to 11th grade and the railroad depot, which served as his campaign headquarters during the 1976 election, are part of a 71-acre national historic site. (The Carters' current residence is not open to the public.) Much of the surrounding town and its environs make up the Jimmy Carter National Preservation District.

Facilities: *Plains High School – Museum and visitor center with restored classrooms and exhibits about the Carters' lives in Plains. Depot – museum with exhibits about the 1976 Presidential campaign. Farm – Carter's boyhood home and farm commissary restored to its 1937 appearance.* **Days/Hours**: *Open daily, 9 a.m. to 5 p.m. Closed New Year's Day, Thanksgiving and Christmas.* **Directions**: *Sumter County. From Americus, take US 280 west about 10 miles to Plains. Go to Bond Street and turn right. Plains High School, where the Visitor's Center is located, is on the right.* **More Information**: *Jimmy Carter National Historic Site, Plains High School, 300 N. Bond St., Plains, GA 31780. 229/824-4104.*

Kolomoki Mounds

Indians lived in this land between the rivers for thousands of years before the first European explorers walked the continent, bringing disease and ultimate conflict. Located along Kolomoki Creek, just a few miles from the Chattahoochee River, was Kolomoki, a major population and ceremonial center in North America. Here, at this site, was a Woodland Indian village where as many as 3,000 Indians may have lived and worshiped during the 13th century.

The Kolomoki inhabitants created huge mounds of earth upon which they practiced their religion and buried their dead. It is estimated that it took 2 million basket loads of dirt carried by perhaps 1,000 workers to build the largest of the mounds, the Great Temple Mound. The mound rises 56 feet above the surrounding plain and covers nearly an acre and a half. From its summit, the chief priest led the riverine agriculturists in the elaborate religious rituals that governed not only their lives, but their deaths, as well. Directly in front of the Great Temple Mound was a large plaza which served as a village commons and a playing field. Scattered around the perimeter of the plaza are two burial mounds and four ceremonial mounds. The Woodland Indians placed their dead in carefully prepared log-lined

What It Means to be "Indian"

In the truest sense, the Indians who lived in the Land Between the Rivers during the Woodland Period existed in the wilderness, depending on nature and their own skills to survive.

"The Woodland people roamed the [Chattahoochee-Flint] Valley in search of game and wild plants, from which they got almost all their daily needs. Aided by the development of the bow and arrow, which became the weapon of choice during the Woodland Period, the Valley Indians became supremely accomplished hunters. Mastery of the forest and of the plants and creatures within it made them at home in the wilderness. As such, they probably came as close as any native Americans to the idealized concept most people have of what it means to be 'Indian'—to exist in a state of nature entirely dependent upon wild game and plants for sustenance and upon one's wits and physical skills for survival and domestic comforts."

The Old Beloved Path by William W. Winn

graves which they covered with a layer of rock and a thick mantle of earth. Typical of the Woodland culture, a variety of goods, such as beads, pottery bowls and clay effigies, were buried with the dead.

The 300-acre historic site lies within the Kolomoki Mounds State Historic Park.

Facilities: *Kolomoki Mounds State Historic Park (see page 214).* **Days/Hours**: *Open daily. Park – 7 a.m. to 10 p.m. Park office – 8 a.m. to 5 p.m. Fishing lake – 7 a.m. to sunset. Swimming Pool – Tuesday through Sunday from Memorial Day to Labor Day, 11 a.m. to 6 p.m. Museum – Tuesday through Saturday, 9 a.m. to 5 p.m.; Sunday, 2 p.m. to 5:30 p.m.; closed Monday.* **Fees**: *$2 Park Pass required daily for vehicles under 13 persons. All other facilities subject to user fees. Contact the state park office for the latest information on fees and reservations.* **Directions**: *Early County. From Blakely, take US 27 about 2 miles to Upper Kolomoki Road. Turn left and follow for 4 miles to the entrance and park office.* **More Information**: *Kolomoki Mounds State Historic Park, Route 1, Box 114, Blakely, GA 31723. 229/724-2150. For reservations and fees, call 229/723-3398. Website: www.gastateparks.org. Central Reservations Center, 800/864-7275, Monday through Friday, 8 a.m. to 5 p.m.*

Little White House State Historic Site

One of the first reactions that comes to mind on a visit to the Little White House is how unassuming the house is. It is a small—just six rooms—colonnaded, wood frame house designed in the Southern Greek Revival style. Nearly dwarfed by its own natural setting, it sits on the north slope of Pine Mountain overlooking a deep, wooded ravine of pine, oak, hickory, magnolia, mountain laurel and wild azalea. But small and secluded as it is, this is where one of our greatest presidents, Franklin Delano Roosevelt, spent many of his happier moments.

The way that FDR lived at the Little White House greatly reflected the ideas, principles and policies of the man. His independent spirit led him here to swim in the warm spring waters and hopefully cure, or at least improve, the condition of his polio-crippled legs. Slipping away from his Secret Service men in a specially designed car, he could drive around the countryside to visit the people of his rural Georgia neighborhood—Manchester, Greenville, the Cove. He enjoyed their friendship and learned their problems, which were typical of rural communities all over the nation—lack of jobs, lack of money or financial security, poor roads, high electricity rates or no service at all, farm lands exhausted from poor agricultural practices, depleted natural resources. From here he formulated many of the New Deal policies that are recorded in history books—policies that led the nation out of its worst depression. The Civilian Conservation Corps. The Works Progress Administration. The Rural Electrification Administration. The Agricultural Adjustment Act. The Soil Conservation Service. And from here, during some of his darkest

The Little White House
In 1932, the same year he was elected president, Franklin D. Roosevelt built a house in Warm Springs, Georgia, that became known as The Little White House.

"*The Little White House was based on a house Roosevelt had seen in the nearby town of Greenville. He was a strong believer in copying local styles. He persuaded his mother to build a small cottage to rent to patients and families of patients. He persuaded Toombs [Henry Toombs, FDR's friend and architect] to design it in the style of an old Meriwether Inn servant cabin. The Little White House was located at the brow of a hill, on the very edge of a ravine. Roosevelt wanted a sun porch overlooking the ravine, where he would work (often at a card table) in nice weather. The simplicity of what came to be on occasion the headquarters of the United States government is suggested by the fact that when he wanted to work indoors in chilly weather, he had the card table moved in in front of the fireplace.*"

The Squire of Warm Springs by Theo Lippman, Jr.

 (continued on page 205)

Striped bass

Striped Bass

The striped bass is a saltwater fish that originally migrated up the Flint and Chattahoochee Rivers to spawn. When the Jim Woodruff Dam was completed in 1957, some stripers were trapped in both rivers. They continue to spawn at several places on the Flint from Newton up to the Georgia Power Dam below Lake Chehaw at Albany. Some stripers continue to enter Lake Seminole by swimming through the lock at the Woodruff Dam. Once they have spawned in the Seminole-Flint-Chattahoochee system, they tend to stay there. In summer, mature fish, which require cooler oxygenated water, congregate around Flint River springs where the water temperature is between 68 and 70 degrees. It's estimated that there are between 200 and 500 adult stripers in the Flint—"adult" being fish four-to-six years old and weighing 9 to 12 pounds. Eight-and nine-year-old fish are not uncommon, and some live to be 15 years old and reach a weight of 60 pounds and a length of three feet.

Dry Creek Preserve

A 20-acre preserve owned by the Nature Conservancy to protect a roadside population of the Cooley Meadowrue plant. An endangered species, there are only nine recorded populations in existence. This is the only one in Georgia. Tall and spindly, it has white flowers.

e Bend

Double Spring

③

Double Spring (also wn as Shaft Spring) t side of river 20' 13.3" 84° 15' 08.7"

ith and Paul DeLoach on Cooleewahee Creek

Cooleewahee Creek

Mill Creek

Lake Chehaw and Albany

Abrams Creek

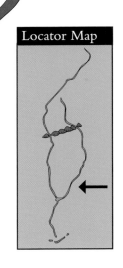
Locator Map

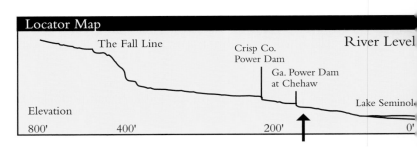
Locator Map

The Fall Line

Crisp Co.
Power Dam

Ga. Power Dam
at Chehaw

River Level

Lake Seminole

Elevation

800'   400'   200'   0'

Fisherman Haywood Parrish and Jimmy Clements between Albany and Newton

Plantation Country and the Swamp of Toa

Pine Hill Plantation quail hunt

Red Bluff   Buzzards Roost

Flint River Plantations

Large hunting plantations, encompassing thousands of acres each, line both banks of the Flint in Lee, Dougherty, Baker, Miller and Mitchell Counties. Most of these are private lands open only to owners and their guests. Some cater to corporate and private customers. For a listing of plantations that welcome guests, see page 227.

Plant Mitchell

2. The Wall Spring

West side of river

31° 25' 54.7"   84° 08' 37.8"

Locator Map

River Level

The Fall Line

Crisp Co.
Power Dam

Ga. Power Dam
at Chehaw

Lake Seminole

Elevation

| 800' | 400' | 200' | 0' |

1. Wilson's Blue Hole Spring

West side of river

31° 27' 14"   84° 09' 24.0"

Locator Map

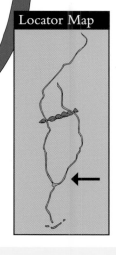

Chickasawhatchee Wildlife Management Area

9,836 acres operated by the Georgia Department of Natural Resources for hunting deer, turkey, squirrel, quail, dove and ducks

15. Radium Springs

Georgia's largest natural springs. Normal flow is 70,000 gallons per minute at an even 68 degrees year round. Developed as a tourist attraction in the 1920s. By the late 1940s and '50s, the springs were promoted as one of Georgia's "Seven Natural Wonders."

14. Marine Corps Canal Road Boat Ramp

On east bank, approximately 1 mile below the Oakridge Drive Bridge

13. Blow Hole Spring

Middle of river 31° 32' 28.0" 84° 08' 30.3"

12. The Boat Spring

West side of river 31° 32' 31.6" 84° 08' 33.8"

Oakridge Drive/GA 234/133 Bridge

11. Oakridge Drive Bridge

The last bridge over the river until Newton, 30.8 miles south

10. Viola Bend

On February 16, 1849, the *Viola*, an 1834, 156-ton paddlewheel steamboat loaded with cotton, sank at the head of Snake Shoals. The cargo was saved, but the vessel—owned by Capt. H. W. Van Vechten—was a total loss.

Broad Avenue Bridge

Oglethorpe Boulevard Bridge

9. Albany Veterans Park

A walking path winds around water oaks and sycamores and out to a wooden overlook that extends out over the river.

Albany

Albany

The river runs through downtown Albany.

Relic Hunters

Between Albany and the County Line Boat Ramp, the river draws diligent, determined relic hunters who successfully scour the river bottom for Native American artifacts, such as arrowheads and pottery shards, and the bones and teeth of animals who roamed this region in prehistoric times.

Broad Avenue Bridge
River miles above mouth: 102.2
County: Dougherty

GA 234
River miles above mouth: 100.3
County: Dougherty

See the Guidebook sections for additional information and directions to locations listed on this page.

Turner Field Park

18-acre golf course and recreation area, including clubhouse, picnic pavilion, picnic tables, playground, gymnasium, racquetball courts, softball fields, restrooms and drinking water

1. Turner Field Boat Ramp

On east bank, approximately 3.5 miles from the power dam

2. Cromartie Beach Landing Boat Ramp

On east bank, approximately 1.5 miles above the power dam

Lake Chehaw

3. Lake Chehaw

In 1921 Georgia Power impounded this reservoir at the junction of the Flint River and Muckalee and Kinchafoonee Creeks. The lake encompasses 1,400 acres and 36 miles of shoreline.

4. The Parks at Chehaw

An 800-acre recreational area with nature trails, picnic areas, fishing ponds, play park, RV park for campers, BMX bicycle track, bike park for recreational and mountain bikers and zoo

Muckalee Creek

Kinchafoonee Creek

Boat Trip

Boats with small outboard motors can navigate the Flint from the Marine Corps Landing Boat Ramp all the way to Lake Seminole below Bainbridge. Then, by going through the lock at Jim Woodruff Dam, they can continue on the Apalachicola River to Apalachicola, Florida. By looking at the boat ramps between here and Bainbridge—Marine Corps Landing, GA 37 and County Line boat ramps—boaters can plan good one-day turnaround trips with time for fishing, picnicking, sightseeing or photography.

6. Georgia Power Dam Park

Hiking, fishing, boating and biking in a heavily wooded day use area maintained by the Georgia Power Company

5. Georgia Power Dam

Built in 1921 as part of Georgia Power's Flint River Project, this concrete slab and buttress power dam measures 464 feet long with a structural height of 46 feet. Its three units generate an annual average of 34,000 megawatt hours.

US 19/82 Bypass Bridge

7. Georgia Power Com Dam Boat Ramp

On west bank, just below the power dam

8. Cleve Cox Landing Boat Ramp

On Muckafoonee Creek, below the junction of the Kinchafoonee and Muckalee Creeks

F1

US 19/82 Bypass
River miles above mouth: 103.7
County: Dougherty

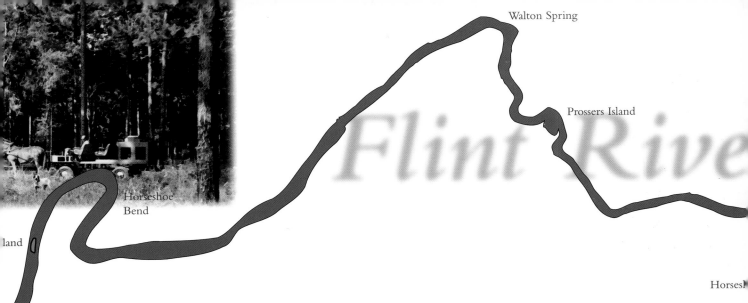

Walton Spring

Prossers Island

Flint Rive

land

Horseshoe
Bend

Horses

land

3.
kn
W
31

Swamp of Toa

30,000 acres of swamps and wetlands, known by some as the Swamp of Toa and by others as Chickasawhatchee Swamp, lie northwest of this section of the river. Teaming with wildlife and a variety of plant species, this area is linked directly to the river through an underground aquifer and is considered to be one of the most important ecosystems in Georgia.

Visitors to Wilderness Pond in the Swamp of Toa

John Sperry, Sherri S.

(continued from page 202

times, he commanded American armies up to the final days of one of the world's worst conflicts, World War II.

President Roosevelt died in the Little White House on April 12, 1945, while sitting in his favorite brown leather chair for a portrait that was just brush strokes away from being completed. He had suffered a cerebral hemorrhage.

On the day of his death, the Little White House was sealed off and carefully preserved.

Facilities: *The Little White House complex includes the house, a guest house, the servants' quarters and garage where Roosevelt's 1938 touring car is kept and sentry houses where 65 U.S. Marines were posted each time Roosevelt visited. Within the park, there is a memorial fountain that is fed by water from the nearby warm springs; the Walk of States with a state flag and native rock from each U.S. state; and a picnic area and a gift shop with snack bar. A museum dedicated to Roosevelt's life features documents and photographs, including one where FDR is picnicking at Flat Shoals and another where he is fishing from his favorite spot at Flat Shoals; the hat he wore while fishing on the Flint River; gifts from foreign embassies; his walking cane collection; and other personal items. A 12-minute film, A Warm Springs Memoir of Franklin Delano Roosevelt, is shown continuously at no additional charge.* **Days/Hours**: *Open daily, 9 a.m. to 5 p.m., last ticket sold at 4:45 p.m. Closed Thanksgiving, Christmas Day and New Year's Day.* **Admission**: *Adults, $5; ages 6 to 18, $2; and 55 and older, $4.* **Directions**: *Meriwether County. From Warm Springs, take US Alt27/GA 85W south about 0.25 mile. The entrance is on the right.* **More Information**: *Little White House State Historic Site, 401 Little White House Road, Warm Springs, GA 31830. 706/655-5870. Website: www.gastateparks.org.*

Rood Creek Indian Mounds

These eight earthen mounds, built during the Mississippian Indian period dating from A.D. 900 to A.D. 1540, formed a village that was the largest Indian settlement in the Chattahoochee River Basin and was probably abandoned before the Spanish came to the area. Indians of the Mississippian culture organized socially into groups that we call chiefdoms. Towns like Rood Mounds were the political, military and religious center of a chiefdom and were supported by surrounding smaller villages.

This site, with its large ceremonial mound and smaller temple mounds, is fortified by two moats, indicating that although these people were farmers, their life was not always peaceful. These are not burial mounds. They are earthen platforms upon which the homes, temples and mortuaries of the elite were placed. They were often arranged around great plazas where ceremonies and markets were held.

The Rood Mounds have remained virtually untouched except for the natural progression of brush and forest that has grown up on and around them. They are named after the Rood family, who once owned a plantation on this land. The U.S. Army Corps of Engineers

Chattahoochee County

This county is named for the river that forms its western border.

"*Chattahoochee County was formed in 1854 from parts of Marion and Muscogee counties. It was named for the Chattahoochee River that forms the county's western boundary. The county seat, and only incorporated municipality, is Cusseta. The city is named for one of the principal tribes of the Lower Creek Indians. The county is home to the Fort Benning Military Reservation, the county's largest employer. Fort Benning was founded at the beginning of the first World War, and was named for General Henry Lewis Benning, a Confederate general who hailed from Columbus. It is the world's largest infantry camp, and is often called the 'West Point of the South.'*"

From *Georgia County Snapshots*, Georgia Department of Community Affairs

For tourism information on towns in Chattahoochee County, see Resources page 300.

now owns the property and has closed it to the public with the exception of a tour that leaves from the Kirbo Educational Museum in Florence Marina State Park (see page 213). The tour explores the eight Indian mounds and the resources available to the Indians along the Chattahoochee River. The one-mile walk through the historic site takes about an hour and a half.

More Information: *Florence Marina State Park, Route 1, Box 36, Omaha, GA 31821. 229/838-6870 or 4244. Kirbo Interpretive Center, 229/838-4706.*

The Bluff at Fort Gaines

The 130-foot bluff that juts out over the Chattahoochee River at Fort Gaines is one of the most interesting physical locations on the entire river. Rising high above the river is the kind of terrain that existed in Eufaula, Franklin and Bainbridge before the building of dams and the impoundment of lakes. This physical location directly relates to the bluff's historical significance as the site of three different forts. Standing here, you'll get a clear understanding of how one cannon atop this bluff could control boat transportation up and down the waterway.

In 1814, after the Battle of Horseshoe Bend and the end of the Creek Indian War, General Andrew Jackson demanded property from the Creeks to compensate for the cost of fighting the war. This area was part of that property, known as the Tallassee Territory that the Indians were forced to give up. In 1816, General Edmund Pendleton Gaines, Commander of the Eastern Section of the Southern Division, suggested to Jackson that a frontier fort be built here to protect the new lands and the surveyors who would soon be coming to draw the boundary lines. On April 2, 1816, 100 troops arrived at the bluff to construct a stockade, named Fort Gaines after the man who suggested it be built. In 1836 a second fort was built to protect settlers from Indian attacks, and a third one was built in 1863 to prevent Union troops from getting upriver to the Confederate shipbuilding, iron works and textile plants at Columbus.

This site is now part of the Fort Gaines Historic Bluff Street area. The Cornelia Club House, a large white building, occupies the location of the three forts. Behind the building to the left is a good spot to look out at the river. Behind the building and to the right, you will see one of the three Confederate cannons that guarded the fort, still in the same position as it was during the war. From here, Confederate artillerymen had a commanding view of the river. The second cannon was located a few yards to the south and the third was below the bluff in a bend of the river.

A self-guided walking tour, written by resident James Edgar Coleman, relates the history of the entire Fort Gaines Historic Bluff Street area, including the Fort Gaines Frontier Village and the Otis Micco statue (see page 209). The walking tour is available at the Clay County Library.

Clay County

Fort Gaines sits on a high bluff overlooking the Chattahoochee River, the county's western border.

"Clay County was created from parts of Early and Randolph counties in 1854. It was named for Senator Henry Clay of Kentucky. There are two incorporated municipalities within the county: Fort Gaines, the county seat, and Bluffton. Fort Gaines grew up around a fort on the Chattahoochee River established to protect settlers during the Creek Indian Wars. The town, named for the fort's builder, General Edmund Pendleton Gaines, became a shipping point for cotton planters for many miles on both sides of the Chattahoochee River, remaining a key market until about 1858 when railroads replaced river freight. The Walter F. George Lock and Dam in George T. Bagby State Park is just north of Fort Gaines on the Chattahoochee River. Under construction from 1955 until 1963, the dam stretches two and a half miles from Alabama. The lock, second highest east of the Mississippi, forms a lake called Lake George of Lake Chattahoochee. The lake extends 85 miles upriver. Walter F. George, a notable Clay County resident, rose from tenant farmer beginnings to serve in the U.S. Senate from 1923 to 1956."

From *Georgia County Snapshots*, Georgia Department of Community Affairs

For tourism information on towns in Clay County, see Resources page 300.

As a side note, Fort Gaines has the distinction of being the only one of all the frontier forts created in Georgia to be a present-day incorporated municipality.

Directions: *Clay County. In Fort Gaines from the intersection of GA 37 and GA 39, take GA 37 (Hartford Street) west about 0.25 mile to Jackson Street. Turn right. Go to the next street, Carroll Street and turn left. Go until it dead ends into Bluff Street. The white building straight ahead, the Cornelia Club House, occupies the site where the three forts were located.* **More Information**: *Clay County Economic Development Council, P.O. Box 298, Fort Gaines, GA 31751. Clay County Library, 208 S. Hancock, Fort Gaines, GA 31751. 229/768-2248.*

Warm Springs Pools Complex

About a mile from the Little White House are the spring-fed pools that attracted Franklin D. Roosevelt to the Warm Springs area in 1924 and kept him coming back until he died there in 1945. The original pools and bath houses built on this site were part of the Warm Springs summer resort area, which grew up around the therapeutic springs (see page 198) once Meriwether County was created in 1827 and the threat of Indians removed. By 1832 the resort town was known to have had two bath houses, 10 x 12 feet and 4 x 12 feet, located a few feet from two of the largest springs. By lowering a gate, the water level could be raised to about four feet within a few minutes—the length of time for someone to undress.

At first, the springs were visited by nearby plantation owners, who built summer cottages at Warm Springs. But as the springs became known for their medicinal qualities, others came from across the young country—by horse and carriage and later by stage and then train—to enjoy the spring water and the cool Pine Mountain breezes. By 1875 there were six 10 x 10 open-air masonry pools, capturing the warm springs water. In 1893 two new pools were built, one for men and one for women.

The resort area itself survived several owners, fires and the Civil War. It's most fashionable era came during the Gay Nineties, when the Victorian-styled, three-story Meriwether Inn was built overlooking the pools.

By the time Roosevelt arrived in 1924, however, the resort's heyday was long gone and the pools were somewhat run down. Roosevelt hoped the pools would help him rebuild the muscles in his legs that polio had destroyed three years earlier. After one day of exercise in the pool, he was able to stand up in four feet of water—something he considered a major accomplishment. In 1926, Roosevelt spent two-thirds of his personal fortune to buy the $200,000 resort and turn it into a health spa for treating polio patients. Among other improvements, he built the changing rooms and three hydrotherapy pools, which were used for therapy until 1942, when an indoor pool was built.

The Pool Ruins

Once the indoor therapy pool was built in 1942 at Warm Springs, the outdoor hydrotherapy pools were seldom used and over the years fell into disrepair. Today, the restored pools are part of the state historic site.

"I surely wish that I had had my camera with me the first time we examined the pools in 1980. There was a huge pine tree that had fallen through the back wall and roof and the top was in the pool. There was several feet of mud and muck in the pools with a stream of warm water meandering through. There were cattails and bay bushes growing all over the place. This was in midwinter and the warm water had established a micro-climate and there were huge tadpoles in the warm pools and bull frogs everywhere. It was really a spectacular ruin."

Billy Townsend, Chief Historian, Georgia Department of Natural Resources

Now drained, except for during an annual hydrotherapy session, these pools are part of the state historic site. You can walk down into the pools where a basin-type fountain pumps water from the 11 springs beneath the concrete—just enough for you to dip in your hands and feel the water's 88-degree warmth. The changing rooms and doctor's office have been converted into a small interpretive center. If you are lucky, park employee Suzanne Pike, who was a four-year-old polio patient at Warm Springs on FDR's last Thanksgiving visit, will be on hand to tell you stories about that era.

Facilities: *Historic pools and interpretive museum.* **Days/Hours**: *Open daily, 9 a.m. to 4:45 p.m.* **Admission**: *Free.* **Directions**: *Meriwether County. From Warm Springs, take GA 41/US 27Alt north for 0.25 miles. Entrance on left at the 4th paved road.* **More Information**: *Little White House Historic Site, 401 Little White House Road, Warm Springs, GA 31830. 706/655-5851. Website: www.gastateparks.org*

MUSEUMS

Andersonville Village

During the Civil War, the village of Andersonville sat near the end of the Southwestern Railroad. It was here that 45,000 Union prisoners of war arrived by train during 1864 and early 1865 and were marched the the quarter mile to Camp Sumter, the Civil War prison. It was natural for the village to become the supply center for the prison, which would later become known by the town's name of Andersonville.

In the 1970s, Andersonville became a living history museum through the efforts of its 300 citizens, who organized as the private, non-profit Andersonville Guild. Some of the town's 19th-century structures were moved from other locations, like the restored railroad depot on Church Street that serves as a visitor center and museum. The town has a seven-acre pioneer farm complete with mostly authentic structures, such as a blacksmith shop, gristmill, liquor still, smokehouse, barn, petting zoo, mule-powered sugar cane mill and syrup kettle and log cabins.

The Andersonville Historic Fair, the first weekend in October, draws thousands of visitors to see blacksmiths, potters, glassblowers, quilters, basketmakers, cloggers, musicians and two large-scale Civil War reenactments.

Facilities: *Visitor center and museum, 7-acre park with pioneer farm and picnic area.* **Days/Hours**: *Open daily, October 1 through April 30, 9 a.m. to 5 p.m.; May 1 through September 30, 9 a.m. to 5:30 p.m. Closed Christmas.* **Directions**: *Sumter County. From Americus, take GA 49 northeast 10 miles to Andersonville. At Church Street, turn left. The Visitor Center is on the right, just across the railroad tracks.* **More Information**: *Andersonville Guild, P.O. Box 6, Andersonville, GA 31711. 229/924-2558.*

Marion County

Marion County sits in both the Flint and the Chattahoochee watersheds in The Land Between the Rivers.

"Marion County was created in 1827. Georgia's 72nd county was named for the Revolutionary War hero General Francis Marion. Known as the 'Swamp Fox,' Marion campaigned successfully against the British in South Carolina. The county seat, and only incorporated municipality, is Buena Vista. Originally known as Pea Ridge, the city was renamed in honor of a famous battle in the Mexican War. Two antebellum courthouses still stand in Marion County: the Old Courthouse in Tazewell, erected in 1848 at a cost of $1,637, and the present courthouse built in 1850 in Buena Vista. Fort Perry was built in Marion County by General John Floyd, on the old Alabama Road. It was named in honor of the hero of the Lake Erie Battle in 1812."

From *Georgia County Snapshots*, Georgia Department of Community Affairs

For tourism information on towns in Marion County, see Resources page 300.

Columbus Museum

The Columbus Museum is unique in the Southeast because it offers both American art and regional history. One permanent exhibit, *Chattahoochee Legacy*, is of particular interest because it depicts the cultural history of the Chattahoochee Valley in a chronological format, ranging from prehistoric times to the present. As you walk through the exhibit, you will see replicas of a pre-Columbian Native American dwelling, a turn-of-the-century schoolroom, a 1930s shotgun house, Native American artifacts, Civil War-era weapons and early textile and metal foundries artifacts. A film that traces the area's development is shown several times a day.

Facilities: *30,000 square feet of exhibit space, two classrooms, a teaching darkroom, meeting room and multi-use theater, 298-seat auditorium, gift shop and reception areas.* **Days/Hours**: *Tuesday through Saturday, 10 a.m. to 5 p.m.; Sunday, 1 to 5 p.m. Open until 8 p.m. the third Thursday of each month. Closed Mondays and Legal Holidays.* **Admission**: *Free.* **Directions**: *Muscogee County. In Columbus, take I-185 to Exit 4. Turn west onto Wynnton/Macon Road. Go about 2.5 miles. The museum is on the right.* **More Information**: *The Columbus Museum, 1251 Wynnton Road, Columbus, GA 31906. 706/649-0713; fax, 706/649-1070. Website: www.columbusmuseum.com.*

Fort Gaines Frontier Village and Otis Micco Statue

In 1816, when General Gaines arrived to build the frontier fort of Fort Gaines on bluffs overlooking the Chattahoochee River and clear the area of hostile Indians, Creek Indian Chief Otis Micco and his people were living in the area, possibly on some flat land abutting the bluffs or directly across the river.

Rather than swear allegiance to America and live "under the guns of Fort Gaines," the Indians abandoned their village and crops and fled south to Spanish Florida to join other refugees, who called themselves Seminoles. This statue to Otis Micco, which was carved from a live oak tree by artist Phillip Andrews in 1988, is the only Creek Indian statue located in the old Creek Nation.

The Frontier Village adjacent to the statue is a collection of authentic frontier structures that recreates Fort Gaines as it might have looked during its earliest days. Seven log structures, including two houses, a corn crib, gristmill, smokehouse and cane press, were all moved from other locations in Clay County.

This outdoor museum and the Otis Micco statue are part of the historic bluff area at Fort Gaines. A self-guided walking tour, written by resident James Edgar Coleman, of the Fort Gaines Historic Bluff Street area is available at the Clay County Library.

Directions: *Clay County. In Fort Gaines from the intersection of GA 37 and GA 39, take GA 37 (Hartford Street) west about 0.25 mile to Jackson Street. Turn right. Go to the next street, Carroll Street and turn left. Go until it dead ends into Bluff Street. Turn left down the steep hill. The Otis Micco*

Bear and the Indian

Prehistoric Indians once hunted bear throughout the Chattahoochee and Flint River Valleys.

"Bear could be found closer to home. In the winter, their customary den was in the hollows of trees. The Indians located them by searching for telltale signs of claw marks on the tree trunks. Once located, it was fairly easy to smoke the bears out of their dens and shoot them as they emerged. They might also be trapped at such times. After the delicious fat was rendered into oil, it was stored in gourds or deerskin containers. The Indians used it for frying and flavoring, anointed their bodies and hair with it, and rubbed it on their bows. The hides made good bedding and warm winter coats. The meat was eaten well done—Southeastern Indians ate all their meat cooked thoroughly. There is no evidence that the Indians made bacon out of bear until they were taught to do so by Europeans. It is also not true that the Indians of the Valley [Flint-Chattahoochee] hunted for bear in honey trees, at least during prehistoric times. There were no honey bees in the Valley until bee cultivation began in the historic period."

The Old Beloved Path by William W. Winn

statue is at the end of the road and the Frontier Village is to the left of the statue. **More Information**: *Clay County Economic Development Council, P.O. Box 298, Fort Gaines, GA 31751. Clay County Library, 208 S. Hancock, Fort Gaines, GA 31751. 229/768-2248.*

Kirbo Interpretive Center

This educational museum, located on the grounds of the Florence Marina State Park, sits in the midst of a rich cultural history. Just five miles south are eight earthen Indian mounds dating from A.D. 900 to A.D. 1540. Known as the Rood Creek Indian Mounds, the site was the largest Indian settlement in the Chattahoochee River Basin. About three miles south of the park is the site of Roanoke, one of the earliest European settlements in the area, which was destroyed by Creek Indians in 1836 (see sidebar this page). To the north in Omaha is Fort McCreary. Rebuilt in 1996 by the Daughters of the American Revolution, the wooden block house is an exact replica of the 1836 fort that garrisoned Georgia Militia sent to protect the frontier settlers during the Creek Indian uprising. The Florence Marina area itself was once the site of a flourishing river town that was a port for steamboats traveling the Chattahoochee.

The museum displays artifacts from the prehistoric Paleo-Indian period through the early-20th century. Exhibits depict the removal of the Creek Indians from the Florence area from 1715 to 1836, the influence of cotton on the development of towns along the Chattahoochee; and the story of the steamboats that traveled the river from 1828 to the 1930s. Ranger-led tours to the Rood Creek Indian Mounds and to Fort McCreary leave from the Kirbo Center. Other programs include pioneer weapons, frontier life demonstrations and life in a river town. Educational program packets and a video are available upon request.

Facilities: *For state park facilities, see page 213.* **Days/Hours**: *Open daily, 8 a.m. to 5 p.m. Tours to Rood Creek Indian Mounds leave every Saturday beginning at 10 a.m. Other tours are available upon request.* **Fees**: *$2 Park Pass required daily for vehicles under 13 persons. All other facilities subject to user fees. Contact the state park office for the latest information on fees and reservations.* **Directions**: *Stewart County. From Lumpkin, take GA 39C west for 16 miles. Park entrance located at end of 39C.* **More Information**: *Florence Marina State Park, Route 1, Box 36, Omaha, GA 31821. 229/838-6870 or 4244. Kirbo Interpretive Center, 229/838-4706. Website: www.gastateparks.org. Central Reservations Center, 800/864-7275, Monday through Friday, 8 a.m. to 5 p.m.*

Westville

Back in the 1850s, people grew their own food. They built their homes from pine trees that were several hundred years old and

The Burning of Roanoke

The massacre of settlers at Roanoke on the banks of the Chattahoochee in Stewart County was one of the first battles of the Creek Indian War of 1836 in Georgia.

"About two miles south of the Florence Community, Stewart County, was once the site of Roanoke, a very busy settlement. Before it was destroyed by Creek Indian warriors, Roanoke was located on the eastern bank of the Chattahoochee River just west of today's GA 39.

"Roanoke was originally an Indian village, but after settlement by the whites, it was incorporated in 1832 with about 30 families living there. It had a post office, and several stores and was considered to be a thriving white settlement. Roanoke was attacked by a small band of Creek Indians on May 13, 1836. They were easily defeated but two nights later, about 300 Creeks in a surprise attack, burned the town. It was never rebuilt and nothing of the settlement remains today".

Indian Heritage of Georgia by Marion R. Hemperley

secured them with rectangular nails forged by the local blacksmith. They cooked over open fires and they read by the light of candles that they had made from beeswax or tallow. Life was not easy in the land between the rivers and Westville, an outdoor living history village, realistically depicts this pre-industrial life and culture.

At Westville, there are more than 30 pre-Civil War buildings, including a church, a schoolhouse, shops and homes. This private, non-profit educational museum has relocated original structures from around the state, authentically restored them and placed them in the landscape of an early Georgia town. It is said to be the only living history museum in America that features authentic, original structures—not recreations.

On any day at Westville, you'll find craftspersons demonstrating their circa 1850 trades: tilling, spinning, quilting, weaving, woodworking, blacksmithing and basket and pottery making. Annual events at Westville accurately reflect the period: a Spring Festival with demonstrations of farm activities that went on in the spring, such as plowing and planting; a Memorial Day Weekend with reenactments of the 1836 Creek Indian Battles—the Battle of Roanoke and the Battle of Shepherd's Plantation—as well as demonstrations on Indian tools, art, crafts, housing and weapons at the Creek Indian Camps; and a July Fourth Celebration with 1850s food and family games, as well as a vintage baseball game.

For a small cost, Westville will provide teachers with background information on social customs, architecture, religion, travel, Indians and agriculture of the 1850 period before a classroom visit.

Days/Hours: *Tuesday through Saturday, 10 a.m. to 5 p.m.; Sunday, 1 p.m. to 5 p.m. Closed New Year's Day, Thanksgiving and Christmas.* **Admission**: *Adults, $8; seniors, college students and military personnel, $7; and students (K-12), $4. Group rates available with reservations.* **Directions**: *Stewart County. In Lumpkin at the intersection of US 27 and GA 27.* **More Information**: *Westville, MLK Drive, Lumpkin, GA 31815. 229/838-6310 or 888/733-1850. Website: www.westville.org.*

PARKS

Franklin D. Roosevelt State Park
Layers of human history have left their imprint on these 10,000 acres that straddle the pine and laurel slopes of Pine Mountain. Creek Indians once roamed this land, using the old buffalo trail which followed the natural gap through the mountain. The trail, which is now GA 340, was one of their main north-south routes. Their village stood in the vicinity of the park's Liberty Bell Pool. In the early 1800s a trader by the name of King pitched his tent near the site where the Roosevelt Memorial Bridge now spans the gap. His trade with the Creeks lasted until the Indian Springs Treaties of 1825 and 1826, when the Creeks ceded their land between the rivers to the state of

The Founding of Westville
Towns, very much like the outdoor living history village of Westville, sprang up all over the Land Between the Rivers in the mid-1800s.

"*By and large they came with a single consuming idea—to plant cotton. They had no time to waste. In an amazingly short period, they ripped the china briar roots from the rich soil in the creek bottoms, cut down the canebrakes, cleared the forest and got cotton seed in the ground, often before the rude huts in which they slept were finished. Almost simultaneously with the establishment of the cotton farms and plantations, towns such as Roanoke sprang up on the Chattahoochee River on the county's western border and others like Lumpkin developed inland where two major Indian trails or horse paths intersected. We may imagine that, by 1830, at a point where the old Slash Eye Trail crossed the path from Fort Perry near the center of the county, the village of Westville was founded.*"

The Magic and Mystery of Westville essay by William W. Winn

Georgia and were forced west of the Chattahoochee. But trader King stayed and in the waning days of Indian occupation established a trading post where the Indian village had been. Soon white settlers made their way through the gap and a frontier town sprang up around the trading post. It flourished—a gristmill, cotton gin, cobbler's shop, tanning yard, chair factory, schoolhouse, church and tavern, which housed the town's post office. The townspeople honored the trader by calling the town and the gap, King's Gap. No trace of the Indians and their village could be found. And by the 1900s, the town, too, disappeared. Only the ruins of King's trading post—where the thriving little settlement got its start—remained.

By the time Franklin D. Roosevelt moved into the Little White House at Warm Springs in 1932, the area, as well as the rest of the country, was suffering from the Great Depression. Many of Roosevelt's ideas to help hungry, jobless Americans took shape as he picnicked at Dowdell's Knob; and the land that had been King's Gap benefited from his solutions. Using picks, shovels, and wheelbarrows—not machinery—the Civilian Conservation Corps (CCC) dug the 15-acre Lake Delano and 25-acre Lake Franklin. The less machinery used, the more hands needed—all part of Roosevelt's plan to create more jobs for young men left unemployed by the Great Depression. Trees cleared for building the lakes became the wood for building the group camp dining halls, kitchens and barracks and log cabins along Lake Delano. Stone blasted from the mountain was used to construct the Roosevelt Inn (which is now the park's information center), the Liberty Bell Pool and the Roosevelt Memorial Bridge, which crosses King's Gap.

All was done under the President's watchful eye. Roosevelt personally designed the 500,000-gallon Liberty Pool and helped decide the route of GA 190 along the top of Pine Mountain, which the Works Progress Administration (WPA) built. Seemingly, the President never saw a blueprint that his pencil could not improve. A story is told that when workers balked at building an unsupported stone arch under the stairway at the Inn, from his wheelchair Roosevelt directed the placement of each rock until the arch was finished.

In less than three years, the CCC built the entire park—lakes, cabins, group camps, inn, pool, bathhouse, the Roosevelt Memorial Bridge, fish hatcheries, hiking trails, roads, spring houses, and the boathouse. The park was national property until 1942, when it became Georgia's largest state park. Each year former CCC workers who built the park return for a reunion.

The spring, which once furnished water to buffalo, Native Americans, European traders and pioneer Americans, now serves FDR State Park and fills the 500,000-gallon Liberty Bell Pool.

Facilities: *21 cottages, campgrounds (see page 220), the 23-mile Pine Mountain Trail (see page 224), visitor's center, trading post, amphitheater, two lakes (Franklin and Delano), Liberty Bell Pool, boat rental and fishing on*

Harris County

Harris County and Pine Mountain are part of the gateway to The Land Between the Rivers.

"Harris County was created in 1827 from portions of Muscogee and Troup counties. Georgia's 71st county was named for Charles Harris, a lawyer who served as mayor of Savannah. The county seat is Hamilton. Other municipalities are Pine Mountain, Shiloh and Waverly Hall. The nationally known Callaway Gardens Resort is located in the county. The 12,000-acre resort features 63 holes of golf, a 1,000-acre hunting preserve and one of the largest botanical gardens in the world… The Chattahoochee River and Lake Harding form the western border of Harris County, providing ample opportunity for fishing, swimming, boating and other outdoor activities.

From *Georgia County Snapshots*, Georgia Department of Community Affairs

For tourism information on towns in Harris County, see Resources page 300.

Lake Delano, horseback riding trails, short nature trails, picnic shelters with tables and grills and playgrounds. **Days/Hours**: *Open daily. Park – 7 a.m. to 10 p.m. Office – Monday through Thursday, 8 a.m. to 5 p.m.; Friday, 8 a.m. to 10 p.m.; Saturday and Sunday 8 a.m. to 6 p.m.* **Fees**: *$2 park pass required daily for vehicles under 13 persons. All other facilities subject to user fees. Contact the state park office for the latest information on fees and reservations.* **Directions**: *Harris and Meriwether Counties. From Pine Mountain, take US 27 east about 5 miles to GA 354. Turn left and follow the signs.* **More Information**: *F. D. Roosevelt State Park, 2970 Georgia Highway 190, Pine Mountain, GA 31822; 706/663-4858. Or Georgia State Parks and Historic Sites, 205 Butler Street, Suite 1352 East, Atlanta, GA 30334. Website: www.gastateparks.org. Central Reservations Center, 800/864-7275, Monday through Friday, 8 a.m. to 5 p.m.*

Florence Marina State Park

In 1836 steamboats traveling the Chattahoochee River would stop here at a landing and river town known as Florence. Today, Florence Marina is a 173-acre state park, and the natural deep-water marina that lies adjacent to it still serves as a landing for boats traveling the Chattahoochee and the 48,000-acre Lake Walter F. George.

The Kirbo Interpretive Center is a museum located on the park grounds with displays about Native Americans, nature and local history (see page 210). Special annual events at the park include Archaeology on the River in May, All About Alligators in June and an Early American Festival in September.

Facilities: *Marina with 66 boat slips and gas; 6 cottages and 8 efficiency units for rent; campground (see page 220); 125-person group shelter with heating and air, complete kitchen, steam table, fireplace, table and chairs and restrooms; picnic shelter; picnic tables; jon boat and canoe rentals; swimming pool; tennis courts; lighted fishing pier; miniature golf; and trading post with snacks, fishing supplies and restrooms.* **Days/Hours**: *Open daily. Park – 7 a.m. to 10 p.m. Park Office – 8 a.m. to 5 p.m. Kirbo Interpretive Center – 8 a.m. to 5 p.m.* **Fees**: *$2 park pass required daily for vehicles under 13 persons. All other facilities subject to user fees. Contact the state park office for the latest information on fees and reservations.* **Directions**: *Stewart County. From Lumpkin, take GA 39C west for 16 miles. Park entrance located at end of 39C.* **More Information**: *Florence Marina State Park, Route 1, Box 36, Omaha, GA 31821. 229/838-6870 or 4244. Kirbo Interpretive Center, 229/838-4706. Website: www.gastateparks.org. Central Reservations Center, 800/864-7275, Monday through Friday, 8 a.m. to 5 p.m.*

George T. Bagby State Park

The dock at George T. Bagby State Park is a good place to launch your boat if you are anticipating a trip down the Chattahoochee to Apalachicola. This 700-acre Georgia state park, located about two miles north of the Walter F. George Lock and Dam, has a marina with slips available for monthly or daily rental and a public boat ramp, which is open for use by all park visitors. Meadow Links, the park's 18-hole golf course, is the newest of the Georgia State Park golf courses. Bagby's 30-room lodge has meeting room space for up to 125 people and its Pilothouse Restaurant overlooks the lake and serves a-la-carte and buffet-style meals. Special events hosted here include a Bass Fishing Tournament in May, an Independence Day Celebration, a Labor Day Tennis Tournament and a Fun Fest in October.

Facilities: Marina with 34 boat slips and gas dock; 30-room guest lodge with meeting rooms; Pilothouse Restaurant; 5 fully-equipped, 2-bedroom cottages; 1 covered picnic shelter; 50 picnic sites; swimming beach; pedal boat, canoe and fishing boat rental; public boat ramp; bait and tackle shop and 3-mile nature trail. **Days/Hours**: *Open daily. Park – 7 a.m. to 10 p.m. Park Office – 8 a.m. to 5 p.m. Swimming beach–Memorial Day through Labor Day.* **Fees**: *$2 park pass required daily for vehicles under 13 persons. All other facilities subject to user fees. Contact the state park office for the latest information on fees and reservations.* **Directions**: *Clay County. From Fort Gaines, take GA 30 north for 4 miles. Entrance on left side of road.* **More Information**: *George T. Bagby State Park and Lodge, Route 1, Box 201, Fort Gaines, GA 31751. Park and Lodge, 229/768-2571; Meadow Links Golf Course, 229/768-3714. Website: www.gastateparks.org. Central Reservations, 800/864-7275, Monday through Friday, 8 a.m. to 5 p.m.*

Kolomoki Mounds State Historic Park

In 1938, the citizens of Early County presented the state of Georgia with a gift of archaeological and prehistoric significance—the Kolomoki Indian Mounds, seven earthen mounds built during the 12th and 13th centuries by the Swift Creek and Weeden Island Indians. Today, the site, which the U.S. Department of the Interior designated as a National Historic Landmark, is a 1,293-acre state historic park where you can learn about these people who once lived in and cultivated this river basin by exploring the mounds and visiting the museum which houses artifacts from mound excavations (see page 201).

Kolomoki offers a group program that includes a museum tour, film, brief description of Kolomoki's history and Q&A session. Staff demonstrate primitive skills, such as the blowgun, pump drill and bullroarer. Teachers are given a sheet describing the self-guided tour of the mound area so they can lead students at their own pace. Annual events at the park include astronomy programs in April and October, an Easter Egg Hunt, the Kolomoki Festival in October and Christmas Lights at Kolomoki throughout December.

Facilities: Campground (see page 220), 2 group shelters, 7 picnic shelters, picnic sites, 2 fishing lakes (Kolomoki and Yohola) with boat ramps and docks,

Early County

Early County's western border sits along the Chattahoochee River, while the eastern portion of the county lies within the Flint River watershed.

"Early County was created in 1818 from land obtained from the Creek Indians. The counties of Calhoun, Clay, Decatur, Dougherty, Grady, Miller, Mitchell, and Seminole were all created from territory originally belonging to Early County. Georgia's 41st county was named for Peter Early, Governor of Georgia from 1813 to 1815, Superior Court Judge, and member of Congress. Blakely, the county seat, was named for Captain Johnson Blakely, a North Carolinian lost at sea during the War of 1812. In the north central Early County is a row of mounds of Native American origin dating to around the year 800... Kolomoki Mounds State Park preserves the site... The southernmost covered bridge in the United States, Coheelee Creek Bridge, is located in the western part of the county (see page 200)."

From *Georgia County Snapshots*, Georgia Department of Community Affairs

For tourism information on towns in Early County, see Resources page 299.

fishing and canoe boat rental, swimming pool, 5 miles of nature trails (see page XXX), museum, 18-hole miniature golf, playground and restrooms. **Days/Hours**: *Open daily. Park – 7 a.m. to 10 p.m. Park office – 8 a.m. to 5 p.m. Fishing lake – 7 a.m. to sunset. Swimming pool – Tuesday through Sunday from Memorial Day to Labor Day, 11 a.m. to 6 p.m. Museum – Tuesday through Saturday, 9 a.m. to 5 p.m.; Sunday, 2 to 5:30 p.m.; closed Monday.* **Fees**: *$2 park pass required daily for vehicles under 13 persons. All other facilities subject to user fees. Contact the state park office for the latest information on fees and reservations.* **Directions**: *Early County. From Blakely, take US 27 about 2 miles to Upper Kolomoki Road. Turn left and follow for 4 miles to the entrance and park office.* **More Information**: *Kolomoki Mounds State Historic Park, Route 1, Box 114, Blakely, GA, 31723. 229/724-2150. For program reservations and fees, call 229/723-3398. Website: www.gastateparks.org. Central Reservations Center, 800/864-7275, Monday through Friday, 8 a.m. to 5 p.m.*

Providence Canyon State Conservation Park

Two hundred years ago, Providence Canyon did not exist. The pink, red, orange and purple maze of sheer walls, butts and cliffs that rise 150 feet above the main canyon floor of what is sometimes called "Georgia's Little Grand Canyon" was just ordinary farm land owned by three families, the Worthingtons, the Woodalls and the Humbers.

Legend has it that the canyons began with water dripping from the roof of a barn. But historical accounts suggest that it was really the result of poor soil management practices. During the early 1800s, farmers growing cotton, the South's most lucrative cash crop, stripped the forests and worked the top soil to sheer exhaustion. (This was before the development of contour plowing and strip cropping, standard measures which protect the soil today.) Once this natural vegetation was removed, there was nothing to diminish the erosive action of the rainfall that flowed unimpeded across the barren landscape, cutting into the sandy soils of this Coastal Plain region and forming gullies. The gullies deepened at an alarming pace in these soft soils and served to concentrate the runoff into small wet weather streams, which increased the rate of erosion even further. By 1850, the gullies reached down vertically three to five feet. Today, many are as deep as 150 feet.

For groups, the park offers a 13-minute video and guided hikes. Reservations can also be made for programs on honey bees, wildflowers, birds and canyon geology. Special events at Providence Canyon include spring and fall Wildflower Days and a Kudzu Takeover Day in August.

Facilities: *Primitive camping (see page 221), 65 picnic sites, 2 picnic shelters, group picnic shelters, interpretive center, 3-mile loop hiking trail and 7-mile backcountry trail (see page 223).* **Days/Hours**: *Open daily. Interpretive Center – 8 a.m. to 5 p.m. Park – September. 15 through April 14, 7 a.m. to 6 p.m.; April 15 through September 14, 7 a.m. to 9 p.m.*

Stewart County

The beautiful and rare plumleaf azalea grows in this Land Between the Rivers County.

"Stewart County was named for General Daniel Stewart, an officer in the Revolutionary War and War of 1812, and grandfather of President Theodore Roosevelt. There are two incorporated municipalities in the county, Lumpkin, the county seat, and Richland. Lumpkin was named for Wilson Lumpkin, a two-term governor of Georgia, U.S. Congressman and Senator. He was a leading advocate of state rights and 'Indian Removal.' Providence Canyon State Park, located in Stewart County, is a collection of canyons and gullies. The largest of these is 'Grandfather Canyon,' which is a half mile long, 300 feet wide and 150 feet deep... The 1,061-acre park also has the largest natural collection of the rare 'Plumleaf Azalea' (see sidebar page 223) in the world. The historic community of Westville (see page 211) is also located in the county. This was never actually a town, but is made up of more than 25 historic homes, shops and public buildings moved to the site from the surrounding counties... The Woodland, Mississippian, and Creek Indians were all inhabitants of Stewart County at one time or another. Two of the six largest Indian mounds in Georgia are located in the county."

From *Georgia County Snapshots*, Georgia Department of Community Affairs

For tourism information on towns in Stewart County, see Resources page 300.

Fees: *$2 park pass required daily for vehicles under 13 persons. All other facilities subject to user fees. Contact the state park office for the latest information on fees and reservations.* **Directions**: *Stewart County. From Lumpkin, take GA 39C west for 7 miles. Park entrance on left.* **More Information**: *Providence Canyon State Conservation Park, Route 1, Box 158, Lumpkin, GA 31815. 229/838-6202. Website: www.gastateparks.org. Central Reservations, 800/864-7275, Monday through Friday, 8 a.m. to 5 p.m.*

Smiths Landing Park

It's a pleasant rural drive on Day Road to Smiths Landing, past South Georgia farms with fields of cotton and watermelon. The park itself lies on a quiet bend of Spring Creek right above Decatur Lake, shaded by a canopy of live oaks and Spanish moss.

Facilities: *Boat ramp (see map page 239), picnic tables, grills, a pit toilet and gravel parking area.* **Days/Hours**: *Open daily, 24 hours.* **Directions**: *Decatur County. From Bainbridge, take GA 253 west about 9 miles. Turn right onto Day Road, a 2-lane dirt road. Go about 3 miles to Smiths Landing Road. Turn left. The park is at the end of the road.* **More Information**: *See Lake Seminole Resource Manager's Office on page 163.*

Spring Creek Park

A wonderful feature of this park along Spring Creek in Colquitt is the 1,409 foot-elevated boardwalk that winds around lowlands adjacent to the creek. More than 35 plant species, including cypress, maple and oak shade the walk and line the creek banks of this wetlands forest. Two paths stem from the main passageway lead to fishing decks. The scenic boardwalk was the result of numerous individuals and volunteers working together to create a unique environment for fishing, nature study and relaxing.

Facilities: *Boardwalk, nature trail and picnic area.* **Days/Hours**: *Open daily, 8 a.m. to 10 p.m.* **Directions**: *Miller County. From Colquitt town square, take GA 91 south about 0.25 mile to West Street. Turn right. Park entrance is on the left about a block. You can also reach the boardwalk by taking US 27 west from Colquitt to the bridge over Spring Creek. On the right, just before the bridge, is a small picnic and parking area. You can walk to the creek and the boardwalk from there.* **More Information**: *City of Colquitt, 181 S. Cuthbert, Colquitt, GA 31737. 229/758-3412; fax, 229/758-4181.*

Spring Creek

The beautiful, spring-fed Spring Creek runs through the middle of the Land Between the Rivers before it empties into Lake Seminole.

"Spring Creek has its headwaters in Clay and Calhoun Counties and flows directly south draining portions of Early, Miller, Seminole and Decatur Counties before emptying into Lake Seminole. Exotic and beautiful, Spring Creek is vastly different from other Coastal Plains streams. First, it is largely spring fed, and when high water subsides following the spring rains, the water in the upper sections is crystal clear and reveals a beautiful array of underwater plant life, spring 'boils,' and a bottom that is often solid limestone, sometimes pitted by erosion with jagged cutting edges. Fish and mollusks are plentiful and can be observed from a canoe. Cypress and planertrees line the banks, which rise high from the stream thereby eliminating much of the usual wet floodplain flora. Pine and hardwood forests surround the stream. Except in the spring, and in the lake pool of Lake Seminole, the water is too shallow for powerboat traffic, but it is perfect for paddle craft. Limestone outcroppings add to the wilderness beauty of the partially shaded stream, and small shoals and rocky shallows enliven the paddling."

A Paddler's Guide to Southern Georgia by Bob Sehlinger and Don Otey

WILDLIFE MANAGEMENT AREAS

Eufaula National Wildlife Refuge

In 1964, the U. S. Fish and Wildlife Service established the Eufaula National Wildlife Refuge in cooperation with the Corps of Engineers to provide habitat for wintering migratory waterfowl and other migratory and resident species. The 11,160-acre refuge lies on the upper reaches of the Walter F. George Reservoir on either side of the Chattahoochee River in Alabama and Georgia. Past agricultural and clear cutting land practices has changed the landscape and wildlife in this once heavily forested area. The refuge is now managed to protect diverse species in greater numbers than the area could under natural conditions. This is accomplished by managed farmlands, grasslands, woodlands and wetlands.

Eufaula National Wildlife Refuge is one of more than 500 refuges in the United States dedicated to meeting needs of migratory birds and endangered species. Several hundred acres of open cropland are rotated with grassland acres to provide the early succession growth and grains that provide valuable food for these birds. Crops grown include corn, soybeans, wheat, peanuts and other selected plantings. Cooperative farmers cultivate the refuge and leave unharvested shares of crops in refuge fields for wildlife consumption. Harvested crop residues are left in fields throughout the fall and winter for food, cover and erosion control. Many agricultural acres have been converted through the years to forested habitat to provide needed habitat for species that require woodlands. The long-range goal is to provide mixed stands of uneven age timber with special emphasis placed on restoring contiguous blocks of hardwoods. Pump systems, dikes and water control structures are used to manage a man-made system of impoundments to created hundreds of wetland acres. Water levels are raised and lowered seasonally to produce natural foods for waterfowl, feeding areas for marsh and waterbirds, and mudflats for shorebirds and wood storks.

There's a self-guided wildlife drive and interpretive trail and observation tower. Fishing is allowed throughout the refuge. Doves, ducks and deer may be hunted on the refuge during special refuge-conducted hunts. Boat ramps are available at the Florence Marina State Park and Rood Creek Landing Recreation Areas adjacent to the refuge and the Gammage Road access point located on the refuge. Camping is not permitted. Bicycles and horseback riding are permitted on the gravel roads only.

For general refuge regulations, license requirements and hunting seasons, hunters should obtain a current copy of the "Georgia Hunting Seasons & Regulations" booklet, available at local outdoors stores and the Georgia DNR. Hikers and birdwatchers should also check the booklet for the schedule of seasonal hunts. All visitors are encouraged to wear fluorescent orange during hunting season.

Facilities: *Boat ramps, observation tower, wildlife driving trail, interpretive nature trail, refuge headquarters.* **Days/Hours**: *Open daily, 24 hours. Headquarters – Monday through Friday, 7:30 a.m. to 4 p.m. CST.* **Directions**: *Quitman County. From Georgetown, take US 82 west across the Chattahoochee River to US 431. Turn right and go 2 miles. The entrance to the refuge is on the right. Follow the signs.* **More Information**: *Refuge Manager, Eufaula National Wildlife Refuge, Route 2, Box 97-B, Eufaula, AL 36027-9294. 334/687-4065.*

The Winter Hunt

Hunting was the means of survival for Indians in the Flint-Chattahoochee River Valley.

"For Valley Indians in historic times the winter hunt usually began in October, although preparations for it were started much sooner, and ended in March. The women were busy for weeks in advance, preparing food and clothing for the men to take along. Each man was provisioned with an adequate supply of dried meat, persimmon bread, and, toward the end of the Woodland Period, parched corn. The men reworked their weapons, tested and polished their bows, and selected only their best and truest arrows for the hunt. Sometimes women accompanied their husbands so they could bring the meat back to camp and begin the process of cleaning and curing the skins immediately. No matter who went, they were expected to be able to cover 25 to 30 miles a day at a steady trot and to be able to endure all the discomforts of winter while on the move."

The Old Beloved Path by William W. Winn

Hannahatchee Creek Wildlife Management Area

This WMA in the northwestern part of Stewart County is a good place for camping, hiking, bird watching and hunting. Named for Hannahatchee Creek, which flows into the Chattahoochee north of here, this 5,640-acre WMA is home to deer, turkey, fox, bobcat, raccoon, opossum and dove.

For general WMA regulations, license requirements and hunting seasons, hunters should obtain a current copy of the "Georgia Hunting Seasons & Regulations" booklet, available at local outdoors stores and the Georgia DNR. Hikers and birdwatchers should also check the booklet for the schedule of seasonal hunts. All visitors are encouraged to wear fluorescent orange during hunting season.

Facilities: *Campground, hiking trails, pistol and rifle ranges.* **Days/Hours**: *Open daily, 24 hours. All visitors must sign in at the check station.* **Directions**: *Stewart County. From Richland, take GA 27 west about 4 miles to Pleasant Valley Road. Turn right and go about 3.5 miles to Store Road, a dirt road on the right that leads into the WMA. Turn right and go about 0.5 mile to the check station.* **More Information**: *Georgia Department of Natural Resources, Game Management Section, 2024 Newton Road, Albany, GA 31708. 229/430-4254.*

Lake Walter F. George Wildlife Management Area

Hunting, fishing, hiking, bird watching and boating are activities that you can enjoy at this wildlife management area, which stretches along Lake Walter F. George from Fort Benning south to Fort Gaines. Eight different tracts, totaling 1,957 acres of land, make up the area: River Bend Tract, River Bluff Tract, Tobannee Creek Tract, Cool Branch Tract, Pataula Creek Tract, Pataula Creek Park Tract, Sandy Branch Tract and Gravel Point Tract.

The topography varies from almost level to very steep, depending on the tract. Most of the area is mixed pine-hardwood with scattered openings. Access to the various tracts is by improved dirt or paved roads. Access to the interior of most tracts is limited to foot travel. A boat may be helpful in getting to some areas, and is essential for accessing the Pataula Creek and Sandy Branch tracts.

Hunters will find white-tailed deer, turkey, squirrel, rabbit, quail, mourning dove and waterfowl, including Canada geese. Deer hunting is limited to archery only, and small game hunting is limited to shotguns only.

For general WMA regulations, license requirements and hunting seasons, hunters should obtain a current copy of the "Georgia Hunting Seasons & Regulations" booklet, available at local outdoors stores and the Georgia DNR. Hikers and birdwatchers should also check the booklet for the schedule of seasonal hunts. All visitors are encouraged to wear fluorescent orange during hunting season.

Facilities: *Boat ramps at Pataula Creek Park, Sandy Branch, River Bluff, River Bend, and Cool Branch Tracts. Camping is available all around the lake*

Archaic Indians and the White-tailed Deer

For Archaic Indians living in the Land Between the Rivers, hunting for white-tailed deer meant survival.

"…As important as nuts and acorns were in the diet of Archaic people in the Valley, the essential element was the white-tailed deer, a valuable source of food, clothing, tools, and more. About half of a deer could be eaten; the rest was used in home manufacture. Its antlers and bones were fashioned into needles, fishhooks, spear points, awls and drills, flakers, pins, saws, scrapers, hammers, and ornaments. The animal's hide was fleshed, de-haired, and cured to be made into moccasins, containers, and clothing. The sinews and gut could be cured and made into thongs and twining. The heads of bucks were dried and, along with the cured hide, were probably worn by hunters when stalking wild deer or as headdresses on ceremonial occasions."

The Old Beloved Path by William W. Winn

at Corp of Engineers Campgrounds. **Days/Hours**: *Open daily, 24 hours. Hunting is from 30 minutes before sunrise until 30 minutes after sunset, unless otherwise specified.* **Directions**: *Clay, Quitman and Chattahoochee Counties. From Ft. Gaines, take GA 39 north to access most of the tracts, which occur along the lakeshore. Directions to and maps of the various tracts can be obtained from the Albany Game Management Office. WMA land is marked by a combination of red painted bands and yellow WMA signs on boundary trees.* **More Information**: *Georgia Department of Natural Resources, Game Management Section, 2024 Newton Road, Albany, GA 31708. 229/430-4254.*

Mayhaw Wildlife Management Area

Named for the small, red berry that grows in the area and is used for making jams and jellies, Mayhaw is a 4,681-acre wildlife management area in Southwest Georgia just three miles northwest of Colquitt in Miller County. There are three separate tracts—Holt Old House, Willoughby and Fire Tower—where you can enjoy hunting, hiking and bird watching. Cypress Creek runs through the Willoughby Tract, where a campground and the check station for the WMA are also located. An archery and firearm range is located on the Fire Tower Tract.

Populations of deer, quail, turkey, feral hog, fox, bobcat, raccoon, opossum and other small game can all be found at Mayhaw. Waterfowl found is mostly wood duck.

For general WMA regulations, license requirements and hunting seasons, hunters should obtain a current copy of the "Georgia Hunting Seasons & Regulations" booklet, available at local outdoors stores and the Georgia DNR. Hikers and birdwatchers should also check the booklet for the schedule of seasonal hunts. All visitors are encouraged to wear fluorescent orange during hunting season.

Facilities: *Campground on Willoughby Tract, archery and firearm range on Fire Tower Tract and hiking trails.* **Days/Hours**: *Open daily, 24 hours. Hunting hours are from 30 minutes before sunrise until 30 minutes after sunset, unless otherwise specified. All visitors must sign in at the check station.* **Directions**: *Miller County. Fire House Tract – From Colquitt, take GA 91 west about 1 mile. Tract lies on both sides of highway. Willoughby and Holt Old House Tracts – From Colquitt, take US 27 northwest 2 miles to first paved road. Turn left and go 1 mile to Willoughby and 2 miles to Old House. Check station is located near entrance to Willoughby Tract.* **More Information**: *Georgia Department of Natural Resources, Game Management Section, 2024 Newton Road, Albany, GA 31708. 229/430-4254.*

CAMPGROUNDS

Franklin D. Roosevelt Campground

From a single sleeping bag next to a stream on Pine Mountain Ridge to a group campsite for 120 people along Lake Franklin,

---

Miller County

Miller County sits in the Flint River Watershed in the Land Between the Rivers.

"Miller County was created in 1856 from parts of Baker and Early counties. It was named after Judge Andrew J. Miller, who served as a commander of the Oglethorpe Infantry, served in the legislature for more than 20 years, and several times as president of the Senate. Miller is best remembered for introducing a bill to give property rights to married women. The county seat is Colquitt. It is the only incorporated municipality within the county, and was named for U.S. Senator Walter Colquitt, who was previously a clergyman, attorney and judge."

From *Georgia County Snapshots*, Georgia Department of Community Affairs

For tourism information on towns in Miller County, see Resources page 300.

Franklin D. Roosevelt State Park offers about any type of camping experience you desire.

Facilities: *140 tent, trailer and RV sites, all with water and electrical hookups, grills and fire rings; five comfort stations with hot showers and flush toilets; sanitary disposal station; and laundry facilities. Two group camps next to Lake Franklin with shower houses, lake swimming and activity areas. Four pioneer campsites with water provided. Primitive overnight camping available on the 23-mile Pine Mountain Trail (see page 224) with campsites limited to 15 people. For state park facilities, see page 211.* **Days/Hours**: *Open daily, 7 a.m. to 10 p.m.* **Fees**: *$2 park pass required daily for vehicles under 13 persons. All other facilities subject to user fees. Contact the state park office for the latest information on fees and reservations.* **Directions**: *Harris and Meriwether Counties. From Pine Mountain, take US 27 east about 5 miles to GA 354. Turn left and follow the signs.* **More Information**: *Franklin D. Roosevelt State Park, 2970 Georgia Highway 190, Pine Mountain, GA 31822. 706/663-4858. Georgia State Parks and Historic Sites, 205 Butler Street, Suite 1352 East, Atlanta, GA 30334. Website: www.gastateparks.org. Central Reservations Center, 800/864-7275, Monday through Friday, 8 a.m. to 5 p.m.*

Florence Marina Campgrounds

These wooded campsites at Florence Marina, on the north end of Lake Walter F. George on the Chattahoochee River, lie adjacent to the natural deepwater marina and fishing pier that are part of the Florence Marina State Park facility.

Facilities: *44 tent, trailer and RV sites, each with water, electric, sewage and cable TV hookups, picnic table and fire ring. Comfort station with restrooms, hot showers and laundry facilities. For state park facilities, see page 213.* **Days/Hours**: *Open daily, 7 a.m. to 10 p.m.* **Fees**: *$2 park pass required daily for vehicles under 13 persons. All other facilities subject to user fees. Contact the state park office for the latest information on fees and reservations.* **Directions**: *Stewart County. From Lumpkin, take GA 39C west for 16 miles. Park entrance located at end of 39C.* **More Information**: *Florence Marina State Park, Route 1, Box 36, Omaha, GA 31821. 229/838-6870 or 4244. Kirbo Interpretive Center, 229/838-4706. Website: www.gastateparks.org. Central Reservations Center, 800/864-7275, Monday through Friday, 8 a.m. to 5 p.m.*

Kolomoki Mounds Campground

Five different camping areas at Kolomoki Mounds State Historic Park offer a range of camping experiences: Lakeside Campground and Rustic Campground for recreational vehicles and tents, two pioneer camping areas and Camp Hicita for group camping of up to 135 people.

Facilities: *Lakeside and Rustic campgrounds — 43 campsites for RVs and tents with water and electrical hookups, picnic tables, fire rings and grills; bathhouses with hot showers and laundry facilities; and dump station. Pioneer*

Webster County

The bald eagle and the red-cockaded woodpecker are two protected species found within this county in the Flint River Watershed.

"Webster County was created in 1853 from part of Stewart County. Georgia's 103rd county originally had an Indian name, Kinchafoonee, for a principal creek that crosses it. After outsiders made fun of the name, the county's citizens petitioned to change it to honor Daniel Webster. Preston, the county seat, was known as Lannahassee and was the first white settlement after Creek Indians left the area. When the county was created, its name changed to honor William O. Preston of South Carolina."

From *Georgia County Snapshots*, Georgia Department of Community Affairs

For tourism information on towns in Webster County, see Resources page 300.

campgrounds — picnic tables, grills and a fire ring; no electricity or restrooms; one pioneer area with fresh water, one without. Camp Hicita — 4 sleeping cabins with counselor rooms in each, staff quarters, infirmary, commercial kitchen, dining hall, 2 craft cabins, open chapel, private swimming pool, amphitheater, softball field, basketball goal and volleyball net. For state park facilities see page 214. **Days/Hours**: *Open daily, 7 a.m. to 10 p.m. Check out time is 1 p.m. for campsites.* **Fees**: *$2 park pass required daily for vehicles under 13 persons. All other facilities subject to user fees. Contact the state park office for the latest information on fees and reservations.* **Directions**: *Early County. From Blakely, take US 27 about 2 miles to Upper Kolomoki Road. Turn left and follow for 4 miles to the entrance and park office.* **More Information**: *Kolomoki Mounds State Historic Park, Route 1, Box 114, Blakely, GA 31723. 229/724-2150. Website: www.gastateparks.org. Central Reservations Center, 800/864-7275, Monday through Friday, 8 a.m. to   5 p.m.*

Providence Canyon Camping

Camping in Georgia's "Little Grand Canyon" is primitive only. Two sites are available for pioneer camping, which Georgia State Parks defines as camping for organized groups under the active supervision of adult leaders. Six other campsites sit along the back portion of the seven-mile backpacking trail where campers must have a permit to hike and camp. Creek beds here are prone to have water and/or mud, so campers and hikers should dress appropriately.

Facilities: *Two pioneer camping areas and 6 camping sites on backcountry trail (see page 223). Sites are semi-remote and without shower facilities. For state park facilities, see page 215.* **Days/Hours**: *Open daily. Park — September 15 through April 14, 7 a.m. to 6 p.m.; April 15 through September 14, 7 a.m. to 9 p.m.* **Fees**: *$2 park pass required daily for vehicles under 13 persons. All other facilities subject to user fees. Contact the state park office for the latest information on fees and reservations.* **Directions**: *Stewart County. From Lumpkin, take GA 39C west for 7 miles. Park entrance on left.* **More Information**: *Providence Canyon State Conservation Park, Route 1, Box 158, Lumpkin, GA 31815. 229/838-6202. Website: www.gastateparks.org. Central Reservations Center, 800/864-7275, Monday through Friday, 8 a.m. to 5 p.m.*

FISHING

Steve Cocke Hatchery

Catfish, brim and bass are the fish grown and distributed at this state fish hatchery near Dawson. The 46-acre hatchery produces fish for private waters within a 32-county region.

Programs at the hatchery include producing fingerling shoal bass for the Flint River, and Gulf Coast striped bass for the Chattahoochee-Flint-Apalachicola River System, to re-establish populations due to habitat loss. The hatchery also provides hybrid bass to reservoirs statewide and Channel Catfish to Kid's Fishing Events, a statewide program for teaching kids to fish.

Quitman County

The Chattahoochee River flows along the western border of Quitman County.

"Quitman County was created from parts of Randolph and Stewart counties in 1858. The county was named for General John A. Quitman, a leader in the Mexican War, once Governor of Mississippi, and an avid spokesman for states rights. The county's only incorporated municipality is Georgetown, the county seat. It was named for the area in Washington, D.C. It was originally called Tobanana after a nearby creek. The county has several endangered species living within its borders, including the Gray Bat, the Indiana Bat, and the Bald Eagle."

From *Georgia County Snapshots*, Georgia Department of Community Affairs

For tourism information on towns in Quitman County, see Resources page 300.

The best time to visit the hatchery is in April and May when the fish and newborn Canada geese are abundant. Tours of the hatchery are available on a limited basis and are targeted to younger kids, scouts and church groups.

Facilities: *17 ponds with 15.5 acres of water.* **Days/Hours**: *Open Monday through Friday, 8 a.m. to 4:30 p.m. Special group tours can be arranged in advance. Call for reservations.* **Directions**: *Terrell County. From Dawson, take US 82 west about 2 miles. Entrance is on the left.* **More Information**: *Steve Cocke Hatchery, 109 Hatchery Road, Dawson, GA 31742. 229/955-4486.*

Warm Springs Regional Fisheries Center

Established in 1899 by Congress, the National Fish Hatchery at Warm Springs is the second-oldest hatchery in the nation. This warm-water hatchery, operated by the U.S. Fish and Wildlife Service, raises striped bass, sturgeon, paddlefish, channel catfish, bluegill and mussels in 40 production ponds separated by dikes along the 56-acre grounds. Two concrete display pools feature, respectively, goldfish and native warm-water fish, such as longnose gar, spotted gar, striped bass, hybrid bass, largemouth bass, crappie, bluegill and redear sunfish.

Cold Spring, which supplies the town of Warm Springs with its drinking water, also supplies the 63 degree Fahrenheit water that fills the ponds and flows through the stream in front of the visitor center. The visitor center features several aquariums and exhibits with native fish, such as gar, largemouth bass, crappie, catfish, bluegill, and redear sunfish, and a 3-mile wooded hiking trail, which is a good place for viewing white-tailed deer, wild turkeys, rabbits, turtles, frogs, songbirds and hawks.

In 1990, the National Fish Hatchery combined with a Fish Health Laboratory and Fish Technology Center to form the Warm Springs Regional Fisheries Center, the Southeast headquarters for aquaculture research and information.

Facilities: *Aquarium, picnic area and hiking trail.* **Days/Hours**: *Open daily, 8 a.m. to 4 p.m.; closed on federal holidays. Special group tours can be arranged in advance.* **Directions**: *Meriwether County. From Warm Springs, take GA 41 east 1 mile to the entrance.* **More Information**: *Warm Springs Regional Fisheries Center, 5308 Spring Street, Warm Springs, GA 31830-9712. 706/655-3382 or 3620.*

HIKES AND WALKS

Backcountry Trail

You must have a permit to hike this red-blazed trail that winds through the backcountry of Providence Canyon, delivering a view of all 16 canyons in the state park.

Randolph County

Randolph County lies within both the Flint and the Chattahoochee River watersheds.

"Randolph County was created in 1828 from a portion of Lee County. Georgia's 75th Georgia county was named for John Randolph of Virginia, a Republican Congressman and a descendent of Pocahontas. There are three incorporated municipalities in the county: Coleman, Shellman, and Cuthbert, the county seat. Cuthbert was named for John A. Cuthbert, editor, congressman, and judge. Randolph's first county seat was Lumpkin. Lumpkin, however, became the seat of government for Stewart County, when it was created from a portion of Randolph. One of the first pecan trees brought to Georgia from Texas was planted in Cuthbert. The tree eventually became known as the 'mother of the Georgia pecan industry' in honor of its great age and size."

From *Georgia County Snapshots*, Georgia Department of Community Affairs

For tourism information on towns in Randolph County, see Resources page 300.

Distance: This red-blazed trail makes a 7-mile loop.

Trailhead: Providence Canyon State Conservation Park (see page 215). Trail begins and ends at the visitor center, where you can pick up permits and trail maps.

Features: From this trail you can see the nine deeper canyons along the Canyon Loop Trail (see below), as well as the seven canyons of the backcountry. There are six campsites for hikers located at different points along this backpacking trail. These areas are fairly remote and without facilities.

Canyon Loop Trail

This trail in the Providence Canyon State Park day-use area winds through the most scenic portion of this unique state park, whose unusual geological features have earned it the nickname of Georgia's Little Grand Canyon.

Distance: This is a 3-mile, white-blazed loop trail.

Trailhead Location: Providence Canyon State Conservation Park (see page 215). Trail begins and ends at the Visitor Center.

Features: The best way to see Providence Canyon is from this trail, which encircles nine of the park's 16 canyons. Numerous overlooks provide views of the canyon walls, which like Neapolitan ice cream, divide into three layers, each with unique coloring and qualities. These three layers make up two distinctive geologic formations (recognizable bodies of rock or sediment), the Providence Formation and the Clayton Formation.

Look closely at the bottom of the canyon for the three to nine foot wide layer of silt and sand. This brownish, dark grey-colored layer is geologically known as the Perote member of the Providence Formation. It feels like a mixture of play-dough and beach sand, and contains pieces of the shiny, flaky, glittering mineral known as mica, which is used in the manufacture of table tops and other board surfaces.

The next layer, about 120 feet high, is the Providence Formation member known as the Providence Sand. This sandy soil contains streaks of white, buff, tan and even salmon, pink and lavender. Within these massive horizontal layers are smaller layers with a different angle, a sign that an ocean deposited the sand between 65 million and 85 million years ago. The Providence Sand section contains white clay, which, when rubbed between the hands, feels gritty and leaves a slippery stain that seems like baby powder. It's kaolin, a substance mined for many industrial uses from a rich belt just south of the Fall Line, which runs east to west in the middle of the state from Augusta to Columbus, marking the ancient coastline.

Above the Providence Sand at the top of the canyon, a thin layer, the Clayton Formation, appears as a red-orange sand and clay mix. Near the bottom of the Clayton, a hard heavy layer resembling rusted metal indicates a layer of high-grade iron ore, which is mined in some

Azalea

The azalea, with its flowing, beautiful flowering branches that announce spring time to the south, is the name given to a group of flowering deciduous shrubs that grow mainly in eastern North America and China. Azaleas are grown in gardens and occur wild in woodland and swamp areas, living best in acid soil and partial shade.

Shaped like a trumpet, with five tapering petals, their fragrant flowers bloom before their leaves open and are a favorite flower of bees. Azalea blossoms range in color through all shades of pink, red, white, yellow and purple. Their long pollen stalks extend beyond the petals. A long, slender container covered with hairs holds the seeds. In some azaleas, the flower has a covering of sticky hairs which keeps ants away from the nectar.

About 40 species of azaleas grow in North America, blooming early in May and June. Many of these can be found in the Flint and Chattahoochee River Valley, including the Alabama, flame and Piedmont azalea.

One in particular, the plumleaf (*Rhododendron prunifolium*), is one of the showiest native azaleas; and the lower Chattahoochee River Basin in the Land Between the Rivers is one of the few places in the world it can be found. The plumleaf has an unusually late flowering period, producing its yellow-orange to deep red flowers at a time when few, if any, other azaleas are in bloom. The plumleaf was Cason and Virginia Callaway's inspiration for Callaway Gardens (see page 197) and is featured on the garden's logo. The finest natural display of plumleaf azalea is found within Providence Canyon State Park (see page 215), where more than a thousand plants bloom in July and August.

areas for the manufacture of steel. Once the newly formed gullies cut through the red-orange sand and clay of the Clayton, they easily eroded away the Providence Sand. The small wet weather streams can be seen in the canyon bottom where they collect at times of abundant rainfall. Groundwater flowing through the porous earth also shapes the canyons, collecting over layers of impermeable clay and under-mining the overlying sediments, which from time to time come crashing down over the weakened layers underneath. The canyon continually grows wider as nature works away the walls, at the rate of about six feet per year.

Beneath the Providence Formation is the Ripley Formation, a very erosion-resistant, clay-like soil that slows the erosion process to a hardly measurable rate, while the sides of the canyon continue to wash downstream.

Besides the unusual geology, beautiful and unusual wildflowers grow in the canyons, including the plumleaf azalea, which grows close to the watercourses far below the canyon rims.

Pine Mountain Trail

Two of President Roosevelt's favorite places to picnic and relax when he was at the Little White House were "the wolf's den," a spot by a waterfall on his farm, and Dowdell's Knob, which overlooks Pine Mountain Valley. Both can be seen from the Pine Mountain Trail, a 23-mile hiking trail that traverses Pine Mountain Ridge, meandering across the mountain's summit, ridges and valleys.

Volunteers of the Pine Mountain Trail Association, an incorporated, non-profit organization dedicated to enhancing, preserving and promoting the Pine Mountain Trail, built and maintain the trail, its loops and connectors. The trail is extremely well-marked and easy to moderate to hike; but it's a good idea to purchase a map of the trail system, available at the FDR State Park office.

Distance: There are three, well-marked trails: the 23-mile, blue-blazed Pine Mountain Trail; the 3.2-mile, red-blazed Mountain Creek Nature Trail; and 38.7 miles of white-blazed loops and connecting loop trails.

Trailhead Location: Franklin D. Roosevelt State Park (see page 211). Western terminus of trail starts at park entrance at US 27 and GA 190 across from the Callaway Gardens Country Store in Harris County. Eastern terminus of trail starts beneath the WJSP-TV tower on GA 85 in Meriwether County. The trail crisscrosses GA 190 several times, offering hikers multiple entry points.

Features: Unusual rock outcroppings, waterfalls, beaver dams, historic sites, mountain vegetation – all can be seen along this trail. Hard Hollis quartzite makes up most of Pine Mountain, and anytime rock is exposed, look for the whitish crystals of quartz. Vegetation along the summit and hillsides of the mountain is more typical of an Appalachian mixed hardwood forest than the Georgia Piedmont.

Calhoun County

The gopher tortoise makes its home in this county in the Flint River Watershed.

"Calhoun County was created in 1854 from parts of Baker and Early counties. It was named for Senator John C. Calhoun of South Carolina, who had resigned as Vice President of the U.S. in 1832 so that he could return to the Senate to debate Daniel Webster on state rights. Calhoun County has four incorporated municipalities: Morgan, Arlington, Edison, and Leary. Morgan, the county seat, was named for General Daniel Morgan, a Revolutionary War figure."

From *Georgia County Snapshots*, Georgia Department of Community Affairs

For tourism information on towns in Calhoun County, see Resources page 300.

Shortleaf pine, hickory, chestnut and black oak grow along the drier ridge tops, while the moist coves and creek bottoms support sweet gum, yellow poplar and maple. In spring, the forest blazes with the colors of Piedmont azalea, rhododendron and mountain laurel.

There are 11 designated campsites, all near water, located at various places a short distance off the trail. Camping on the trail is by permit only and these must be obtained from the park office before starting out on the trail. Shuttles are available; just ask at the park office for information.

HUNTING

In this part of southwest Georgia, the hunt is for the bobwhite quail. Large hunting plantations, encompassing thousands of acres each, line both banks of the Flint River in Lee, Dougherty, Baker, Miller and Mitchell Counties. Most of these are private lands open only to owners and their guests. Some cater to corporate and private customers. To learn more about the hunting experience on a quail plantation, turn the page.

Bobwhite Quail

The bobwhite quail is one of the most extensively hunted game birds in all of America. Although they weigh only five to six ounces, these fast little birds with their crafty survival instincts and impressive numbers have won the respect of many hunters. They are among the most widespread of the quail species, with more than 20 subspecies ranging from Canada to southern Mexico.

The bobwhite quail is found in a variety of habitats—from suburban parks to fields, open woodlands, savannas and grasslands. They prefer farmlands where wheat and other grains are cultivated, while farmers enjoy their presence because they eat harmful insects and destroy certain weeds. In winter, the bobwhite quail form large groups called coveys. Consisting of about five to 30 birds, they roam areas up to 40 acres. Coveys are created for protection and warmth. Packed tightly together, the birds on the inside of the bunch are kept insulated by those on the outside of the group, who face outwards—on watch for predators. The birds rotate positions, taking turns spending time in the warm middle of the covey. If danger does approach, the covey will burst into flight, briefly startling and confusing the predator.

The male bobwhite quail has a white throat and eyeline with a black line separating the two. The lower breast is speckled white and dark brown. The rest of the bird is a muted brown, except for the tail, which is gray. Females are similar, the only differences being a lighter color overall, and a brownish throat and eyeline instead of white.

The Quail Plantations of South Georgia

"The year's first frost and occasional rains accompany the cooler air of late November. Broom sedge ripens to a golden brown, and the fields emit the earthy smells of a late, southern fall. Bird season is here. Guns are oiled and the dogs are ready. Matched buckskin mules stand waiting, their harnesses festooned with polished brass. The scene is set for quail hunting in the grand plantation style."

Joseph Kitchens, *Quail Hunting Plantations of South Georgia and North Florida*

The large plantation culture—perpetuated by cotton—that flourished in the expanse of land from Tallahassee north to Albany and the Flint River Basin in the early 1800s continued even after the Civil War. Plantation properties did not break up as they did in other parts of the state. Owners managed to hang on to their properties and continued to plant cotton, which was fast depleting the soil.

The 1870s saw an influx of northern money and investment into the region. Northern industrialists and newly wealthy entrepreneurs began buying up large tracts of land from owners who were realizing financial difficulties due to the eroded and depleted land and the agricultural depression of that time. With this change of hands, the focus of the plantations began to change—from cotton and agriculture to the hunting of game birds—as the new owners treated their newly acquired property as winter retreats and sporting lands for family and friends.

Quail and dove were the most plentiful game birds in this region. Primarily migratory, doves were shot on the wing over harvested fields or fields left unharvested to entice the birds. Quail, however, were abundant year-round.

Non-migratory bobwhite quails, the best-known species in the United States, gather into coveys—large groups that may exceed 100 birds. They disperse during the day for feeding and gather again at night or in adverse weather. The covey members seek warmth and protection by huddling in a circle, with their heads turned outward.

"Although many other types of game were plentiful, quail shooting became the favored sport. Perhaps this was because it occurred during the fall, a season of traditional holiday festivities and reunions. Or perhaps it was the spectacular autumn weather, with its crisp November skies and golden-brown terrain; or that indescribable sensation of a covey rise over a pair of rock-steady pointers. While not all plantation owners came for the shooting, most did enjoy the social aspects of the event: leisure rides in the hunting wagons, bird-dog field trials, catered lunches in the field, and, of course, the pleasure of visiting with family and houseguests."

Joseph Kitchens, *Quail Hunting Plantations of South Georgia and North Florida*

The quail plantation of today is a large property whose most important product over the years has been quail for the hunting pleasure of owners and their guests. Fire has destroyed many of the classic southern plantation homes that once graced the properties. Today's residences vary in style from tudor to contemporary to rustic. But the hunting plantations and game preserves have kept many of the cultural traditions of the old cotton plantations. Elegant southern meals, cocktails, stables, barns, hunt wagons, mules and kennels of pointers and setters are all part of the quail plantation scene.

"It is cold and damp in the gray light of dawn as the men and women gather in the 'big house.' Breakfast is hurried but plentiful—black coffee and country ham awaken the senses. Outside there is barking in the kennels as the dog handlers make their choices for the day's shooting. "Load up," they command as eager pointers leap into cages mounted on the hunting wagons. Others yelp and surge against the kennel fences, frustrated to be left behind."

Joseph Kitchens, *Quail Hunting Plantations of South Georgia and North Florida*

Known as "the quail capital of the world," the South Georgia and Florida Panhandle region today contains more than 100 working quail plantations, many covering thousands of acres each. It has been found that quail plantations are good employers of an area and good stewards of the land. Studies comparing the quail plantation form of land use to both forestry and agriculture indicate that the quail plantation provides more jobs in an area and that the diversity of plant life, habitats and associated wildlife of the plantations is, from an ecological point of view, far superior to that of most modern farms and tree farms. Quail plantations are lands that are rich in their variety of vegetation, game and birds. They are operated on sound ecological principles and they offer some of the more pleasant vistas to be found anywhere on the Coastal Plains.

In the Flint River Basin, these plantations range from the private and exclusive, where only owners and their "by invitation only" guests hunt, to plantations that specialize in week-long corporate retreats to ones that welcome families and all levels and ages of hunters. All in all, these quail plantations strive to preserve the grand tradition of the hunt.

"With their handlers yelling commands, pairs of hunting dogs are set loose to range in a criss-cross pattern ahead of the wagon and riders, until a dog freezes in a rigid point, tail in the air and nose aimed at the scent of a covey of quail. The hunters dismount and creep forward until the covey flushes and the shooting begins ..."

Pine Hill Plantation Brochure

The following are quail plantations in the Flint and Chattahoochee watershed that market themselves as quail plantations open to the public upon reservation.

Big Pine Plantation

Quail hunting is the specialty on the 1,000 acres at Big Pine Plantation in Blakely. Big Pine offers guided quail hunts for one or two people, half-day professional and businessman special hunts, and "do-it-yourself" quail hunts where you can bring your own dogs. Big Pine also offers discount prices for corporate or group quail hunts. These hunts are designed so businesses can entertain an unlimited number of clients and friends. Packages are available for full- and half-day hunts that include guides, dogs, field transportation, lodging, country-cooked noon meals and refreshments in the field. Hunters can also shoot sporting clays at a designated time for a nominal fee. Big Pine will dress and package quail and has insulated coolers available for purchase to ship dressed quail, packed in ice on airlines.

Facilities: *Lodge with 2-person rooms.* **Season**: *Open daily, Monday through Friday, 9 a.m. to 5 p.m. Quail hunting season is October 15 through March 15.* **Rates**: *Contact Big Pine for packages and prices. Non-refundable deposits are required.* **More Information**: *Donnie Crawford, manager, Big Pine Plantation, 218 Magnolia Street, Blakely, GA 31723. 229/723-3166; fax 229/723-3430.*

Big Red Oak Plantation

Once a cotton plantation along the banks of Big Red Oak Creek and the Flint River, Big Red Oak Plantation in Meriwether County is now a quail hunting plantation where pine trees and sage fields are maintained for wildlife habitat and partridge peas, clover, wheat, chufer, millet and other grains are planted. The original home, located on a site across the lake from the lodge, burned in the early 1900s, but the family cemetery attests to the fact that it has been family-owned for six generations. Hunting packages for quail and chukar include full- and half-day hunts with guide, jeep, dogs, refreshments and license for quail and chukar. Guided and unguided wild turkey hunting is also available and the lake is stocked with bass and bream.

Facilities: *Lodge with 3 bedrooms and 3 baths sleeps 6, regulation pool table and wet bar; 25-acre fishing lake; rifle, skeet and trap ranges; gun rental.* **Seasons**: *Quail and chukar – October 1 to March 31; turkey – mid March to mid May.* **Rates**: *Contact Big Red Oak for current rates.* **More Information**: *Arthur Estes, owner, Big Red Oak Plantation, P.O. Box 247, Gay, GA 30218. 706/538-6870.*

Chancey Mill Hunting Preserve

This privately owned, fourth-generation 3,000-acre farm in Early County was opened up for guided deer and turkey hunts for the first time in 1999. There is a variety of terrain to hunt: woods of native pine and hardwood, natural streams and creeks and more than 100 acres of beaver ponds. Chancey Mill offers full- and half-day hunts with guides, jeep and dogs. Lodging is also available in Grist Lodge, a rustic cypress cabin overlooking a small catfish pond near Grist Farm headquarters, the preserve's main house.

Facilities: *Cabin – sleeps 4 and includes a kitchen and dining area. Lodging, with special rates for hunters, is also available at the Sparks House Bed and Breakfast in nearby*

Blakely. **Rates***: Contact Chancey Mill for packages and prices.* **More Information***: Richard (Dee) Grist, owner, Chancey Mill, P.O. Box 818, Blakely, GA 31723. 229/723-6626; fax, 229/723-8773. Website: www.chanceymill.com.*

Hilton Hunting Preserve

Besides quail, chukar, pheasant, dove and deer hunting, Hilton Hunting Preserve in Early County offers week-long summer youth camps for ages 16 and under. At the camp, children learn about hunting, fishing, boating, hiking, archery, gun safety and the proper way to call a turkey. Hilton has packages for full- and half-day quail hunts with guides, jeep, dogs, box lunch and refreshments as well as combination and economy hunts. There are also liberated quail, wild quail and fishing memberships available. The preserve charges extra for meals and for bird cleaning.

Facilities*: Hunting lodge.* **Rates***: Contact Hilton for packages and prices. 24-hour notice required for all guided hunts.* **More Information***: John P. Chambers, owner, Hilton Hunting Preserve, Rt. 5, Box 2095, Blakely, GA 31723. 229/723-8349 or 229/723-7268.*

Llewellin's Point Hunting Preserve

This 1,100-acre traditional southern quail hunting plantation, which gets its name from the Llewellin setter, is located in Pine Mountain near Callaway Gardens. Low rolling hills, open fields and low brush habitat make this a good terrain for hunting bobwhite quail, ringneck pheasant, chukar partridge and mallard ducks. Llewellin's specializes in corporate hunts but welcomes all hunters. The hunting preserve puts together both full- and half-day hunts for groups. Packages include guide, dogs, field transportation, refreshments in the field and licenses. There are also do-it-yourself quail hunts, pheasant-only hunts and chukar-only hunts.

Facilities*: Hunting lodge with 2 private dining rooms and spacious den; kennels; and pro shop with all hunting needs, including 12-and-20-gauge rental guns and shells of all gauges, earplugs, safety glasses and orange safety vests. Other facilities, including accommodations, restaurants and other recreational activities are available at nearby Callaway Gardens (see page 197).* **Season***: October 1 through March 31. Reservations are required and should be made*

as far in advance as possible. **Rates***: Contact Llewellin's for packages and prices.* **More Information***: Floyd and Rebecca Clements, managers, Llewellin's Point Hunting Preserve, 7729 Hamilton Pleasant Grove Road, Pine Mountain, GA 31822. 800/636-9819 or 706/663-8215. Website: www.llewellins-point.com.*

Pine Hill Plantation

This is a family-owned working plantation with cotton, peanuts and livestock that hosts guided quail hunts the traditional way on horseback or mule-drawn wagons. Pine Hill owns or leases thousands of acres of rolling wiregrass terrain, longleaf pine and live oak woods interspersed with crop fields and food plots in Miller, Decatur and Seminole Counties. The plantation only hosts one party at a time. Three guides (a scout, a dog-handler and a wagon master) will take a party of up to six for one day to a week. Guided hunts on Lake Seminole and various ponds in the area are also available. Pine Hill is a member of Quail Unlimited and helps host the Celebrity Quail Hunt each year.

Facilities*: Lodge with 3 bedrooms and 2 1/2 baths accommodates 6 hunters; dining hall; kennels with more than 30 pointers and setters; shells and other supplies available, but no clothing or boots.* **Season***: Peak season is November 1 to March 10.* **Rates***: Contact Pine Hill for rates and open dates.* **More Information***: G. J. and Kathy Kimbrel, owners, Pine Hill Plantation, 255 Kimbrel Road, Colquitt, GA 31737. 229/758-6602; fax, 229/758-6608.*

Pinewood Plantation Lodge and Conference Center

Located in the pine woods of Mitchell County, this quail hunting lodge caters to corporate clients as well as hunters of all levels. Pinewood's full- and half-day hunts include guides, jeeps, wagons, dogs, lunch and hunting license. Pinewood Lake is stocked with bream and bass.

Facilities*: Lodge with bunk house, single and double rooms (sleeps 24 people); recreation room; conference room with fax and internet access; dining room; fishing lake; trap range; gun rental and shells for sale.* **Season***: October 1 through March 31.* **Rates***: Contact Pinewood for current packages and rates. Pinewood offers 5- and 10-hunt packages.* **More Information***: Ronnie Smith, manager, Pinewood Plantation Lodge and Conference Center, 744*

Pleasant Grove Church Road, Albany, GA 31705. Lodge, 229/483-0770; office, 229/446-0617. Website: pinewoodplantation.com.

Pretoria Station Hunting Preserve

Quail hunting is the specialty at Pretoria Station in Dougherty County, but the preserve also offers a diverse hunting experience that includes dove shoots over peanut fields, waterholes and specially planted plots; spring turkey hunts; whitetail deer in the fall and winter; and year-round wild hog hunts. Sporting clays and fishing are also available on the 1,800-acre plantation. Full- and half-day hunt packages are with guides, jeep and dogs. Pretoria Station will customize hunts for families and for corporate retreats.

Facilities*: Lodge and dining room, campground; country store with shells and other hunting accessories; and fishing lake.* **Season***: Open year-round.* **Rates***: Contact Pretoria Station for rates.* **More Information***: Pretoria Station Hunting Preserve, 4601 Leary Road, Albany, GA 31707. 229/439-4132. Website: pretoriastation.com.*

Quail Country Lodge and Conference Center

Quail Country manages more than 9,500 acres, with 1,000 acres in the Quail Country preserve, for deer, turkey, dove or pheasant hunting. Quail Country definitely caters to large corporate groups who want to mix hunting with business. All quail hunts are conducted with trained guides and dogs and specially equipped jeeps or from a custom designed "hunting buggy." Horseback quail hunting is also available.

Facilities*: 1,200-square-foot lodge with 15 bedrooms, conference room with visual aids for meetings, dining room, lounges with satellite TVs, fireplaces, sitting rooms, telephone rooms and country store; 13-station sporting clays course; and creeks and lakes for fishing.* **Season***: October 1 to March 31. Native quail hunting season runs from about Thanksgiving through February.* **Rates***: Contact Quail Country for packages and prices.* **More Information***: Quail Country Lodge and Conference Center, Rt. 1, Box 745, Arlington, GA 31713. 229/725-4645; fax 229/725-5443. Website: www.quailcountry.com.*

Rio Piedra Plantation

Rio Piedra Plantation is located on the banks of the Flint River in Mitchell County in a classic South Georgia quail hunting terrain of Spanish moss-draped oaks and hardwoods. The plantation supplements native quail with bobwhite quail, raised and early-released to covey like native birds. An Orvis-endorsed wingshooting destination, Rio Piedra packages range from half-day to three-day hunts with guide, dogs, jeep and meals, with and without lodging. The plantation also will arrange individual packages.

Facilities*: 9-bedroom lodge, private baths, dining room, Orvis Pro Shop, gun rental, shells for purchase and 10-station sporting clays course.* **Season***: October through March.* **Rates***: Contact Rio Piedra for current packages and rates.* **More Information***: Rio Piedra Plantation, 5749 Turkey Road, Camilla, GA 31730. 229/336-1677 or 800/538-8559; fax, 229/336-0058. Website: www.riopiedraplantation.com.*

Riverview Plantation

Stretching for miles along the Flint River in Mitchell County is Riverview Plantation, one of South Georgia's classic quail-hunting plantations. Home to five generations of the Cox family, Riverview's fertile soil has yielded cotton, peanuts, tobacco, pecans and grains and has been a refuge for wild game, fish and birds. In 1958, the Cox family opened their land to an exclusive clientele of sportsmen and began focusing on developing a substantial quail habitat. Riverview constantly grooms and cultivates the land for maximum quail production—planting corn, grain, millet, sorghum, peas, lespedezas and winter greens to supplement the native acorns, partridge pea, pine mast and beggar-lice. Riverview offers full-day hunts with guides, jeep and dogs. Trap shooting, skeet and trout fishing are also available.

Facilities*: 42 single rooms in 8 cottages; meals; pro shop with hunting clothes, accessories, shells, and gift items; gun rentals; skeet field; and ponds stocked with rainbow trout.* **Season***: Mid-October through March. Non-refundable deposits required. Reservations are necessary and must be booked early—many book a year or two ahead of time. Riverview hosts 30 guests at one time.* **Rates***: Contact Riverview for current rates.* **More Information***: Riverview Plantation, 11991 Riverview Road, Camilla, GA 31730. 229/294-4904; fax, 229/294-9851. Website: www.riverviewplantation.com.*

Southern Farms Hunting Lodge and Guide Service

Quail, deer and turkey can all be hunted on this working farm and hunting plantation. Southern Farms has more than 3,000 acres of red and white oak ridges, pine thickets and hardwood creek bottom and 1,500 acres of agricultural fields where corn, soybean, peanuts and summer and winter wheat is grown. Full- and half-day hunts with guides, jeep and dogs are offered. Both archery and gun deer hunting are available. Turkey hunting is for spring gobblers only. Harvested game will be quartered, packed in ice or frozen for full lodging guests.

Facilities: *Lodge includes meals; gun rental available; 15-foot towers and ground blinds.* **Rates**: *Contact Southern Farms for packages and prices. Deposits are required. Group discounts are available.* **More Information**: *Troy Kilby, owner, Southern Farms Hunting Lodge and Guide Service, 1080 Ivy Mill Road, Parrott, GA 31777. 888/326-3295 or 229/623-5206.*

Southpoint Plantation

In the same family for five generations, this 3,500-acre plantation was opened to the public for quail hunting in 1990. F&W Agriservices of Albany manages this Terrell County plantation. Full- and half-day hunts at Southpoint include guides, jeep, dogs, hunting license and lunch.

Facilities: *Lodge with main living area and meals, gun rentals, shells and practice targets.* **Season**: *October 1 to March 31.* **Rates**: *Contact Southpoint for packages and prices. Reservations required as amount of space is limited. There is an extra charge for cleaning, dressing and packaging birds.* **More Information**: *Jimmy Harris, manager, Southpoint Plantation, P.O. Box 4309, Albany, GA 31706. 229/888-6598.*

Wise Olde Pine Hunting Preserve

The folks at Wise Olde Pine say that everything is flexible except gun safety. There is no set schedule. Clay target shooting is always available. Hunters can bring their own dogs if they prefer. Quail hunting is the specialty at this Sumter County plantation but deer and turkey hunting are available, including deer bow season. The hunting preserve offers full- and half-day hunts with guides, jeep and dogs. Wise Olde Pine is a host for the Quail Unlimited Celebrity Hunt and the Lancaster Outdoor Bobwhite Classic every year.

Facilities: *Restored 3-bedroom 1850 log house with 2 fireplaces, central air and heat and kitchen; Big House dining room; gun rental and shells for sale.* **Season**: *October 15 through March 31.* **Rates**: *Contact Wise Olde Pine for current rates. Non-refundable deposits will guarantee reservation.* **More Information**: *Mickey and Connie Wise, owners, Wise Olde Pine Hunting Preserve, 590 Three Bridges Road, Americus, GA 31709. 229/846-5491.*

Wynfield Plantation

Piney woods, wiregrass meadows, fields of broomsage and brush and bottomlands dotted with hardwoods make up the diverse terrain at Wynfield Plantation. Wynfield, which is Orvis-endorsed, specializes in quail hunting, but also offers deer, turkey and wild boar. Full- and half-day hunts for quail include guides, jeep, dogs, lunch and hunting license. There are also combination hunts with quail and deer, turkey or wild boar. The sporting clays course at Wynfield has 21 shooting boxes spread over seven different fields and covering 10 acres of natural habitat. Each station is designed to match the environment encountered during a live hunt.

Facilities: *2-bedroom cabins with living room, wet bar, TV, bath, telephone and private porch; lodge with dining room and pro shop; lake; boats and tackle; and 21-station sporting clays course.* **Season**: *Open year-round.* **Rates**: *Contact Wynfield for current packages and rates.* **More Information**: *Larry L. Ruis, owner, Wynfield Plantation, 2413 Tarva Road, P.O. Box 71686, Albany, GA 31708. 229/889-0193. Website: www.wynfieldplantation.com.*

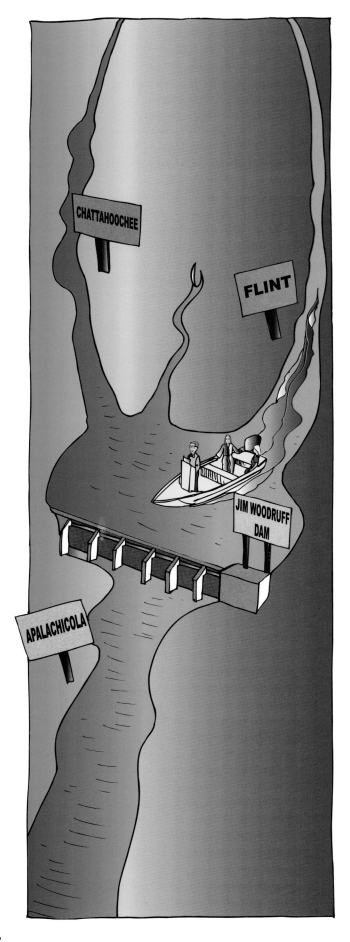

Section 8

Apalachicola River

WE FOLLOW RIO'S DIRECTIONS and "lock through" at Jim Woodruff Lock and Dam to begin a 106-mile journey down the remarkable Apalachicola River to the Gulf of Mexico.

On the Apalachicola River, use the Guidebook Section beginning on page 236 to explore: Torreya State Park Natural Area and its hiking trails, Apalachicola Bluff and Ravines Preserve, Apalachicola National Forest, Apalachicola River Wildlife and Environmental Area, Apalachicola Wildlife Management Area, Ed Ball Wildlife Management Area, Robert Brent Wildlife Management Area, Panhandle Pioneer Settlement near Blountstown, Fort Gadsden State Historic Site, Dead Lakes, the town of Apalachicola via a self-guided walking tour, Apalachicola National Estuarine Research Reserve, plus, the landings and marinas on the river and in the area around Apalachicola.

LOCKING THROUGH*

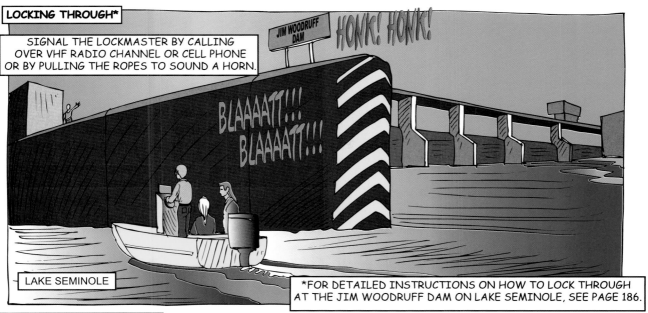

SIGNAL THE LOCKMASTER BY CALLING OVER VHF RADIO CHANNEL OR CELL PHONE OR BY PULLING THE ROPES TO SOUND A HORN.

JIM WOODRUFF DAM

HONK! HONK!

BLAAAATT!!!
BLAAAATT!!!

LAKE SEMINOLE

*FOR DETAILED INSTRUCTIONS ON HOW TO LOCK THROUGH AT THE JIM WOODRUFF DAM ON LAKE SEMINOLE, SEE PAGE 186.

THE LOWERING AND LIFTING PROCESS IS FAIRLY SLOW.

JIM WOODRUFF LOCK IS 82 FEET BY 450 FEET WITH A MAXIMUM LIFT OF 33 FEET.
IT OPERATES 24 HOURS A DAY, SEVEN DAYS A WEEK.

WHEN "LOCKING THROUGH" IS COMPLETED, YOU ARE ON THE SAME LEVEL AS THE RIVER.

APALACHICOLA RIVER

233

235

Section 8

Apalachicola River

SIGNIFICANT NATURAL AREAS

Torreya State Park Natural Area

Much of this park, which sits on the high bluffs overlooking the Apalachicola River, resembles the Appalachian Mountains, not only because of the steepness of the ravines, but because of the many flora that migrated to this region during the Ice Age and remained here at its end, perfectly at home in the cool, shaded climate. Further adding to the mountain illusion are several uncommonly clear creeks which bubble over tiny shoals of limestone rocks covered in moss. The creeks have shaped the ravines by cutting away the remains of ancient coast-line dunes here. Similarly, the Apalachicola River is working furiously on the adjacent sand hills to create the most visually stunning vistas in the state, the Apalachicola Bluffs. Several overlooks 125 feet or higher in the park illustrate the river's eastward migration over the ages. On the west bank is land the river has ground into submission eons ago—a vast expanse of wet and low floodplains covered in marshes and swamps. On the east bank is terrain the river is just beginning to sculpt—the high walls of multicolored sand, limestone and clay, which rise straight up from the river's edge.

From the surface of the river to the top of the bluffs and ravines, the floral scenery changes dramatically. Swamp forests of tupelo, willow and bald-cypress grow in standing water along the river. Large water hickory, swamp-chestnut oak and the rare U.S. Champion winged-elm rise above the floodplain, seasonally covered with nutrient-rich waters. Diminutive rare Florida yews and Torreya trees, which only grow here, hide out in the steep bluffs and narrow ravines. Giant magnolias, hickories and beech rise majestically above the hilltops.

More than 100 species of birds, including bald eagle, osprey (see page 257), white ibis, egret and great blue heron, can be seen in the area. Common wildlife include otter, bobcat, white-tailed deer, beaver, raccoon and the unusual Barbours map turtle.

The best way to see this natural area is to hike one of the three trails at Torreya State Park (see page 246).

How the Apalachicola Got its Name

Apalachicola, "meaning people of the ruling place," was an ancient Indian capital town located on the Chattahoochee River about 30 miles below present-day Columbus, Georgia. The Spanish built a fort there in 1689 and referred to the whole river as Rio de Los Apalachicolas after the Indian town.

When the English came to the area, however, they referred to the river as the Chattahoochee after the name of the Creek settlement, Chattahoochee Old Town, at today's Franklin, Georgia. So the name of the river at any one place and time depended on who controlled it militarily and who was drawing the maps.

Today, the river's name officially changes from Chattahoochee to Apalachicola at the Georgia-Florida state line, because that was the border established in 1781 between the English and Spanish territories.

 (continued on page 241)

...mpground

...s – family, youth
...e campgrounds –
...nes of Torreya

...d Hiking Trails

...most biologically
...nusual areas of
...reya tree, a
...clings to life in
...east bank of the
...hicola River.
...e river here with
...ar against the

2. Apalachicola Bluffs and Ravines Preserve

The Apalachicola River Bluffs originate in Southwest Georgia. They extend along the Flint River, from about 10 miles above the Woodruff Dam downstream along the east bank of the Apalachicola River for a distance of about 25 miles into Florida. Alum Bluff, which can be reached by the Garden of Eden Trail, is near the southern limit of the series of cliffs. This escarpment marks the western edge of the Tallahassee Hills, known as the Tifton Upland.

Robert Brent Wildlife Management Area

This 83,233-acre wildlife management area is one of the most popular deer and turkey hunting areas in the Florida Panhandle.

Florida National Scenic Trail in the Apalachicola National Forest

A 55-mile section of the Florida National Scenic Trail passes from west to east in the Apalachicola National Forest. The Apalachicola West Section, 34 miles, goes through the Apalachicola Ranger District. One of the longest and most remote hikes in Florida, this level, mostly single-lane track offers a true wilderness experience. The trailhead is in Camel Lake Campground.

Apalachicola National Forest

Water, trees and savannas cover most of ... national forest, the largest in Florida. Si... through it, including the Apalachicola, ... western boundary of the forest, and th...

Apalachicola River Wildlife and E...

More than 55,600 acres comprises thre... Apalachicola below Wewahitchka. Attra... deer hunters, most of whom like to hu... by boat.

Apalachicola Wildlife Managemen...

Hunters stalk deer, wild hog, gray squir... mink and otter in this 558,000-acre wi... is prevalent in the area, but they are pr...

4. Fort Gadsden State Historic Sit...

Between 1812 and 1852, four different ... nations occupied two forts on this strat... overlook to fight enemies either up or ... down the river.

Bristol

3

...Bridge
...ed the
...Bridge

Blountstown

Big Gully Landing

Camel Lake Campground

Estiffanulga

Wright Lake Cam...

4

Cotton Landing Campground

White Oak Landing

Ed Ball Wildlife M...

Deer, turkey, gray squ...
rabbit, raccoon, oposs...
coyote, beaver, armad...
and otter and migrato...
hunted in this 66,272...
management area.

Apalachicola River

...Pioneer
...t

...tory outdoor
...th 11 period
...hat reflect
...as it was in this
...840 to 1940

Dead Lakes State Recreation Area

Fishing, picnic area, hiking trails, showers and restrooms

Dead Lakes

Dead Lakes is an area created naturally when currents of the Apalachicola River formed a sandbar, partially blocking the mouth of its tributary, the Chipola River. Water flooded approximately 12,000 acres of river swamp, killing thousands of trees in the floodplain and giving the lake its name. The levees were later stabilized by a dam, which maintains the flooded swamp.

Dead Lakes State Recreation Area Campground

Wewahitchka

Jackson R...

...orida

...ge
...ove mouth: 79.4
...ty

Corps of Engineers Campgrounds

East Bank Campground (3)

River Junction Landing Campground (6)

Faceville Landing Campground (8)

Hales Landing Campground (14)

Neals Landing Campground (35)

State Parks

Seminole State Park (25)

Three Rivers State Recreation Area (41)

Commercial Marinas

(★ Indicates Boat Fuel Available)

★Wingate's Lodge (7)

Big Jim's Landing (22)

★Seminole Sportsman's Lodge (29)

★Trails End Marina (31)

★Seminole Lodge (44)

Corps of Engineers Day Use Areas

Jim Woodruff Dam Fishing Area (1)

Chattahoochee Park (4)

River Junction Landing (6)

Faceville Landing Park (8)

Hales Landing Park (14)

Reynoldsville Park (20)

Spring Creek Park (21)

Cypress Pond Park (27)

Rays Lake Park (28)

Cummings Landing Park (30)

Butlers Ferry Landing (32)

Fairchilds Park (33)

Desser Landing (34)

Neals Landing Park (35)

Parramore Landing (37)

Sneads Park (43)

Westbank Overlook (45)

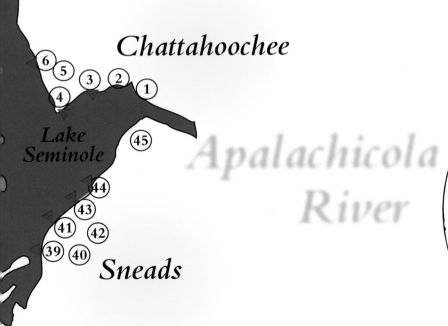

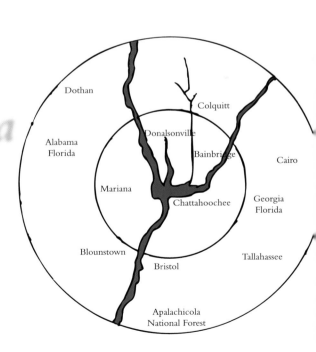

Jim Woodruff Dam
River miles above mouth:0
County: Seminole

County, Municipal Recreation Areas

Chattahoochee Athletic Park (2)

Horseshoe Bend Landing (9)

Earl May Boat Basin Park (10)

Cheney Griffin Park (11)

Big Slough Landing (12)

Flint River Landing (13)

Ten Mile Still Landing (16)

Ralph King Landing (17)

Smith Landing (18)

Decatur Landing (19)

Sealy Point Park (23)

Harvel Pond (24)

Buena Vista Park (36)

Arnold Landing (38)

Howells Landing (39)

Hiking Trails

Turkey Flight Overlook Trail (5)

Gopher Tortoise Trails (26)

Lakeside Trail (40)

Half Dry Creek Trail (42)

Wildlife Management Areas

Lake Seminole Wildlife Management Area (15)

Lake Seminole Wildlife Management Area

This wildlife management area consists of 16,895 acres, stretching across both Seminole and Decatur Counties and bordering much of Lake Seminole. Hunting, fishing, hiking, bird watching and boating can all be enjoyed within the WMA boundaries.

There are numerous park areas around the lake.

From Bainbridge take GA 253 south about 3 miles to Ten Mile Still Road. Turn left and go about 2 miles to Hales Landing on the left. There is a map there of each of the tracts of the WMA. Or contact the Georgia Department of Natural Resources, Wildlife Resources Division, 2024 Newton Road, Albany, GA 31707-3576. 229/430-4254.

Apalachee Wildlife Management Area

Covers 7,952 acres of land in Jackson County, Florida, and more than five miles along the lake's western shoreline. Fishing, wildlife viewing and seasonal hunting.

Other Features

Jim Woodruff Lock and Dam

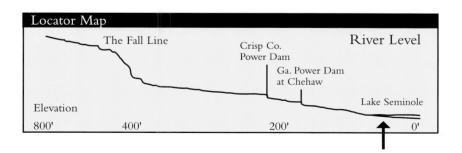

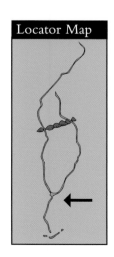

Apalachicola River from Woodruff Dam to the Bay

Flint River

Spring Creek

Chattahoochee

Chattahoochee River

Lake Seminole

US 90 Bridge

I-10 Bridge

Torreya State Par

Four different camp
and scout and two
sit amid the bluffs a
State Park.

1. Torreya State P

Located within one
diverse and topolog
Florida. Named for
nearly extinct speci
the steep ravines al
first 20 miles of the
Andrew Jackson cro
his army during the
Seminoles in 1818.

US 90 Bridge

Known as the
"Victory Bridge,"
this is the first bridge on
the Apalachicola River. The
old Works Progress
Administration Bridge, built in
the 1930s during the
Roosevelt Administration, is
visible just downstream.

3. Garden of Eden Trail and Alum Bluff Overlook

Amazed by the diversity, an early botanist
jested that this area was the original
Garden of Eden and that Noah made his
ark out of the Torreya tree. This "paleorefugia" or sanctuary for ancient flora and
fauna is perhaps the best place to explore
this part of Florida's scenery and notable
variety of rare and endangered species.
3.5 miles including an optional 0.5-mile
loop at Alum Bluff.

Biodiversity

The Apalachicola River corridor is one of the
most remarkable natural regions in the entire
United States. Habitats include pitcher plant
bogs, cypress swamps and hardwood forests. In
the upper part of the river is the highest diversity of reptile and amphibian species in the
country. The river basin contains America's
largest diversity of woody plant species. On a
square-mile basis, Apalachicola Bay is the most
productive estuary in the United States. It is a
breeding ground and an incubator for all types
of marine life.

Par
Set

A li
mus
stru
Flor
area

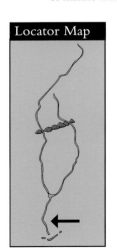

Locator Map

Locator Map

River Level

The Fall Line

Crisp Co.
Power Dam

Ga. Power Dam
at Chehaw

Lake Seminole

Elevation

800'   400'   200'

Jim Woodruff Lock and Dam
River miles above mouth: 106.3
Counties: Decatur (GA) Gadsden (FL)

I-10 Bridge
River miles above mouth: 100
Counties: Jackson and Gadsden

FL 20
River m
County

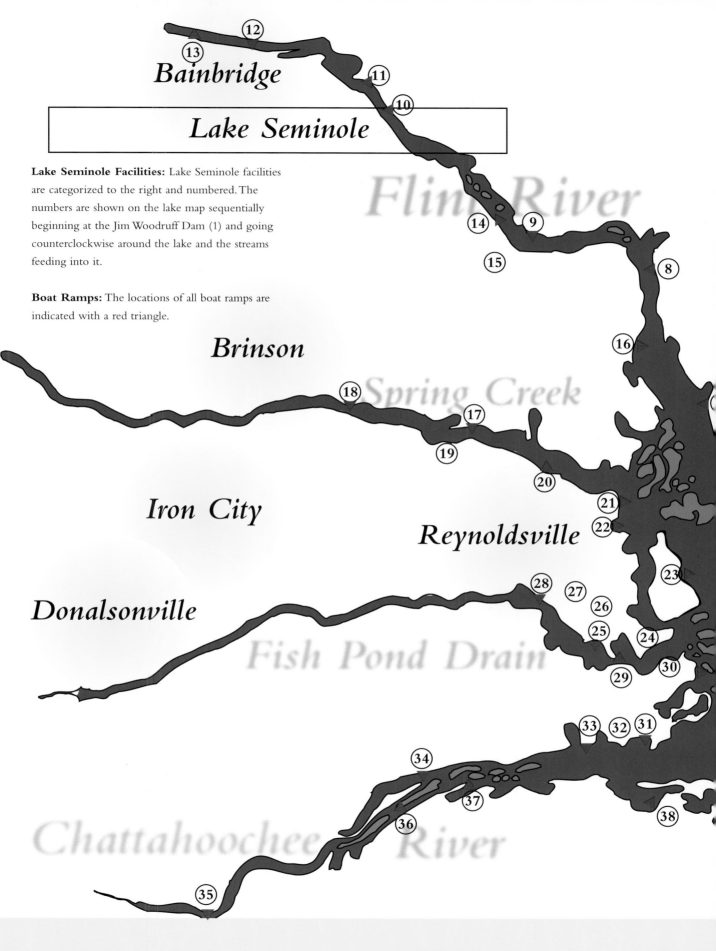

Bainbridge

Lake Seminole

Lake Seminole Facilities: Lake Seminole facilities are categorized to the right and numbered. The numbers are shown on the lake map sequentially beginning at the Jim Woodruff Dam (1) and going counterclockwise around the lake and the streams feeding into it.

Boat Ramps: The locations of all boat ramps are indicated with a red triangle.

Flint River

Brinson

Spring Creek

Iron City

Reynoldsville

Donalsonville

Fish Pond Drain

Chattahoochee River

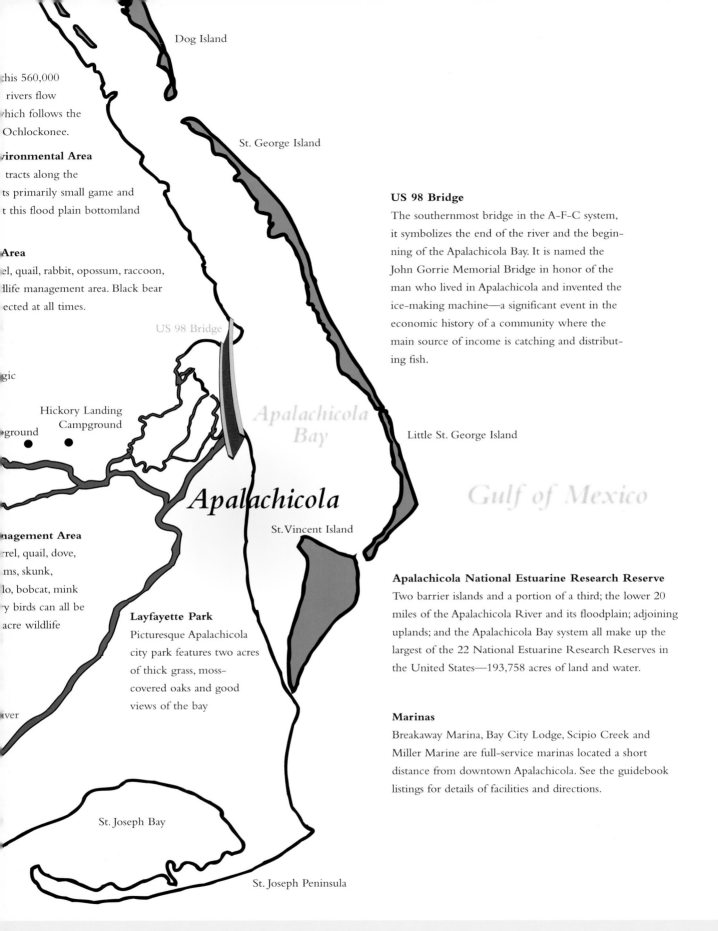

Dog Island

St. George Island

this 560,000
rivers flow
which follows the
Ochlockonee.

ironmental Area
tracts along the
ts primarily small game and
t this flood plain bottomland

Area
el, quail, rabbit, opossum, raccoon,
llife management area. Black bear
ected at all times.

US 98 Bridge

gic

Hickory Landing
Campground

ground

Apalachicola Bay

US 98 Bridge
The southernmost bridge in the A-F-C system,
it symbolizes the end of the river and the beginning of the Apalachicola Bay. It is named the
John Gorrie Memorial Bridge in honor of the
man who lived in Apalachicola and invented the
ice-making machine—a significant event in the
economic history of a community where the
main source of income is catching and distributing fish.

Little St. George Island

Gulf of Mexico

Apalachicola

St. Vincent Island

nagement Area
rel, quail, dove,
ms, skunk,
lo, bobcat, mink
y birds can all be
acre wildlife

iver

Layfayette Park
Picturesque Apalachicola
city park features two acres
of thick grass, moss-
covered oaks and good
views of the bay

Apalachicola National Estuarine Research Reserve
Two barrier islands and a portion of a third; the lower 20
miles of the Apalachicola River and its floodplain; adjoining
uplands; and the Apalachicola Bay system all make up the
largest of the 22 National Estuarine Research Reserves in
the United States—193,758 acres of land and water.

Marinas
Breakaway Marina, Bay City Lodge, Scipio Creek and
Miller Marine are full-service marinas located a short
distance from downtown Apalachicola. See the guidebook
listings for details of facilities and directions.

St. Joseph Bay

St. Joseph Peninsula

John Gorrie Bridge (US 98)
River miles above mouth: 0
County: Gulf

Cheney Griffin Park in Bainbridge

Bainbridge

Bainbridge

The river runs through Bainbridge.

Old Power Dam on Spring Creek at Decatur Landing

5. Cheney Griffin Park

Spanish moss-covered live oaks grace the 50-foot boardwalk that overlooks a bend in the river. From this strategic location, all four bridges that cross the river in Bainbridge are visible: the US 27 Business Bridge and the CSX Railroad Bridge upstream, and the US 27/82 Bypass Bridge and the CSX Railroad Bridge downstream.

Earl May Boat Basin Boat Ramp

east bank inlet, just below the US 27/84 Bridge

7. Earl May Boat Basin

Boat ramp, campsites, picnic shelters with grills, picnic tables, playground, fishing ponds, steam-powered sawmill, historic steam-powered train engine, baseball and softball fields, restrooms and drinking water

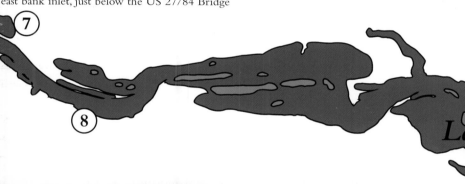

Lake Seminole

8. State Docks Spring

West bank. Marked with buoys. 31° 53' 21.6" 84° 36' 48.6"

Boat Trips

Wingate's Lodge on Lake Seminole is a good location to begin a boat trip to Apalachicola Bay. Boats go through the lock at Jim Woodruff Dam on Lake Seminole. From there it's 106 miles to Apalachicola Bay. A caution: There is no gas on the Apalachicola until boaters reach the marinas just north of the Bay.

GA 37 Bridge to the County Line Boat Ramp

Camilla

Locator Map

The Fall Line

Elevation

800'   400'

Camilla

About 10 miles east of the river via GA Hwy 37

Flint River

1. GA 37 Boat Ramp

On east bank, just above the GA 37 Bridge

GA 37 Bridge

①

Newton

Boat Trip

Newton is a good starting point for trips in small motor boats up and down the river. Limestone banks, grand cypress and sycamore trees and occasional springs characterize the trip in both directions.

Paul L

Newton

About 1 mile west of the river via GA 37

GA 37

River miles above mouth: 69.5

Counties: Baker and Mitchell

Bainbridge

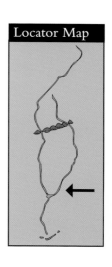

Locator Map

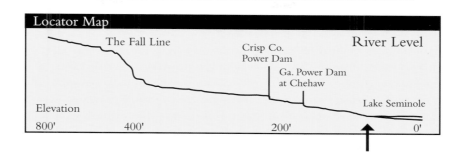

Locator Map

The Fall Line

Crisp Co.
Power Dam

Ga. Power Dam
at Chehaw

River Level

Lake Seminole

Elevation

800'   400'   200'   0'

1. Hog Parlor Spring

So called because hogs from a nearby farm once
frequented this spring and the surrounding banks

①

Flin

Alligators

Boat slips at Lunker Lodge on

Mussels

With its temperate climate and diverse topography, Georgia has one of the richest and most diverse freshwater mussel populations in the world—more than 100 species. Purple bankclimber, southern fatmucket, washboard, little spectaclecase, green floater, gulf moccasinshell, sculptured pigtoe and elephantear are some of the 29 species of mussels that live in the Flint.

3. County Line Boat Ramp
On east bank, 24.5 miles below the GA 37 Bridge

2. Bovine Spring
So called because cows, coming here to drink from the river, have scarred and eroded the bank. West bank 31° 06' 07.1" 84° 30' 31.2"

Boat Trip
From the County Line Boat Ramp, small motor boats can navigate as far upstream as Albany or go downstream to Bainbridge and Lake Seminole.

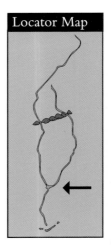

Locator Map

River Level

Crisp Co.
Power Dam

Ga. Power Dam
at Chehaw

Lake Seminole

200'   0'

Horseshoe Bend

Double Spring

eLoach at Bovine Springs

Ichawaynochaway Creek

Cypress pond

Boat ramps at C[...]

3. Big Slough Boat Ramp

On east bank, about 3.5 miles above the US 27 (Bus) Bridge

4. Cheney Griffin Park Boat Ramp

On east bank, just below the US 27 (Bus) Bridge

US 27 (Bus) Bridge

2. Flint River Landing

On west bank, 4.5 miles above the US 27 (Bus) Bridge. Above Bainbridge the river begins to back up, forming the Flint River arm of Lake Seminole. Flint River Landing, about 4.5 miles north of the city, is considered to be the northernmost "Seminole" boat ramp on the river.

US 27/84 Bypass Bridge

6. [...]
Or[...]

 e Seminole

US 27 Business
River miles above mouth: 29.0
County: Decatur

(continued from page 236

Apalachicola Bluffs and Ravines Preserve

The Apalachicola River Bluffs originate in Southwest Georgia and extend along the Flint River, from about 10 miles above the Woodruff Dam (see page 163) downstream along the east bank of the Apalachicola River for a distance of about 25 miles, into Florida. Alum Bluff, which can be reached by the Garden of Eden Trail, is near the southern limit of the cliffs. This escarpment marks the western edge of the Tallahassee Hills, also known as the Tifton Upland.

During its long geologic history, the river has migrated eastward, eroding these highlands and leaving behind a broad floodplain of alluvial deposits. Erosion by the river's eastern streams has caused a series of deep ravines, many of which form steepheads, or natural amphitheaters, at the edge of the uplands. An unusual physical feature, a steephead is formed when riverbeds cut beneath the water table and the seeping water undercuts the slope.

The Apalachicola Bluffs and Ravines Preserve is located within this region of Florida. Owned by the Nature Conservancy of Florida, the preserve protects 6,267 acres of pine and sandhill uplands, river bluffs, spring-fed creeks, steepheads and ravines—this being one of the few areas where steephead ravines exist. It also provides a refuge for gopher tortoise (see page 160), indigo snake and several rare plants, some found nowhere else on Earth, such as the Florida Torreya and the Florida yew.

The region is biologically unique to Florida and is home to many species more commonly found in the Appalachian Mountains, such as mountain laurel and wild hydrangea. Plants are believed to have continuously occupied the highlands above the Apalachicola River since the formation of the Apalachicola River Valley, roughly 18 million years ago. This is unlike other parts of Florida that have been inundated with sea water since that time. Much of the unusual floristic diversity of the Apalachicola River region is attributable to the continuity of the region with the Southern Appalachians, both in space and time. The fact that the Chattahoochee and the Flint Rivers, which form the Apalachicola River at Chattahoochee, Florida, have their headwaters in the lower Appalachians and the adjacent Piedmont respectively, adds further significance to this region's connection with areas of northern influence. It is also interesting to note that all other rivers draining into Florida have their origin with the Coastal Plain.

The best way to explore the preserve is to hike the Garden of Eden Trail (see page 256).

Directions to Preserve Offices: *Liberty County. From Bristol, Florida, take SR 12 3.9 miles northeast to CR 270. Turn left and go 2.8 miles to the Apalachicola Bluffs and Ravines sign on the left. Turn left onto the dirt road and go 0.9 miles to the preserve offices.* **More Information**: *The Nature Conservancy, 625 N. Adams St., Tallahassee, FL 32301. 850/222-0199. The preserve is open for self-guided tours during daylight hours only. There is no water, facilities or staff with regular hours on-site. The local preserve caretaker can be reached at 850/643-2756.*

The Torreya Tree

"The Torreya is found only within a 25-mile radius on the Apalachicola, and its only close relatives are in California, China, and Japan. An evergreen, it has shining rigid narrow needles an inch long, spreading wide from its branches in double ranks. Its fruit is dark purple, the shape of a plum and the size of an olive. Insects rarely attack it. It has been transplanted successfully as far east as Tallahassee, 60 miles away, and has been grown there from seed. But to see the Torreya in its natural habitat, you must go to Torreya State Park....

"Among the park's pines and magnolias and deciduous hardwoods, the Torreya grows on angled hillsides leading down to the Apalachicola. Two other rare specimens also grow in Torreya State Park. One of them, the Florida yew, is rarer even than the Torreya; its needles are shorter, and it bears its nutlike fruit in a pulpy red cup. The other, Chapman's rhododendron, an evergreen shrub with tiny pink flowers, is found only in a few parts of the northern panhandle and can be seen in spring bloom in the park."

The Other Florida by Gloria Jahoda

The Dead Lakes

The bleached skeletons of thousands of dead cypress trees rise from the water at Dead Lakes, a monument to how rivers shape the terrain over thousands of years. Dead Lakes is an area created naturally when currents of the Apalachicola River, particularly those flowing during a bad flood in 1860, formed a sandbar, or point bar, partially blocking the mouth of its tributary, the Chipola River. (See page 275 of "How Rivers Work" for more on point bars.) Water flooded approximately 12,000 acres of river swamp, killing thousands of trees in the floodplain and giving the lake its name. Later, a logjam from beavers and lumberjacks at the mouth of the Chipola worsened the blockage. The swamp cypresses, accustomed to seasonal dry periods, withered and died in droves. Their carcasses, still standing, inspired the area's name.

The best way to see the Dead Lakes area is to visit the Dead Lakes State Recreation Area (see page 247). Numerous animals find refuge in the park—fox, cotton rat, raccoon, opossum, deer, rabbit, skunk, beaver, turtle, snake and alligator. The primary plant communities found at Dead Lakes are river swamp, swamp forest and pine flatwood. The uplands are covered with longleaf pines, while Southern magnolia, sweetbay and cypress trees border the wetlands. Other hardwoods include tupelo, sycamore, red maple, sweet gum, Southern red oak, sand post oak and turkey oak. Titi and other water-loving species grow along the border of the lake near the boat ramp. Former residents of the area introduced non-native plants, which can still be found in the park. But, in keeping with Florida Park Service land management philosophy, the practice of removing the exotic plants to make room for native plants is ongoing.

Directions: *Gulf County. From Wewahitchka, Florida, take FL 71 about 2 miles north. Park entrance is on the right.* **More Information**: *Dead Lakes State Recreation Area, P.O. Box 989, Wewahitchka, FL 32465. 850/639-2702.*

NATURE-BASED EDUCATIONAL CENTERS

Apalachicola National Estuarine Research Reserve

The lower 20 miles of the Apalachicola River. Its floodplain and adjoining uplands. The Apalachicola Bay system. Two barrier islands and a portion of a third. These all comprise the Apalachicola National Estuarine Research Reserve—193,758 acres of land and water—the largest of the 22 national estuarine research reserves in the United States.

Beaches, oyster bars, marshes, forested floodplains and sandhills are some of the habitats found within these environments and living within them are dozens and dozens of amphibians, reptiles and mammals, as well as more than 1,300 plant species, 103 of them threatened or endangered. The reserve and surrounding drainage basin are among the most important bird habitats in the Southeast United

Chipola Cutoff

In the late 1800s—several years after Apalachicola River currents formed a sandbar at the mouth of the Chipola River—the U.S. Army Corps of Engineers dug a two-mile shortcut from the Apalachicola to the Chipola River near the eastern edge of the town of Wewahitchka, Florida. The Chipola Cutoff, as it was called, saved steamboats dozens of miles going from the Chipola River to the Apalachicola, but also allowed the faster-flowing Apalachicola a release valve to push large volumes of water into the slower moving Chipola. In fact, the Apalachicola sends more water into the cutoff than into its natural channel. You can actually see the muddy waters of the Apalachicola boil into the clear waters of the Chipola. The cutoff ensures that the Dead Lakes area remains flooded.

The Corps has informally talked about putting in a dike to redirect more water flow down the Apalachicola, but opposition by locals and state officials precludes that action, as well as closing the cutoff altogether. Taking away the cutoff might seriously affect the Dead Lakes, a favorite hangout for fishermen, and dry up the nearby swamps, one of the richest sources of tupelo honey nectar (see sidebar page 249).

States—more than 300 species, with 20 designated as endangered, threatened or species of special concern. And then there are the fish—more than 180 species have been documented in the river and bay systems, including American eel, striped basse, shoal bass, striped mullet, speckled trout, flounder and red drum.

Two goals of the reserve are to educate the public about these estuarine ecosystems and promote resource protection. Through hands-on exhibits; a guest lecture series; interpretive field trips and hikes into the river, bay and barrier island habitats; teacher workshops; classroom curriculum materials; traveling displays and publications, the reserve reaches an audience that includes school groups, environmental management professionals and the general public.

Facilities*: Robert L. Howell Building with reserve headquarters and 100-seat auditorium; research building with 150-square-foot lab facility; and the estuarine walk with freshwater, brackish water and salt water tanks.* **Days/Hours***: Open weekdays, 8 a.m. to 5 p.m. Guests are welcome during regular hours, and educational groups may call to schedule a program for your group.* **Directions***: Franklin County. From downtown Apalachicola, take Market Street northwest (away from the Bay) to "M" Avenue. Turn left and go 2 blocks to 7th Street. Turn right. ANERR is on the right.* **More Information***: Apalachicola National Estuarine Research Reserve, 261 7th Street, Apalachicola, FL 32320. 850/653-8063. Website: www.apalachicola.com/apalachicola/reserve.html.*

HISTORIC SITES

Gregory House

In 1849 planter James Gregory built this impressive home at Ocheesee Landing, across the river and a short distance downstream from its current location. There Gregory operated a cotton plantation in the fertile river floodplains. By 1851, the well-established estate included a steamboat landing, cotton gin, warehouse and many slave quarters.

After the Civil War, Gregory lost his estate, but established another successful plantation in Gainesville, Florida, using freed slaves as share-croppers. He never went back to Ocheesee, but his youngest daughter Chaffa, after paying back taxes and repairing the house, returned to live in the home until her death in 1916. The house then fell into disrepair. Outlaws, tramps and river rats hid out on the property until 1935 when the Florida government acquired it from the Neal Lumber Company of Blountstown.

Over the next three years, the state undertook an ambitious project to dismantle the house, float it across the river and reassemble it where it currently stands, on a high bluff overlooking the river in Torreya State Park. The house looks the same as before the Civil War, except for the five-foot high brick pillars to keep it above floodwaters. It has authentic 1850s furnishings and the original lumber,

Mullet Fishing

Mullet is a common name for the small, spiny-finned fishes found in coastal marine and brackish water in all tropical and temperate seas. It is the lowest-priced fish in the market, not surprising considering that it teems everywhere near the Apalachicola Bay, in saltwater and fresh. Mullets live near shore, often around islands, feeding on minute organisms filtered from the water through their sievelike gill rakers. There are about 95 known species of mullet, all edible and tasty. Just ask the locals who like to catch them out of the bay, particularly with a cast net.

Whether from a dock, pier, boat or while wading in the water, anyone can catch a mullet. Look for schools of mullet running near the surface, their heads poking out of the water. Take a net and with as much skill and technique as possible—sort of like a lasso—fling it out to make it spread fully. Casting the perfect net has been described as a zen-like pleasure. It almost doesn't matter if the fish are hauled in, it's how the net spreads, some say. Want to give it a spin? Most local hardware and bait-and-tackle stores sell the nets.

complete with wooden pegs instead of nails. To see the original Gregory House site, look down the river from the edge of the lawn. Swamp hardwoods like cypress cover the former cotton fields.

Entrance to the house is limited to regular 45-minute tours led by park rangers. Rangers dress in 19th-century clothing and give candlelight tours of the home one evening each year, generally the second week of May.

Facilities: *See Torreya State Park, page 246.* **Days/Hours**: *Tours begin at 10 a.m. weekdays and at 10 a.m., 2 p.m. and 4 p.m. weekends and holidays.* **Fees**: *Adults, $1; children under 13, 50¢.* **Directions to Torreya State Park**: *Liberty County. From Bristol, Florida, go north on FL 12 for 4 miles. Turn left on FL 270 and continue for about 7.5 miles. Turn left on CR 1641, which soon enters Torreya State Park.*

Fort Gadsden State Historic Site

On Prospect Bluff, 18 miles upstream of Apalachicola on the east bank of the Apalachicola River, only small earthen walls give testament to the site's bloody history. Between 1812 and 1852, four nations occupied two forts on this strategic overlook to fight enemies either up or down the river. The British constructed the first fortification at the beginning of the War of 1812 to recruit free blacks, ex-slaves and Seminoles to aid in their fight against the United States, whose territory extended to what is today the southern border of Georgia, about 50 miles due north.

Whether sympathizing with the former slaves, or relishing the trouble they might cause his former foes, the British post commander Lt. Col. Edward Nicholls, at the end of the war in 1815, turned the fort over to a group of ex-slaves and free blacks under the leadership of a mulatto from Pensacola. Little is known about him except his name, Garçon. Along with the fort, the British handed over nine cannons, 2,500 muskets, 500 carbines, 500 pistols, 500 swords and 700 kegs of gunpowder.

Over the next year, runaway slaves, free blacks and Seminoles joined forces with those at the fort to create a quasi-independent state of about 1,000 settlers who farmed and traded along a 50-mile strip of the Apalachicola River Valley.

The United States considered them a danger and threatened destruction of the fort. General Andrew Jackson complained to the Spanish, then nominal authorities of Florida. He claimed that the Negro Fort, as it was called, protected renegades, pirates and Seminoles who plundered the American border as well as slaves who were the rightful property of American owners.

The Spanish governor in Pensacola responded that the blacks' only crime was wanting to live freely. And Seminoles who lived just south of the United States countered that it was the Americans who crossed the border to attack them. Nevertheless, Jackson pressed on, ordering the construction of Fort Scott near present-day Chattahoochee,

Seminole Indians

After the Creek Indian War of 1814, thousands of Indians from Georgia and Alabama fled south into Spanish La Florida. There, they joined other tribes whose members had been scattered throughout the peninsula for thousands of years. The core group of these tribes called themselves *yat'siminoli* or "free people" due to the fact that their ancestors had resisted Spanish and English attempts at conquering and converting them for so many years. English speakers referred to these tribes as *Seminolies*, or Seminoles—a word thought to be an English corruption of the Spanish word *cimmarones*, which means wild ones.

Runaway slaves joined forces with the Seminoles, receiving protection in exchange for a portion of their crops. Known as "Black Seminoles," they were fierce fighters who, like their Indian counterparts, were determined to preserve their freedom.

Spurred by Andrew Jackson's vigorous policy of Indian removal, three wars took place between the Seminoles and U.S. forces. Jackson invaded Florida in pursuit of the Seminoles, forcing some of them to Indian Territory during the First Seminole War from 1817 to 1819.

The Second Seminole War broke out in 1835. Lasting seven years, it was the longest and most costly of the Indian-removal wars fought east of the Mississippi. In the end, most Seminoles surrendered and moved to Indian Territory while a small group fled into the Everglades. From 1855 to 1858, those remaining fought on, but in the end, most were sent west. In 1970, the U.S. government awarded the Seminoles more than $12 million for land taken from them.

Florida, a border town between Spanish Territory and the United States on the Apalachicola River. Supplies for the new fort had to come from New Orleans up the Apalachicola River, meaning naval ships would pass under the guns of the Negro Fort.

In early July 1816, the Americans—with two supply ships and two gunboats—dropped anchor in the Apalachicola Bay. Blacks and Indians ambushed five sailors sent to shore for water, killing all but one, who escaped back to his ship. From Fort Scott, Col. Duncan Clinch dispatched two companies of soldiers and a band of Seminole allies to rendezvous with the gunboats.

On July 27 a Negro Fort cannon took aim at an American vessel, but the 24-pound shot fell short, falling harmlessly in the water. The U.S. gunboats returned fire. After several near misses, a 12-pound "hot shot" heated by an onboard stove landed directly in the fort's magazine. Shaking the ground for miles and reportedly heard as far away as Pensacola, the explosion blew the Negro Fort to oblivion. Of the 300—many woman and children—who took refuge at the fort from the American force, only 30 survived.

"The scene ... was horrible beyond description," recalled one U.S. soldier. "Hundreds of lifeless bodies were stretched on the plains, buried in sand and rubbish or suspended from the top of pines."

Garçon and an Indian leader survived the blast, but the American-allied Seminoles burned them at the stake. The blacks along the river-banks abandoned their settlements, many fleeing to the central Florida wilderness. Native Americans who lived in villages on the river soon suffered the same fate as the blacks. Two years later, while leading a force down the river to destroy Seminole villages, Andrew Jackson instructed Lt. James Gadsden to build the fort which bears his name on the same site.

The United States maintained Fort Gadsden until Spain ceded Florida to the United States in 1821. It remained unused until 1862, when the Confederate Army occupied the site to defend the Florida interior from Union ships running up the Apalachicola River. The troops abandoned the position a year later because of the threat of malaria, a common illness in the lowland swamps of Florida. Today, the King's Colors and the Twenty Star Stars and Stripes, the flags of 19th-century England and the United States, respectively, fly over the graveyard near the museum.

Facilities: *Small outdoor museum with interpretive exhibits on its history, picnic area with grills, restrooms and drinking water.* **Days/Hours**: *Open daily, year-round, 8 a.m. to 8 p.m., but usually closes around sunset in the winter.* **Fees**: *None.* **Directions**: *Liberty County. From Sumatra, go south on FL 65 for about 4 miles, then turn right on FSR 129 and drive about 2 miles.* **More Information**: *Apalachicola Ranger District, USDA Forest Service, P.O Box 579, FL 20, Bristol, FL 32321. 850/643-2282.*

Apalachicola River History

The arrival of the Spanish in the 1500s transformed Native American society in the Florida Territory. As Franciscan friars opened missions across the Panhandle, Indian populations plummeted, mostly due to exposure to European diseases.

Armed conflict added to the disruption of Indian life for the next three centuries as Spain, England and the United States maneuvered for control of north Florida. Georgia Creeks, in cooperation with the British, raided the Spanish and their allies, the Apalachee tribe from Tallahassee and the smaller Apalachicola tribe, who lived in the Apalachicola River Valley. During this time, these tribes continued to visit the islands and coast for hunting, fishing and shellfish harvesting.

In the 1830s and '40s, the United States forcibly removed from northwest Florida most of the remaining Creeks, Apalachee, Apalachicola and related tribes, who together were known as the Seminoles (see sidebar page 244). The descendants of those who continued to resist populate several towns on the river, including Blountstown, named after an Indian chief whose royal lineage has since continued for more than 100 years.

MUSEUMS

Panhandle Pioneer Settlement

This living history outdoor museum proves what a community can do when they have a vision and good volunteer help. The town of Blountstown has relocated more than 11 period structures, including a post office, high school gymnasium, blacksmith shop, church, school and several homes, to this site to establish a pioneer settlement that reflects Florida life as it was in the area around the turn of the 19th century. Tours feature volunteers in period dress giving folklife demonstrations. Annual events include a Pioneer Day, the third Saturday in October.

Facilities: *Period structures dating from 1840 to 1940.* **Days/Hours**: *Open to the general public, September 1 through May 31, Tuesday, Thursday, Friday and Saturday, noon to 4 p.m. CST; June 1 through Aug. 31, open Tuesday, Thursday and Saturday, 9 a.m. until 1 p.m. CST. Private group tours are available by appointment.* **Fees**: *Adults, $2; children, $1.* **Directions**: *Calhoun County. In Blountstown, Florida, take FL 20 west to 19 Street. Turn right and follow to Sam Atkins Park. Follow the signs. The settlement is located on the north side of the park.* **More Information**: *Panhandle Pioneer Settlement, P.O. Box 215, Blountstown, FL 32424. 850/674-8055 or 850/674-4516. Or Calhoun County Chamber of Commerce, 340-B E. Central Avenue, Blountstown, FL 32424. 850/674-4519; fax, 850/674-4962.*

PARKS

Torreya State Park

Located within one of the most biologically diverse and topologically unusual areas in the state, this park has a long and distinguished natural history (see page 236). The park is named after the Torreya tree, a nearly extinct species that clings to life in the steep ravines along the east bank of the first 20 miles of the Apalachicola River (see sidebar page 255).

When humans first came to this area is uncertain, but a number of Indian sites have been discovered in the park. General Andrew Jackson crossed the river here with his army during the first war against the Seminoles in 1818. From 1840 to 1910, when the Apalachicola served as a commercial transportation corridor, more than 200 steamboats loaded with cotton, timber or other goods traveled its channel. Planter James Gregory built a grand estate across the river from the park at Ocheesee Landing in 1849. During the Civil War, six Confederate cannons stood guard over the highest bluff; the remains of the gun pit can be seen along the Apalachicola River Bluffs Trail. In 1935 the Civilian Conservation Corps moved the Gregory House to its present location overlooking the river in the state park.

Facilities: *Campground (see page 251), picnic shelters, picnic area, hiking*

Longleaf Pine

"The longleaf pine is an unusual tree. Its seedling remains for as long as six years or more in what is called the 'grass stage.' The bud of the seedling tree stays close to the ground, sometimes buried in sand, while a plume of long, dark green, shiny needles waves above it like a shaving brush. During this time the tree is sending its life support system—its taproot—down several feet before beginning its above-ground growth.

"This unusual growth pattern is a safety feature against the frequent lightning fires that often swept through Florida's pine flatwoods in earlier days. The long, moist needles of the grass stage protect the bud from heat. When it finally starts to grow, the longleaf pine shoots up quickly, growing as much as a meter or more (three to four feet) in a year, raising the bud out of reach of the next low-burning forest fire.

"Mature longleaf pines can reach 500 years of age and have tall, straight trunks about half a meter or more in diameter (about two feet). The bark is thick, insulating the trunk from fire. The needles grow in clusters of three, from 25 to 51 centimeters (10–20 inches) long, the longest needles of any pine. Cones are large—sometimes 30 cm (a foot) long—and have thick scales with small, curved prickles."

The Young Naturalist's Guide to Florida by Peggy Sias Lantz and Wendy A. Hale

trails (see page 255), guided tours of the Gregory House (see page 243). **Days/Hours**: *Open daily, 8 a.m. until sunset.* **Fees**: *$2 per vehicle.* **Directions**: *Liberty County. From Bristol, Florida, go north on FL 12 for 4 miles. Turn left on FL 270 and continue for about 7.5 miles. Turn left on CR 1641 and follow to the end (about 7 miles).* **More Information**: *Torreya State Park, Route 2, Box 70, Bristol, FL 32321. 850/643-2674. Website: www.dep.state.fl.us/parks.*

Dead Lakes State Recreation Area

Before becoming a park in 1974, this 83-acre state recreation area was a fish hatchery built by the Works Progress Administration—a New Deal agency—and operated by the Florida Game Commission from 1936 to 1951. A variety of activities have taken place here. As late as 1944, Spanish moss was collected from trees, hung to dry and used for packing material and furniture stuffing (see sidebar this page). Cedar shake shingles for roofing were once made here. A still for turpentining (see sidebar page 248), a major industry in the 1950s, was just outside the park's boundaries. (In the park, you can still see "cat faces," V-shaped cuts in a pine tree that allowed the sap to drip out and collect into buckets that hung just below the cuts.) Tupelos, one of the most common hardwoods in the park, once supported a thriving beekeeping industry. Bees kept here produced 1,000 barrels of tupelo honey (see sidebar page 249) annually.

Two ponds and one of the two structures constructed by the WPA —a house for the resident biologist—remain standing. The ponds have the same fish found in the Dead Lakes (see page 242)—bass, bream, crappie, gar and carp.

Facilities: *Boat ramp into the West Arm Creek section of the Dead Lakes, campground (see page 253), fishing, picnic area, hiking trails, showers and restrooms.* **Days/Hours**: *Open daily, year-round, 8 a.m. until sunset. The gate is locked at sunset, but arrangements can be made ahead of time to enter the park after dark.* **Fees**: *Day use, $2 per vehicle. The entrance station on the park brochure map does not exist; payment is on the honor system.* **Directions**: *Gulf County. From Wewahitchka, Florida, take FL 71 about 2 miles north. Park entrance on right.* **More Information**: *Dead Lakes State Recreation Area, P.O. Box 989, Wewahitchka, FL 32465. 850/639-2702.*

Lafayette Park

This picturesque Apalachicola city park features two acres of thick grass and moss-covered oaks. When it opened in 1832, the park was out in the country. The original city grew along the riverside, not the bay shore. Stately homes on the park perimeter came later, beginning in the 1890s timber boom. Marsh grass runs along the water now, but there was a sandy beach here before the 1935 causeway for the bay bridge altered the bay current.

Facilities: *Picnic tables, 100-foot pier for cast net fishing, gazebo, interpretive signage and playground.* **Days/Hours**: *Open daily, year-round for day*

Spanish Moss

A rootless plant, Spanish moss is often seen hanging in long, gray strands from the trunks and branches of trees, especially live oak. A member of the pineapple family, Spanish moss is a flowering, perennial, mosslike epiphyte —a plant that grows on another plant but is not a parasite and produces its own food by photosynthesis. It is native to the western hemisphere from Argentina to the southern United States and is the only species of the pineapple family indigenous to the United States. The stem of the plant, which attains a length of six feet, is slender and threadlike and is covered with small scales that enable it to absorb moisture. The leaves and yellow flowers are inconspicuous. The fruit is a capsule.

As late as 1944, Spanish moss was collected from trees, hung to dry in the sun or sheds like tobacco and used for packing material and furniture stuffing. Moss gatherers would reach up with bamboo poles to take down from live oak trees strands of the moss. For half a year the moss dried, often on wire fences in the yards of the collectors. After that they would take the moss to a nearby city where the strands would be ginned, or separated from their outer husks. Mostly poor rural farmers, both black and white, these moss collectors received pennies a pound for their labor. Sporadic moss collecting continued for a number of years to supply the few upholsterers who still preferred moss to other filler.

use only. **Directions**: *Franklin County. In the Apalachicola Historic District on Avenue B between 13th and 15th Streets.* **More Information**: *Apalachicola City Hall, 1 Avenue E, Apalachicola, FL 32320. 850/653-9319.*

WILDLIFE MANAGEMENT AREAS

Robert Brent Wildlife Management Area

At 83,233-acres, this is one of the most popular deer hunting areas in the Florida Panhandle. One of its natural draws is the diverse habitat of pine woodlands and hardwood steephead ravines, which tend to provide drainage to the creeks in the area. These ravines are found mostly in the northwestern corner of the WMA—the part that is in the Apalachicola River watershed, just below Torreya State Park. Roads here tend to be sandy and are generally accessible by both two- and four-wheel drive vehicles.

Besides deer, there is a good turkey population. Other wildlife available here are wild hog, gray squirrel, quail, rabbit, raccoon, opossum, coyote, skunk, beaver, bobcat, mink, otter and migratory birds.

Camping is prohibited. Be sure to check on local regulations before hunting. Hunting permits, state licenses and migratory waterfowl stamps may be required. Fishing and hunting regulation booklets are available free of charge from the Florida Fish and Wildlife Commission.

Facilities: *None.* **Days/Hours**: *Open daily, 24 hours.* **Directions**: *Gadsden and Liberty Counties, Florida. There are several points of access. It is best to get a map of the WMA.* **More Information**: *Florida Fish and Wildlife Conservation Commission, Northwest Region, 1911 Highway 2321, Panama City, FL 32409-1658. 850/265-3677. Website: www.state.fl.us/fwc.*

Apalachicola National Forest

Water, trees and savannas cover most of this 560,000-acre national forest, the largest in Florida. Six rivers flow through it, including the Apalachicola, which follows the western boundary of the forest, and the Ochlockonee, which divides the forest into two administrative sections, the Wakulla and Apalachicola Ranger Districts.

Historical evidence suggests few Indians lived in this forest, although the Apalachee Indians settled north and south of it. Creeks and Seminoles traveled to those areas in the 1700s and early 1800s. But after the United States gained control of Florida from Spain in 1821, most of the area went into private hands. After extensive turpentining and logging exhausted the pine and hardwood forests between 1880 and 1920, much of the land was abandoned and small towns along the Apalachicola Northern Railroad line disappeared. The federal government acquired most of the property during the Depression and established the national forest in 1936.

Several paved state highways pass through the national forest, as do

Turpentining

Tapping sap from pine trees produced so many useful substances for wooden shipbuilding that the practice became known as the naval store industry. One substance in particular, turpentine, became the livelihood for many in South Georgia and the Florida Panhandle.

Until the 1940s, scores of black turpentiners scratched a living from the pines, placing nails at the bottom of V-shaped cuts where gum dripped into waiting buckets. Making rounds between hundreds of trees, turpentiners collected the sap and distilled the rich ooze into turpentine, resin and pitch in their work camp stills. The trees, unless completely exhausted, were cut higher for new sap geysers the following year. Some survivors bear turpentine scars, called cat faces because the cuts resemble whiskers.

The turpentiners slept in windowless shacks, shared a pump house and bought on credit from camp bosses. The children worked the trees, too; labor laws did not apply to what the state declared an agricultural occupation. In more recent times turpentiners sprayed sulfuric acid from flit guns to speed up the gum flow. Droplets of the potion sizzled through their clothes and blistered their skin.

The industry died as modern technology discovered how to extract turpentine from cut-over pine stumps. But as late as 1942, turpentining remained Florida's second-largest employer.

dozens of forest service roads, virtually all graded, maintained and suitable for two-wheel drive vehicles. A few small towns are scattered throughout. Most along the Apalachicola Northern Railroad—Vilas, Liberty, Bon Ami and Central City—remain on maps, but became ghost towns years ago with the decline of the turpentine industry. It's best to pick up supplies in the larger cities around the forest, like Bristol, Quincy, Sopchoppy or Tallahassee.

Camping is permitted throughout the forest, but limited to designated campgrounds (see page 250) or hunt camps during several hunting seasons, which begin in October and end in March. Contact a ranger office to find out the specific dates. Boat landings, campgrounds and primitive campsites are scattered throughout the forest, but most visitors don't stray far from either the Apalachicola or the Ochlockonee Rivers.

More Information: *National Forests in Florida, Woodcrest Office Park, 325 John Knox Road, Suite F-100, Tallahassee, FL 32303. 850/942-9300. The Apalachicola Ranger District Office, P.O. Box 579, Bristol, FL 32321. 850/643-2282. Recreation Director, Apalachicola National Forest, C/O Wakulla Ranger District Office, 1773 Crawfordville Highway, Crawfordville, FL 32327. 850/926-3561. The ranger offices provide detailed maps of the national forest and know where the latest controlled burns have taken place if you are interested in exploring those areas.*

Apalachicola River Wildlife and Environmental Area

This area of more than 55,600 acres is comprised of three tracts along the Apalachicola River below Wewahitchka. It attracts primarily small game and deer hunters. A 121-acre millet field has been planted to attract doves. There is some vehicular access here, but most hunters like to hunt this floodplain bottomland by boat.

Camping here is limited to tents and camping vehicles. Be sure to check on local regulations before hunting. Hunting permits, state licenses and migratory waterfowl stamps may be required. Fishing and hunting regulation booklets are available free of charge from the Florida Fish and Wildlife Commission.

Facilities: *Boat ramps.* **Days/Hours**: *Open daily, 24 hours.* **Directions**: *Franklin and Gulf Counties, Florida. There are numerous points of access. It is best to get a map of the WEA.* **More Information**: *Florida Fish and Wildlife Conservation Commission, Northwest Region, 1911 Highway 2321, Panama City, FL 32409-1658. 850/265-3677. Website: www.state.fl.us/fwc.*

Apalachicola Wildlife Management Area

Covering more than 558,000 acres, this is one of the largest public WMAs in Florida, having the same borders as the Apalachicola National Forest. An area in the western portion of the WMA falls in the Apalachicola watershed. Due to its size and the fact that most of the area is open to deer-dog running, deer hunters flock here from all

Tupelo Honey

Some of Florida's major nectar plants include gallberry, citrus, saw palmetto, cabbage palm and black mangrove—but none compare in importance to the tupelo blossom. The largest and densest stands of water tupelo, or tupelo gum, trees grow in the swamps of the lower Apalachicola and Chipola rivers. Each spring beekeepers from all over the Florida Panhandle mine their unusually sweet blossoms. A constant buzz resounds for three weeks as bees work the flowers, little green marbles covered in tiny green and pale white petals. The entire river basin has the aroma of tupelo honey, one of the sweetest, purest varieties of honey in the world.

Tupelos grow elsewhere, like along the Altamaha River in Georgia, but nowhere so densely that honey made from them can be certified pure tupelo, a honey packed with fruit sugars that never hardens, granulates or sours. For this reason, it is used for some medicinal purposes. Doctors often recommend tupelo honey for their diabetic patients who can tolerate fruit sugars

To create pure tupelo honey, combs must be stripped of all stored honey before the tupelo blooms begin. The bees are given clear nesting boxes before being moved to a beeyard nearer the honey source. As soon as the bloom ends, beekeepers must harvest the product before it is mixed with different honey sources.

over the state. Wild hog, gray squirrel, quail, rabbit, opossum, raccoon, beaver, coyote, skunk, armadillo, migratory game birds, bobcat, mink and otter can all be hunted here. Black bear is also prevalent, but they are protected at all times.

Camping is permitted here only in designated campsites during the general gun season. Be sure to check on local regulations before hunting. Hunting permits, state licenses and migratory waterfowl stamps may be required. Fishing and hunting regulation booklets are available free of charge from the Florida Fish and Wildlife Commission.

Facilities: *Boat ramps and several camping areas maintained by the US Forest Service, including Big Gully Landing, White Oak Landing, Cotton Landing and Hickory Landing. For boat ramps, see map page 240.* **Days/Hours**: *Open daily, 24 hours.* **Directions**: *Franklin, Leon, Liberty and Wakulla Counties, Florida. There are numerous points of access. It is best to get a map of the WMA.* **More Information**: *Florida Fish and Wildlife Conservation Commission, Northwest Region, 1911 Highway 2321, Panama City, FL 32409-1658. 850/265-3677. Website: www.state.fl.us/fwc.*

Ed Ball Wildlife Management Area

This wildlife management area, covering 66,270 acres—part of which is in the Apalachicola River watershed—surrounds Lake Wimico west of the river. The area here is generally low and swampy and travel can be frustrating, especially during rainy weather.

Deer, turkey, gray squirrel, quail, rabbit, raccoon, opossum, skunk, coyote, beaver, armadillo, bobcat, mink, otter and migratory birds can all be hunted here. The area has both dog and still hunting. The Florida Wildlife Commission has planted a field for dove hunters who purchase a special permit.

Camping is prohibited. Be sure to check on local regulations before hunting. Hunting permits, state licenses and migratory waterfowl stamps may be required. Fishing and hunting regulation booklets are available free of charge from the Florida Fish and Wildlife Commission.

Facilities: *Boat ramp.* **Days/Hours**: *Open daily, 24 hours.* **Directions**: *Franklin and Gulf Counties, Florida. There are several points of access. It is best to get a map of the WMA.* **More Information**: *Florida Fish and Wildlife Conservation Commission, Northwest Region, 1911 Highway 2321, Panama City, FL 32409-1658. 850/265-3677. Website: www.state.fl.us/fwc.*

Quail Hunting's Emotional

"'Quail hunting's emotional,' one of the northerners tries to explain to me. 'It's a question of feeling, pure and simple. You're tramping along with your dogs, and suddenly one of them freezes into a point. His heart may be pounding with eagerness to flush the covey, but there he stands like a statue, his nose ahead and his front paw lifted. Your backing dog honors that point and doesn't move a muscle. The control is a sort of miracle of training and intelligence and love on the part of dog and man. And then you give the sign, and all at once there's an explosion of wings beating away in every direction. You've got to choose your bird in a split second and aim for him before he gets to cover. It starts the electricity in your blood. No man yet can think like a quail, do you understand? Where they'll go, whether they'll run or fly, how your retrieving dog is going to fight his way into a swamp and out again with your birds—the challenge is never the same twice.' The hunter pauses, peering at me narrowly. 'Afterwards—well, I don't know how to describe it except to tell you a man feels more whole than he was. Something's become a part of him. Maybe the country or the dogs or the sight of the birds or his skill with a gun, I don't know.' He shrugs hopelessly at my skepticism. 'It's God's own glory to be out there, that's all. If you'd come you'd know.'"

The Other Florida by Gloria Jahoda

CAMPGROUNDS

Torreya State Park Campground

Four different campgrounds sit amid the bluffs and ravines of Torreya State Park: a family campground in the shady hardwoods near the Weeping Ridge Trail, two primitive campsites in designated areas along the hiking trail for registered hikers and a youth camp for scout groups and youth organizations.

Facilities*: 24 campsites with electric and water hookups; 2 primitive campsites with 4 ground grills and without water; and a youth camp with picnic tables, fire rings, water and restrooms. For state park facilities, see page 246.* **Days/Hours***: Open daily, 8 a.m. until sunset. Arrangements can be made ahead of time to enter the park after dark. Anyone planning to camp must first register with a park ranger. Primitive campers must locate and be registered by a Park Ranger at least one hour prior to sunset and before setting out on the trail to camp.* **Fees***: Campsites with water, $8 - $10 per night; campsites with water and electricity, $10 - $12 per night; primitive camping, $3 nightly per person. The park doesn't take reservations.* **Directions***: Liberty County. From Bristol, Florida, go north on FL 12 for 4 miles. Turn left on FL 270 and continue for about 7.5 miles. Turn left on CR 1641, which soon enters the park.* **More Information***: Torreya State Park, Route 2, Box 70, Bristol, FL 32321. 850/643-2674. Website: www.dep.state.fl.us/parks.*

Camel Lake Campground

A pleasant, mostly pine-shaded place within the Apalachicola National Forest to pitch a tent or park an RV next to a 25-acre freshwater lake.

Facilities*: 6 campsites with tables and fire rings, boat ramp with 10hp motor limit, picnic area with tables and grills, unsupervised swimming beach, flush toilets, drinking water and trails suitable for hiking or off-road biking. Interpretive displays and trail maps are all but nonexistent.* **Days/Hours***: Open daily, year-round. There is no entrance station or gate.* **Fees***: $4 per day; day use, $2 per vehicle.* **Directions***: Liberty County. From Bristol, take CR 12 south for about 11 miles. Turn left on FSR 105 and drive 2 miles.*

Big Gully Landing

This is a no-frills facility, used primarily by fishermen and hunters and located in the Apalachicola National Forest on Equaloxic Creek, just downstream of where Big Gully and Little Gully creeks meet. Unless you know the area and the many meandering creeks, you are better off putting-in elsewhere to reach the Apalachicola River. A lot of logs and roots clog the creek when it is low.

Facilities*: Primitive camping and boat ramp allows motorized crafts. No water, toilets or other public conveniences.* **Days/Hours***: Open daily, year-round. There is no entrance station or gate.* **Directions***: Liberty County. From Bristol, Florida, go 12 miles south on CR 12, which then forks to the left. Bear right on CR 379 and 1 mile later go right on FSR 133. The landing is at the end of the road, which is less than a mile long.*

Water Tupelo

The water tupelo, or tupelo gum, is common in river swamps of the lower Coastal Plain where it is often inundated for long periods of time in winter and spring. Frequently, water tupelo occurs in pure stands or mixed with bald cypress and wetland hardwoods.

The water tupelo is a large tree, often more then 100 feet tall and three to four feet in diameter, with large swollen buttresses. It has large leaves— five to 10 inches long and two to four inches wide.

In areas along the lower Apalachicola and Chipola Rivers, tupelo honey (see sidebar page 249) is the prized commodity from this tree.

White Oak Landing

A primitive camp often used as a base for hunting or fishing, White Oak Landing is on the deep, slow-moving River Styx, several miles upstream from where it joins with the Apalachicola River within the boundaries of the Apalachicola National Forest.

Facilities: *Primitive camping and concrete boat ramp (one of the best in the national forest)*. **Days/Hours**: *Open daily, year-round. There is no entrance station or gate.* **Directions**: *Liberty County. From Sumatra, Florida, go north on CR 379 for about 7.5 miles. Turn left on CR 115 and proceed 3.5 miles.*

Cotton Landing Campground

This site, a designated hunt camp in the Apalachicola National Forest, is slightly more developed than Big Gully and offers primitive camping, fishing and boating along Kennedy Creek, about four miles upstream from where it meets the Apalachicola River.

Facilities: *7 primitive campsites, boat ramp with no horsepower limits and chemical toilets.* **Days/Hours**: *Open daily, year-round. There is no entrance station or gate.* **Directions**: *Liberty County. From Sumatra, Florida, take CR 379 northwest for 3.2 miles. Turn left onto FSR 123 and follow it for 2.8 miles, then turn left on FSR 123B and go 0.7 mile.*

Wright Lake Campground

This cypress-lined, five-acre freshwater lake is in a secluded pine forest and has some of the best camping facilities and interpretive trails in the Apalachicola National Forest. It's home to some notable inhabitants, such as the endangered red-cockaded woodpecker and the harper's beauty, a rare flower found nowhere else in the world. Hunters who used this campground in the past tend not to anymore since camping fees began in 1996.

Facilities: *19 RV and tent sites with water, picnic tables and grills; small unsupervised swimming beach; two interpretive loop trails around the lake; handicap-accessible bathhouse with flush toilets and warm showers; dump station; and drinking water.* **Days/Hours**: *Open daily, year-round. There is no entrance station or gate, only a self-service fee station.* **Fees**: *$8 nightly per day; day use, $2 per vehicle.* **Directions**: *Franklin County. From Sumatra, Florida, take FL 65 south for 2 miles. Turn right on FSR 101 and drive for about 2 miles. Turn right at the sign and go 0.25 mile.*

Hickory Landing Campground

This flat area, shaded by thick pines next to Owl Creek, a deep, blackwater channel lined with cypress swamps, is one of the best places to access the Apalachicola River, little more than a mile downstream. Hickory Landing is a designated hunt camp in the Apalachicola National Forest.

Facilities: *12 RV and tent campsites with picnic tables and fire rings, boat ramp with no horsepower limit on motors, "vault" toilets which resemble*

Florida Springs

Natural water oozes, bubbles and gushes into pools, creeks and rivers all over Florida, the state with the largest collection of springs in the nation. The springs' clear, mild waters attract swimmers, cave divers and paddlers. The springs vary greatly in size and duration—some small ones seep into the soil only once in awhile, large ones issue forth millions of gallons a day, forming the headwaters of major rivers.

The state's largest springs concentrate in east central Florida, but there are a few of note on the Chipola River (see sidebar page 253), a tributary of the Apalachicola and almost entirely spring fed. Some run into the river on the west bank just below I-10. Countless minor ones originate just upstream of the city of Marianna, Florida. One large exception, Bozell Springs, with rocky limestone ledges and a crystal-clear bottom 25 feet deep, is popular with cave divers. It feeds a creek that quickly empties into the Chipola.

There are two springs associated with the upper Apalachicola River, the first about 100 yards below the Jim Woodruff Lock and Dam on Lake Seminole (see page 163). It's invisible in the muddy waters of the Apalachicola, but state fish and game officials have cleared out its path to enhance the flow because sport fish, such as striped and hybrid bass, like the spring water. The other spring, about a mile further downstream, originates in the woods.

outhouses and drinking water. **Days/Hours**: *Open daily, year-round. There is no entrance station or gate.* **Fees**: *$3 per day.* **Directions**: *Franklin County. From Sumatra, Florida, take FL 65 south for 2 miles. Turn right on FSR 101 and go 1.5 miles, and then left on FSR 101B for 1 mile.*

Dead Lakes State Recreation Area Campground

Shaded by longleaf pines and carpeted with a cushion of wiregrass, this campsite sits on a hill at Dead Lakes State Recreation Area on the Chipola River (see sidebar this page).

Facilities: *10 campsites with electricity, 10 primitive campsites. For other park facilities see page 247.* **Days/Hours**: *Open daily, year-round, 8 a.m. until sunset. The gate is locked at sunset, but arrangements can be made ahead of time to enter the park after dark.* **Fees**: *Camping, $8 per night; with electricity, $2 more.* **Directions**: *Gulf County. From Wewahitchka, Florida, take FL 71 about 2 miles north. Park entrance is on right.* **More Information**: *Dead Lakes State Recreation Area, P.O. Box 989, Wewahitchka, FL 32465. 850/639-2702.*

MARINAS AND FISH CAMPS

Breakaway Marina, Motel & Restaurant

Operating since 1966, this is a full–service marina with a ship store, Evinrude dealership, motel, restaurant, service shop and guides. About 4 miles upstream of Apalachicola Bay, Breakaway caters to salt and freshwater fishers alike.

Facilities: *15 transient wet slips; covered and open slips with electricity and water; boat ramp; dry stack storage; gas; guided boats for rent; 15 motel rooms; 4 open RV spaces with complete hookups, restrooms and showers; restaurant; store with most marine supplies, snacks and drinks.* **Days/Hours**: *Marina – open daily, year-round, 6:30 a.m. to 6 p.m.; closed for lunch, noon to 1 p.m. Restaurant – 6:30 a.m. to 6 p.m.; closed noon to 1 p.m. except Saturday and Sunday.* **Fees**: *Motel – $48 a night for double occupancy; RV spaces – $10 a night. The lodge doesn't directly book guides, but generally, they run $350 a day for inshore and $450 a day for offshore trips for up to 4.* **Directions**: *Gulf County. From Apalachicola, Florida, take 12th Street north for 3 miles to Waddell Road. Turn right and go about 1 mile to the end of the road.* **Location on River**: *On the west bank of the Apalachicola River just below mile marker 4.* **More Information**: *Manager Jerry Cathen or owner Gorrie Wilson, 200 Waddell Road, Apalachicola, FL 32320. 850/653-8897. Website: www.breakawaymarina.com.*

Bay City Lodge

This fishing lodge sits on a picturesque, swamp-canopied canal leading into the river at mile marker 3.5. It's a prime starting point for saltwater and freshwater fishing excursions or barrier island sightseeing tours.

Facilities: *35 transient wet slips, dry dock storage, gas, charter guides and*

Chipola River

The main tributary of the Apalachicola River, the Chipola, begins in southeast Alabama. Sometimes it runs swiftly along tree-lined banks with a limestone bottom. Other times it slows the pace, and marshes and swamps with occasional bluffs take up either horizon. The name is Indian for "clear water," and much of the river has a clear emerald color. A little rain turns it smoky green; a lot makes it tan. Springs bubble forth along the way. The Chipola becomes navigable a few miles north of Marianna, Florida, but soon goes underground for one-half mile underneath Florida Caverns State Park.

Most trees native to the panhandle grow along some part of its path. Wild azalea, daisies and cardinal flowers bloom in the spring. Turtles and alligators sun in the river. Bird life is abundant, especially in the lower section. Catfish, bream and bass are the most common catches.

Near the end of its 80-mile journey, a sandbar transformed the increasingly swampy river into the Dead Lakes (see page 242), five connected bodies of water littered with the standing remains of thousands of dead trees.

guide boats, 10 motel rooms, 6 cottages, boat ramp, restaurant, tennis court and bait-and-tackle store. **Days/Hours**: *The restaurant is generally open all year except winter and serves breakfast and dinner only. Inshore fishing guides are available in spring, summer and autumn.* **Fees**: *Motel rooms, $45; cottages $55 a night. Guides, including 22-ft boat rentals, run $275 for 4 people for a full day.* **Directions**: *Gulf County. From Apalachicola, go north on 12th Street for 2 miles. Turn right on Bay City Road and continue for 1 mile. Location on river: On west bank of the Apalachicola River at mile marker 3.5.* **Location on River**: *On the west bank of the Apalachicola River between mile markers 3 and 4.* **More Information**: *Manager Tom Gordon, P.O. Box 172, Apalachicola, FL 32329. 850/653-9294.*

Scipio Creek Marina

This newly established, family-owned business is the largest marina in Apalachicola and is within walking distance of many of the town's, restaurants, shops and bed-and-breakfast establishments.

Facilities: *More than 500 feet of parallel dockage with 385 feet for transient boats; dry storage; shore power; gas dock with diesel fuel; restaurant; ship store with marine supplies, bait and tackle, outdoor clothing, hunting supplies, snacks and drinks; pump out station; and showers. Several fishing guides as well as Eco-Tours sightseeing boats work out of Scipio.* **Days/Hours**: *Open daily, 6 a.m. to 6 p.m.* **Fees**: *$1 a foot for transient boat docks.* **Directions**: *Franklin County. From the flashing light in downtown Apalachicola, take Market Street northwest about a 0.5 mile straight to Scipio Creek and the marina.* **Location on the River**: *Heading downstream toward Apalachicola, go to mile marker 2. Turn to the right and follow the docks back north up into Scipio Creek. Turn up the creek.* **More Information**: *Scipio Creek Marina, Inc., 301 Market Street, P.O. Box 398, Apalachicola, FL 32329. 850/653-8030; fax 850/653-4280. Website: www.scipiocreekmarina.com.*

Miller Marine

Miller's specializes as a complete marine fuel-service facility, including emergency after-hours service on request. It is within walking distance of historic Apalachicola restaurants and shops.

Facilities: *Boat dock; gas and diesel fuel; and store with nautical charts, marine supplies, filters, batteries and lubricants.* **Days/Hours**: *Open daily, Monday through Saturday, 7:30 a.m. to 5:30 p.m.; Sunday, 1:30 to 5 p.m.* **Directions**: *Franklin County. From the flashing light in downtown Apalachicola, take Avenue E east 2 blocks to Water Street. Turn right. Miller Marine is on the left, 1 block north of the US 98 Bridge.* **Location on the River**: *On the right at mile marker 2 at the mouth of Apalachicola River, just north of the US 98 Bridge. Dock is at the big Chevron sign.* **More Information**: *Miller Marine, Inc., 119 Water Street, P. O. Box 308, Apalachicola, FL 32320. 850/653-9521.*

Skipper's Terms

Distinguishing between port (left) and starboard (right) can be confusing for new boaters. Remember that "port" and "left" match up as four-letter words, while "right" and "starboard" have more letters. Port and starboard colors follow the same rule: port is red (short); starboard is green (longer). Port, left and red are all short words. Starboard, right and green are longer words.

HIKES AND WALKS

Apalachicola River Bluffs Trail

A Florida National Recreational Trail located in Torreya State Park, this is also known as the original loop trail. Similar to the Garden of Eden trail, this hike crosses through many different natural features and habitats in the most ecologically unique part of Florida—the bluffs and ravines of the upper Apalachicola River. The view from the bluffs is not quite as spectacular as from Alum Bluff, but it does offer a descent to the river floodplain and passes close enough to Torreya trees to examine them.

Distance: Trail makes a 7-mile loop.

Trailhead Location: Torreya State Park (see page 246). Park in front of the old Gregory House. Access to the loop trail begins at the south end of the parking lot.

Features: Once plentiful, Torreyas are now on the brink of extinction. Formerly, trees 50 feet in height and eight feet in circumference were not uncommon. Today, only a few tiny specimens remain in the wild, none more than a couple of feet in height or of reproductive age. Some are by the trail near the river. Some botanists believe that they could die out before too long. Smoke from once plentiful wildfires, which traveled up the river corridor, protected them from fungal epidemics. Modern human fire suppression to protect timber stands, however, has inadvertently promoted unchecked epidemics for the past several decades. Many other rare species reside in the park as well, some found elsewhere only in the southern Appalachians, which is what this steep, cool and moist terrain resembles. Visitors don't have to hike the entire trail to see the Torreyas. A smaller, 45-minute loop along the river offers that opportunity. A good place to see Florida Yews is the trail near the Rock Creek stone bridge. Many rare wildflowers bloom in early spring, including Indian pink, white baneberry, rue-anemone, wild comphrey, eastern leatherwood, trout lily, mountain laurel, orange azalea and narrow-leaved trillium. Most also occur in the Alum Bluffs preserve.

During the Civil War, the Apalachicola River was an important route into the South that had to be protected. Located on one bluff here was a six cannon battery in place to prevent Union gun boats from passing. The remains of the gun pit can be seen along the trail. The trail also passes by the Gregory House (see page 243), a 1849 plantation house that once stood across the river from the park at Ocheesee Landing.

There are two primitive campsites along this trail—Rock Bluff and Rock Creek. Each site has four ground grills. Campers must be registered to stay in the campgrounds.

Hazards: Private property used for hunting borders some of the park, which also is a habitat for several venomous snake species. Biting insects make summer trips difficult.

Torreya Trees

Nearly extinct, Torreya (Tor REY a) trees cling to life in the cool, shaded ravines and bluffs on the east bank of the upper Apalachicola River. Found elsewhere only in China, Japan and California, the widely scattered trees could be remnants of a once-continuous forest across North America and East Asia when the two continents were part of the supercontinent Pangaea millions of years ago. The Torreyas share living quarters among the bluffs with their cousins, the rare Florida Yews.

Though once plentiful, Torreyas might not last much longer in the wild. In the past, trees commonly grew to 50 feet high and eight feet around. Today, only a few tiny specimens remain in their natural environment, none more than a couple of feet high, and none of reproductive age. The tree does well as an ornamental; one of the largest such specimens in the world is in the gardens of the Biltmore Estate in Asheville, North Carolina.

Fungal epidemics have decimated the Torreya over the past 40 years. Traditionally, smoke from periodic wildfires swept down the river basin and acted as a natural fumigant to keep the Torreyas healthy. But human fire suppression to protect timber stands has allowed the blight to multiply unchecked.

The Torreya Challenge Trail

Opened in 1985, this trail is often referred to as the new loop trail. It closely resembles the old loop trail as it passes through similar deep ravines along Rock Creek. Hardwoods make a canopy in the lower sections, pine trees in the higher. There are Torreyas, but not near the trail. Unlike the older loop, it doesn't go near the river.

Distance: This orange-blazed trail makes an 8-mile loop.

Trailhead Location: Torreya State Park (see page 246). Access the trail from the park's picnic area. Take the trail past the old youth camp restroom, turn left down service road to fork. Take right fork to Stone Bridge. The trail starts past the bridge on the left. From December to April, during eagle nesting season, the new hiking trail can only be accessed from the Torreya hiking loop, not the stone bridge trailhead.

Features: The trail's remoteness and mean the terrain is less trampled underfoot than the river bluffs trail. The Torreya Challenge Back Pack Camp, a primitive campsite with four ground grills, is located on the trail. You must be registered to stay at the campsite.

Hazards: The trail is habitat to several kinds of venomous snakes. Biting insects make summer trips difficult.

Torreya State Park / Weeping Ridge Trail

This trail leads to a ledge in a deep ravine where water seeps out of the ground and forms a small waterfall during the rainy season.

Distance: This trail takes about one hour to walk roundtrip.

Trailhead Location: Torreya State Park (see page 246). Liberty County. From Bristol, take FL 12 north for 4 miles. Turn left on FL 270 and continue for about 7.5 miles. Turn left on CR 1641, which soon enters Torreya State Park. Trailhead is at the entrance to the main campground.

Features: Southern magnolia, white oak and spruce are common along the trail.

Hazards: Biting insects in the summer.

Garden of Eden Trail

Amazed by the diversity, early botanists jested that this area was the original Garden of Eden and that Noah made his ark out of the Torreya tree. This "paleorefugia," or sanctuary for ancient flora and fauna, is perhaps the best place to explore Florida's most breathtaking scenery and notable variety of rare and endangered species. The topography along the trail is similar to Torreya State Park (see page 246), but this trail in the Apalachicola Bluffs and Ravines Preserve generally offers a more peaceful setting because of less foot traffic.

After going up and down several steep ravines, the trail abruptly halts on the sudden and sheer Alum Bluff, which gets its name from the alum-like taste of one of its layers. The view of the wide expanse of Florida, Alabama and Georgia offers evidence of the river's long history as a natural shaper of the land. As the river erodes the

Hiking the Garden of Eden Trail

"The last time I went to Torreya State Park was on a summer afternoon in the rainy season. There were a number of blooming flowers to be seen. The main trail was hazardously slippery and from time to time I was caught in a shower, remnant of the thunderstorm that had greeted me at the park gate after my drive over in bright sun. I was glad I had worn rough-soled sneakers, for the trails at Torreya are steep, winding over exposed tree roots down to the river bottom with its slick coating of clay. Among the flowering magnolias and the Torreya trees I found the perennial cardinal flower, Lobelia cardinalis, with its spike of brilliant red. It is the only red lobelia, and a lover of riverbanks. Wild hydrangeas were beginning to turn from the white of their peak bloom to pink. Blue dayflowers and dog violets appeared along the trail, and elderberries were turning purple. In the distance I could hear the harsh honking of great blue herons. Red and white and pink morning glories twined near the low ground at the river's edge. In the deep green of the woods, towhees and Carolina chickadees were calling. I climbed up a hill covered with bluestem palms and small holly trees and listened to the soft running of an invisible spring. Iridescent dragonflies alighted on branches before me. The smell of the leafmold was woody and rich. A pileated woodpecker cried in a flash of red and black and white from a wild pecan tree before I saw the beating of his wings as he flew into far green shadows. Near me was an iron-wood log that had been felled by a storm; from it were growing new green shoots as the tree struggled to stay alive in a tangle of abundance. From a single stump I saw two hickory trunks growing. The path wound upward. Everywhere resurrection ferns were bright green on tree trunks. Under a magnolia I found a Chapman's rhododendron, and not far away a Florida yew."

The Other Florida by Gloria Jahoda

highlands to the east, it leaves behind a broad, low plain to the west. Of all the limestone and clay cliffs along the upper Apalachicola, Alum Bluff arguably offers the most dramatic view of the river and plains. It certainly exposes the oldest geological layers in the state—the bottom yellow to gray band at the base dates back 18 million years—and probably reaches the highest elevation from the river's edge. (Some people with Torreya State Park speculate one of their bluffs is higher, but other sources consider Alum the highest.) Height estimates for Alum Bluff and its Torreya Park rivals, from the river's surface, range from 100 to 210 feet. More likely, Alum's true height is just about in the middle.

You can hear nature's land cutting process at work. Even on the calmest days, clumps of clay slip down the side of the cliff. Some trees leaning over the edge of the precipice, their roots racing back to find firmer ground, demonstrate that the soil avalanches can be much more severe. The hike follows the bluff edge for a short while, then loops around back to the main trail for a return trip.

Like the bluff, the ravines you pass through offer exhilarating scenery. The uncharacteristic clearness of the streams, steepness of the ravine and character of the plant life makes much of this hike seem like it passes through the Appalachian Mountains rather than the Florida Panhandle. In fact, many of the rare or unusual species—like mountain laurel, white baneberry, wild ginger, bay star vine and wild hydrangea—did come from Appalachia, taking refuge here during the last ice age. The shade and cool temperatures allowed them to stay when the earth warmed up.

Like Torreya State Park, Torreya trees and Florida yews, two of the oldest and rarest species in the state, live in the bluffs and ravines in the preserve.

Other trees flourish here. One magnolia (see sidebar page 179) in a ravine has a trunk so wide three adults might not reach their arms around it. And protected longleaf pines are making a comeback in a wiregrass savanna near the beginning of the trail.

Animals living here include deer, wild turkey, gopher tortoise, indigo snakes and dusky salamanders, and otters and alligators in a pond on the preserve. Bird watchers should look for bald eagles, kites, red-eyed vireo and several species of warblers.

Distance: The hike is 3.5 miles round-trip, including an optional 0.5-mile loop at Alum Bluff. The trail usually takes several hours because most of it covers steep terrain.

Trailhead Location: Apalachicola Bluffs and Ravines Preserve (see page 236). From Bristol, Florida, take FL 12 east about 1.6 miles to Garden of Eden Road, a dirt road. Turn left at large "Apalachicola Bluffs Garden of Eden Trail" sign. A short distance down the road, you will come to a parking lot for hikers.

The trailhead, with an interpretive display and map, is a couple hundred yards down the sandy road past the parking area.

Osprey

The osprey is a large bird of prey in the hawk family. Its name comes from a Latin word that means bonebreaker. It is also called fish hawk and fishing eagle. Ospreys feed only on fish, particularly those that stay close to the surface and are of little value to man. The bird hovers over the water, then sets it wings and dives feet first, hitting the water with a great splash and grasping the fish with its long, sharp talons. The osprey will often go completely under water, but it's feathers are close, firm and slightly oily, so it can plunge into water without becoming soaked.

The bird is about two feet long with a wingspread of nearly six feet. It is dark brown above and has some white on its head. It is white below with a few streaks of dark brown. An osprey is easy to spot—usually nesting in the tops of tall trees near large bodies of water. Sometimes they nest in chimney tops, on telephone pole crossbars, on ledges, in dead stumps and even on the ground. They usually lay three eggs, colored whitish and spotted with shades of brown.

Ospreys live near both fresh and saltwater in almost every temperate and tropical country in the world. The American osprey breeds from northwestern Alaska to Newfoundland, and south to Lower California, western Mexico and the Gulf States. It winters from the southern United States to northern Argentina and Paraguay. You'll see ospreys all along the Flint River Corridor, particularly from Lake Blackshear to Apalachicola Bay.

Features: Evidence of Civil War gun pits remain on the edge of Alum Bluff. Two Confederate companies, totaling up to 150 soldiers, manned seven heavy guns, the largest weighing more than three tons, on the bluff beginning in the spring of 1862. The artillery was meant to stop Federal raiders from moving deep into Georgia and Alabama on the Apalachicola-Flint-Chattahoochee River System. The guns would have had an easy shot had Union gunboats attempted to navigate the sharp river bend below the bluff. But they remained silent and the risk of Union attack sharply declined in late 1862 when the Confederates sank obstructions in the Apalachicola River near present-day Wewahitchka, 26 miles to the south. The bulk of the garrison moved inland a few miles because of the threat of tropical illnesses in July of 1863, but the bluff remained manned until at least autumn of that year when the entire 1st Florida Battalion was ordered to Savannah, Georgia. At that time, a new Confederate position was being prepared upriver a number of miles at a bluff in present-day Torreya State Park.

Hazards: The trail sometimes runs along the preserve border and there is hunting in the winter on the surrounding private property. Insects and heat make summer a poor time to visit.

Apalachicola Walking Tour

Nestled between the Apalachicola River to the east and the Apalachicola Bay to the south, this town took its name from the Apalachicola Indians, a small tribe related to the Creeks that were living in small villages along the river when the first Europeans and Spanish missionaries arrived in the 1500s. Apalachicola has been translated to "land of the friendly people" and "the people who live on the other side." The second reference might have come from the much-larger Apalachee tribe, who were centered around present-day Tallahassee. They were in close contact with the Spanish friars, who explored and mapped the area.

The city was first settled in 1821 by Americans when cotton grown in the Chattahoochee and Flint River valleys needed to find a way to world markets. In that year a port custom house was built. And soon after incorporating in 1832, Apalachicola became the third-largest port city on the gulf and the third-largest cotton port in the United States. For decades steamboats chugged up and down the Apalachicola River, bringing cotton down to the port and manufactured goods to upriver cities and plantations. A growing sponge industry, which became the third largest in the state, gave the economy a boost, as well. By 1840, about $17 million worth of goods passed through Apalachicola, more than the rest of the ports in the state combined. The city boasted an opera house, a racetrack, two banks and plenty of mansions, one the residence of a Dr. John Gorrie. Gorrie, the city's most-honored son, served as bank director, postmaster, city treasurer, city councilman and as a physician. Yet, Gorrie was not fully recog-

Steamboats

For more than a century, riverboats chugged up and down the waterway between the Gulf of Mexico port of Apalachicola and the Columbus steamboat wharf on the Chattahoochee and the Albany landing on the Flint. The first was the *Fanny*, coming to Bainbridge in 1827 and to Columbus in 1828. The last to dock was the *George W. Miller* in Columbus in 1939.

A paddlewheel was a large wheel used by steamboats on which flat boards (buckets) were so arranged that when the wheels turned, the boards came in contact with the water, thus propelling the boat. If the vessel was a sidewheeler, the paddlewheels were located on the sides. If it was a sternwheeler, the paddlewheel was suspended aft of (behind) the hull (the body of the vessel).

Stacked high with cotton bales on the trip down and loaded with groceries, manufactured goods and Apalachicola Bay oysters—kept alive with cornmeal sprinkled in wooden barrels—on the way up, the riverboats stopped at any number of 240 landings or towns along the way. Boiler explosions, fires, changing river currents and sandbars made steamboating on the river dangerous. The sunken remains of some lie hidden in the muddy depths.

As with boating today, steamboating had its own language. A roustabout was a man who worked on rivers; mark twain was a river depth of two (twain) fathoms or 12 feet; hitting a snag meant a boat had run into a fallen tree in the river; and a diper dredge was a steam shovel mounted on a float and used to dig in the river.

nized for his greatest contribution until after his death. While trying to cool the rooms of patients with yellow fever, he invented the first ice-making machine. Gorrie entertained guests during the summer by putting ice in their drinks, but he was unable to market his invention. In part, he had no success because the contraption produced ice so slowly. But another reason was opposition from the powerful Northeast ice industry. Storing and shipping giant blocks of ice as far south as the Caribbean was big, profitable business. After Gorrie's death in 1855, however, the novelty caught on, making possible modern refrigeration and air conditioning.

But Apalachicola's good times didn't last. In the 1850s, the city took a hit when cotton began to ride the rails. During the Civil War, the economy collapsed when Union ships blockaded the port. After the war, the town rode the crest of a lumber boom, but by the late 1920s, the vast swampy plains to the north had been completely stripped of cypress. Since then, Apalachicola has turned to harvesting and process-ing seafood to make a living, which can easily be seen by a stroll down Water Street. Shrimp boats and deep sea charters crowd the docks. Large tin buildings that process seafood line the street, spitting out mounds of shell from their sides. Amid the standing remains of several, crumbling brick cotton and sponge warehouses, there have sprung up trendy art galleries, antique stores, coffee shops and restau-rants, serving seafood right off the boat.

A distant—but growing—second industry is tourism, increasingly playing an important role to the local economy. Apalachicola, a town of 3,000, has all the charm of historic coastal cities like Savannah or Mobile, but none of the urban blight. There's plenty of historical landmarks, antebellum homes and oyster bars, but no shopping malls, few convenience stores and only one traffic signal. (Actually, it's a caution light.)

In the historic district, about 200 19th-century homes remain, many shaded by oaks and magnolias and spread out along wide streets and historic parks. The city was built with plans from Philadelphia, which in turn was based on the old grid streets of ancient Rome. The square block streets in the historic district are broken up with a number of open squares, originally serving as fire breaks and animal grazing areas.

Most of the historic homes and buildings are within a two-square mile area, offering an opportunity to take an easy stroll back through time. The Chamber of Commerce downtown on Market Street has self-guided walking tour maps. Some notable stops include:

Cotton Warehouse. This is one of the original 42 cotton warehouses built in 1838. Around the first-story front door are some of the origi-nal granite posts and lintels which earned Apalachicola the name "the city of granite fronts." Nearby City Hall is housed in the other remaining cotton warehouse.

Sponge Warehouse. Built around 1840, this is one of the original sponge trade warehouses. When fast-talking auctioneers sold the stuff

Apalachicola and Cotton

In 1822 Apalachicola exported its first bale of cotton. Sitting at the mouth of the Apalachicola-Flint-Chattahoochee River System, the largest and longest in the southeastern United States, Apalachicola was, within 15 years, the third largest cotton port on the Gulf of Mexico behind New Orleans and Mobile.

"Apalachicola was a flurry of activity during the commercial season. Hundreds of bales of cotton spilled out of the warehouses and clogged the streets. The auction bell clanged as draymen rushed the bales from the wharves to the compresses to the warehouses and back again. Cotton factors, whose job it was to sell the cotton, held court in their counting rooms on the second floor of their warehouses. Here they laid out samples for prospective buyers, and they dashed off letters to their associates in New York and Europe notifying them of an ensuing shipment. They arranged for the bales to be mended or repacked, insured, and stored. They dickered over the lowest ocean freightage, and they arranged financ-ing so that neither they nor their clients had to wait for the cotton to reach the English textiles mill before they received compensa-tion. They sent other letters upriver to the farmer who waited to hear what his year's labor would bring. All day long their clerks bent over the precious accounting books that brought order to the entire operation. Long into the night, lamplights glowed from the upstairs windows of the counting rooms on Water Street."

Fair to Middlin'—The Antebellum Cotton Trade of the Apalachicola/Chattahoochee River Valley by Lynn Willoughby

by the crateload in the late 1800s, thousands of sponges spilled out from the door and clear across the street. In 1895 the sponge trade employed 100 men.

Raney House. David Raney, a wealthy commission merchant, built this Greek Revival home in 1838. The city owns and restored the house, which contains many original furnishings. The site of the local historical society, Raney House is on the National Register of Historic Places and open to the public on Saturday, 1 to 5 p.m. or by appointment.

Orman House. Planter and merchant Thomas Orman sometimes put a keg of nails on the roof during the Civil War, but not for home repairs. If Union troops came through town, Confederate sympathizers hiding upriver would see the keg and stay in the woods. The restored house is now the Magnolia Hall Bed and Breakfast.

Marks-Bruce House. Built in 1804 in St. Joe, the cottage house was abandoned during a Yellow Fever epidemic and in 1854, like many of its neighbors, was relocated by barge to Apalachicola.

Chapman House. Dr. Alvin W. Chapman, renowned 19th-century botanist who wrote the *Flora of the Southern United States*, built the house in the 1840s. He was a secret Union sympathizer and reportedly helped federal prisoners escape from a nearby prison.

Chestnut Street Cemetery. Dating from 1832, the cemetery has brought together in eternal peace a rainbow of peoples: Confederate and Union soldiers, blacks, whites, Jews, Irish, Italians and yellow fever victims. The rundown condition—along with wrought-iron gates and moss-covered trees—adds to the eerie charm.

John Gorrie Museum and Grave. His original ice-making machine is in the Smithsonian, but a replica resides in the museum. The museum is open daily except Tuesday, Wednesday and holidays, 9 a.m. to 5 p.m. **More Information***: 850/653-9347.*

Trinity Episcopal Church. The circa 1838 Greek Revival building was shipped in sections from New York and assembled with wooden pegs. It's on the National Registry of Historic Places. Drs. Chapman and Gorrie were active in the parish.

The Coombs House Inn. This 1905 Victorian mansion has been restored into a bed and breakfast.

Wefing House. The Queen Anne style of this circa 1896 home was popular with many timber barons who built near the town's bayshore from the 1890s to 1920s.

The Gibson Hotel. This 1907 Victorian hotel is one of few inns on the Federal Register of Historic Places still operating. This local landmark has good seafood, a full bar, 31 luxurious rooms and a two-story, three-sided porch with bay and river views.

More Information*: Apalachicola Area Historical Society, 128 Market Street, Apalachicola, FL 32320. Apalachicola Bay Chamber of Commerce, 84 Market Street, Apalachicola, FL 32320. 850/653-9419.*

Apalachicola Bay Facts

Between 65 and 85 percent of local residents make a living "directly from the sea."

The retail value of the bay's seafood is about $100 million a year.

The bay yield of four-to-six million tons of oyster meat a year provides 90 percent of Florida's, and 10 percent of the country's, oyster harvest.

The bay is 55 miles long and, at most, six miles long. The bay averages only nine feet in depth.

Fourteen percent, or 21,860 acres, of the total water area in the bay is covered in estuary marshes.

Almost 84 percent of the bay's freshwater originates in Georgia; a much smaller percentage comes from Alabama.

One million tons of river sediments wash into the bay every year.

Daily average flow into the bay is 16 billion gallons.

Maximum flow is more than 200 billion gallons.

When tides go out, 700 billion gallons leave the bay.

SCENIC DRIVES

Apalachee Savannas Scenic Byway

This mostly easy drive on a narrow, winding paved road goes through some botanically unique pine forests, grasslands and swamps of the Apalachicola National Forest. There are three different stops you can make toward the end of the drive that will add to your trip: a swamp lake interpretive trail, a historic fort on the Apalachicola River, and a small area rich in botanical diversity.

Distance: Reset your odometer for this 32-mile driving tour.

The Drive: The trip begins with gently rolling to flat terrain. The sandy hills are what's left of ancient sand dunes when the coast was here. As ice ages come and go, ocean levels fall and rise, dramatically altering the coastline of flat areas like Florida. During the last big chill 12,000 years ago, when much of Earth's water was locked up in the polar caps, Florida had twice as much land mass as now. Much earlier, during a warmer period than now, the coast came this far north.

Pines and oaks flourish in the hills and flat lands. Many of the former are planted slash pines, which continue to be harvested for timber. There are stands of cypress, magnolias, titi, sweetbay and silverbay in the large, wet depressions in the forest, known as bays. Most of them are far from the road or obscured by adjoining pines, which prefer slightly higher, drier ground; but the road crosses several streams (for example Big Gully Creek at mile 4, Kennedy Creek at mile 16 and Little Owl Creek at mile 21) that offer close-up views of swamp hardwoods and shrubs. Immediately after Big Gully Creek when the road forks, bear right (west) on FL 379 to stay on the scenic drive.

A few miles before Kennedy Creek, the heavily forested hills begin to fade and give way to vast savannas, or natural fields of grass. In this case its wiregrass, a thick, tan stalk that grows to about three or four feet high in moist ground. Along the savanna edges grow longleaf pines, whose needles can reach 12 or 14 inches in length. At mile 16, you begin to see to the left (east) Post Office Bay, which includes one of the largest remaining and best-preserved longleaf pine and wiregrass plant communities.

Longleaf pines don't grow as fast as slash pines, which accounts for their widespread disappearance during the logging booms of the early 20th century, but they are extremely adapted to survive the wildfires that historically consumed the wiregrass fields during periodic droughts. For almost the first 10 years, a longleaf pine resembles a big, thick grass stalk. But should a fire come, its long fleshy taproot goes quick action. Taking advantage of the rich, ashy soil and the absence of shade, the tree shoots up over the next several years in a stage of accelerated growth. By the time the next fire hits a number of years later, the tree has a good chance of being thick and tall enough to avoid the lethal heat; their bark is much deeper than other pines and they grow up to 75 feet.

Shrimp

The elegant lines of shrimp boats can be seen combing the waters around Apalachicola Bay, their lights crisscrossing the horizon at night when shrimp, generally nocturnal creatures, leave the sand or mud burrows that protect them during the day. Shrimp inhabit saltwater and freshwater and are mostly found on shallow seafloors, where they feed on small animals and plants. They can grow up to eight inches (larger shrimp are called prawns). There are about 2,000 species of this small crustacean; the most common variety in waters near the United States is the white shrimp.

Mild gulf waters in the Apalachicola area allow at least limited shrimping year-round, but as the mouth of the Apalachicola River is rather shallow, most shrimp boats anchor in nearby Carrabelle, which has one of the deepest ports in the gulf. Small bay boats usually stay within the barrier island perimeter on short daily trips, but offshore shrimp boats, 65 feet in length or longer with refrigerated cargo holds, roam the gulf for up to a month at a time.

Given the cheapness and abundance of commercial shrimp in the region, recreational shrimping is uncommon—but some Floridians are still hooked on the hobby. From mid-December until early May, the shrimp are often near the surface of the water. During their nightly runs, they can be caught from bridges, piers, bulkheads or boats along salt marshes of the Apalachicola Bay by dipping a shrimp net—21 feet is a good size—as they swim or float through an area lighted by flashlight.

It's a game of chance trying to figure out where the shrimp will run, but hit a mother lode that fills up a five-gallon bucket and, well, supermarket shrimp just won't taste the same again.

Rare red-cockaded woodpeckers, the only birds to burrow in living trees, live exclusively in longleaf pines (see sidebar this page). The largest recorded colony of 500 lives in the Apalachicola Ranger District, many around Post Office Bay or other longleaf pines stands along this drive. The trees in which the woodpeckers live are easy to spot because rangers have marked their trunks with white bands.

Wildflowers in the wiregrass savannas take advantage of the ash-rich soil and bloom after a fire, particularly if it coincides with their natural flowering times. Consider contacting the ranger district office to find out if a controlled burn has taken place recently and visit the spot for better than usual floral displays. Among the notable spring blossoms are pitcher plants, which grow in large numbers in the savannas, and, right along the sunken road shoulders, pine lilies, Chapman's buttorwort, and a variety of rare blue, pink and purple orchids. Yellow and white orchids show later in summer and autumn.

At the end of FL 379 at mile 23.5, bear right (south) onto FL 65. The intersection marks the beginning of Sumatra. Little more than a clearing in the woods, the tiny town's most prominent landmark is a picturesque, old white shack that serves as the post office. It's only open in the morning.

Three possible stops near the end of the trip are:

Wright Lake Campground. At mile 26 turn right (west) on FSR 101 for two miles. One of the most developed camping and recreational sites in the national forest, Wright Lake has two excellent interpretive loop trails around a freshwater lake and nearby swamps, plus a swimming beach.

Fort Gadsden Historic Site (see page 244). At mile 28 turn right (west) on FSR 129 for two miles. In the 19th century, English, Americans, Indians and free blacks all fought for control of a military installation on Prospect Bluff overlooking the Apalachicola River. Few signs remain, but an outdoor museum marks the spot where, in one terrible explosion in July of 1816, almost 300 Seminoles, free blacks and ex-slaves lost their lives when an American gunboat fired a cannon shot that struck the fort's powder magazine.

FSR 143. At mile 31 turn left (east) on the 4-mile loop road, which offers one of the best places to explore a wiregrass, pine and swamp area that most resembles its original condition. To the east and north of the loop are a cypress swamp and savannas that, for the most part, escaped logging.

Drive Directions: *Liberty County. From Bristol, Florida, head south on FL 12 for about 10 miles. The scenic drive begins as you enter the Apalachicola National Forest. Four miles later the road forks. To remain on the Scenic Byway, bear right (west) on FL 379, which toward the end of the trip joins FL 65. Go right (south) on FL 65 for 8 miles until you exit the national forest, which concludes the drive.*

Red-cockaded Woodpecker

Once a common bird of the pine flatwoods, the endangered red-cockaded woodpecker can now be found only in a few remaining old-growth pine forests of southeastern United States, including the Flint River Corridor from Veterans Memorial State Park (see page 116) into the Apalachicola Bluffs.

Named for the red ear patch, or cockade, of the adult male, this small woodpecker's best field marks (colors and markings that help identify an animal) are its white cheek patches and black and white 'ladder'-striped back.

The most distinctive feature of this woodpecker is its choice of home sites. Most woodpecker species peck cavities, or holes, in decaying tree trunks with their chisel-like beaks, but the red-cockaded is the only wood-pecker to perform this construction activity almost exclusively in living pine trees. Around each cavity it drills several holes from which sticky sap continually drips, helping to repel predators, such as the climbing black racer and other snakes, or the great horned owl.

The red-cockaded woodpecker excavates cavities in several species of pines, though longleaf pine (see page 246) is most often selected. A type of plant fungus called red heart often afflicts longleaf pines that are 60 years and older. While it does not kill the tree, red heart fungus weakens the heartwood of the tree, making the woodpecker's job of cavity excavation easier.

Barrier Saints Drive

This drive along the gulf coast offers a view of different land forms, water channels and coastal forests. It passes through Apalachicola, at the mouth of the Apalachicola River.

Distance: This is a 50-mile driving tour.

The Drive: From the entrance of St. George Island State Park, known for its beautiful beaches, drive west 4 miles on Gulf Beach Drive toward the middle of the island. Turn right on Franklin Road, which becomes the bridge crossing St. George Sound. As you approach the mainland, you'll often see many small boats cruising the sound to the east of the bridge. They are oystermen, who in crews of one or two pick up the shellfish by the bushel. One scoops them up with the tongs, which resemble two rakes put together like pliers. The other breaks the clumps apart into single oysters. Their 20-foot vessels loaded by late afternoon, they go to the seafood processing houses on the gulf to deliver the goods. Many of the seafood processing plants are in Eastpoint, the city you enter after crossing this 4.5-mile section of the bay. When you reach the mainland, turn left on South Bay Shore Drive. Less than a mile later, turn left again on US 98, which soon crosses over the Apalachicola Bay on the 4-mile long John Gorrie Memorial Bridge. Near the end, the bridge finds ground briefly on Towhead Island, mostly a collection of marsh grass, then rises up in an arc over the mouth of the Apalachicola River, which allows large ships to pass underneath, and descends to dump you into downtown Apalachicola. For several decades before the Civil War, the city was the third-busiest port on the gulf. Cotton from plantations in Georgia, Alabama and North Florida came down the river to Apalachicola, where it was traded and stored before heading to textile mills in New England and Europe. You might want to stop and walk around the city (see page 258) or eat in one of the downtown restaurants such as the Boss Oyster Raw Bar or the Owl Cafe. A few blocks north of downtown, turn left at the caution light to remain on US 98. If you need to pick up refreshments, there's a number of convenience and grocery stores over the next several miles, but this is the last city you will pass through on the drive. Once you pass the row of seafood businesses on the left, there's few urban signs and lots of natural beauty, including a nice view of the St. Vincent Sound and St. Vincent Island. Eight miles west of Apalachicola, bear left on C30 when US 98 forks to the right. A little more than 10 miles later, turn left (west) on C30E. Through the pines on the right, you'll begin to see St. Joseph Bay; on the left, the Gulf of Mexico.

Approximately 2 miles later on the right (north) side of the road is a historical marker near the site of a major Confederate saltworks. The road to the rental cabin community there leads to a small shop that has information about the old saltworks, which were on the property. It produced up to 150 bushels of salt a day through seawater evaporation. The only trace of the saltworks, destroyed in 1862 by a Union

Oysters

The oyster's life isn't an easy one. Most are swallowed up as small free-swimming larvae. If they survive their two-week larval stage, they sink to the bottom and attach themselves to rocks and other hard surfaces. They start out life as males, but later become females. As adults, they feed on tiny organisms filtered in from the water in tissue that doubles as breathing gills. Their hard shells provide secure quarters—not necessarily secure enought to protect them from the snails, starfish and birds that have evolved ways to bore, suck or pick their ways in. Oysters average an inch of growth a year, although the ones in the Apalachicola Bay tend to increase in size faster because of ideal growing conditions. Ninety percent of Florida's, and 10 percent of the country's, oysters come from the bay.

These oysters are considered some of the finest tasting in the world. The blend of salt-and freshwater in the bay gives them their ideal slightly salty or iodine flavor. In the 1800s the prized mollusks were fed cornmeal in barrels as they were taken by steamboat up the Apalachicola and Chattahoochee Rivers. Today, fine restaurants as far away as Hawaii fly them in on ice.

In and around Apalachicola, many restaurants take them right out of the bay. The Boss Oyster Raw Bar and the Gibson Hotel are popular, as is the Indian Pass Trading Post Raw Bar, 18 miles west of Apalachicola.

More important than where an oyster is eaten, however, is when an oyster is eaten. Winter months are the best. That's the season they store fat and are plumpest. Also important is what is put on an oyster. Fresh from Apalachicola Bay with a drop or two of Tabasco on a saltine cracker is the preferred eating method by the natives.

landing party and the U.S.S. *Kingfisher's* guns, are a few bricks in the ground. Soon after the saltworks, you pass a military radar installation on the right. There will be a U.S. Air Force/Cape San Blas sign in front of a road that forks to the left. State and military authorities in the area assure that the road is open to the public if the gate is unlocked. You can take the short road to the end and walk 200 yards straight ahead to the cape. The buildings and metal-framed lighthouse to the right of the road, however, are off-limits government property. The lighthouse served as a beacon on the cape for 79 years until its retirement in 1996. The cape has an excellent swimming beach, and is noted for the variety of shells which wash ashore. Back on C30E right after the cape, the road turns sharply right (north) and continues about five miles to the entrance of St. Joseph Peninsula State Park.

One of the best places to see fiddler and horseshoe crabs and large water birds like pelicans, herons and egrets is the short, interpretive loop trail that begins at the picnic area next to Eagle Harbor, about 1 mile north of the entrance station. It's best to watch as the tide goes out, when small fish are swept out from a large marsh creek into St. Joseph Bay where the hungry birds wait.

BRIDGES

US 90 Bridge
Known as the "Victory Bridge," this is the first bridge on the Apalachicola River. The old Works Progress Administration Bridge, built in the 1930s during the Roosevelt administration, is visible just downstream. **Location**: *On the Jackson and Gadsden County Line where US 90 crosses the Apalachicola River between Sneads and Chattahoochee, Florida.*

I-10 Bridge
Location: *On the Jackson and Gadsden County Line where I-10 crosses the Apalachicola River south of Chattahoochee, Florida.*

FL 20 Bridge
Location: *In Liberty County where FL 20 crosses the Apalachicola River between Bristol and Blountstown, Florida.*

US 98 Bridge
This four-mile long bridge, built in 1988, is the southernmost in the A-F-C River System and symbolizes the end of the river and the beginning of Apalachicola Bay. It is named the John Gorrie Memorial Bridge, in honor of John Gorrie, who invented the ice-making machine in Apalachicola. **Location**: *In Gulf County where US 98 crosses the mouth of the Apalachicola River at Apalachicola Bay between Apalachicola and Eastpoint.*

Oystermen
A fiercely independent breed, oyster-folk keep irregular hours, work for themselves and hate being cooped up indoors. They usually go out into the bay in the morning in simple boats about 22 feet long and congregate in oyster beds east of the St. George Island Bridge. Most work in crews of two. One attacks the oysters with 12-foot poles, or tongs, connected like pliers with rakes on both ends. He tongs up oyster clumps known as burrs. His partner on the other end of the boat splits the burrs into single oysters on a culling board, a thick, strong length of wood attached to the boat, with an iron rod that resembles a giant ice pick.

They work in shallows, usually four- or five-feet deep. And after they've cleaned out an oyster bed, they move into the next one, dragging along the bottom a mini-anchor—usually an automobile crankshaft. Cramming every inch of the boat with oysters, they can collect 10 or more bushels on a good day.

Anyone can launch a boat and work the same oyster bars as the pros. But if you want to hunt more convenient mollusks, you can go oyster hogging—picking over with a culling iron the oyster bars exposed near the shoreline during low tides. Generally, oysters from coon bars, as they are called, have skinnier and longer shells than those further out in the bay. The latter grow better as they are always underwater.

Oyster season is year-round, but the best months are those with an R in them, especially the winter ones. The bag limit is one bushel (60 pounds or two five-gallon buckets) per person, and the oysters must be three inches in their greatest dimension. Out-of-staters must have at least a temporary license for recreational saltwater fishing.

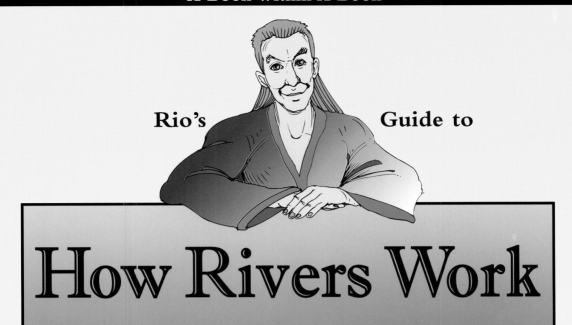

Rio's Guide to

How Rivers Work

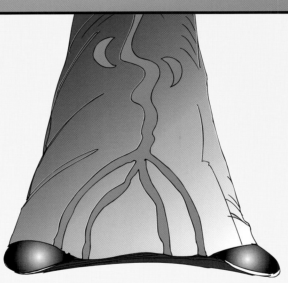

Contents

The Water Cycle

"Water is the main difference between Earth and other planets in the solar system. Earth is just the right distance from the sun to have water. Any closer and it would be too hot. Water would evaporate. Any farther away and it would be too cold. Everything would freeze. Approximately 71 percent of the earth is covered with water. It's for good reason that Earth has been called the water planet.

"If you look into outer space, you can see that there's no magic pipeline supplying water to Earth from somewhere else. The water that is here is all the water that has ever been here—for billions of years—and all the water that will ever be here.

"All of the water on Earth is recycled again and again through what is called the hydrologic cycle, or simply, the water cycle."

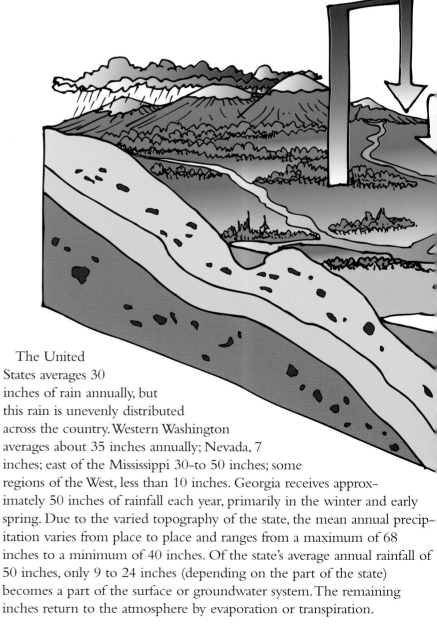

A plant draws water from the ground through its roots. Then, the plant passes the water out through its leaves as vapor in a process called transpiration. A birch tree gives off about 70 gallons of water a day. An acre of corn gives off about 4,000 gallons of water per day.

The United States averages 30 inches of rain annually, but this rain is unevenly distributed across the country. Western Washington averages about 35 inches annually; Nevada, 7 inches; east of the Mississippi 30-to 50 inches; some regions of the West, less than 10 inches. Georgia receives approximately 50 inches of rainfall each year, primarily in the winter and early spring. Due to the varied topography of the state, the mean annual precipitation varies from place to place and ranges from a maximum of 68 inches to a minimum of 40 inches. Of the state's average annual rainfall of 50 inches, only 9 to 24 inches (depending on the part of the state) becomes a part of the surface or groundwater system. The remaining inches return to the atmosphere by evaporation or transpiration.

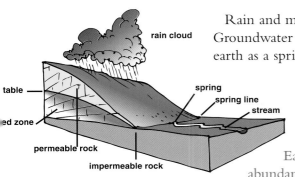

Rain and melted snow seep into the ground. Groundwater emerges from the surface of the earth as a spring. It may be a trickle or a gusher.

"On the Moon, Mercury and Mars, craters dominate the landscape. But on the continents of Earth, stream valleys are the most abundant landforms. All of these mountains, hills and valleys were shaped by flowing water. Rivers are the primary shapers of the Earth's surface.

"The water that falls on land comes from about 10 percent of the water evaporated from the oceans. That combines with water taken up from the land by a process called "evapotranspiration," and returns to the earth as rain, snow, sleet or hail.

"Evaporation is when water goes into the atmosphere as a vapor. Transpiration is the water given off by plants. The combination is called, "evapotranspiration.""

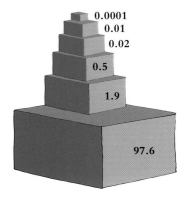

Where is the Earth's water?

0.0001 percent is in the atmosphere.
0.01 percent is soil moisture
0.02 percent is in rivers, lakes and inland seas
0.5 percent is groundwater
1.9 percent is in ice caps and glaciers
97.6 percent is in the oceans

Once water evaporates from the ocean, 90 percent of it returns directly back to the oceans in the form of rainfall.

Some of the water that falls on land does not evaporate but forms streams and rivers, which run to the ocean.

As ocean water evaporates, it loses its salt content.

The River System

"Look at the drawing on the facing page. We've all witnessed how one creek flows into another creek to form a larger stream, then observed how that stream flows downhill to join the main channel of the river. But what about the magnified view —the tiny network of water channels that look like the veins in a leaf?

"The next time it rains, walk out into your backyard. Watch how the raindrops gather in tiny rivulets even on flat ground. One trickle flows into another and that flows into another until they form a small stream. The new stream merges with another and that with another until they eventually flow into a creek and from there into a river."

RIVER SYSTEM

A river system is a network of connecting water channels. Water from rain, snow and other sources collects into the channels and flows to the ocean. A river system has three parts: a collecting system, a transporting system and a dispersing system.

THE COLLECTING SYSTEM

A river's collecting system consists of a network of tributaries in the headwaters region. This network collects and funnels water and sediment to the main stream. One of the most surprising characteristics of a collecting system is its intricate network of innumerable tributaries. Look at the illustration on this page. This is not the entire collecting system. It is a very tiny portion of it. Even the smallest tributary has its own system of smaller and smaller tributaries, until the total number becomes astronomical. In fact, most of the Earth's surface is some type of drainage system.

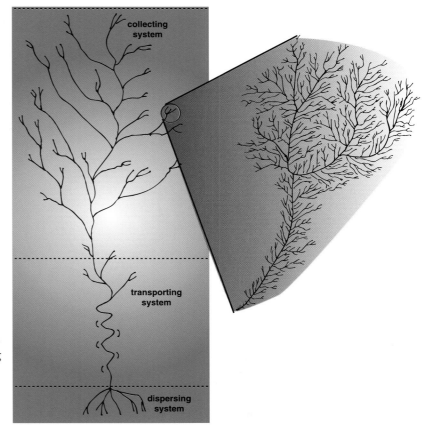

THE TRANSPORTING SYSTEM

The main task of a river's transporting system is to carry water and sediment toward the ocean. But it does other important work as well. More water and sediment are "collected" into the system. The river meanders back and forth eroding its banks. On the inside of the meanders, sediment drops out, forming point bars. More sediment drops out of the river when it overflows its banks during floods, creating floodplains.

THE DISPERSING SYSTEM

A river's dispersing system is a network of channels at a river's mouth where coarse sediment, fine-grained sand and water are dispersed into the ocean.

WHAT IS A WATERSHED?

A ridge of high ground borders every river system. This ridge encloses what is called a watershed—the region draining into a river system. Beyond the ridge, all water flows into another river system. Just as water in a bowl flows downward to a common destination, all rivers, creeks, streams, ponds, lakes, wetlands and other types of water bodies in a watershed drain into the river system. A watershed creates a natural community where every living thing has something important in common—the source and final disposition of their water.

A River's Balancing Act

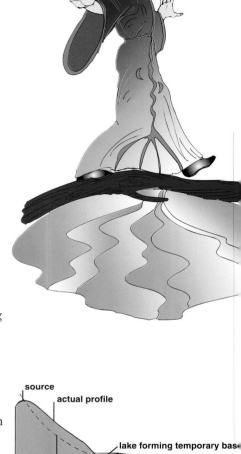

"One of the most important things about a river system—maybe the most important thing—is this: Change one part of the river and the change affects all other parts.

"Knowing this helps to understand how Earth's landscape has evolved over the years. And it has a practical side. If you change rivers to suit your needs with dams and dredging, you should know how the river will react.

"A river is always trying to reach a kind of perfect balance called 'equilibrium,' where it doesn't erode the banks or deposit any sediment. Of course, the river never reaches that balance, but it is always trying."

Here are the most important variables in stream flow. These variables constantly adjust toward a state of equilibrium.

Gradient. The gradient of a stream is its slope. The gradient is usually expressed in the numbers of feet or meters the stream descends for each mile or kilometer of flow. The headwater streams, which drain the Rocky Mountains, can have gradients of over 50m/km; the lower reaches of the Mississippi have a gradient of only 1 or 2 cm/km. One way a river changes its gradient is by lengthening itself through the creation of meanders.

Velocity. The speed of flow, which varies depending on gradient, volume of water and the location of water in a stream channel.

Sediment Load. The combination of dissolved material, fine particles and coarse material moving in the stream channel.

Discharge. The amount of water passing a given point during a given interval of time. Usually measured in cubic feet per second (cfs).

Base Level. The base level of a stream is the lowest level to which the stream can erode its channel. It is a key feature in the study of stream activity. A temporary base level may be a lake. The ultimate base level is where the stream enters the ocean.

When a river reaches a hollow in the landscape, the water may build up to form a lake. The river current slows down and the rocky debris is deposited on the lake bottom. When the river leaves the lake, the water is clearer than when it went in.

Lakes tend to be comparatively temporary features. A river deposits sediments on a lakebed, which builds up and eventually fills in. At the same time, reeds and other water plants grow around the edges, and when they die, the vegetable matter builds up, trapping even more sediment. The lake will fill up completely and become first a marsh and then dry land. The area then becomes a valley floor or a floodplain with the river flowing across it.

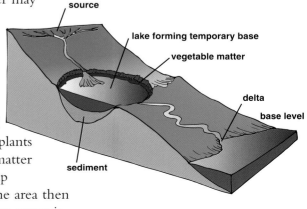

Dam construction greatly affects the equilibrium in a river system. In the reservoir behind a dam, the gradient is reduced to zero. So where the river enters the reservoir, its sediment load is deposited as a delta and layers of silt and mud build up on the reservoir floor. Because most sediment is trapped in the reservoir, the water released downstream of the dam doesn't have much sediment and, therefore, is capable of much more erosion than an undammed river, which carried a sediment load, adjusted to its gradient. As a result, extensive scour and erosion commonly occur downstream from a new dam.

To get a better understanding of equilibrium in a river system, let's look at a hypothetical stream in which equilibrium has been established.

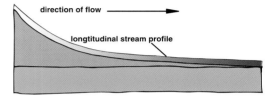

1. The variables in the stream system (discharge, velocity, gradient, base level and load) are all in balance so neither erosion nor sedimentation occurs along the stream's profile. There is just enough water to transport the available sediment down the existing slope. Such a stream is in equilibrium and is known as a "graded" stream.

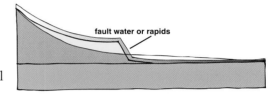

2. The stream's profile is displaced by a disruption that creates a waterfall. An example of this actually occurred at Cabin Creek, a small tributary on the Madison River in Montana, in 1959 during the Hebgen Lake Earthquake when the creekbed dropped about three meters.

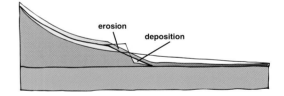

3. The increased gradient across the falls greatly increases the stream's velocity at that point so rapid erosion occurs and the waterfall, or rapid, begins to migrate upstream. The eroded sediment added to the stream segment on the dropped fault block is more than the stream can transport because the system was already at equilibrium before the faulting occurred.

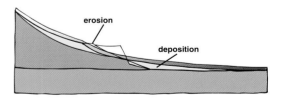

4. The river, therefore, deposits part of its load at that point, thus building up the channel gradient until a new profile of equilibrium is established.

5. By June 1960 erosion by Montana's Cabin Creek had erased the waterfall at the cliff formed by the fault, and only a small rapid was left. By 1965, the rapid was completely removed and equilibrium was reestablished.

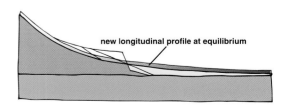

Waterfalls

Tumbling water does not wear away the riverbed rock at an even rate. Some rocks are less resistant to erosion than others. When the river reaches a layer of harder, more resistant rock, it runs across it and drops off the end as a waterfall. The softer, less resistant rock beyond the hard rock is eroded quickly by the force of water and the stones dropped upon it. A deep plunge pool forms at the foot of the waterfall. The swirling water in the plunge pool undercuts the hard rock and the rock face of the waterfall. A new waterfall then forms slightly upstream on the newly exposed rock face. This erosion gradually moves the position of the waterfall upstream and eventually the vertical drop disappears altogether. (See "A River's Balancing Act" on the previous page.)

hard rock

soft rock

plunge pool

Niagara Falls is a good illustration of the action of waterfalls.

The Niagara River originated as the last glacier receded from the area and water flowed from Lake Erie to Lake Ontario over the Niagara Cliffs. Erosion causes the waterfalls to migrate upstream at an average of 1.3 meters a year, as the action of Niagara Falls undercuts the weak shale beneath the harder limestone.

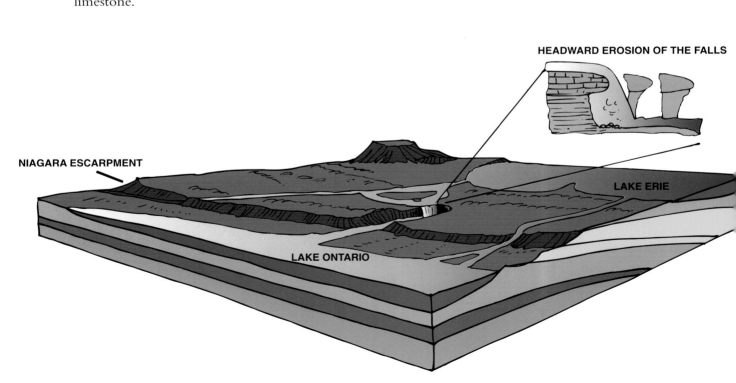

HEADWARD EROSION OF THE FALLS

NIAGARA ESCARPMENT

LAKE ERIE

LAKE ONTARIO

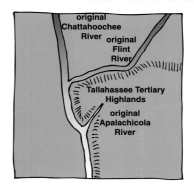

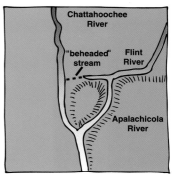

STREAM PIRACY

All streams have a tendency to erode upstream at the headwaters. When this occurs, the tributaries of one stream can extend upslope and intersect the middle course of another stream, thus diverting the headwaters on one stream to another. This process is known as stream piracy. Stream piracy is most likely to occur if one stream has a steeper gradient or more easily eroded rocks than another.

Here is an example of double stream piracy that occurred on the Flint, Chattahoochee and Apalachicola Rivers millions of years ago. Geological evidence suggests that the Apalachicola River was once only a small tributary of the Chattahoochee River. The Apalachicola actually captured the Flint River. Then the Flint captured the Chattahoochee.

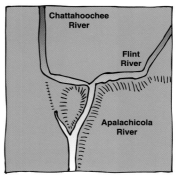

1. Originally, the Flint and Chattahoochee Rivers flowed west around what is known as the Tallahassee Highlands. At this point in time, the Apalachicola, a small tributary of the Chattahoochee, was just beginning to cut into the Highlands.

2. Still a tributary of the Chattahoochee, the Apalachicola cut through the Highlands, capturing the Flint and diverting its waters southward along the newer channel.

Meanwhile, the "beheaded" section of the Flint became an inverted stream, flowing back into the Apalachicola while slowly cutting headwaters to the west.

3. The beheaded portion of the Flint itself became a pirate and captured the Chattahoochee, rapidly enlarging the Apalachicola River Valley.

DRAINAGE PATTERNS

Tributaries of a river usually form one of three types of drainage patterns.

The dendritic pattern is the simplest drainage pattern. This forms when the tributaries flow at random so that a map of the river and its tributaries look like a tree with the river itself forming the trunk and the tributaries forming the branches.

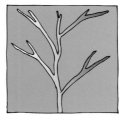

Dendritic Pattern

Geography has an affect on the drainage. If the landscape consists of a number of parallel ridges—which happens frequently where there are beds of hard rock alternating with beds of soft rock—the result is a trellis pattern. The rivers and tributaries either follow the parallel valleys formed in the soft rock or they cut directly through the ridges of hard rock. As a result, the tributaries and rivers meet each other at right angles in a square, block-shaped arrangement.

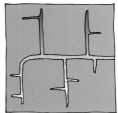

Trellis Pattern

When a new hill is pushed up in the form of a dome, the rivers will flow down the sides of the dome away from the high center. The result is a radial drainage pattern with all the rivers flowing outward.

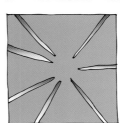

Radial Pattern

Major Features of a Floodplain

"These floodplain features occur all along the Flint River Corridor, especially in the section between Po Biddy Road Bridge and the GA 49 Bridge between Oglethorpe and Montezuma."

FLOODPLAIN

A floodplain is a relatively flat area adjacent to a stream, creek or river that is frequently covered by water during flooding. A flooded stream has the capacity to carry more and larger sediments in its channel due to the high velocity. As the stream overflows its banks, the velocity of the overflow water decreases and some of the stream's sediment load is deposited adjacent to the stream in the floodplain.

NATURAL LEVEES

Natural levees are natural dikes, or flood barriers, that build up on the banks of a river each time it overflows onto the floodplain and deposits sediment. Of all the sediment suspended in floodwaters, the finest sediment is carried by the floodwaters farther out into the floodplain. The coarsest sediment drops out first, closest to the river channel where it builds up a high embankment. With each flooding, the river dumps more and more material on the edges and the natural levees continue to grow higher. At the same time, the river channel is also rising due to the deposit of sediment. In time, the river can actually be higher than the surrounding floodplain. The natural levees of the Hun Huaang River in China are so high that the riverbed is 15 feet above the floodplain.

BACKSWAMP

As a result of the growth and development of natural levees, much of the floodplain may be lower than the river flowing across it. This area, known as a backswamp, is poorly drained and commonly the site of marshes and swamps.

YAZOO STREAMS

Tributary streams in the backswamp are unable to flow up the slope of the natural levees, so they are forced either to empty into the backswamp or to flow as Yazoo streams that run parallel to the main stream, sometimes for many miles. Yazoo streams are named after the river of that name in Mississippi.

POINT BARS

As the stream rounds a curve, the water on the outside of the curve has to flow faster than the water on the inside. This causes the bank on the outside of the river bank to erode. Conversely, on the inside of the curve the stream is going very slow and part of the sediment it is carrying drops out, creating a point bar. (More on point bars on the next page.)

OXBOW LAKES

An oxbow lake is an abandoned meander that has been cut off from the river's main channel. The river shortens its course by cutting across the neck of a meander instead of flowing around it. Oxbow lakes soon become filled with mud and silt, which aid the growth of reeds, and eventually disappear. Under normal conditions, it may take hundreds, or even thousands, of years for a river to create an oxbow lake, but, at the height of a flood, it can create one in less than an hour.

Crevasse Splay

At times the levee may be breached and the water will flow out over the floodplain, forming a Crevasse Splay across the plain from the breach.

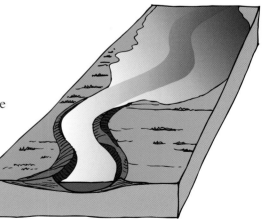

Stream Flow

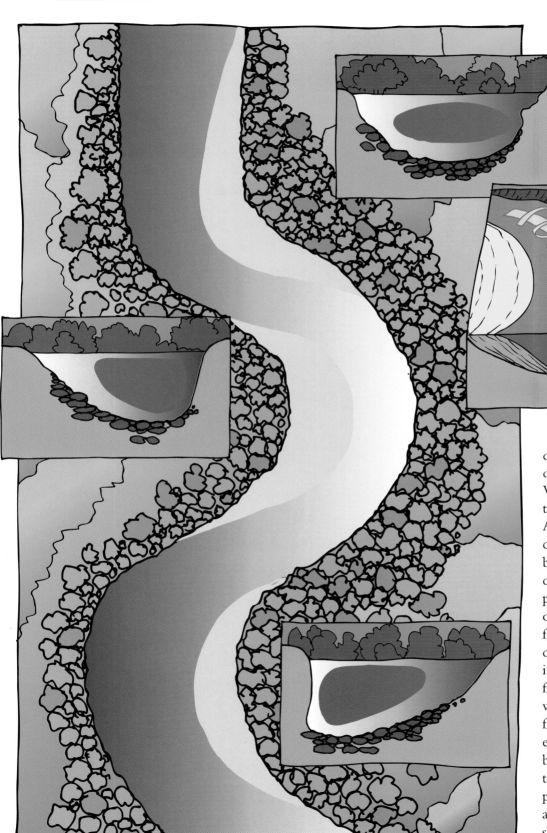

The location of a river's channel depends on the configuration of the stream. Where the stream is straight, the channel is in the middle. As the stream turns, the channel shifts to the outside bend or curve. The flow in a channel follows a corkscrew pattern. Water on the outside of the curve is forced to flow faster than on the inside of the curve. This difference in velocity, together with normal frictional drag on the channel walls, produces a corkscrew flow pattern. As a result, erosion occurs on the outer bank and deposition occurs on the inside of the bend. These processes produce an asymmetrical channel, which slowly migrates laterally.

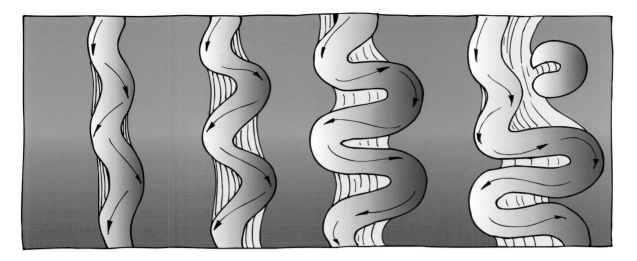

MEANDERS

Meanders begin where the stream's flow is deflected by an irregularity, and moves to the opposite bank where erosion begins. The meander enlarges and migrates laterally. At the same time, a point bar is growing on the opposite side of the river.

There is a general downslope migration of meanders as they grow larger and ultimately cut themselves off to form oxbow lakes.

The new straighter channel will not remain straight for long. Any curve in it will begin to erode on the outside and build up sediment on the inside, and the process will start again.

EDDIES

Confronted with a boulder, water—which can't be compressed like air can—piles up on the upstream side. When it flows around the boulder, it creates an eddy. Since the water in the eddy downstream is lower than the water piled up in front, the water flows back upstream toward the boulder to fill the resulting depression. We usually think of everything in a river flowing downstream, but even in the swiftest whitewater river, there are strong upstream currents.

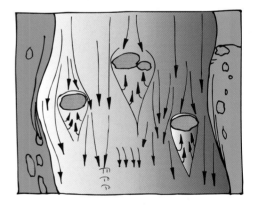

BRAIDED STREAMS

Braided streams have channels that run in various ways. They split up and come together, creating little islands called bars. These intricate patterns can be the result of melted water from glaciers or because a river is so choked with sediment it can't maintain a single channel.

Transporting Sediment

Running water is such a powerful force in shaping the Earth, not only because it can abrade and erode its channel, but also because of its enormous power to transport loose sediment produced by weathering.

The capacity of a stream to transport sediment increases to a third or fourth power of its velocity. That is, if the velocity is doubled, the stream can move eight to 16 times as much sediment.

Within a stream system, sediment is transported three ways.

The suspended load is the most obvious, and generally the largest, fraction of material moved by a river. In most major streams, silt and clay-sized particles remain in suspension most of the time and move downstream at the same velocity as the flowing water to be deposited in a lake or on a floodplain.

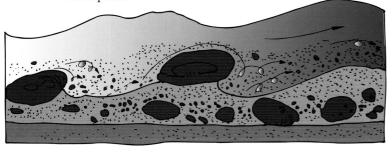

Particles of sediment too large to remain in suspension collect on the stream bottom and form the **bed load,** or **traction load.** These particles move by sliding, rolling and saltation (short leaps). The bed load moves only if there is sufficient velocity to move the large particles. It thus differs fundamentally from the suspended load, which moves constantly. There is not always a sharp distinction between the largest particles of the suspended load and the smallest particles of the bed load because the velocity of a stream fluctuates constantly. Part of the bed load can suddenly move in suspension, or part of the suspended load can settle.

The bed load can constitute 50 percent of the total load in some rivers, but it usually ranges from 7 to 10 percent of the total sediment load. The movement of the bed load is one of the major tools of stream abrasion because as the sand and gravel move, they wear away the sides and bottom of the stream channel. In some rivers, such as the Colorado and Little River, the grinding action of the bed load can be heard as large boulders are moved along the river's bottom.

The dissolved load is matter transported in the form of chemical ions; it is essentially invisible. All streams carry some dissolved material, which is derived principally from the groundwater that emerges from seeps and springs along the riverbanks. The most abundant material in solution are calcium and bicarbonate ions, but sodium, magnesium, chloride, ferric and sulfate ions are also common. Various amounts of organic matter are present and some streams are brown with organic acids from the decay of plant material.

Running water is the major agent of erosion. Rivers in the United States transport an average of 1.3 million tons of sediment per day to the oceans. The rivers of the world combine to unload about 10 billion tons of sediment into the sea every year, including the weathered remains of the mountains, where some of them were born.

POTHOLES

Potholes are erosional features usually found in the rocks of fast-moving streams. These circular depressions in rocks are formed by the grinding action of trapped sand and gravel being swirled around by strong currents within the river. Starting points for potholes are usually niches or breaks in the rocks, such as poorly developed joints along foliation planes, where water flow becomes disturbed and begins to swirl and erode.

" Since as long as I can remember—and that's a long time—rocks have been splitting and crumbling, forming smaller and smaller pieces and finally cobbles, pebbles, sand and mud. Some of this debris becomes a vital part of life-giving soil. Sooner or later, most of it reaches the edge of the continent."

REGOLITH

One of the most important processes of erosion is the removal and transport of rock debris, or regolith, produced by weathering. The process is simple but important. Loose rock debris is washed downslope into the drainage system and is transported as sediment load in streams and rivers. In addition, soluble material is carried in solution. The net result is that the blanket of regolith created by weathering is continually being removed and transported to the sea by stream action. As it is being removed, however, the weathering of fresh bedrock is also continually regenerating it.

Measurements of the amount of sediment carried by rivers indicate that the surface of the land is being lowered by on the average of 6cm (2.4 in) every 1,000 years.

RIVER ROCKS AND PEBBLES

Stones carried along by a river tend to have their corners knocked off. After being carried long distances, they are worn to a round shape and polished. If we look at a river sediment that consists of jagged lumps of rock, we can be sure that this material has not been carried very far. River gravel formed of spherical pebbles has been brought great distances.

If the river suddenly slows down, perhaps because it is coming out of a mountain gorge and onto a plain, most of the material it carries along is dropped suddenly. If we find a river sediment in which course stones and muds are jumbled together, we can say that the current suddenly slowed here. On the other hand, distinct layers of particles that are all the same size means that the current has a steady flow.

"A beach is made up of whatever a stream carries to the shore. Each beach has its own special material. The Flint and Chattahoochee Rivers form the Apalachicola, which drains straight out into Apalachicola Bay, forming a delta. If you trace those rivers back to where they came from, you'll see that they came from the Piedmont and Blue Ridge. The Piedmont and Blue Ridge are made out of schists and gneiss and other rocks. If you get rain falling and weathering, falling on granite—which is made of mica, feldspar and quartz—the mica and feldspar start to deteriorate and turn into clay, and so they wash away. Then all you have left is little grains of quartz. Quartz is very stable and tends not to break down chemically, partly because it is such a simple composition—the silicon oxygen bond that holds quartz is one of the strongest in nature. Now these little grains are loose. They are no longer part of a rock. So the stream transports them as sand and they'll end up on a beach at St. George or St. Vincent Island or somewhere else.

"If you get far enough down into Florida and look at the beaches down there, they are not made of material transported from the Piedmont and Blue Ridge because they are being fed by streams coming off the Florida Peninsula, which is covered with limestone. So the Florida beaches are just eroded limestone. They have particles of limestone, little shell fragments and fossils.

"The beaches are made of whatever the rivers carry to the shore."

Stream Terraces

Stream terraces develop along the sides of floodplain valleys when geological forces raise the riverbed. The river cuts downward and gradually forms a new floodplain. If the riverbed is raised again, the process is repeated. A river may erode stream terraces as it meanders across the valley, or a river can bury a stream terrace under sediment.

1. A stream cuts through a valley by normal down cutting and headward erosion.

2. Changes in climate, base level or other factors that reduce energy flow cause the stream to partially fill its valley with sediments, forming a broad flat floor.

3. An increase in flow energy causes the stream to erode through the previously deposited alluvium. A pair of terraces is left as a remnant of the former floodplain.

4. The stream shifts laterally and forms lower terraces as subsequent changes erode the older valley fill.

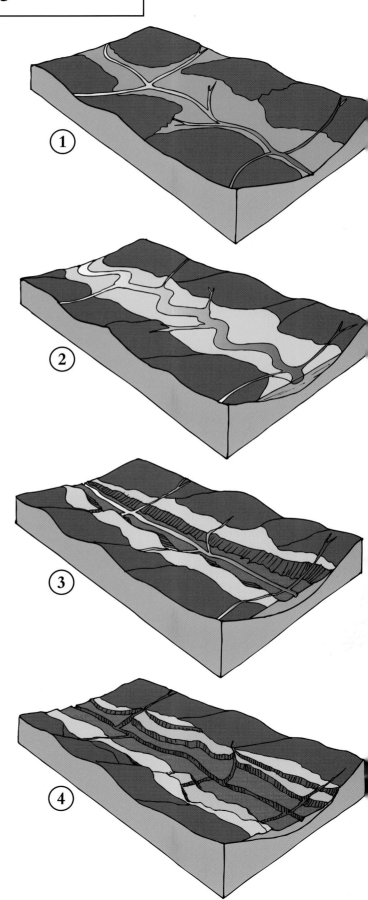

River Facts and Quotes

RUNNING WATER SHAPES THE PLANET

"The most vigorous mover and shaper on terrestrial Earth is running water. Stream valleys are the most abundant and widespread landforms on the continents. Seen in satellite photographs, the vast network of stream valleys resemble in their patterns the shape of an outspread tree without leaves. Intricate, delicate filaments at the top, like twigs at the end of a branch. Strong and thick near the bottom, like the base of a trunk."

From *River Systems, Earth's Dynamic Systems* by Ken Hamblin

HOW MUCH DOES WATER WEIGH?

A gallon of water weighs 8.33 pounds. A cubic foot of water weighs 62.4 pounds.

MEASURING RIVER FLOW

Cubic feet per second, or cfs, is a way of measuring water flow. It is the volume of water moving past a specified point at a specified time. A small river might flow 600 cubic feet per second, meaning that a slice of water containing 600 cubic feet of water and weighing, 37,440 pounds flows past a given point in one second. A large river might run over 100,000 cfs. The Colorado River in the Grand Canyon averages 30,000 to 40,000 cfs. From 1977 through 1992 the discharge of the Flint River based on mean daily flow at Newton, Georgia, was 4,030 cfs. Mean daily discharge ranged from 922 cfs in 1991 to 47,000 cfs in 1990.

DAMMED RIVERS

Nationwide 600,000 miles of rivers are dammed by 68,000 large dams (more than two stories high). The Yellowstone River in Wyoming and Montana (more than 600 miles long) is the only major American river that remains undammed. There are nearly 2 million small dams—dams under two stories —in the United States.

WHERE DOES RIVER FOG COME FROM?

Ever wonder why mists often shroud rivers, creeks and valleys during cloudless nights in the summer and fall?

During these times of year the sun warms up the water, causing it to evaporate a lot of moisture into the air next to it.

Throughout the night, however, the water surface and adjacent humid air lose heat rapidly to the colder atmosphere above. During calm and clear nights, the temperature of the humid surface air often falls below the dew point. When this change happens the air cannot hold as much moisture as before and condenses to form innumerable water droplets, which form a fog.

If the air is windy, the fog tends to blow over the water and dissipate. If the sky is overcast, there is usually enough heat radiating from the clouds back to the earth to prevent cooling of the surface air to the dew point, and thus preventing the consequent formation of fog.

LAND USE AND RIVERS

Land use is the most important factor in a river's water quality. Although urban and suburban land use accounts for only five percent of the Apalachicola, Chattahoochee and Flint Basin, it has the most important effect on stream-water quality. The intensity of the land use effect on water quality varies in proportion to various measures of urbanization, such as impervious area, population density and percent of industrial and transportation land use. As the percentage of urban land use increases within a watershed, nutrients, pesticides, trace elements and organic compounds are more prevalent and occur at higher concentrations in streams. Source: U. S. Geological Survey Circular 1164.

FREE FLOWING RIVERS

The Yellowstone is the longest free-flowing river in the lower 48 states.

With 153 miles of free-flowing water, the Flint River is one of only 42 free-flowing river reaches longer than 125 miles remaining in the contiguous 48 states. Other Georgia rivers with 125 miles or more of free-flowing water are: the Alapaha (125), Altamaha (128) Ocmulgee (184), Oconee (134) and Savannah (170).

DON'T MESS WITH RIVERS

"In the world there is nothing more submissive and weak than water. Yet, for attacking that which is hard and strong nothing can surpass it."

Loa-Tzu (Chinese philosopher of the 6th century B.C.)

Early Industry on Rivers

"Early settlers harnessed the power of rivers to operate their gristmills. The first textile mills were water powered."

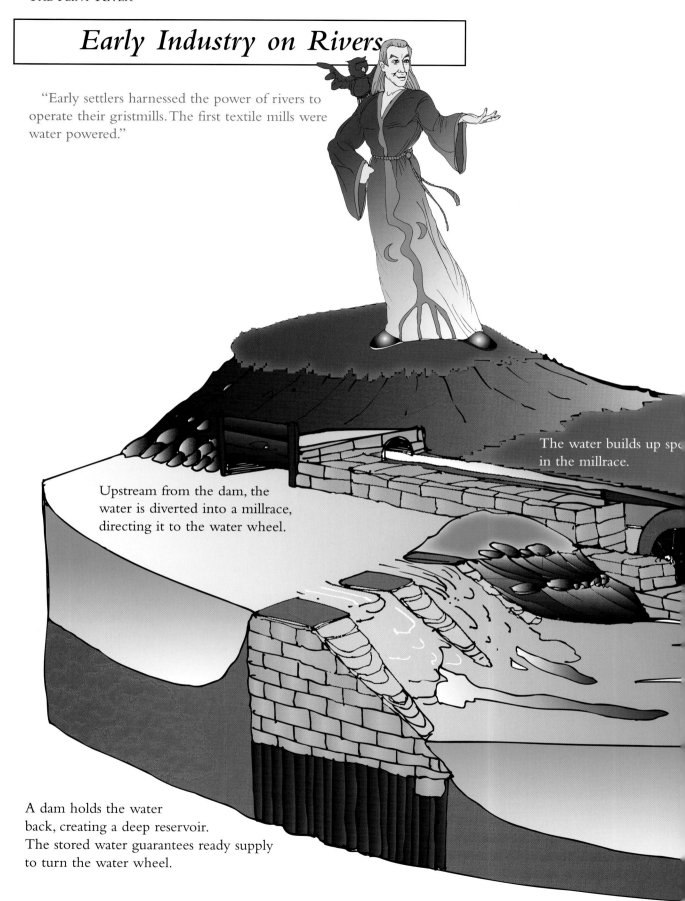

The water builds up spe[...]
in the millrace.

Upstream from the dam, the water is diverted into a millrace, directing it to the water wheel.

A dam holds the water back, creating a deep reservoir. The stored water guarantees ready supply to turn the water wheel.

"In building first their mills and then their cities along rivers, the pioneers of this part of America were following a pattern of settlement as old as civilization. The first great civilizations arose in the valleys of great rivers: in the Nile Valley of Egypt, the Tigris Euphrates Valley of Mesopotamia, the Indus Valley of Pakistan and the Hwang Ho Valley of China. All of these civilizations built large irrigation systems, made the land productive and prospered."

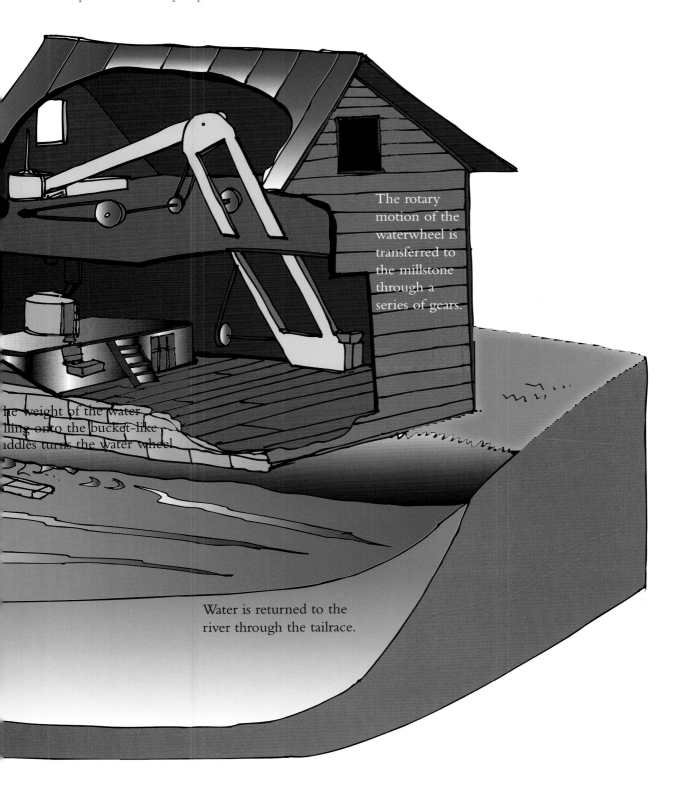

The rotary motion of the waterwheel is transferred to the millstone through a series of gears.

The weight of the water falling onto the bucket-like paddles turns the water wheel.

Water is returned to the river through the tailrace.

Hydroelectric Power

"Building dams across river valleys means that running water can be contained so it can be used how and where it is most needed—whether it is to prevent flooding, divert water into irrigation channels for agriculture, provide reservoirs for water storage or provide a source of power for electricity.

"Hydroelectric power is one of the most important benefits of river regulations. The general construction of dams and the generation of hydroelectric power changes the normal dynamic of river flows."

HYDROELECTRIC TURBINE

Today, the principle of the water wheel is used for producing electricity. Water pressure turns a turbine, which is connected to an electric generator.

HOW HYDROELECTRICITY WORKS

The principles used in a modern hydroelectric plant are the same as those used centuries ago. Back then, the natural energy of falling or flowing water was harnessed and changed into mechanical energy by paddle wheels, such as those seen on old gristmills. The water turned the wheels and the wheels turned the machinery.

In the late 1800s hydro energy was first changed into electric energy by allowing water to spin turbines connected to electric generators instead of paddle wheels. To meet the ever-growing demand for energy, dams were built to hold and store the enormous amounts of water, called reservoirs, needed to produce thousands of kilowatts of electricity. In this illustration, you can see how a hydroelectric power plant generates electricity.

Falling water from the reservoir (1) passes through the penstock (2) to enter the powerhouse. The flowing water turns the propeller-like water wheel or turbine (3), which is connected by a shaft to the generator (4), which spins and produces electricity.

The same water that flowed through the turbine (3) is then discharged through the draft tube (5) where it enters the tailrace (6) and returns unaltered to the river below the dam.

The electricity produced by the spinning generator (4) is conducted to the power transformer (7) where the voltage is increased. The high-voltage electricity is then fed into transmission lines for distribution to electricity customers.

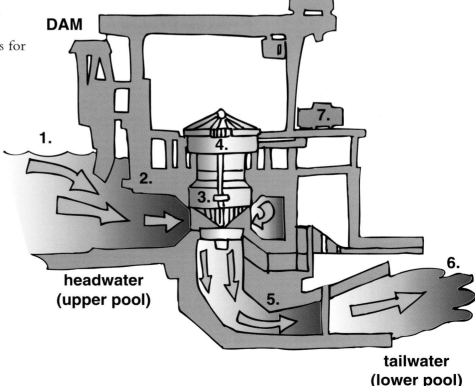

DAM

1.

2.

3.

4.

5.

6.

7.

headwater (upper pool)

tailwater (lower pool)

Water for Cities

"Rivers and streams are the primary sources of water for cities and the way that cities dispose of their wastes.

"The water system of a modern city is designed to provide 130 gallons of water per person, per day. That's used for bathing, washing dishes, flushing toilets, doing laundry, watering the grass and drinking. In most water systems, up to 30 percent of the water pumped from the river is lost because of leaks. In the treatment plant, impurities are removed and germs destroyed to make the water safe for drinking. Sedimentation, filtering and the addition of chemicals are the main methods of treatment."

Water is stored in a reservoir. Th height of the reservoir provides pressure for water distribution. The water is distributed from the reservoir to the buildings in the

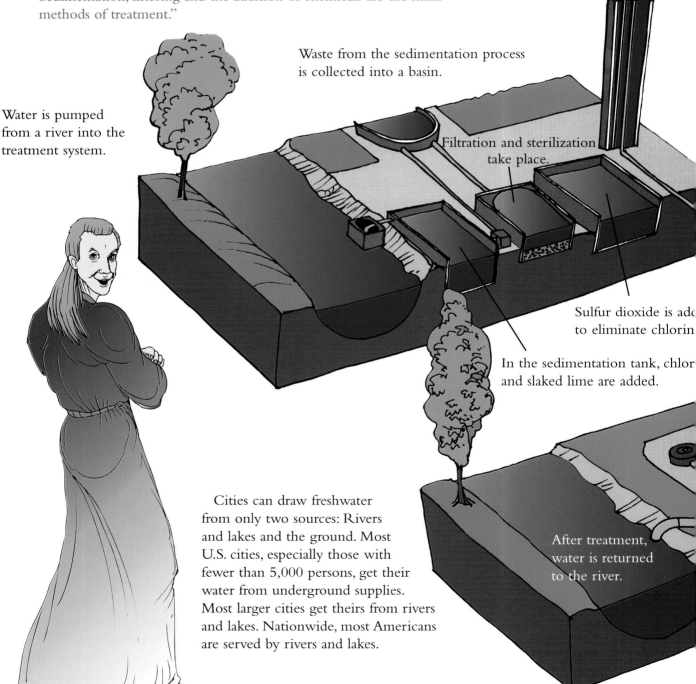

Waste from the sedimentation process is collected into a basin.

Water is pumped from a river into the treatment system.

Filtration and sterilization take place.

Sulfur dioxide is add to eliminate chlorin

In the sedimentation tank, chlor and slaked lime are added.

After treatment, water is returned to the river.

Cities can draw freshwater from only two sources: Rivers and lakes and the ground. Most U.S. cities, especially those with fewer than 5,000 persons, get their water from underground supplies. Most larger cities get theirs from rivers and lakes. Nationwide, most Americans are served by rivers and lakes.

Pressure in the system sends water to
the top of the buildings.

What comes in must go out.
Drainpipes send water to the
sewer system.

Sewer pipes are oval, an efficient shape
for carrying away waste.

Solid waste settles to the bottom of the tank.

Sewage and sludge are separated.

is treated.

Several stages of sedimentation and aeration take place during the
treatment process. Some communities have created "wetlands" where
natural processes do much of the work of the sewage treatment plant.

Development Affects Rivers

"According to my best sources, the earth is about 4,500 million years old. And rivers have been around just about that long, too. Humans have been here only a tiny, tiny fraction of that time… Maybe 2.5 million years? For most of that time, they had little effect on the way rivers worked. But just in the last 200 or so years, humans have had a major impact on the natural river system. Since the industrial revolution, the growth of tons and tons of discharges from factories has added to the problem and has changed rivers.

"It's becoming harder and harder for Earth's finite water supply to purify itself. Nature now has to cope with new chemical compounds that won't break down, such as plastics; chemical wastes produced by industrial plants; and loads of sewage from growing cities. An increasing percentage of the world's limited water supply is being rendered unfit for human use.

"Urbanization changes the surface of the earth and affects the way the water runs off the land. Roads and sidewalks repel water; they don't take in water. Water is channeled through gutters, storm drains and sewers. As a result, flooding increases in intensity and frequency."

Industries and vehicle exhausts give off gasses (including sulfur dioxide and nitrogen oxides), which combine with water vapo in the air to form acid rain. This rain, which is diluted sulfuric acid, is fatal to vegetation. Acid rain has killed many of the trees in the mountains along the East Coast in the United States.

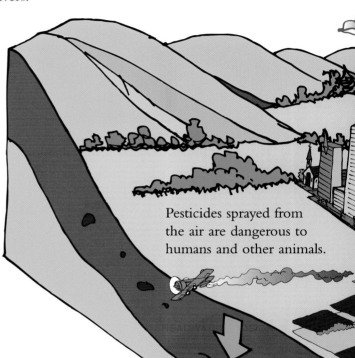

Pesticides sprayed from the air are dangerous to humans and other animals.

The most influential factor in water quality is land use. Storm water runoff from various land uses transports pollutants to streams.

Many cities are not near rivers or lakes large enough to meet their needs. These cities use water that is stored underground. This water comes from rain that soaks into the ground. As it trickles downward, it fills spaces between grains of sand and cracks and pores in rocks. In time, the water reaches a layer of rock or other material that is watertight. The water collects above that watertight layer and the ground becomes saturated. This saturated zone is called an aquifer. The top of the zone is called the water table. Cities obtain underground water by drilling wells below the water table and pumping up the water.

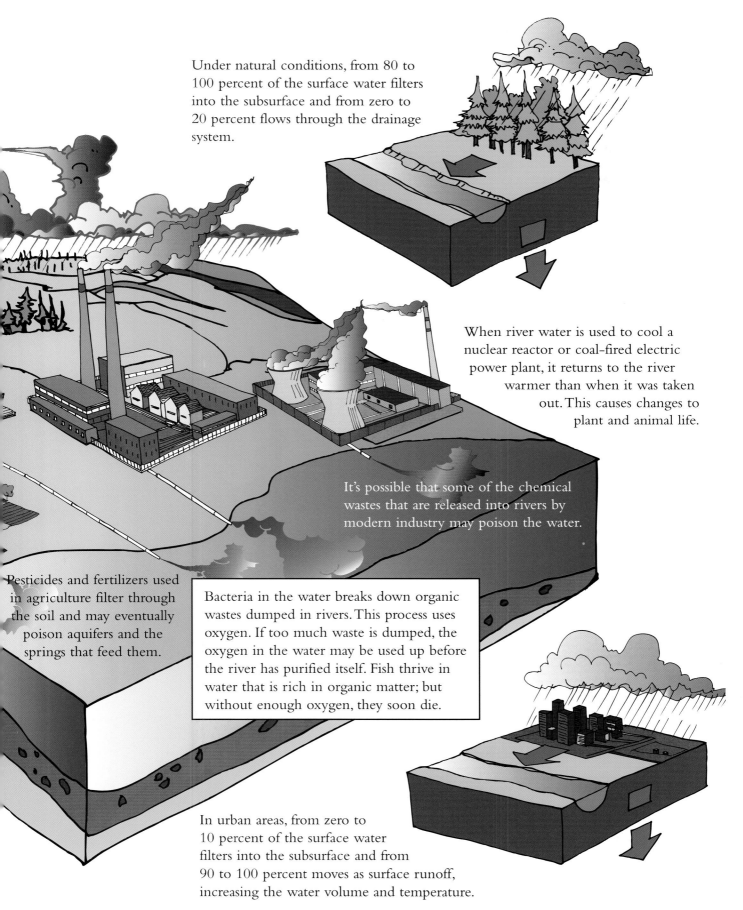

Under natural conditions, from 80 to 100 percent of the surface water filters into the subsurface and from zero to 20 percent flows through the drainage system.

When river water is used to cool a nuclear reactor or coal-fired electric power plant, it returns to the river warmer than when it was taken out. This causes changes to plant and animal life.

It's possible that some of the chemical wastes that are released into rivers by modern industry may poison the water.

Pesticides and fertilizers used in agriculture filter through the soil and may eventually poison aquifers and the springs that feed them.

Bacteria in the water breaks down organic wastes dumped in rivers. This process uses oxygen. If too much waste is dumped, the oxygen in the water may be used up before the river has purified itself. Fish thrive in water that is rich in organic matter; but without enough oxygen, they soon die.

In urban areas, from zero to 10 percent of the surface water filters into the subsurface and from 90 to 100 percent moves as surface runoff, increasing the water volume and temperature.

Wetlands

Wetlands are natural areas that hold water. There are many different kinds of wetlands: swamps, marshes, bogs and mangrove swamps are some of them. Generally found in low-lying areas, wetlands may be as small as a wading pool or as big as a lake. Water is an essential ingredient of a wetland—but it isn't always there. Some wetlands stay wet all year, while others dry out for months at a time. Wetlands on the coast fill up and drain twice a day because of the ocean's tides.

Wetlands benefit people by providing free services that are worth billions of dollars each year.

Wetlands help clean our water. Because water moves slowly in wetlands, silt and sediments settle out. Wetland plants absorb certain nutrients and chemicals that pollute rivers, ponds and lakes.

Wetlands help control floods. When rivers overflow, wetlands hold excess waste and slow the fast currents of overflowing rivers.

Wetlands provide recreation. They provide opportunities for fishing, canoeing, hiking and bird watching.

Wetlands provide homes for wildlife. On a per-acre basis, more plants and animals live in wetlands than anywhere else. About 35 percent of all plant and animals listed as threatened or endangered in the United States either live in wetlands or rely on them in some way. In wetlands, you see birds, ducks, turtles, fish, muskrats, beavers, deer, raccoons and a host of other animals.

Wetlands, particularly coastal wetlands, are breeding grounds for many fish. Most of the fish and shellfish that we eat live in wetlands, where they find food and protection from larger fish when they are young. Wetlands along the Gulf and Atlantic coasts are especially important as fish nurseries. Wetlands support a multi-billion dollar commercial and recreational fishing industry.

Over the past 200 years, expansion of human development has caused the destruction of valuable wetlands. Of the approximately 215 million acres of wetlands originally existing in the lower 48 states, fewer than half remain.

Estuaries

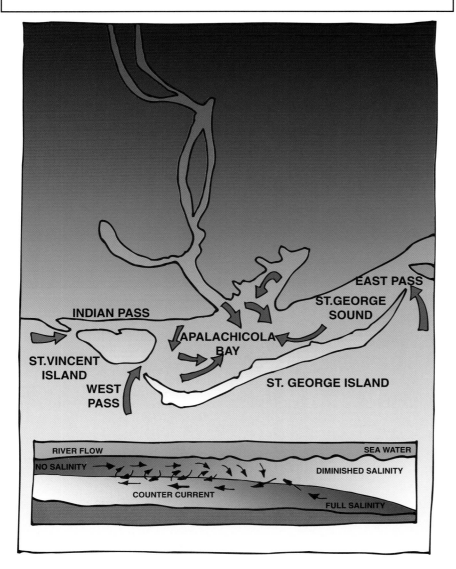

"The Flint and Chattahoochee Rivers meet to form the Apalachicola River, which flows 106 miles through Florida to Apalachicola Bay. The estuary where the Apalachicola River meets the ocean is not only beautiful, it is one of the most productive estuaries on a per-acre basis in all of North America. Shrimp, oysters and many types of fish are either born here or spend part of their early life in this estuary. More than 90 percent of Florida's oysters are harvested in Apalachicola Bay."

A constantly changing mix of freshwater and saltwater at the junction of rivers and oceans, estuaries are home to an abundance of life. River currents send freshwater downstream and ocean currents push saltwater upstream. When the two meet, they form a wedge; the lighter freshwater continues flowing on top toward the ocean, and the heavier saltwater is driven downward and up the channel. If the freshwater is clear, the wedge can easily be seen. Clear water flows downstream on the surface, but, underneath, dark muddy water flows in the opposite direction. The location of the wedge within an estuary zone changes often—sometimes within a matter of minutes—depending on tides, seasons and weather conditions. Strong incoming tides and storms can push it far up the channel. So can low river flows during summer and winter. Conversely,

outgoing tides or spring river floods send it far into the bay. Temperatures in the wedge vary as well. In summer and autumn, incoming freshwater is warmer than the ocean. In the winter and spring, the opposite is true. Life is extremely difficult in the estuary because of rapidly changing water levels, currents, salinity content and temperatures. Despite the harsh conditions, there is plenty of food for estuary life. Much of the nutrient load that comes with rivers is slowed or stopped by the incoming ocean current. The settling organic matter feeds marsh grasses, algae and microscopic plants and continues up the food chain. Estuaries support more life than any other natural environment. They serve as a spawning ground for more than 75 percent of all commercially harvested shrimp, crabs, oysters and fishes.

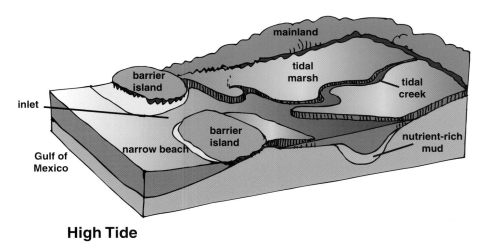

High Tide

inlet

Gulf of Mexico

narrow beach

barrier island

barrier island

mainland

tidal marsh

tidal creek

nutrient-rich mud

MARSHES

The coastal marshes are up to seven times as productive as cultivated wheat fields, complete with irrigation and fertilizer. Economic evaluation of the marshes shows that from a production value they are worth $89,000 per acre—a renewable resource with no overhead.

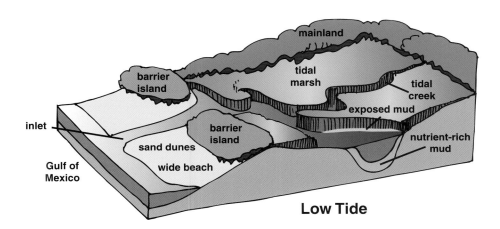

inlet

Gulf of Mexico

barrier island

sand dunes

wide beach

barrier island

mainland

tidal marsh

tidal creek

exposed mud

nutrient-rich mud

Low Tide

DELTAS

When a river is full of rocky debris and sediment and enters a sea that is quiet and has no strong currents, the sediment is deposited at the river mouth. Layers of silt and sand are built up and the river breaks into several channels winding around the sandbanks and enters the sea by a number of mouths. The result is a delta.

TYPES OF DELTAS

Sometimes, such as at the mouth of the Mississippi, the delta consists of levees that extend out into the sea. The individual channels are lined by long narrow banks, producing a levee that resembles a bird's foot.

When the sediment is dumped immediately, the channels are continually being blocked and the water finds new outlets. The constantly changing patterns of channels produces a rounded front, an arcuate delta like that of the Nile.

When a delta builds out into the sea gradually, there may be only a single mouth to the river with the delta sands curving back to the land on each side. This is a cuspate delta, such as that of the Tiber River in Italy and the delta found at Apalachicola Bay.

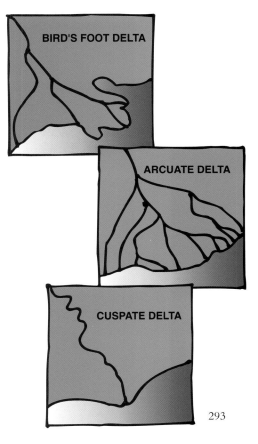

BIRD'S FOOT DELTA

ARCUATE DELTA

CUSPATE DELTA

Glossary

Aquifer

Underground rock layer, which collects and holds water. Aquifers may consist of sedimentary and porous rocks, fractured and cracked rocks and loose deposits of sand and gravel.

Base Level

The level below which a stream cannot effectively erode. Sea level is the ultimate base level, but lakes form temporary base levels for inland drainage systems.

Bed Load

Material transported by currents along the bottom of a stream or river by rolling or sliding, in contrast to material carried in suspension or solution.

Buffer Zones

The protective margins mandated by most states and federal resource agencies to protect stream banks from logging and development. Opinions differ as to how wide minimum buffer zones should be. Georgia buffer zones are 25 feet for warm water streams and 50 feet for trout streams.

Discharge

Rate of flow. The volume of water moving through a given cross section of a stream in a given unit of time.

Drainage Basin

Area of land in which all water falling as rain or snow runs via ditches, streams or other water courses into a single river or lake or into the sea.

Drainage System

An integrated system of tributaries and a trunk system which collect and funnel surface water to the sea, a lake or some other body of water. The drainage basin is the total area that contributes water to a single drainage system.

Erosion

The process that loosens sediment and moves it from one place to another on the Earth's surface. Agents of erosion include water, ice, wind and gravity. In the case of water, it breaks off fragments of rock on sloping ground, carries them away and eventually breaks them down into smaller pieces.

Estuary

A bay at the mouth of a river formed by deposition of the sand or by a rise in sea level. Freshwater from the river mixes with and dilutes seawater in an estuary.

Floodplain

The land adjacent to streams that is subject to periodic flooding is called a floodplain. Floodplains function as emergency storage space—seepage areas and passageways for storm water during floods. Flood plains hold the excess flows until the streams normalize again.

Floodplains are often more diverse than the adjacent upland areas. This unique environment represents a gradient in vegetation, moisture and soils, which create a number of habitats. Twigs, branches and leaves, falling from the floodplain vegetation, provide important instream habitat for insects and fish. Additionally, this vegetation provides a food or energy source that is important to the entire aquatic food web. Land is often referred to as being in the 100-year flood plain or the 500-year flood plain. These terms may be misleading. The term does not mean that a 100-year flood will occur only once over a 100-year period. The 100-year flood has a one percent chance of occurring in any given year. Likewise the 500-year flood has a one-in-500 chance of occurring in any given year. Extensive floodplains border the Flint River.

Groundwater

Water below the Earth's surface. It generally occurs in pore spaces of rocks and soil.

Headwater Erosion

Extension of a stream headward, up the regional slope of erosion.

Karst Topography

A landscape characterized by sinks, solution valleys and other features produced by groundwater activity.

Load

The total amount of sediment carried at any given time by a stream.

Marsh

Wet low-lying ground that is temporarily or permanently covered with water, characterized by aquatic, grasslike vegetation.

Runoff

The process by which water that has fallen on land runs from higher ground to lower and eventually makes its way to the sea.

Sand

Sedimentary material composed of fragments ranging in diameter from 0.0625 to 2 mm. Sand particles are larger than silt particles, but smaller than pebbles. Much sand is composed of quartz grains, because quartz is abundant and resists chemical and mechanical disintegration, but other materials, such as shell fragments and rock fragments, can also form sand.

Sediment

Material—such as gravel, sand, mud and lime—that is transported and deposited by wind and water.

Sedimentation

A natural phenomenon whereby a river, as it reaches lower ground and its speed lessens, deposits the small particles of sand, mud and rocks it was carrying.

Shoal

A bank of sand or rocks just below the surface of a water body. In general, an area of shallow water.

Silt

Sedimentary material composed of fragments, ranging in diameter from 1/265 to 1/16 mm. Silt particles are larger than clay particles but smaller than sand particles.

Slough

Old river channel that now resembles a lake, pond or canal.

Solution Chamber

A hollow in a water-soluble rock layer underlying surface soil, caused by the dissolving action of water percolating from the surface.

Sorting

The natural separation of particles, according to size, shape or weight. It occurs during transportation by running water.

Stream Load

The total amount of sediment carried by a stream at a given time.

Suspended Load

The part of a stream's load that is carried in suspension for a considerable length of time without contact with the streambed. It consists mainly of mud, silt and sand. Contrast with bed load and dissolved load.

Tributary

A stream flowing into or joining a larger stream.

Ultimate Base Level

The lowest possible level to which a stream can erode the Earth's surface: sea level.

Upland

High ground, not wetland.

Watershed

The ridge or crestline separating two drainage basins. Rain falling on either side of the watershed will run off towards one river system or the other.

Water Table

The upper surface of the zone of saturation. Only a certain, sometimes small, percentage of water runs off in stream channels. Usually, water percolates downward through the soil until it reaches a point of complete saturation. Above this level, known as the water table, is filled with air. Water tables fluctuate considerably, according to the amount of water received and absorbed. Some soils hold water for a long time, but others lose it rather quickly.

Wetland

Any area that is more or less regularly wet or flooded, where the water table stands at or above the land surface for at least part of the year. Dr. Eugene Odum, the legendary ecologist at the University of Georgia, quips that the plot should pass the squish test. "If you put a foot in and you hear a squish, it's a wetland." Wetlands are areas with enough surface or ground water to support vegetation adapted to life in saturated soil conditions. Some wetlands are wetter than others. They may hold water permanently or only a few days each year. Marsh, swamp, floodplain forest, bottomland, bog, fen, slough, wet meadow, prairie pothole—each of these names may apply to a wetland, depending on where the wetland is located, what grows in it or how it gets its water.

Zone of Saturation

The zone in the subsurface in which all pore spaces are filled with water.

Here are some things you can do to enjoy, preserve and protect rivers **and help keep them working.**

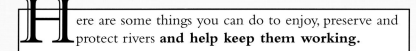

How Rivers Work

☑ Join one of the environmental groups that have a special emphasis on river education and protection, such as a Riverkeeper organization or the Georgia Conservancy. For a listing of river-related environmental groups and phone numbers, see the Resources Section of this book.

☑ Participate in a river cleanup event or local Adopt-A-Stream program. For information, call 888/373-5947.

☑ Buy household products labeled non-toxic, non-phosphorus or water soluble. Toxic chemicals can harm stream life and phosphorus can promote excessive growth of weeds and algae.

☑ Dispose of trash properly. Styrofoam and plastics can kill fish and wildlife and contaminate water sources.

☑ Inspect your home septic tank system annually and pump it out every three to five years.

☑ Never dispose of solvents, hazardous chemicals or waste in storm or home drains.

☑ Use pesticides, herbicides and fertilizers carefully and sparingly—and only when other methods have failed. Do not apply them if rain is in the forecast. Remember, anything entering a storm drain goes directly into streams—untreated.

☑ When watering your lawn and garden, divert water away from paved surfaces and onto the grass.

☑ Do not dump used motor oil or antifreeze down storm drains. Take these used products to designated recycling centers.

☑ Have your car inspected and maintained regularly. Leakage of fluids will eventually reach the nearest stream.

☑ Report any suspicious potential pollutant discharge or illegal dumping activity. Call Toll Free 800/2421-4113.

☑ Use this or some other guide to get out and see, learn about and enjoy rivers!

Resources

BIBLIOGRAPHY

The following is a selected bibliography of books and reports that contain information about the Flint River and environs.

A Brief Historical Sketch of the Town of Woodbury by Charles Sloan Reid. 1948.

A Brief History of Warm Springs published by the City of Warm Springs. 1993.

A History of Georgia edited by Kenneth Coleman. The University of Georgia Press, Athens, GA, 30602. Second Edition, 1991.

A Paddler's Guide to Southern Georgia by Bob Sehlinger and Don Otey. Menasha Ridge Press, Birmingham, AL. 1980.

A Walking or Cycling Tour of Fort Gaines by James Edgar Coleman. Clay County Economic Development Council and First State Bank and Trust, Fort Gaines, GA 31751.

Cornerstone of Georgia, Seminole County 1920–1991 by the Seminole County Historical Society. WH Wolfe Associates, Historical Publications Division, P.O. Box 972, Roswell, GA 30077.

Decatur County Georgia, Past and Present by the Decatur County Historical Society. WH Wolfe Associates, Historical Publications Division, P.O. Box 972, Roswell, GA 30077.

Fair to Middlin'–The Antebellum Cotton Trade of the Apalachicola/Chattahoochee River Valley by Lynn Willoughby. University of Alabama Press, Tuscaloosa, AL 35487-0380. 1993.

Flowing Through Time, A History of the Lower Chattahoochee River by Lynn Willoughby. The University of Alabama Press, Tuscaloosa, AL 34587-0380. 1999.

Generations, The Story of Albany by Dr. Joseph Kitchens and Dr. C. Stephen Gurr. Community Communications, Inc., Montgomery, AL. 1998.

Georgia History in Outline by Kenneth Coleman. University of Georgia Press, Athens, GA. 1960.

Georgia Wildlife Viewing Guide by Jerry McCollum, Betsie Rothermel and Chuck Rabolli. Georgia Wildlife Federation, Conyers, GA. 1996.

Historical Account of Meriwether County, 1827–1974 compiled by Regina P. Pinkston. Published in cooperation with Meriwether County by Meriwether Historical Society, Greenville, GA. 1974.

History of Clayton County Georgia, 1821–1983 edited by Alice Copeland Kilgore, Edith Haynes Smith and Frances Partridge Tuck. Ancestors Unlimited, Inc., P.O. Box 1507, Jonesboro, GA 30237. 1983.

Indian Heritage of Georgia by Marion R. Hemperley. Garden Club of Georgia. 1994.

Inventory of the County Archives of Georgia, No. 47 Dougherty County by the Georgia Historical Records Survey Division of Professional and Service Projects Work Projects Administration. Atlanta, GA. January 1941.

Knights of Spain, Warriors of the Sun by Charles Hudson. The University of Georgia Press, Athens, GA 30602. 1997.

"Little White House Springs and Pools, Staff Report, Interpretive Unit" by Billy Townsend. 1980.

Native Trees of Georgia by G. Norman Bishop. Georgia Forestry Commission. 1990.

Nature's Melody, A Guide to Georgia Wildflowers by Betty L. Benson for The Garden Club of Georgia, Inc. Published by The Garden Club of Georgia, Inc., 325 S. Lumpkin Street, Athens, GA 30602-1865. 1994.

Perilous Journeys: A History of Steamboating on the Chattahoochee, Apalachicola, and Flint Rivers, 1828–1928 by Edward A. Mueller. Historic Chattahoochee Commission, Eufaula, AL. 1990.

Prologue by Maston O'Neal. 1985.

Protected Plants of Georgia by Thomas S. Patrick, James R. Allison and Gregory A. Krakow. Georgia DNR, Wildlife Resources Division, Georgia Natural Heritage Program, 2070 US Highway 278 S. E., Social Circle, GA 30279. 1995.

Quail Plantations of South Georgia and North Florida text by Joseph Kitchens. Photographs by Hank Margeson. The University of Georgia Press, Athens, GA 30602. 1991.

Randolph County Georgia, Volume II by the Randolph County Historical Society. Wolfe Publishing, P.O. Box 8036, Fernandina Beach, FL 32035. 1997.

The Atlas of Georgia by Thomas W. Hodler and Howard A. Schretter. The Institute of Community and Area Development, University of Georgia, Athens, GA 30602. 1986.

The Bluff at Fort Gaines, Georgia by James Edgar Coleman. Clay County Economic Development Council, Fort Gaines, GA. 1997.

The Federal Road through Georgia, the Creek Nation and Alabama, 1806–1836 by Henry deLeon Southerland, Jr., and Jerry Elijah Brown. The University of Alabama Press, Box 870380, Tuscaloosa, AL 35487-0380. 1989.

The Georgia Almanac and Book of Facts edited by James A. Crutchfield. Rutledge Hill Press, Inc., 513 Third Avenue South, Nashville, TN 37210. 1986.

The History of Fayette County edited by Carolyn C. Cary. The Fayette County Historical Society, Inc. 1977.

The Magic and Mystery of Westville photographs by Mike Haskey and text by William W. Winn. Westville Historic Handicrafts, Inc., P.O. Box 1850, Lumpkin, GA 31815. 1999.

The Natural Environments of Georgia by Charles H. Wharton, published jointly by Geologic and Water Resources Division and Resource Planning Section, Office of Planning and Research, Georgia DNR, Atlanta, GA. 1978.

The New Georgia Guide. Steve Gurr, Project Director, and Jane Powers Weldon, Project Coordinator. The University of Georgia Press, Athens, Georgia 30602 and the Georgia Humanities Council, Atlanta, GA 30303. 1996.

The Old Beloved Path: Daily Life Among the Indians of the Chattahoochee River Valley by William W. Winn. The Chattahoochee Historic Commission, Eufaula, AL, and The Columbus Museum, Columbus, GA. 1992.

The Other Florida by Gloria Jahoda. Florida Classics Library, Port Salerno, FL. 1967.

There Was a Land, A History of Talbot County, Georgia by Judge Robert H. Jordan. Talbotton, GA. 1971.

The Squire of Warm Springs by Theo Lippman, Jr. Published by The Roosevelt Warm Springs Institute for Rehabilitation.

The Story of Franklin D. Roosevelt, Warm Springs and The Little White House. Published by the Georgia DNR and Georgia Heritage Association.

The Young Naturalist's Guide to Florida by Peggy Sias Lantz and Wendy A. Hale. Pineapple Press, Inc., P.O. Drawer 16008, Southside Station, Sarasota, FL 34239. 1994.

The Warm Springs of Georgia, Their Geologic Relations and Origins by D. F. Hewett and G. W. Crickmay. U.S. Department of the Interior, Geological Survey, 1937.

This So Remote Frontier: The Chattahoochee Country of Alabama and Georgia by Mark Fretwell. Historic Chattahoochee Commission, Eufaula, AL. 1990.

Thomaston-Upson County Sesquicentennial History compiled by Mrs. J. M. Kellum, Mrs. W. H. Hightower, Jr., Mrs. C. W. Greene and Mrs. George Miller. Thomaston Upson County Sesquicentennial Committee. 1974.

Travels by William Bartram. Penguin Books, New York, NY. 1988.

Trees of Georgia and Adjacent States by Claud L. Brown and L. Katherine Kirkman. Timber Press, Inc., The Haseltine Building, 133 S. W. Second Avenue, Suite 450, Portland, OR 97204. 1990.

BOAT RENTALS AND TOURS

We discovered that the best type of boat to use on the river depends on where you are and what you want to do. Outfitters will rent you a canoe or kayak; but the following businesses give you another choice in enjoying the river.

Benign Boat Works, Inc. 317 Water St., Apalachicola, FL 32320. 850/653-8214; fax, 850/653-3579. Website: www.apalachicola.com/BenignBoats.

Eco Ventures, Inc., 301 Market St. Gibby Conrad, owner, 317 Water St., P.O. Box 578, Apalachicola, FL 32329. 850/653-2593.

Governor Stone. Joe Terrell, Apalachicola Maritime Museum, Inc., P.O. Box 625, Apalachicola, FL 32329-0625. 850/653-8700. Website: www.homtown.com/apalachicola/maritime.html.

Jubilee Paddlewheel Riverboat Tours. Departs from Apalachicola River docks at 329 Water Street. Dan Blake, 850/653-9502.

MAPS

Maps are our single most important tool in researching guidebooks. We also believe they are the single most important tool in enjoying any trip. The following are the major maps we used and places to get them.

Atlantic Mapping Recreation and fishing guide maps. Atlantic Mapping, Inc., P.O. Box 739, Marietta, GA 30065. 770/426-5768.

County Road Maps and Official State Highway Maps. Georgia Department of Transportation, Map Sales Division, 2 Capitol Square, Atlanta, GA 30334. 404/656-5336. Florida

Department of Commerce, Collins Building, Tallahassee, FL 32399-2000. 850/263-3510.

Forest Service Maps. U. S. Department of Agriculture, Forest Service, Visitor's Center, Room 154, 1720 Peachtree Rd., NW, Atlanta, GA 30367-9102. 404/347-2384.

U.S. Army Corps of Engineers Lake Maps. Lake Seminole Resource Management Office, P.O. Box 96, Chattahoochee, FL 32324. 229/662-2001.

USGS Topographical Maps. Powers Elevation Co., Inc., P.O. Box 440889, Aurora, CO 80044-0889. 303/321-2217 or 800/824-2550; fax: 303/321-2218. Website: www.usgs.gov.

To find maps on the internet, visit the following sites: www.topozone.com (for topo maps of the entire country); www.ncrc.nps.gov (for free-flowing river segments in the US categorized by state); and http://ga.water.usgs.gov (for current water levels of Georgia rivers).

RIVER RELATED ORGANIZATIONS

Listed below are organizations and government agencies which advocate river preservation and related topics.

American Rivers, 1025 Vermont Ave., NW, Suite 720, Washington, DC 20005. 202/347-7550. Website: www.amrivers.org/amrivers/.

Apalachicola River and Baykeeper, P.O. Box 484, Eastpoint, FL 32328.

Florida B.A.S.S. Chapter Federation, 210 14th St., NE, Naples, FL 34120. 941/353-7941; e-mail, usbattens@worldnet.att.net.

Florida Defenders of the Environment, 4424 NW 13th St., Suite C-8, Gainesville, FL 32609-1885. 352/378-8465; fax 352/377-0869. Website: www.fladefenders.org.

Florida Wildlife Federation, P.O. Box 6870, Tallahassee, FL 32314-6870. 800/656-3014. Website: www.fwf.usf.edu.

Georgia Adopt-A-Stream, 7 ML King Dr., SW, Suite 643, Atlanta, GA 30334. 404/656-0099 or 0069; fax, 404/657-7031; e-mail, michele_droszez@mail.dnr.state.ga.us.

Georgia B.A.S.S. Chapter Federation, 11575 Northgate Trail, Roswell, GA 30075. 770/993-6597.

Georgia Canoeing Association, P.O. Box 7023, Atlanta, GA 30357. 770/421-9729; e-mail, gacanoe@mindspring.com. Website: www.mindspring.com/~gacanoe.

Georgia Council of Trout Unlimited, 108 Sycamore St., Rome, GA 30165. 706/234-5310 or 706/234-8006.

Georgia Environmental Organization, Inc., 3185 Center St., Smyrna, GA 30080-7039. 404/605-0000; fax: 404/350-9997. Website: www.geoeco.org.

Georgia River Network, 2225 Jefferson Dr., Atlanta, GA 30350. 770-522-8239. Website: www.garivers.org.

Georgia Wildlife Federation, 1930 Iris Dr., Conyers, GA 30207. 770/929-3350; fax, 770/929-3534.

Line Creek Association, 254 Trickum Creek Rd., Tyrone, GA 30290. 770/631-9380; fax 770/631-9272.

Northwest Florida Water Management District, 81 Water Management Dr., Havanna, FL 32333. 850/539-5999; fax 850/539-4380. Website: www.state.fl.us/nwfwmd.gov.

Office of Greenways and Trails, Florida Department of Environmental Protection, 2600 Blair Stone Rd., M. S. 795, Tallahassee, FL 32399-2400. 850/488-3701; fax, 850/922-6302. Website: dep.state.fl.us/gwt.

Sierra Club, 85 2nd St., 2nd Floor, San Francisco, CA 94105-3441. 415/977-5500; fax, 415/977-5799. Website: www.sierraclub.org.

Southern Conservation Trust, Inc., 201 McIntosh Trail, Peachtree City, GA 30269. 770/486-7774; fax, 770/486-7775.

The Chattahoochee Riverkeeper, Inc., P.O. Box 1492, Columbus, GA 31902. 706/317-4837; fax, 706/663-7817.

The Conservation Fund, 1800 N. Kent Street, Suite 1120, Arlington, VA 22209-2156. 703/525-6300; fax, 703/525-4610; e-mail, mail@conservationfund.org. Website: www.conservationfund.org. Southeastern Regional Office, P.O. Box 1362, Tucker, GA 30085-1362. 770/414-0211; fax, 770/938-0585. Florida Office, 4400 PGA Blvd., Suite 900, Palm Beach Gardens, FL 33410. 561/624-4925; fax, 561/624-4948.

The Georgia Conservancy, State Office, 1776 Peachtree St., NW, Suite 400 South, Atlanta, GA 30309. 404/876-2900; fax, 404/872-9229. Website: www. gaconservancy.org.

The Nature Conservancy of Georgia, 1330 W. Peachtree St., Suite 410, Atlanta, GA 30309-2904. 404/873-6946; fax, 404/873-6984. Website: www.tnc.org/Georgia/index.html.

The Nature Conservancy of Florida, 222 S. Westmonte Dr., Suite 300, Altamonte Springs, FL 32714. 407/682-3664; fax: 407/682-3077. Website: www.tnc.org.

The Trust for Public Land, Atlanta Field Office, 1447 Peachtree St., NE, Atlanta, GA 30309. 404/873-7306; fax, 404/875-9099.

Upper Chattahoochee Riverkeeper, 1900 Emery St., Suite 450, Atlanta, GA 30318. 404/352-9828; fax, 404/352-8676; e-mail, rivrkeep@mindspring.com. Website: www.chattahoochee.org.

OUTFITTERS, CHARTERS AND GUIDES

Bear Paw Canoe Trails. Rickie and Anna McAlpin, owners, 2100 Bear Paw Lane, Marianna, FL 32448. 850/482-4948; fax: 850/482-3141.

Boss Charters. Docked at the Apalachicola River Inn Marina, 123 Walter St., Apalachicola, FL 32320. Dennis Crosby, captain. 850/653-8055.

Broke-A-Toes Outdoor Supplies & Service. Tom Brocato, owner, 1151 Cape San Blas Rd., Port St. Joe, FL 32457. 850/229-WAVE; fax 850/229-8991. Website: www.capesanblas.com/broke-a-toes.

Captain Charles Charters. Charles Wilson, captain, 449 24th Ave., Apalachicola, FL 32320. 850/653-9008. Website: www.CaptCharlesCharters.com.

Captain Tony's Charters. Tony Thompson, captain, 258 Paradise Lane, Apalachicola, FL 32320. 850/653-3560. Website: www.members.xoom.com/captaintony.

DBI Scuba. Julian Winchester, guide, 1921 Dawson Rd., Albany, GA 31707. 229/438-7030. Website: www.dbiscuba.com.

Flint River Outdoor Center. Jim McDaniel, owner, 4429 Woodland Rd., GA 36 at Flint River, Thomaston, GA 30286-3235. 706/647-2633; fax, 706/674-2897.

Flint River Outpost. John Singletary, owner, 1678 Highway 32 East, Leesburg, GA 31763. 229/759-9170. Website: www.flint-river-outpost.bigstep.com

Gerald I. Lawhorn Canoe Base Training Center. Thunder Scout Reservation, 1166 Dripping Rock Rd., Molena, GA 30258. 706/646-2255; fax 706/646-2120. Website: www.thunderbsa.org.

High Country Outfitters, Inc. Gerald Marshall and Bubba Sloan, owners. Three locations: 3906 Roswell Rd., Atlanta, 404/814-0999; Perimeter Mall, Atlanta, 770/391-9657; Riverchase Galleria, Birmingham, 205/985-3215. Website: highcountryoutfitters.com.

Hooked On Charter Fishing. Ronald Walters, captain, US 98 & 2nd St., P.O. Box 875, Eastpoint, FL 32328. 800/446-1639 or 904/670-8371.

Jack Wingate. Wingate's Lunker Lodge, 139 Wingate Rd., Bainbridge, GA 31717. 229/246-0658.

Jeanni's Journeys, Inc. Jeanni McMillan, owner, 139 E. Gorrie, St. George Island, FL 32328. 850/927-3259; fax, 850/927-3831. Website: www.hometown.com/jjinc.

REI. Location #1: 1800 NE Expressway, Atlanta, GA 30329; 404/633-6508. Location #2: 1165 Perimeter Center West, Suite 200, Atlanta, GA 30346. 770/901-9200.

River Dog Flyfishing. Todd Rogers, guide, P.O. Box 423, Newton, GA 31770. 229/435-6390.

Robinson Brothers Guide Service. Tommy Robinson and Chris Robinson, owners, PO 248, 94 Market St., Apalachicola, FL 32329. 850/653-9669. Website: www.floridaredfish.com.

RockFish Charters. Hull Dickenson, captain, 925 East Gulf Beach Dr., St. George Island, FL 32328. 850/927-3839. Website: www.RockFishCharters.com.

Stringer, Jim, P.O. Box 253, Gay, GA 30218. 706/538-6359.

TOWNS, CHAMBERS AND TOURISM ORGANIZATIONS

Americus. Americus Downtown Development Authority, 101 West Lamar Street, P.O. Box M, Americus, GA 31709. 229/924-4421; fax, 229/928-0430. Americus-Sumter County Chamber of Commerce, 400 West Lamar Street, P.O. Box 724, Americus, Georgia 31709. 229/924-2646; fax, 229/924-8784. Website: Webserver.americus.net/~chamber/.

Apalachicola. Apalachicola Area Historical Society, 128 Market St., Apalachicola, FL 32320. Apalachicola Bay Chamber of Commerce, 84 Market St., Apalachicola, FL 32320. 850/653-9419. Website: www.apalachicola.com.

Bainbridge. Bainbridge-Decatur County Chamber of Commerce, P.O. Box 736, Bainbridge, GA 31718. 800/243-4774 or 229/246-4774; fax 229/243-7633. Website: www.bainbridgega.com/chamber.

Blakely. Blakely-Early County Chamber of Commerce, P.O. Box 189, Blakely, GA 31723. 229/723-3741.

Brooks. City of Brooks, 951 85 Connector, P.O. Box 96, Brooks, GA 30205. 770/719-7666.

Buena Vista. Buena Vista-Marion County Chamber of Commerce. 229/649-2842.

Butler. City of Butler, P.O. Box 476, Butler, GA 31006. 478/862-5435; fax, 478/862-5083.

Camilla Chamber of Commerce, P.O. Box 226, Camilla, GA 31730. 229/336-5255.

Clayton County Convention and Visitors Bureau, 104 North Main Street, Jonesboro, GA 30236. 770/478-4800 or 800-662-STAY.

Columbus. Columbus Convention and Visitors Bureau, 1000 Bay Ave., Columbus, GA 31902. 706/322-1613 or 800/999-1613. Historic Columbus Foundation, 700 Broadway, Columbus, GA 31906. 706/323-7979. Website: www.columbusga.com.

Colquitt. Colquitt/Miller Arts Council, P.O. Box 567, Colquitt, GA 31737. 229/758-5450. Website: www.swamp-gravy.com. Colquitt/Miller County Chamber of Commerce, 166 First Street, Colquitt, GA 31737. 229/758-2400; fax, 229/758-8140.

Concord. City of Concord, P.O. Box 175, Concord, GA 30206. 770/884-5221; fax, 770/884-9666.

Cordele. Cordele-Crisp Chamber of Commerce, P.O. Box 158, Cordele, GA 31010. 229/273-1668; fax 229/273-5132. Website: www.cordele-crisp-chamber.com. Cordele Main Street, P.O. Box 5739, Cordele, GA 31010. 229/273-3102; 229/273-6773.

Cusseta. City of Cusseta, P.O. Box 240, Cusseta, GA 31804. 706/989-3156 or 3421.

Dooly County Chamber of Commerce, 204 A W. Union Street, P.O. Box 394, Vienna, GA 31092. 229/268-8275.

Donalsonville-Seminole County Chamber of Commerce, P. O. Box 713, Donalsonville, GA 31745. 229/524-2588; fax, 229/524-8406.

Fayetteville. City of Fayetteville, 240 South Glynn Street, Fayetteville, GA 30214. 770/461-6029; fax, 770/460-4238.

Fort Gaines. Clay County Library, 208 S. Hancock, Fort Gaines, GA 31751. 229/768-2248.

Fort Valley. Fort Valley Main Street, P.O. Box 1864, Fort Valley, GA 31030. 478/825-5986; 478/825-7711.

Gay. City of Gay, P.O. Box 216, Gay, GA 30218. 706/538-6097.

Greenville. City of Greenville, P.O. Box 236, Greenville, GA 30222. 706/672-1216; fax, 706/672-1940.

Griffin. Main Street Griffin, P.O. Box T, Griffin, GA 30223. 770/228-5356; fax, 770/229-6630.

Historic Chattahoochee Commission. P.O. Box 33, Eufaula, AL 36072-0033. 334/687-9755. Website: www.hcc-al-ga.org.

Jonesboro. City of Jonesboro, 124 North Avenue, Jonesboro, GA 30236. 770/478-3800. Website: www.jonesboroga.com. Historical Jonesboro—Clayton County, Inc., P.O. Box 922, Jonesboro, GA 30237. 770/473-0197. Website: www.gwtw-jonesboro.org.

Leesburg. Leesburg Chamber of Commerce, P.O. Box 439, Leesburg, GA 31763. 229/759-2422.

Macon County. Macon County Chamber of Commerce, 316 South Dooly Street, P.O. Box 308, Montezuma, GA

31063. 229/472-2391. Website: www.maconcountyga.org.

Manchester. Manchester Development Authority, 101 Broad Street, P.O. Box 583, Manchester, GA 31816. 706/846-5341; fax, 706/846-2255. Website: www.manchester-ga.com

Meriwether County Chamber of Commerce, 91 Broad Street, P.O. Box 9, Warm Springs, GA 31830. 706/655-2558; fax, 706/655-2812. Tourism Information, 800/FDR-1927.

Molena. City of Molena, P.O. Box 194, Molena, GA 30258. 770/884-9711; fax, 770/884-0344.

Newton. Baker County Chamber of Commerce, P.O. Box 238, Newton, GA 31770. 229/734-5421.

Peachtree City. City of Peachtree City, 151 Willowbend Road, Peachtree City, GA 30269. 770/487-7657.

Pine Mountain. Pine Mountain Chamber of Commerce, P.O. Box 483, Pine Mountain, GA 31822. 706/663-8850. Website: www.pinemtn.org.

Preston. City of Preston, P.O. Box 37, Preston, GA 31824. 229/828-2975.

Riverdale. City of Riverdale, 6690 Church Street, Riverdale, GA 30274. 770/997-8989; fax, 770/997-8992. Website: www.cityofriverdale.com.

Roberta. Roberta-Crawford County Chamber of Commerce, P.O. Box 417, Roberta, GA 31078. 478/836-3825.

Southwest Georgia Chamber of Commerce (Calhoun, Clay, Quitman, Randolph and Stewart Counties), P.O. Box 31, Cuthbert, GA 31740. 229/732-2683 or 2785; fax, 229/732-6590.

Talbot County Chamber of Commerce, P.O. Box 98, Talbotton, GA 31827. 706/665-8079.

Terrell County Chamber of Commerce, 127 West Lee Street, P.O. Box 405, Dawson, GA 31742. 229/995-2011.

Thomaston. Thomaston Main Street, P.O. Box 703, Thomaston, GA 30286. 706/647-8311; fax, 706/646-2653.

Warm Springs. City of Warm Springs, P.O. Box 156, Warm Springs, GA 31830. 706/655-9096, fax, 706/655-2814. Meriwether County Chamber of Commerce, 91 Broad Street, P.O. Box 9, Warm Springs, GA 31830. 706/655-2558; fax, 706/655-2812. Tourism Information, 800/FDR-1927.

Woodbury. City of Woodbury, P.O. Box 297, Woodbury, GA 30293. 706/553-5480.

Woodland. City of Woodland, P.O. Box 187, Woodland, GA 31836. 706/674-2200.

Zebulon. City of Zebulon, 500 Highway 19, P.O. Box 385, Zebulon, GA 30295. 770/567-8748; fax, 770/567-8802.

Index